HEART IN CONFLICT

MICHAEL GRIMWOOD

HEART IN CONFLICT

FAULKNER'S STRUGGLES
WITH VOCATION

THE UNIVERSITY OF GEORGIA PRESS
ATHENS AND LONDON

© 1987 by the University of Georgia Press
Athens, Georgia 30602
All rights reserved

Designed by Kathi L. Dailey
Set in 10½ on 13 Mergenthaler Electra with Gill Sans
The paper in this book meets the guidelines for
permanence and durability of the Committee on
Production Guidelines for Book Longevity of the
Council on Library Resources.

Printed in the United States of America

91 90 89 88 87   5 4 3 2 1

Library of Congress Cataloging in Publication Data

Grimwood, Michael.
    Heart in conflict.

    Bibliography: p.
    Includes index.
    1. Faulkner, William, 1897–1962—Criticism and
interpretation. 2. Authorship—Psychological aspects.
3. Literature—Psychology. 4. Creation (Literary, artistic,
etc.) 5. Authors in literature. 6. Self in literature. I. Title.
PS3511.A86Z78416 1987   813'.52   85-29022
ISBN 0-8203-0855-2 (alk. paper)

FOR LINDA WOOTTON

The problems of the human heart in conflict
with itself . . . alone can make good writing.

William Faulkner

This publication has been supported by the National Endowment for the Humanities, a federal agency which supports the study of such fields as history, philosophy, literature, and languages.

CONTENTS

PREFACE

My subject is two periods of crisis in William Faulkner's literary career. During the first, in his youth, he struggled to fashion a vocation for himself. Part One of this book explores the unconscious motives underlying Faulkner's predisposition to a career as an imaginative writer. During the second, which extended throughout his fifth decade, those motives seemed ready to collapse under the weight of the particular social fabric and literary traditions within which his career had necessarily proceeded. Part Two treats his struggle to maintain his vocation against—or amid— that collapse. These two struggles correspond roughly to the two vocational phases of Erik Erikson's "life cycle": the "crisis of identity" and the "crisis of generativity." Faulkner weathered the first crisis in relative solitude, but once he had fully declared his vocation it defined him as a social being. The second crisis consequently tested a culture as well as an individual.

If I seem to use the words *vocation* and *career* interchangeably, I actually assume an important distinction: *vocation* is a synchronic, *career* a diachronic model of authorship. Faulkner's *career* is divisible into biographical periods; his *vocation* is a constant principle which may have entered his consciousness—and his fiction—more clearly during some periods than others. The developmental chronology of the career has been ably anatomized by Gary Lee Stonum, David Minter, and others. I am more interested here in attempting to characterize the vocation. Insofar as I attend to the career, then, I concentrate on those periods of it when his vocation emerged most fully into view: the beginning and the climax. I do not pretend that Faulkner never entertained questions about his vocation at other times: the Reverend Shegog's sermon in *The Sound and the Fury* (1929), Addie Bundren's monologue in *As I Lay Dying* (1930), and Quentin Compson's construction of Thomas Sutpen's narrative in *Absalom, Absalom!* (1936) all refer more or less directly to Faulkner's own activities as an author. But these are not my subject, though they are related to it. I have tried to isolate the components of Faulkner's vocation by focusing in some detail on two significant parts of his career, rather than to sketch, comprehensively but perhaps shallowly, the full history of his representations of that vocation.

I begin *in medias res*, on a summer day in 1937 when Faulkner looked across the threshold of middle age toward his literary posterity and recoiled at what he saw. I then seek the origins of—and some precedents for—that anxious outlook in a group of early stories and poems through which he attempted to define his reasons for becoming a writer. By applying Freudian as well as Eriksonian theories of personality to his apprenticeship, I suggest that the psychological sources of Faulkner's vocation contained the seeds of its potential undoing. In *The Marble Faun*, "Carcassonne," "The Leg," and other works, he created a private iconography through which to express the tensions he had tried to resolve by becoming a writer. In images counterpoising passivity against action, confinement against escape, restraint against release, and silence against sound, he manifested an urge toward negation that accompanied the evolution of his creativity.

Through a company of parodic doubles for himself, moreover, he voiced his suspicion of the radical fraudulence of his authority. His commitment to literature originated in a hunger for impersonation—and for disguises of his impersonations. To deny his membership in the middle class, he devised a "pastoral" identity for himself, combining the "upper" and the "lower" levels of his society into a precariously false unity. To neutralize his neighbors' low opinion of the writer's role, he invented more honorable descriptions of himself, from "wounded veteran" to "farmer." Thus, the structure of his professional constitution came to reflect—and invert—the realities and the expectations of his community.

In Part Two, therefore, I shift from a primarily psychological to a primarily sociological investigation of Faulkner's vocation. I trace the emergence of Faulkner's vocational self-doubt and the disintegration of his "pastoral identity" through four books he wrote between 1937 and 1950, a period during which he reevaluated his career and made partial adjustments in it to accord with depleted resources and diminished hopes. All of these books—*The Wild Palms* (1939), *The Hamlet* (1940), *Knight's Gambit* (published in 1949, but written mostly before 1941), and *Go Down, Moses* (1942)—share a structural principle that distinguishes them from most of Faulkner's other works. They might be called "anthology novels," as they belong to a hybrid form midway between story collection and novel proper: each combines, more or less loosely, several discrete narrative units into a roughly integrated whole. I have left undiscussed one other book published during the same period, *Intruder in the Dust* (1948), because it does not negotiate the same conspicuous compromise between continuity and discontinuity as the other four.

I contend that the dialectical character of these anthology novels mirrored divisions within Faulkner, which in turn derived partly from his perception of the structure of his community. For the purposes of analyzing these books, I assume a complex formal correspondence among text, personality, and society. Disturbances in the actual composition of "Yoknapatawpha County" evoked imbalances in the hierarchical chemistry of Faulkner's self-image, resulting in articulately disordered narratives. In these fractured texts, Faulkner dramatized the public origins and consequences of his internal duplicity.

As I have stated, that duplicity was "pastoral." The basic argument of this book is that the degeneration many readers attribute to Faulkner's writing in the forties resulted not from superficial difficulties imposed upon him from outside but from psychic and social pressures that are inherent in pastoralism—the literary mode in which he characteristically worked. The concept of pastoralism I employ here derives variously from William Empson, Raymond Williams, Renato Poggioli, and Lewis Simpson; and I have applied it in a different way to each of the four books under consideration. In its most general sense, the concept refers to an author's application of relatively literate and sophisticated perception to the rendering of relatively nonliterate and simple experience. Specifically, here, it pertains to those books in which Faulkner wrote about the poor whites and Negroes of rural Mississippi.

Part One explores the ways in which his relationship with such people became incorporated into his literary identity. Part Two examines a midlife upheaval in that social construction. The first two chapters of Part Two discuss the shifting distance between Faulkner and the people he usually wrote about: they suggest that in *The Wild Palms* and *The Hamlet* he came to write *about* that distance, embodying it in the structure of one book and in the language of the other. The third chapter of Part Two asserts that, between the time when he wrote the original stories of *Knight's Gambit*, before 1943, and the time when he revised its title story, in 1949, this distance had evolved into a gap between the writer and his work and between the writer and his readers. The final chapter offers as partial explanation for this transformation the apparent fact that, in *Go Down, Moses*, writing about illiterate people had made Faulkner suspicious of the value of literacy itself and of his vocation to writing. He expressed this suspicion in burlesque exaggerations of his distinctive literary style, which by now he had made gratuitously inaccessible to the very people whose lives he was trying with only mixed results to penetrate. His self-doubt led him to rehearse his predicament through elaborate metaphors for writer, text, and audience. Pastoralism culminated in its logical result, self-parody.

Thus, Faulkner's "decline" resulted less from financial worry and public neglect (or acclaim) than from his recognition of contradictions within himself and within his cultural heritage. During the late thirties and the forties, Faulkner increasingly acknowledged a fact that he had mostly suppressed while writing the masterpieces of 1929 through 1936: that he had built his career on a foundation of imposture. Reviving the native traditions of Southern literature, furthermore, he increasingly found them untrue to his experience as a writer. Particularly in adapting the century-old traditions of Southwestern humor and plantation fiction to his own purposes, he confronted the falsity of their representational conventions. Turning to the formulae of popular fiction and film, in contemporary American culture generally, he fared no better: Faulkner's anthology novels offer a measured repudiation of the storyteller's calling.

I hasten to add that they remain masterful products of that calling. Except for *Knight's Gambit*, I believe that these books are among Faulkner's best. If they represent confessions of failure, they remain eloquently successful confessions. If they reveal the fraudulence of their origins, they attest to an authenticity that transcends those origins. If they are elaborately self-parodic, the author who thus calls himself into question still rewards the closest attention: our vicarious experience of the writing of these books, which is perhaps their central common subject, is complex and moving. If they are not "unified" neatly, neither is the truth they convey. The story they all tell, in their various ways, is the story of their own telling—and untelling. Their final subject is a drama of genius divided against itself.

ACKNOWLEDGMENTS

I am grateful to Carlos Baker for his guidance, his encouragement, and his example. He helped me launch this study years ago, and he ignited the slow-burning fuse that finished the job. Richard M. Ludwig, Louis D. Rubin, Jr., Arthur Kinney, and John Matthews all have provided generously intelligent reactions to my ideas and to my prose. A. Walton Litz sent me unsolicited encouragement and sympathetic criticism at a crucial time. I have valued the good advice and the good offices of my colleagues Lucinda MacKethan and John Bassett. As my notes will confirm, I am indebted to the whole myriad of scholars who have written about Faulkner, but I must single out Joseph Blotner for special thanks. Without his meticulously reliable biographies, my work would have been impossible. I am also indebted to the editors of *Southern Review, Southern Literary Journal*, and *Notes on Mississippi Writers* for publishing early versions of some of the materials in this book; and to Max Webb, Gail Mortimer, and William Howard for providing me with audiences before which to try out other parts of it. Students in my courses in Faulkner and in Southern Writers suffered through trial versions of some of my arguments, and their responses affected my final exposition. The National Endowment for the Humanities provided me funds during one summer; the Department of English of North Carolina State University granted me a semester leave. The libraries of North Carolina State University, Princeton University, the University of Virginia, Duke University, and the University of North Carolina at Chapel Hill were indispensable to my research. The William Faulkner Foundation gave me access to the manuscripts collection at Alderman Library. Expert typing by Veronica Norris, Elaine Hocutt, and—especially—Charlene Turner made my life measurably easier. Malcolm Call has been an energetic, forthright, and efficient publisher; Ellen Harris, Debbie Winter, and Nancy Holmes have proven to be exemplary editors.

My wife, Linda, to whom this book is gratefully dedicated, has been my first and wisest critic, my most forceful advocate, and my enduring companion.

ABBREVIATIONS

ALG	Meta Carpenter Wilde and Orin Borsten, *A Loving Gentleman: The Love Story of William Faulkner and Meta Carpenter.*
BL	Joseph Blotner, *Faulkner: A Biography*, 2 volumes (1974).
BL1	Joseph Blotner, *Faulkner: A Biography*, 1 volume (1984).
BLRO	Malcolm Franklin, *Bitterweeds: Life with William Faulkner at Rowan Oak.*
BW	*The Big Woods.*
CNC	Ben Wasson, *Count No 'Count: Flashbacks to Faulkner.*
CS	*Collected Stories of William Faulkner.*
ELM	*Elmer.*
EPP	*William Faulkner: Early Prose and Poetry.*
ESPL	*Essays, Speeches and Public Letters.*
FA	*Father Abraham.*
FAB	*A Fable.*
FCF	Malcolm Cowley, *The Faulkner-Cowley File: Letters and Memories, 1944–1962.*
FU	*Faulkner in the University.*
FWP	*Faulkner at West Point.*
GB	*A Green Bough.*
GDM	*Go Down, Moses.*
HAM	*The Hamlet.*
HEL	*Helen: A Courtship.*
IID	*Intruder in the Dust.*
KG	*Knight's Gambit.*
LA	*Light in August.*
LG	*Lion in the Garden.*
MBB	John Faulkner, *My Brother Bill: An Affectionate Reminiscence.*

MF	*The Marble Faun.*
MOS	*Mosquitoes.*
NOS	*New Orleans Sketches.*
PY	*Pylon.*
REQ	*Requiem for a Nun.*
SAR	*Sartoris.*
SF	*The Sound and the Fury.*
SL	*Selected Letters.*
SP	*Soldiers' Pay.*
SY	*Sanctuary.*
TN	*The Town.*
UNV	*The Unvanquished.*
US	*Uncollected Stories.*
VS	*Vision in Spring.*
WP	*The Wild Palms.*

PART ONE

BILLY'S LIMP

THE ORIGINS OF FAULKNER'S SENSE OF VOCATION

CHAPTER ONE

"WILLIAM FAULKNER" AND "ERNEST V. TRUEBLOOD"

"Sister Jane" is still selling, but Lord! it's poor stuff. No doubt
that's because the brother represents my inner—my inner—oh,
well! my inner spezerinktum; I can't think of the other word. It
isn't "self" and it isn't—oh, yes! it's the other fellow inside of me,
the fellow who does all my literary work while I get the reputation,
being really nothing but a cornfield journalist. . . . I wish I could
trot the other fellow out when company comes. But he shrinks to
nothing and is gone. But the cornfield journalist pursues me and
stays on top.

Joel Chandler Harris, 1897

"Afternoon of a Cow"

On Friday, June 25, 1937, William Faulkner gathered a small group of
male acquaintances in his rented house in Beverly Hills, California. After
a luncheon of Southern food prepared by his cook, "Mammy" Narcissus
McEwen, and before the poker game that was to constitute the afternoon's
principal business, Faulkner surprised his friends by reading aloud a story
he had written, seemingly for the occasion. He called it "Afternoon of a
Cow" and pretended facetiously that it was the work of his "secretary,"
"Ernest V. Trueblood" (BL, 953, 961). It was only an entertainment, in
fact a rather coarse one befitting the masculine company, and Faulkner's
startled audience did not consider it successful or even comprehensible.
Nor, since its first whimsical publication in an obscure journal in 1947,[1]
have the few scholars who bothered to search it out lingered to admire or
ponder it. As a work of fiction, objectively evaluated, it well deserves the
neglect it has suffered. As a document in Faulkner's literary biography,
however, "Afternoon of a Cow" is significant. It contains the germ of a

locus classicus of Faulknerian prose style, the Ike Snopes section of *The Hamlet*; more important, it expresses as directly as anything else Faulkner ever wrote his own perception of his situation as a writer.

Faulkner had written the story toward the end of 1935, soon after the accidental death of his favorite brother, Dean. He had just arrived in Hollywood to begin the second of his three protracted exiles there, and he had just initiated an affair with Meta Carpenter, the personal secretary of film director Howard Hawks. When he had composed "Afternoon," he had been struggling to complete *Absalom, Absalom!* (BL1, 362–63). He resurrected it for his friends' amusement during a period of even greater frustration. His wife, Estelle, had recently abandoned him to California, depriving him of his daughter Jill's company, after discovering his affair. His lover, in turn, had married another man after she realized that Faulkner would not seek a divorce. The handsome salary he received at the studio was insufficient to meet the expenses of his two households, and he jeopardized this necessary income by drinking on the job and by writing scenes for the wrong movies. Worse, the screenwriting interfered with his "real" work, his fiction. Although he had managed to complete *Absalom, Absalom!* in Hollywood the previous year, it had failed to attract the attention he felt it deserved. The book that he immodestly called "the best novel yet written by an American" received a lukewarm and uncomprehending critical response in the last months of 1936, and its sales were meager. The author's disappointments in love and in work encouraged him to indulge his most morbid inclinations. He still grieved over his brother, and now over the more recent deaths of three close friends as well: Vernon Omlie, General James Stone, and the General's son, Jim Junior. Moreover, not yet forty years old, he was becoming obsessed with his own mortality. Lonely and depressed, his thoughts turned to self-pity, age, and death. [2]

Faulkner's guest of honor that afternoon was Maurice Coindreau, a Princeton professor who had undertaken to be the novelist's French translator. Coindreau had stayed with Faulkner for a week to consult with him about a translation of *The Sound and the Fury*. The "stag party" occurred on the evening before Coindreau's departure. Faulkner invited four men: Ben Wasson, an old friend from Mississippi; a wealthy neighbor named Davenport; and "two painters" he had met at one or another Hollywood party. After dinner, Faulkner produced the typescript and offered to read it aloud, declaring, "This is a very original story. It was written by a boy who has talent. I'm the hero, and I find it very comic" (BL, 961). None of them recognized the talented boy's name, "Ernest V. Trueblood." As Faulkner read, Coindreau quickly understood why not. Intimately familiar with Faulkner's prose style, he recognized its characteristics at once. "The text," he explained later, "was one of those that necessitate a sustained effort; the tangled sentences, interrupted by digressions and parentheses, enveloped thought in perfidious arabesques."[3] In other words, it was Faulknerian.

If Coindreau alone saw through Faulkner's hoax, however, he understood no better than the other listeners what effect their host intended to achieve. Did Faulkner mean for his lie about "Trueblood" to be transparent, or had he actually hoped to fool these men? How did he expect them to respond? If the story was comic, as Faulkner promised, the point of the humor escaped all of the guests, who—digesting the poorly prepared dinner (BL, 961) and anticipating a casual card game—should not have been expected to discern literary subtleties anyway. Faulkner's voice was generally so soft and uninflected that his friends may have had trouble even construing his words. "We were all too attentive to be able even to dream of laughing," Coindreau recounted.[4]

As Faulkner intoned his text, his narrator made some very incriminating revelations about him. "Ernest V. Trueblood" claims to serve "Mr. Faulkner" as a literary secretary, composing the author's fiction for him each day according to instructions received over juleps the previous afternoon. On the afternoon of the narration, however, "Mr. Faulkner" is so distracted by an incident in the management of his "farm," which is his chief occupation, that instead of making up a story he allows his amanuensis to "venture into fact and employ the material which we ourselves have this afternoon created" and to write it in his "own diction and style" (US, 434). The story Trueblood tells is a barnyard joke, but he tells it in a wholly inappropriate way, as if it were the stuff of high romance.

What has distracted "Mr. Faulkner" in Trueblood's sketch is the result of an adolescent prank. His son Malcolm, his nephew James, and his servant Jack Oliver's son Grover (all real names of real people) have accidentally set fire to a pasture behind his antebellum home in Mississippi, presumably Faulkner's Rowan Oak. "Faulkner," Trueblood, and Oliver run there to rescue two horses and a cow, Beulah. Nearing the smoke, they hear Beulah lowing, but her voice seems to come from within the earth. The two horses then materialize out of the smoke, run toward the men, and swerve back across the line of flames, disappearing. Running ahead of the others, "Mr. Faulkner" suddenly vanishes from their sight, and Trueblood recognizes that Beulah and Beulah's master have both fallen into a ravine. Trueblood and Oliver follow them into it, and there they find "sanctuary" from the brush fire, which passes over them. Once safe, they attempt to extricate Beulah from the ravine, but she slides back upon "Mr. Faulkner" and, fearstricken, defecates in his lap. After removing himself from beneath Beulah, reprimanding the three boys, and cleaning himself with saddle soap and "pail after pail of water" (US, 433–34), "Mr. Faulkner" resumes his interrupted julep. Too embarrassed to do anything more than nurse his sullied dignity, however, he refrains from literary invention and authorizes Trueblood to recount the day's mishap in his own way.

This is the complete plot of "Afternoon of a Cow." Faulkner's guests naturally failed to appreciate it that summer evening in 1937. For the value of this rural farce lies not in itself—except as a documentation of the author's chronic sense of degradation—but in Trueblood's inappropriate treatment of it. The story is significant mainly because of its style, or rather because of its two styles: that of Trueblood and that of "Mr. Faulkner."

Trueblood tells his story in a stilted, polysyllabic idiom. By contrast, "Mr. Faulkner" is a vulgarian whose speech is more or less "unprintable." Left unsupervised, Trueblood condescends only once to anything but proper English. When "Faulkner" orders a drink after washing himself, Trueblood orders one too, apologizing in the process for his use of the blandest colloquialism: " 'Make it two,' said I; I felt that the occasion justified, even though it may not have warranted, that temporary aberration into the vernacular of the fleeting moment" (US, 434). [5] Otherwise, he tries to sound as pedantic and as prudish as he can, lavishing an elevated vocabulary and portentous syntax upon his ridiculous rural farce. Thus, he describes a September vegetable garden as "innocent of edible matter" (US, 426). The burnt ground of the pasture is "a stygian plain" (US, 428). Sitting is "sedentation" (US, 431). At the moment of Beulah's incontinence, "Mr. Faulkner underneath received the full discharge of the poor creature's afternoon of anguish and despair" (US, 430). The cow then knew "by woman's sacred instinct that the future held for her that which is to a female far worse than any fear of bodily injury or suffering: one of those invasions of female privacy . . . even the more bitter for the fact that they who are to witness it are gentlemen, people of her own class" (US, 430). After the men "quitted the sable plain which had witnessed our Gethsemane," they "led the cow into its private and detached domicile"— a barn—where she "ruminated, maiden meditant and . . . once more fancy free" (US, 433). In short, Ernest V. Trueblood's style exhibits the rhetorical extremism we typically associate with William Faulkner.

Faulkner read for about twenty-five minutes; then he invited discussion. In Joseph Blotner's reconstruction of the ensuing conversation, the guests admitted that they found the story unamusing, unclear, "overwritten." Dauntlessly, Faulkner defended his ghost-writer: "I have a lot of sympathy for Ernest V. Trueblood," he said. "He has always been so faithful to me, and remember that when the critics were howling at me, it always reflected back on him. I owed it to him at least one time to let him write under his own name. You've been able to see how conscientious he is and how much he cares about 'le mot juste,' and how he is honest and prudish. But, since you didn't seem to find him funny, maybe I'll have to dispense with his services in the future." Recognizing that his friends were not enjoying the sport he had prepared for them, he put away the typescript and got out the cards and poker chips (BL, 963).[6]

The matter might have died there, except that Faulkner did not quite want it to. The next morning, as Coindreau was packing, Faulkner brought him as gifts an inscribed first edition of *Absalom, Absalom!* and a carbon copy of "Afternoon of a Cow" bound between two pieces of blue paper. "I would like you to take this volume as a souvenir of your visit," he said, "and take this story too. . . . This way you will have the complete works of Ernest V. Trueblood."[7] Perhaps Faulkner meant that "Afternoon" was Trueblood's only story; but perhaps he meant that Trueblood had also written *Absalom*.

In 1943 Coindreau published his French translation of the story, "L'Après-Midi d'une Vache," in an Algerian journal called *Fontaine*. Four years later, Reed Whittemore, having heard about the story from Coindreau, offered $75 for permission to publish the original text in his small quarterly *Furioso*. When Faulkner's agent approached him with this news, Faulkner wrote an indifferent assent: "It's all right. . . about the story. . . . I wrote it one afternoon when I felt rotten with a terrible hangover, with no thought of publication, since the story is a ribald one. . . . I have tried it on various people (Americans) who seemed to think it not funny at all but (apparently, as I realise now, they thought it was true) in bad taste" (BL, 1225; SL, 245). Whittemore published it as the work of "Ernest V. Trueblood, William Faulkner's Ghostwriter," but appended to it an appreciation of "Mr. Faulkner's other work."[8] There the matter has rested for four decades.

As a purely biographical document, "Afternoon of a Cow" reinforces an impression that Faulkner felt defeated and threatened. He was reacting sardonically to marital, amatory, financial, and vocational woes by holding himself up to ridicule. His fantasy of being covered with cow manure must have resulted in part from humiliation or shame.[9] More than an ironic expression of Faulkner's melancholy, however, "Afternoon of a Cow" is a story about how Faulkner wrote stories. Indeed, it is an exposé, a confession of fraud. At a moment when his defenses were down and his confidence shaken, Faulkner allowed his most deeply repressed misgivings about his literary vocation to rise toward consciousness.

Most fundamentally, "Afternoon of a Cow" is Faulkner's dissection of his authorial identity—both before the public and within the mirror of his fiction. For most of his life, Faulkner cultivated two opposite images of himself as a writer: one folksy and down-home, the other sophisticated and almost stuffy. When answering questions about his place in American letters, he sometimes assumed a pose not just of amateurism but of functional illiteracy. By the 1950s he deflected questions about his membership among the literati with a formulaic denial. "I'm a farmer," he told an interviewer in 1951. "I ain't a writer. . . . Why, I don't even know any writers. I don't pay no attention to publishers, either" (LG, 64). To a Japanese questioner in 1955, Faulkner responded more grammatically: "I am not really a writer in the sense you mean—my life was established before I began to write. I'm a countryman. My life is farmland and horses and the raising of grain and feed. . . . so in that sense, I'm not a writer because that doesn't come first" (LG, 169). Perhaps. But no other Mississippi "farmer" that same year could have told a Parisian interviewer, "Je suis fermier," while wearing the rosette of the *Légion d'honneur*, into which he had been inducted for his "contribution to the literary art" (LG, 234; BL, 1380).

At the same time that he played the farmer, he also fostered an image of himself as a man of letters. The interviews in which he protested his amateurism also contain plentiful evidence of his wide reading, of his intellectual credentials, and of his total devotion to the craft of fiction. Not long after claiming that writing "doesn't come first," he told another interviewer that writing is "the worst vocation" because "[y]ou're demon-run, under compulsion, always being driven" (LG, 220). Elsewhere, he said that his goal was "to make something that . . . a hundred or two hundred or five hundred, a thousand years later will make people feel what they feel when they read Homer, or read Dickens or Balzac, Tolstoy" (FU, 61). Some farmer.

The apparent contradiction between self-deprecatory false humility and frankly arrogant aspiration did not originate in the fifties, when Faulkner spoke these words. Nor were the "farming" statements as disingenuous as they sound. Such assertions were intended for public consumption, of course, and they formed a cornerstone of the Faulkner mystique. But they also satisfied a deep requirement within the man. He needed to persuade himself as well as his audience that he was "primarily a farmer and after that . . . a writer" (LG, 192). Only if his writing were subordinate to his "farming" could he attain his highest literary ambition. Were he to declare himself a "writer" first and foremost, his sense of himself *as a writer* would somehow have suffered.

Ordinarily, Faulkner enacted this paradox without seeming to notice its illogicality. He played both the farmer and the artist with equal sincerity, and he could switch roles with equanimity. Thus, for example, he concluded a literary interview in 1947 by excusing himself so that he could "go home and let the cow out" (BL, 1231). In fact, his peace of mind depended on the compatibility of the two opposite performances. However, "Afternoon of a Cow" reveals that, at least once, he was onto himself. For in this story both versions of himself—the rube and the aesthete—are manifestly false. "Mr. Faulkner" is a personification of the farmer Faulkner pretended to be, even in 1935, four years before he bought his farm; Ernest V. Trueblood is Faulkner's projection of himself as artist, but this character epitomizes affectation rather than real artistry. Together, they demonstrate Faulkner's momentary awareness that the identity he presented to the world, and to himself, was double—and that both its halves were false. Insofar as Faulkner attributed his fiction to the collaboration of these two characters, the story constitutes his genuine, though facetious, investigation of his own creativity.

In "Afternoon of a Cow" Faulkner located the origins of his fiction in twin acts of self-betrayal. The Trueblood in him—his artistic instrument—had to subordinate his talents to a coarse sensibility he little respected, while the "farmer" had so little confidence in his own articulateness that he surrendered his experience to an exotic voice. Their partnership testified to a fundamental insecurity in Faulkner's mind about writing. He seemed to be confessing, perhaps unconsciously, to a suspicion that his literary career was only a grand impersonation: that, when he sat down to write, he became someone he was not. Yet he could not decide whether he was "Faulkner" pretending to be Trueblood or Trueblood pretending to be "Faulkner," a native intelligence affecting highfalutin' language or a premier literary talent stooping to unworthy subjects. Either way, the fact that he cast "himself" as the inarticulate rube, while allowing someone else—Trueblood—to do the actual writing, suggests his alienation from the act, and from the product, of composition.

At the least, "Afternoon" signals Faulkner's awareness of just how tortuous his prose style had become. The baroque stylistic excesses we think of as Faulknerian, after all, did not evolve until the mid-thirties. The earliest novels had been merely precious at worst, while *The Sound and the Fury* (1929), *As I Lay Dying* (1930), and *Light in August* (1932) had been stylistically restrained in comparison with what came later. But, with *Absalom, Absalom!* (1936) and its offshoot *Pylon* (1935), Faulkner became the verbal labyrinth-maker whom we think of as "Faulkner"—not Farmer "Faulkner" of "Afternoon," but *our* Faulkner, the virtuoso of verbiage whose sentences vanquish attention and memory, the syntactical sadist of "The Bear" (1942) and *A Fable* (1954). "Afternoon of a Cow" contains Faulkner's critical reflection upon his characteristic style while he was still inventing it. Significantly, he distanced himself from its gratuitous difficulties by assigning them to Ernest Trueblood. He purposely estranged himself from his style, as if to shift the blame for it onto some Truebloodian demon of logorrhea that he was momentarily too weak to suppress.

The Faulkner who wrote "Afternoon of a Cow" recognized fully the artificiality of his professional voice. The source of the story's intended humor lies less in its subject than in the inappropriateness to that subject of Trueblood's inflated style. Had Faulkner told his poker partners a barnyard joke about himself in a straightforwardly profane way, they might have chuckled appreciatively and forgotten it. "Afternoon of a Cow" baffled rather than amused them precisely because they were unable to distinguish its tone from that of Faulkner's serious fiction. What he intended as self-parody, they took at face value.

They were not alone in their obtuseness. In 1947, in an afterword to the story, Reed Whittemore wrote of "those rare moments where, as with the cow, [Faulkner's] judgment, his sense of balance, his control fails him."[10] For Whittemore to apply high critical standards to this apparent jape may now seem absurd. But someone who had just read *Pylon* or *Absalom, Absalom!* or *The Hamlet* (1940) or *Go Down, Moses* (1942) would naturally have approached *anything* by Faulkner soberly. These books apply an increasingly convoluted and grand style to relatively lowly subjects, and all were meant to be taken seriously. "Afternoon of a Cow" is funny not because the incongruity between its style and substance is greater than in his *bona fide* works, but because it is only slightly greater. It is important because it reveals Faulkner's conscious awareness of the radical discontinuity between the mostly inarticulate, mostly rural characters he usually wrote about and his grandiloquent means of describing their experience.

In short, it reveals his attunement to the liabilities of pastoralism, the traditional literary mode in which he most clearly participated. Doubtless, Faulkner himself would not have applied this term to himself; most of his readers as well would associate it with a set of conventions that Faulkner did not directly employ. But, insofar as he typically chose to write about people who worked with their hands rather than with their minds, he was a pastoralist. For pastoralism has always thrived on the infatuation of intellectuals and artists with the imagined joys of physical labor. From Theocritus to Virgil to Sannazzaro to Pope to Wordsworth, the pastoralist has tried to articulate the experience of inarticulate people, has conferred a highly artificial literacy upon the illiterate or scarcely literate shepherd, plowman, fisherman, or . . . idiot child. "Afternoon of a Cow" not only dramatizes the pastoral symbiosis between "farmer" and "writer" but also projects that relationship out of one man's identity. Faulkner was not just a pastoral writer; the very structure of his personality was pastoral as well.

The gap between Trueblood and "Faulkner" is greater than the distance between the library, where the former writes, and the veranda, where the latter supervises his farm while reading detective magazines (US, 431). It separates two social classes, one "low" and the other "high." And it separates two distinct realms of experience: thinking and doing—the one indirect, abstract, and reflective; the other immediate, concrete, and instinctive. All pastoral art proceeds from the attempt to bridge this gap, to enjoy both the natural simplicity of the peasant and the empowering craft of the poet-aristocrat. "Afternoon of a Cow" shows that Faulkner was aware not only of his own attempt to bridge this gap but also of the dangers of failing to do so.

What primarily separates "Faulkner" from Trueblood is language. The "farmer" is profane, ungrammatical, and monosyllabic. The "writer" is euphemistic, punctilious, and bombastic. "Faulkner" lives in direct contact with powerful sensations, unmediated by words; Trueblood prefers, he says in true Truebloodian style, "to acquire my experience from reading what had happened to others or what other men believe or think might have logically happened to creatures of their invention or even in inventing what Mr. Faulkner conceives might have happened to certain and sundry creatures who compose his novels and stories" (US, 431).

Faulkner's division of his identity between these two personae suggests that his writing depended on a cooperation between opposite parts of himself that corresponded to opposite levels of his society. "Mr. Faulkner" "conceives" characters and events to write about; Trueblood commits them to paper. Each seems embarrassed by the other's mode of expression. In Trueblood's description of his employer's first words following Beulah's accident, for example, linguistic difference becomes the principal subject: "'Are you hurt, Mr. Faulkner?' I cried. I shall not attempt to reproduce Mr. Faulkner's reply, other than to indicate that it was couched in that pure ancient classic Saxon which the best of our literature sanctions and authorizes and which, due to the exigencies of Mr. Faulkner's style and subject matter, I often employ but which I myself never use although Mr. Faulkner even in his private life is quite addicted to it and which, when he employs it, indicates what might be called a state of the most robust, even though not at all calm, wellbeing. So I knew that he was not hurt" (US, 429).

This passage indicates Faulkner's distinction—serious, albeit jocular—between words that belong in written discourse and those that do not, even when "sanctioned." It assumes a difference between language appropriate to literature and language suitable to direct experience; and it therefore calls attention to the conditions under which this boundary may be crossed. "Afternoon" derives its comedy from an "unauthorized" crossing. A dialect story in reverse, it applies "high" style to "low" content. Trueblood has translated an almost untranslatably vulgar experience into genteel expression.

Faulkner's division of himself into two characters who use different kinds of language proves especially suggestive in the context of Maurice Coindreau's visit. Coindreau had completed a rough draft of *Le Bruit et la Fureur*—his translation of *The Sound and the Fury*—by late May 1937, and he had written to Faulkner requesting a meeting so that they could discuss textual problems. Faulkner had invited him to Beverly Hills, and the professor had arrived there on June 20 (BL, 956–57, 960). During the evenings of the following week, he questioned Faulkner concerning details of this novel to which Faulkner still felt more closely attached than to any of his others. Somewhat to his surprise, Coindreau found his author eager to elucidate the book's complexities and to make it accessible to French readers; and he observed that Faulkner "seemed to know *The Sound and the Fury* by heart, referring me to such and such a paragraph, to such and such a page, to find the key to some highly enigmatic obscurity."[11] Thus Faulkner revived "Afternoon of a Cow" at a time when he had forced himself to examine his own difficult prose intensively—at a time, in short, when he had had to submit to the trials of reading Faulkner.

The labor of clarifying his own troublesome text for French readers alerted him to the difficulties of communication generally and to the pitfalls in his books particularly. This author who claimed not to have considered his audience while he wrote *The Sound and the Fury*[12] had for once to confront his writing from his audience's point of view. In "Afternoon of a Cow," coincidentally, he had written *about* his writing. Acknowledging his increasing tendency toward stylistic complexity while fabricating *Absalom*, he had parodied his own excessiveness. Coindreau, the reader who had had to struggle more intimately with Faulkner's language than anyone else, was the perfect audience for this veiled confession (or apology).

Coindreau was the appropriate recipient in another way too. For "Afternoon of a Cow" presents Faulkner's creative methodology, allegorically, as a process of translation. In this portrait of the artist as *two* no-longer-young men, Faulkner chose to depict his way of composing as a resoundingly gratuitous rendering of simple, earthy experience into needlessly and conspicuously abstruse verbiage. "Mr. Faulkner," the profane farmer, invents stories out of his plebeian experience; the literary Trueblood translates them from unpublishable rustic discourse into "authorized" texts. Some such internal collaboration surely informed Faulkner's consciousness of his normal *modus operandi*. In "Afternoon," he confessed to misgivings about his instinctive methodology: the partnership had become unbalanced, or the partners no longer found each other compatible, or Faulkner had wearied of the task of harmonizing them. For whatever reason, he had begun to regard his pastoral bilingualism as potentially debilitating rather than enabling. Over the next ten to fifteen years, he explored that debility as one of the main subjects of his fiction.

One final fact supports the hypothesis that "Afternoon of a Cow" constitutes Faulkner's analysis of his own voice. Its title directly parodies Mallarmé's poem "L'Après-Midi d'un Faune," a very loose English *translation* of which had been the first text Faulkner ever succeeded in publishing— under the French title in 1919 in the *New Republic* (EPP, 39–40, 123– 25). Thus, Faulkner's facetious title in the thirties alludes specifically to the inauguration of his career, and by extension to the career as a whole. The tacit subject of the story is the vocation Faulkner entered when his words first found a public. Working over Coindreau's shoulder on *Le Bruit et la Fureur* must have reminded him of his earlier translation from French into English. It sensitized him not only to the gap between a writer and a reader of different languages but also to the gap between *any* writer and *all* readers. In various ways, the books Faulkner wrote during the late thirties and the forties all attempt to measure this gap.

Working over Coindreau's shoulder must have reminded Faulkner, too, of the writer he had been when he composed his version of "L'Après-Midi d'un Faune." The dual self-portrait in "Afternoon of a Cow" originated in a repertoire of poses the younger Faulkner had foisted upon his friends, his neighbors, and himself. In attributing his fiction to ludicrously fictional surrogates of himself, he was confessing halfway seriously to the truth. For various reasons both psychological and cultural, he had based his literary career on an elaborately multiple impersonation, which destined him to eventual self-parody.

In fact, Faulkner was not being honest when he told Maurice Coindreau that he was giving him "the complete works of Ernest V. Trueblood." Actually, this literary *alter ego* already had a long, though sporadic, history; and Faulkner would "employ" him further, well after Coindreau's visit.

Blotner records an example of Trueblood's exploits from the late twenties, when the character was already associated with cow-pie pastoralism and with the difficulties of communication. When Faulkner was living in New York in late 1928, overseeing the publication of *Sartoris* and polishing *The Sound and the Fury*, he attended parties in Greenwich Village at which he was regarded as a minor celebrity, having already published two other novels and a book of poetry. His temporary roommate then, an artist from Louisiana named Owen Crump, has recalled that Faulkner evaded his notoriety in a way that was surely calculated to enhance it, by performing fictions.

> At some of these parties . . . he would seem an intellectual, a dapper figure, and when his silent mood was on him, almost a kind of mystery man. He was always, Crump remembered, an object of curiosity, and so he had developed strategies for bores. If silence or brusque answers failed to daunt them, he would . . . begin by telling a long and involved story. Sometimes a person named E. V. Trueblood would figure in it. The story would purposely have no point and get nowhere, but it would be full of directions about how to get places, going through meadows and across creeks. Sometimes the tale would vary. It might involve a baseball game in a cow pasture in which a runner slid into third base. Faulkner and Crump would covertly watch to see how long the hearer could stand it before he made a lame excuse and moved away. (BL, 594)[13]

Faulkner had already invented Trueblood and had already incorporated him into a misleading impersonation, in which failure to communicate was not only acknowledged but actively sought. Already, too, Faulkner was creating a "Mr. Faulkner," who embodied inaccessible urbanity and rural crudeness alternately. If "Mr. Faulkner" could be "dapper" and "intellectual" by contrast with the slovenly rube of the same name in "Afternoon," the Trueblood character is similarly changeable. In the mid-1930s, Trueblood is effete and fastidious; in the late 1920s, *he* was the one sliding into manure. In 1935 and 1937, he is the teller; in 1928, he was the told. Can we conclude that Faulkner needed to identify with his "writer" pose early in his career and with his "farmer" pose later? What matters, early and late, is that he recognized both as poses.

His brother John has recollected a variation on the Trueblood character, similarly exploited by Faulkner, that belongs to approximately the same period as the pasture-baseball stories: "As soon as his books began to be talked about and his name began appearing in print, he started getting fan mail. Requests for photographs, autographed ones, began coming in too. He invented a secretary for himself and named him Earnest Trueheart. He had some photographs made and borrowed the scratchiest pen he could find from the post office and signed *Earnest Trueheart* across his face in the photograph. He sent them to people who requested a picture and he would bring them by to show Mother, and me too if I was there. Earnest Trueheart became almost a living character among the three of us. That was one of the things no one else thought was funny" (MBB, 172). Perhaps it was the kind of joke one had to "be there" to appreciate; but, then again, even Coindreau did not smile when he heard it in an only somewhat less sophomoric version. Faulkner's self-mockery was too strained, his abuse of his audience too self-destructive, his gratification too ironic to be laughed away. Ernest Trueblood/Trueheart was Faulkner's *private* joke.

He cultivated it, on and off, all the rest of his life. Some time during the thirties or forties, for example, he composed a movie synopsis under the title "One Way to Catch a Horse," in which Ernest Trueblood is an honest but extremely simpleminded farmer from East Texas. The plot of this piece is so absurd that it seems to have been intended as a parody of a screenplay rather than as a serious film proposal.[14] A redneck Trueblood goes to the big city to sell his farm so that he can buy a larger one. Confidence men talk him into betting the proceeds on a fictitious horse race in Moscow. After they take his money, he and his drunken hired man, Pete, trail them back and forth across America and finally to Russia. At an "actual" race course near Moscow, the feckless Trueblood drives a mule-team to victory while Stalin himself watches. Impressed, Stalin appoints him "mule commissar" for the entire U.S.S.R. and assigns the O.G.P.U. to find his money. After completing a year's term in the Soviet bureaucracy and regaining his money, he flies home to a hero's welcome in Washington. Impervious to adulation, he hurries back to his family in Bluebell, Texas, to consummate the land deal he had initiated years earlier. His wife presents him with "his" newest child, a three-month-old boy she has named Roosevelt.[15]

Even toward the end of Faulkner's life, when his career was unassailably established and his livelihood secure, he had occasion to employ Trueblood's services. A year before his death, he sent his editor, Albert Erskine, a blurb "by" the effete, literate Trueblood for his final novel, *The Reivers:* "'An extremely important message. . . . eminently qualified to become the Western World's bible of free will and private enterprise.' Ernest V. Trueblood, Literary & Dramatic Critic, Oxford, (Miss.) Eagle" (SL, 455). A few years earlier, as writer-in-residence at the University of Virginia in the late fifties, he organized a facetious "flying club" among some worshipful members of the English faculty who were Air Corps veterans of World War II. They called one office the "Squadron Room," equipped it with a miniature Sopwith Camel, and engaged in military "playacting," complete with salutes and "inspections" (BL, 1640, 1671–72). To commemorate their camaraderie, Faulkner designed a scroll for each of them, in imitation of the winged insignia of the Royal Air Force, with the motto "Ad Astra Per Jack Daniel's." According to Joseph Blotner, one of the playactors, all the scrolls "were signed by 'Ernest V. Trueblood, Adjutant' in a bold signature with flourishes that completely disguised the penman's usually meticulous style" (BL, 1694).

Once again, Trueblood's name served as the stamp of inauthenticity that validated self-parody. Faulkner had joined the R.A.F. in Canada during World War I by pretending to be English (BL, 210-11). But he had been demobilized as a cadet who had never even flown a training plane (BL1, 64–65), much less the glamorous Camel, and he had not crossed the Atlantic until well after the war. When he returned to Oxford, however, he affected a limp, wore an officer's uniform, and concocted stories about his experience on the front (BL, 231–32). He told people he had a silver plate in his head and a metal disc "close to his hip" (BL, 324, 411). This impersonation continued intermittently through the twenties and beyond, and Faulkner's lies about his service record became part of his official biography. So deeply did he need the wounds he invented for himself—and the heroic identity that went with them—that he lied about them to the people he loved most, as well as to the strangers who wrote them into the public record.[16] Even forty years after the war, he was able to reactivate the R.A.F. pose, with juvenile zest; but he also reactivated his Truebloodian shadow-self to give the lie to his false identity. As always, Trueblood was the tongue in Faulkner's capacious cheek.

Faulkner's falsification of his war record, and his delayed, disguised acknowledgment of its falsity, will concern us further. For now, what matters is that, throughout his career, Faulkner maintained in Trueblood a literary *alter ego* through which he could express his deep fear of his own fraudulence as a writer. In fact, Trueblood was only the most obvious symptom of his lurking suspicion that his literary vocation was as bogus as his limp.

"Count No 'Count" and the "American Boy"

Faulkner's periodic reliance on the Trueblood character is simply one vestige of a repertoire of impersonations that he began to perform early in his youth. Indeed, the first version of Trueblood was not a literary invention but Faulkner himself. Beginning in his teens, as Blotner has amply recorded, he devoted considerable energy to a series of elaborate and interlocking roles. Within the matrix of these poses Faulkner declared his vocation, and his vocation consequently retained an element of imposture.[17] He consolidated his identity as a writer during an adolescence devoted to masquerade.

First and foremost, young Faulkner acted out the role of aesthete. Even when he was a child, according to Blotner, "[t]here was already a touch of the dandy about Billy" (BL, 109). He dressed fastidiously and gazed conspicuously at clouds. In his teens, "his generally remote and dreamy behavior began to be commonly noted, and though he still pitched in baseball season and quarterbacked pick-up football teams, he was decidedly different from the rest. He wrote and drew, and he read. He was silent and tended to keep to himself. Some of the students at the Oxford High School began to tease him and to call him 'quair.' He made no response" (BL, 160). By the time he was fourteen, he was composing poetry "with a good deal of pastoral imagery" (BL, 142). Before he was seventeen, he was teaching himself French and reading Swinburne, Keats, and the Imagists—hardly the normal fare of a Mississippi boyhood (BL, 164, 169).

When he was eighteen, his foppish dress and effete manners earned him the name "Count No 'Count," or just "Count," among less "cultivated" neighbors, who regarded his refined tastes as so many "airs." Though it was a university town, Oxford, Mississippi, knew few nineteen-year-olds so capable as the Count of addressing someone with a polished phrase. "Ah," he told an "excessively polite" Ben Wasson when they first met, "we seem to have a young Sir Galahad on a rocking horse come to our college campus." Listening to classical music on another friend's Victrola, he would turn out all the lights and deliver himself of an apothegm: "Even light can be too much distraction when music is being played." A Beethoven symphony stirred him to Truebloodian heights: "Listen to those horns of triumph and joy . . . crying their golden sounds in a great twilight of sorrow." One of this studiously ornamental young man's motives for writing poetry, clearly, was the opportunity it afforded him to *be* a Poet. He wore a handkerchief in his coat sleeve (BL, 180–83; CNC, 24–26, 34–36). In 1925, he admitted that his "mental life" when he was an adolescent had been "completely and smoothly veneered with surface insincerity—obviously necessary to me at that time, to support intact my personal integrity" (EPP, 114).

World War I gave Faulkner a chance to develop a new, though related, identity. At his friend Phil Stone's Commons table at Yale in mid-1918, he took lessons in pronunciation, diction, and usage from an Englishman, so that he might convince R.A.F. recruiters in New York that he was British (BL, 206). After his ruse succeeded, he perfected his impersonation at cadet school in Toronto. For the first time, he Anglicized his surname by adding the *u*; and he claimed to be a "student" from "Finchley, in the county of Middlesex, England." Even when he reverted to his native drawl, the Canadians in his "wing" thought he was English (BL, 210–11). "[H]e gave signs," Blotner adds, "of constructing a persona that apparently pleased him a good deal better than his own identity. . . . He seemed to be in the process of building a new exterior for himself." He grew a moustache, dressed extravagantly, and wrote brooding poetry in his spare time (BL, 215).

When the Armistice prematurely ended his aviator's career before he had even flown, Faulkner returned to Mississippi with his military persona intact. When he got off the train in Oxford, he exhibited the theatrical limp, which he said had resulted either from an accident in Canada or from combat in France, depending on who was listening (BL, 225, 231–32). For years afterward, he would appear in the streets of Oxford wearing the uniform, the limp, and an air of glamorous fatality (BL, 324, 369).[18] Sometimes he carried a cane or a swagger stick (BL1, 68). According to one account, he even sported a monocle on occasion.[19]

Soon after his return, he began to create a third role for himself. Still identifiably a "Poet," Faulkner now assumed a slovenly bohemianism as often as the exquisite refinement he had affected before the war.[20] Back in Oxford, he dismayed some townspeople, including especially his father, by dressing down rather than up, sometimes walking barefoot through the streets (BL, 292–94). Unlike other veterans who were building careers for themselves, he held a series of odd jobs. When he finally landed a permanent position, as postmaster for the University of Mississippi—a "man of letters" indeed—he made sure that his service was so unsatisfactory that even a sympathetic government inspector would have no choice but to fire him (BL, 327–66). Something of a vagabond, he gravitated toward the capitals of the avant-garde: Greenwich Village, the French Quarter in

New Orleans, the Latin Quarter in Paris. He later admitted to having felt an artist's need "to be with people that have the same problems and the same interests as him, that won't laugh at what he's trying to do, won't laugh at what he says no matter how foolish it might sound to the Philistine" (BL, 368). Yet he always returned to Oxford, as if he needed the Philistines' disdain in order to convince himself that he was the "Poet" he hoped to be.

Faulkner seems to have reserved a fourth pose for his travels, although it was the most closely related to home. On occasions when no one from Oxford could contradict him, he pretended to be the doomed scion of a Southern plantation family. On latrine duty in cadet school, he dropped his English pretense long enough to complain that "in his country there was a special race of people to perform such work" (BL, 213). Three years later in New York, he asked friends "for a loan until he received some money from home, which was a 'Southern plantation'" (BL, 324). When he met Sherwood Anderson in New Orleans in 1924, he managed to convey the impression that he was the tragic son of an aristocratic Southern family (BL, 368n, 369–71).

Anderson's thinly fictionalized account of his early acquaintance with Faulkner amply demonstrates the degree to which Faulkner could combine at will his separately developed personalities. In "A Meeting South," first published in 1925, Anderson recounted a visit from a serious young man whom, "for convenience's sake," he chose to call "David"—a name Faulkner would adopt for fictionalized versions of himself throughout the late 1920s.[21] Anderson's David walked with a limp, tried to disguise a "look of pain that occasionally drifted across his face," and drank prodigiously from a bottle he carried in his hip pocket. The bottle, he explained, contained whiskey made by a "nigger on his father's plantation somewhere over in Alabama." Once, his family had owned "several great plantations," but now they were reduced to "a few hundred acres" through decay and incompetence. David was a poet, who referred to Keats and Shelley as "the two English poets all good Southern men love." Reluctantly, he allowed Anderson to extract from him "[t]he story of how he chanced to be a cripple"—how he had served "all through the war with a British flying squadron, but at the last got into a crash and fell." He suffered constantly, not only because of a pinched nerve in his crippled leg but also because of a "silver plate" embedded in his skull. An insomniac, he could find relief from his agony only by drinking or by lying on the ground near the Negro cabins when "our niggers" are making molasses. "The mosquitoes bite me some," he confided, "but I don't mind much. . . . The little pain makes a kind of rhythm for the bigger pain—like poetry."[22]

Even if we assume that Anderson exaggerated Faulkner's performance, his account tallies with many similar ones collected by Blotner, whose biography presents the young Faulkner as a compulsive actor, capable of orchestrating several privately molded characterizations for public consumption. All of these poses—aesthete, bohemian, wounded veteran, Englishman, poet, drunkard, even the Southern aristocrat in a way—share one trait: they are all foreign to the ordinary life of Oxford, Mississippi.

Clearly, Faulkner's decision to become a writer—not just to write, but to adopt a "literary" identity before the world—was intimately connected to a need for disguises. Just as certainly, the disguises he chose were determined in part by the nature of the community he considered his home and by the range of identities that community sanctioned. By defining himself through departure from the expectations of Oxford, Mississippi, he came paradoxically to mirror the town, internalizing its norms by reacting specifically against *them* rather than against others.

At the beginning of the twentieth century, Oxford offered its citizens an extreme diversity of cultural experiences. In some ways it was scarcely more than a frontier town. The "Big Woods" were still nearby, and a collective memory of Indians was alive, if dim. Violent acts of brutality were commonplace, especially against black people, and would-be gentlemen still sometimes settled their differences according to a vestigial code of honor. Lafayette County was basically agricultural; a large portion of its population were functionally illiterate; and the folkways of a peasant society were clearly visible.

At the same time, however, Oxford was a university town, with an entrepreneurial citizenry eager to embrace "progress" and "culture." Its citizens avidly imported the railroad, the automobile, and the airplane, modern miracles that contrasted sharply with the handmade artifacts and the strenuous tedium of traditional labor. The University of Mississippi may not have lived up to the town's namesake, but Oxford did occasionally bathe in side-eddies of the world's intellectual and artistic currents. Indeed, the town enjoyed an intellectual heritage. During the nineteenth century, it had provided a home for Augustus Baldwin Longstreet, one of the founders of imaginative literature in the South, and for his son-in-law

L. Q. C. Lamar, a statesman of the Confederacy and then an associate justice of the U.S. Supreme Court (BL, 168–69). While Faulkner was growing up there, however, Oxford relied for cultural expression upon performances of *Rip Van Winkle* at the "Opera House" and upon lectures at the University Lyceum Hall (BL, 106). In 1906, for example, when Faulkner was in the first grade, the campus welcomed a "Shakespearean recital" by one "Thomas C. Trueblood, A.M., Prof. of Elocution and Oratory, University of Michigan" (BL, 101).

Whether Thomas Trueblood engendered Ernest somewhere in the circuitry of Faulkner's memory is unknowable. But the uneasy collaboration between erudite Ernest and vulgar "Mr. Faulkner" certainly originated in Oxford's cultural dichotomy. Blotner provides graphic examples of the town's incongruities. In 1907, for instance, students at Ole Miss "enacted Molière's *Le Malade Imaginaire*, a performance hailed as 'the first production of a classic play in any foreign language ever given in the South. . . .' If contrast were needed to show the range of experience available in Lafayette County, it was provided by another item a week later. 'Quite an excitement prevailed in Potlockney neighborhood Saturday,' the report began. 'Charley Mize's hounds gave chase to a wolf-like varmint.' Shot by Ernest Mize, it measured six and a half feet from tip to tip" (BL, 106).

Faulkner knew the "active" side of Oxford life. He hunted and fished, played football and baseball, caught free rides on the railroad, experimented with home-brewed alcohol, launched hand-built airplanes, and lent a curious ear to reports of lynchings and other violence (BL, 111–48 passim). With his brothers, he tried to enact the fantasies purveyed in the popular children's magazines to which they subscribed. The *Youth's Companion* and *St. Nicholas* may have included poetry (the latter even published verse submitted by its young readers), but they devoted most of their pages to adventure, sports, and science: stories with such titles as "Andrew Hastings, Aviator," "Betty and the 'White Water,'" and "Memoirs of a White Indian"; articles about "Foot-ball Under the New Rules" and "Photographing a Glacier." Among these indirect incitements to vigor, *St. Nicholas* inserted more explicit injunctions to "enter the fighting-field of life." And the editor of the *Youth's Companion* praised Mark Twain not for his writing but for paying his debts: even a humorist could "play the manly part."[23] Young William's favorite "companion," however, was an even more purely masculine celebration of adolescent enterprise, the *American Boy:* "He had a subscription, and when each issue of the large magazine came he pored over it—over the short stories, which might be comic, sentimental, or uplifting; the articles on famous men; departments such as 'The Boy Debater' and 'The Boy Coin Collector'; ads for moneymakers a boy could sell; or wonderful items for sale, such as a camera or a real Morse telegraph" (BL, 101).

Yet the premier fact of Faulkner's youth is that, while still poring over each issue of the *American Boy* (a magazine which had been founded as a protest against the "sissified" *Youth's Companion*[24]) and while still attempting to embody its energetic, middle-class ideals, he began to write "pastoral" poetry unlike anything that appeared in any of his magazines (BL, 142).

Out of the total range of identities available in Oxford, Mississippi, at the beginning of the century, young Faulkner gravitated toward one—or several—calculated to test the town's indulgence severely. By setting out to "be" a poet, he declined to become the "American boy" his neighbors expected, negating his own normality and inviting their rejection. Nevertheless, his rebellion was safe, because the role he adopted was officially sanctioned by the community's sponsorship of "cultural" events. Faulkner's original decision to become a writer and his lifelong sense of his literary vocation sprang in part from his need for his hometown to resist and spurn him. He was already making himself Oxford's exile-in-residence.

Just how assiduously Faulkner courted disapproval is revealed in a cultural battle he was forced to join soon after World War I. His artistic pretensions had already won him the "Count" label before 1918, but his athletic efforts may have softened the town's displeasure. When he returned from R.A.F. training in Canada, however—sporting the British accent, the moustache, the *u* in his name, and the cane for his "limp," and submitting aggressively high-falutin' verse to the campus newspaper—he provoked public criticism.

Between November 1919 and May 1920, Faulkner published a dozen poems in the *Mississippian*, the campus newspaper of Ole Miss (EPP, 6–17, 125–29; BL, 252–71). All were ambitious and esoteric, filled with archaic diction, with references to the fauns and nymphs of conventional pastoralism, and with allusions to foreign literature, especially to French

Symbolist poetry. In "Naiads' Song," for example, water nymphs invite mortals to a subaqueous repose (and to suicide by drowning) at the hour of Pan's piping:

> Come ye sorrowful and keep
> Tryst with us here in wedded sleep,
> The silent noon lies over us
> And shaken ripples cover us,
> Our arms are soft as is the stream. . . .
>
> Come ye sorrowful and weep
> No more in waking, come and steep
> Yourselves in us as does the bee
> Plunge in the rose that, singing, he
> Has opened. . . .   (EPP, 55–56)

Faulkner had "translated" four of the poems—"Fantoches," "Clair de Lune," "Streets," and "A Clymène"—from Verlaine (or from Arthur Symons's translations of Verlaine[25]). "Clair de Lune" typifies the whole group of poems in its prosodic clumsiness and in its depiction of a formal garden, frozen into artifice by the touch of an unearthly light:

> Your soul is a lovely garden, and go
> There masque and bergamasque charmingly,
> Playing the lute and dancing and also
> Sad beneath their disguising fanchise [sic].
>
> All are singing in a minor key
> Of conqueror love and life opportune,
> Yet seem to doubt their joyous revelry
> As their song melts in the light of the moon.
>
> In the calm moonlight, so lovely fair
> That makes the birds dream in the slender trees,
> While fountains dream among the statues there;
> Slim fountains sob in silver ecstasies.
>   (EPP, 58)

Most readers of the *Mississippian*—and of the Oxford *Eagle*, which reprinted one or two of the poems—were not accustomed to such fare. They would not have cottoned even to accurate and graceful translations of Verlaine. The verse with which they were familiar treated romantic or inspirational subjects sentimentally, or it tapped a regional humor that depended on rural dialects. They would have recognized and understood, though perhaps not liked, the poetry in their children's magazines:

Billy's Way
   by Harriet Prescott Spofford

The ice was strong and crystal clear,
   And Billy, the dear little man,
Longed for an ice-boat that should sail
   As swift as only ice-boats can.

To think, with Billy, was to do,—
   He called the other fellows in,
And, in no time at all, the boat
   Was built and rigged and bound to win.

Then, as they would have launched their work,
   Down came a swooping whirl of snow,
Covered the pond, and broke their hearts,
   Seeing their labor thus laid low.

Not so with Captain Billy; he
   For brooms and shovels called straitway:
They swept the pond of all the snow,
   And launched the ship and sailed away![26]

The Count's way differed markedly from Billy's, and in early 1920 the community expressed its opinion. One month after Faulkner was black-balled from the Scribblers of Sigma Upsilon (a campus literary society) because of his "airs," the first in a series of parodies appeared. On February 25, the student newspaper presented Faulkner's Verlainesque "Fantoches,"[27] a *commedia dell'arte* fantasy. Across from it, on the same page, appeared an unsigned ditty that more nearly satisfied whatever appetite for poetry existed in Oxford. If it is a response to Faulkner, as seems indubitable, it mocked not "Fantoches" but "Naiads' Song," published three weeks earlier. The parody converts the water-nymphs' languid invitation into a swain's resistance of *his* siren; then, it transmogrifies the seductive maiden into a barnyard animal:

A Pastoral Poem

Ah, fair one, with those dreamy eyes,
That have the raven robbed
Of all his darkened, mystic lustre,

Heed now my sobs and sighs,
Consider my plight
This dreary night
'Neath lowring and blackning skies.

Why must I brave this threatning storm
That rumbling far away
Comes closer to the near-at-hand,
Forebiding [sic] grief and harm.
Consider my plight
This dreary night
And leave me to my fireside warm.
She chews her cud with dainty jaw,
As now I milk her, "saw cow, saw."
                              (BL, 265–66)

This seductive animal runs in the same literary herd with Beulah in "Afternoon of a Cow," and later with Ike's cow in *The Hamlet*. Its juxtaposition with "Fantoches" neatly epitomizes the bifurcation of Oxford culture and the schizophrenic foundation of Faulkner's vocation. The authors of "A Pastoral Poem" were two undergraduates named W. H. Drane Lester and Louis M. Jiggitts, roommates who served on the newspaper staff, belonged to the Scribblers of Sigma Upsilon, and went on to win Rhodes scholarships. Far from the bumpkins their poem implies, they were so well read that they knew the conventions of pastoral poetry thoroughly enough to parody them, and they were confident enough of their literacy to enjoy imitating the vernacular idiom they heard all around them. Together they contributed to the newspaper a regular feature called the "Hayseed Letters," a prose equivalent to their doggerel poem. Just as the poem ridicules not so much pastoral poetry as an uneducated pretension to it, the "Hayseed Letters" ridicule a hick's impersonation of learning—a phenomenon that must have been plentifully evident at Mississippi's state university in the teens. A fictitious Ole Miss student named Hiram Hayseed purportedly wrote home to the farm, describing university life in wide-eyed and ungrammatical letters; and his father, Si, responded with rural news. One of Hiram's favorite subjects was Count No 'Count (BL, 266; CNC, 42).

Similar columns had also appeared in the Oxford *Eagle* for years. "One typical one," according to Blotner, "full of phonetic spellings, was 'Josiah Slick's Letter to his Old Woman.' There was something of the same flavor in the noms de plume of the correspondents from the outlying areas of the county, as when the Live Oak news would be written by 'Clod Knocker,' the Oak Grove news by 'Cucumber Green,' and the Pleasant Ridge news by 'A Peach Bud'" (BL, 101).

When Faulkner submitted his poems to the *Mississippian*, he could only have done so in full knowledge of the poetic taste of its readership and its editorial staff. He knew that most of his readers would be more like Hiram Hayseed than like Lester and Jiggitts; and he knew that people like Lester and Jiggitts stood ready to lambaste any Hiram Hayseeds impudent enough to pretend being cultivated. In short, he submitted his poems purposefully to a hostile audience; he offered them for publication in a specifically satirical context. When satire resulted, he may have been gratified as much as embarrassed.

Faulkner soon suffered more direct parodies than "A Pastoral Poem." When his imitation of Verlaine's "Clair de Lune" was published on March 3, the editors placed it only two inches above something called "Whotouches," by "J," which they introduced as "Just a parody on Count's 'Fantouches' by Count, Jr." Faulkner deigned to respond, grandly, in a letter that the editors published on March 17 under the title "The Ivory Tower." He defended himself by surrendering. "A Pastoral Poem" was stupid, he declared, "for my own poem was stupid." He shrugged off the parodies by affecting indifference to them ("the answer is, of course, simply de gustibus") and by submitting with his letter two more poems: "A Poplar" and "Streets," both imitations of Verlaine. The war continued. When "Streets" appeared on page 2 of the issue for March 17, symmetrically opposite it on page 3 appeared "Meats, A dainty little parody on Count's 'Streets,' by Count, Jr., Duke of Takerchance," with an attribution to "Pall Vaserline." Verlaine's refrain "Dansons la gigue!" Faulkner had translated as "Dance the Jig!"; Jiggitts or Lester turned it into "Hold the Pig!" (BL, 267–68; EPP, 128–29).

The following week, "J" published a letter entitled "The 'Mushroom' Poet," attacking the "peculiar person who calls himself William Faulkner": "[W]ouldn't this be a fine University if all of us were to wear sailor collars, monkey hats, and brilliant pantaloons; if we would 'mose' along the street by the aid of a walking prop; and, ye gods forbid, if we should while away our time singing of lascivious knees, smiling lute strings, and voluptuous toes? Wouldn't that be just too grand?" Another parody, entitled "Eheu! Poetae Miselli" (Oh! Poor Little Poet) and initialled "LMJ," appeared in the same issue; and yet another, "Cane de Looney," by a new parodist, appeared on April 7. More letters appeared also, including an unexpected defense of Faulkner ("The 'Mushroom Muse' and The 'Hayseed Hoodlum,'" by an unknown hand) and a second effort in supercilious self-defense by Faulkner himself (BL, 268–69).

As the spring progressed, *Mississippian* readers could follow a full-blown literary quarrel, which subsided only when the school term ended. Before the campus newspaper shut down for the summer, Faulkner published several more poems in his same vein; "J" wrote more letters; more parodies appeared. One of these, written by Paul Rogers and signed "Lord Greyson" (BL1, 82), was entitled "Une Ballade d'une Vache Perdue" (A Ballad of a Lost Cow), after Faulkner's Villonesque "Ballade des Femmes Perdues." Lord Greyson's three eight-line stanzas, according to Blotner, "described the heifer, Betsy, lost and wandering far from home. The poet had enjoyed himself describing the pastoral scene, and her 'rounded curves' and 'waving tresses' as 'she stood there nude'" (BL, 270–71).

The implications of Faulkner's Pastoral War are far-reaching. The clear resemblance between "Une Ballade d'une Vache Perdue" and "Afternoon of a Cow" demonstrates that between 1920 and 1935 Faulkner had internalized the task of parodying himself for which "J," "Lord Greyson," and the others first assumed responsibility. Long after his work had transcended any legitimate vulnerability to such sophomoric ridicule, Faulkner was capable of inflicting it upon himself. Long after he had proven the genuineness of his artistry, he remembered and perpetuated, very specifically, the accusations of fraudulence that had been leveled against him at the outset of his career.

An American in Paris

Faulkner transformed the parodic attacks into self-parody at least as early as 1925, when he first traveled to Europe. From Paris, he sent to Phil Stone a carbon copy of a poetic spoof he may have submitted to H. L. Mencken, enclosing with it a cover letter purportedly written by "Ernest V. Simms," of the "Baptist Young Peoples Union." Ostensibly addressing Mencken, Simms offered the editor of the *American Mercury* a forty-two-line poem entitled "Ode to the Louver," from the hand of "Wm Faulkner," who "wants to get a start at poetry." After explaining that he has chosen Mencken "because my family is long a reader of your magazine until a train reck 2 years ago," Simms set forth his editorial relationship to the young author: "I onley made corrections in the above poem without changing its sentiments because the poet himself quit schools before learning to write because I have a typewritter."[28]

In the semiliterate doggerel that followed, "Wm Faulkner" leads his readers on a poetic tour of the Louvre:

The Louver is on Rivoli street
You can take the cars or go by feet
The river is very deep and wide
It is more than a 100 metters from either side
The boats on it is called a barge
They are big but not as large
    As the Louver

Five subsequent stanzas recount a garbled history of the museum, describe its dimensions, and recommend it to American tourists. Simms provides helpful information in several "Orthurs notes" at the bottoms of the pages: he identifies the "Louver" as a "Big house in Paris, France. Near city hall"; and he defends the word "feet" at the end of line 2 on the grounds that "Foot dont rhyme with street."[29]

The "Ode to the Louver" preceded "Afternoon of a Cow" by a decade, but these two burlesques have much in common. Most obviously, a character named "Ernest V." appears in both as the amanuensis of "William Faulkner." Ernest Simms is far less sophisticated than Ernest Trueblood, but Simms's footnotes do display a Truebloodian impulse toward erudition and le mot juste. Moreover, Trueblood's convertibility into a dull Texas farmer, as in "One Way to Catch a Horse," suggests that the rube and the fop are simply two opposite results of the same self-parodic urge, resulting from two opposite reactions— a "low" one and a "high" one—against the middling life of Oxford.

This duality is more perfectly realized in "Afternoon," where Trueblood plays one part and "Faulkner," the farmer, plays the other. But the "Ode," because of its particular audience (Stone, not Mencken) and because of the European context of its composition, illuminates the schizophrenic history of Faulkner's vocation in some ways that "Afternoon" does not. Whereas Faulkner had clearly established literary credentials for himself when he wrote "Afternoon," he wrote the "Ode" at a time when he was still trying to persuade himself that he was a writer, not reevaluating a career well advanced. Part of his subject in 1925 was his effort to achieve an autonomous authorship, independent of trainers and managers.

When Phil Stone received the letter containing the "Ode" late in 1925, he surely recognized elements of his own correspondence on Faulkner's behalf. As Simms was writing to H. L. Mencken for his protégé, so Stone had written to many editors, Mencken probably included, in his capacity as Faulkner's unofficial literary agent. Since 1914, he had given his young friend books to read and had shaped his education. He had recited Greek poetry to him and talked politics with him. He had drilled him in English grammar and punctuation (BL, 169). In 1918, while at Yale, he had allowed Faulkner to share his room in New Haven (BL, 196–207). After he opened his law practice back in Mississippi, he had his secretary type Faulkner's poems, and he sent them to various magazines. Between 1918 and 1925, he assigned a filing cabinet in his office to Faulkner's typescripts and rejection letters. Stone also helped Faulkner send Coleridge's "Kubla Khan" to the *New Republic*, in the far-fetched hope that the editor would embarrass himself by publishing it—a prank that anticipated Faulkner's letter to Mencken (BL, 246–47). In 1921, Stone secured Faulkner his job as University of Mississippi postmaster to support the literary career (BL, 325–26).

Stone invested so much energy in making a writer of Faulkner that his support turned subtly into dependency. Relying on Faulkner to provide him vicariously with the literary career he knew he could not achieve himself, he became an aggressive parasite (BL, 325). One of their mutual friends remembered Stone's commitment to Faulkner's vocation as a kind of friendly bullying: "To say that Phil 'encouraged' Bill . . . is gross understatement. He cajoled, browbeat, and swore at him; he threatened and pleaded; encouragement came later" (BL, 336). In 1924 Stone negotiated the publication of Faulkner's first book, *The Marble Faun*, by personally guaranteeing the cost of production. In August, he was explaining to the Four Seas Company that "Mr. Falkner is not so very keen at attending to business and I shall probably have to handle most of the business matters" pertaining to the book (BL, 355, 358). After it was published, with a preface by Stone, Stone wrote to countless friends to promote it. To the Yale *Alumni Weekly* he announced, "This poet is my personal property and I urge all my friends and class-mates to buy his book" (BL, 373). By November, according to Blotner, "Phil Stone was caught up in a paroxysm of letter-writing and promotional activity—so much so that it is difficult to imagine how he could have devoted much time to his law practice" (BL, 374).

If the "Ode to the Louver" is Faulkner's parody of himself as a poet, one year after the publication of his first volume of poetry, then even more surely the letter from Ernest V. Simms is a parody of Phil Stone's services as Faulkner's "secretary" (BL1, 170). While this joke implies gratitude, moreover, it also expresses resentment. Simms may embody Faulkner's debt to a man who "corrected" his grammar, loaned him a "typewritter," and wrote to editors, but he is also an object of ridicule. Whether consciously or not, Faulkner was declaring his independence, refusing to be anyone's "property." His parody in 1926 of another man who helped launch his career, Sherwood Anderson, represented a similar gesture toward autonomy.[30] How significant, then, that a decade later Faulkner should still be exorcising this "influence-anxiety"—long after Stone (and Anderson too) had dropped out of the picture. In "Afternoon of a Cow," however, the foreign voice that Faulkner mocks is his own.

Of course, "Ode to the Louver" already contained self-mockery aplenty. If the urbane Stone was one source of Ernest Simms, Count Faulkner was another. The "Ode" satirized Stone as literary agent, but it satirized the agent's "property" too. And the ridicule that Faulkner aimed at himself by pretending to "South'run" illiteracy derived precisely from the foreignness of his own literary voice to his own middle-class ear.

Faulkner would perform "Afternoon of a Cow" while *The Sound and the Fury* was being translated into French. His first publication had been an English translation of a French poem, "L'Après-Midi d'un Faune." He created his first audience—characteristically, a hostile one—by translating poems of the French author Verlaine into English. He went to France, at Stone's urging, because both considered it the homeland of any writer (BL, 375). In the "Ode to the Louver," itself a translation (or mistranslation) of Parisian words and sights into an American English that the rudest Mississippi farmer could understand, Faulkner parodied his own Francophilia.[31] In Paris in the fifties, he would pretend to a thoroughly disingenuous simplicity: "Je suis fermier." In Paris in the twenties, he had rehearsed the rube's role in *earnest*.

Phil Stone, who had majored in Greek and Latin at Ole Miss, had begun to saturate his young friend in all of the national literatures of Europe as early as 1914—when, of course, Europe was on everyone's mind. He would pack his car with books and send his "American boy" out in it to find a shady spot in the country to read. While Faulkner sampled Greek, Latin, German, and other authors in translation, he made a diligent effort to learn French. During his brief enrollment at the university, the grade he received in English was a D, but he earned a B in Spanish and an A in French. He may have imitated British manners and British speech, but for direct literary models he turned toward the Romance languages (BL, 163, 169, 264).

Faulkner embraced Mediterranean culture as a way to repudiate the vulgarity of Anglo-Saxon America. What he liked best about Europe was that it was not Oxford, Mississippi. He made this preference clear in letters he wrote from Europe to his mother, complaining of the crassness of the middle-class American tourists he encountered and praising the easygoing customs of France and Italy. In Paris, for example, he admired an old man who floated a miniature sailboat in the pool of the Luxembourg Gardens: "Think of a country where an old man, if he wants to, can spend his whole time with toy ships, and no one to call him crazy or make fun of him! In America they laugh at him if he drives a car even, if he does anything except play checkers and sleep in the courthouse yard" (SL, 15).

He felt solidarity with both peasants and aristocrats, scorning only the European middle class, which he identified with the United States. Thus, he disliked Switzerland, "a big country club with a membership principally American," but he relished the town of Sommariva in north Italy, where, he claimed, "I lived with the peasants, going out with them in the morning to cut grass, eating bread and cheese and drinking wine from a leather bottle at noon beneath a faded shrine with a poor little bunch of flowers in it, and then coming down the mountain at sunset" (SL, 19). By the 1950s, his memory had expanded this pastoral interlude from two or three days into a whole summer (BL, 1482). But, in a way, it *had* lasted longer: when he had arrived in Paris, having walked north from Italy, he had rented an apartment in a blue-collar neighborhood. "They are grand people, the working classes," he wrote home, "among whom I live myself." But he could also appreciate the vestiges of royalty he encountered. After visiting Vincennes and the Tuileries Gardens, he declared that "there really should be a king here" (SL, 21, 24). Thus, Faulkner's love affair with France was connected not only to his literary aspirations but also to his social rebelliousness. His identification with peasants and aristocrats was a means toward affirming his artistic vocation—and vice versa.

When an aunt and cousin from Mississippi visited him in Paris, they embodied the small-town, middle-class American culture from which Europe had temporarily liberated him. They represented home, and Faulkner recoiled. "They are very nice," he wrote, ironically, to his mother, whose complicity he seems to have assumed, "of the purest Babbitt ray serene. They carry their guidebooks like you would a handkerchief. They make you think of two people in a picture show who are busy talking to each other all the time. Europe has made no impression on them whatever other than to give them a smug feeling of satisfaction for having 'done' it." To cleanse himself of their influence, he declared his intention to "go down into Burgundy again, and see the peasants make wine . . ." (SL, 22). At roughly the same time, in a story he wrote while in Europe, he praised the virtue of "all peoples who live close to the soil" (BL, 445). [32]

To the Faulknerian false identities we have already collected, let us add one more, which subsumes the rest: I'm not middle-class, and I don't really belong to Oxford, Mississippi, he seemed to be announcing. I can be a "farmer," or I can be a "count," or, better yet, I can be both at once; but what I *must* not be is what I *am*. For Faulkner, writing was a means of achieving selfhood by escaping from it. His success would naturally prove self-cancelling to some degree.

The "Ode to the Louver" is a silly squib, but it is also a more complex and revealing document than Faulkner himself knew. Obviously, it expresses disdain for the average American tourist's blindness to France. It might also be said to ridicule those who had parodied his French-inspired poetry; they were as blind to French culture as "Wm" and "Ernest," despite their learning. One target of Faulkner's satire is the Oxford audience that preferred "Hiram Hayseed" to "L'Après-Midi d'un Faune."

By attributing the "Ode" to himself, however, even if only through Simms, Faulkner also faced the fact that he too was something of a tourist. *He* was "Hiram Hayseed," writing letters home. Through the "Ode," he covertly acknowledged that his own smug affectation of a European (that is, simultaneously working-class, aristocratic, and artistic) identity was false. More significantly, the piece exposes as futile his whole ambition to be a writer—closely allied as it was to English mannerisms and French authors. For the "Wm Faulkner" in the "Ode" is irremediably American and hopelessly unliterary. His attempt to graft himself onto European culture is ludicrous. In the "Ode to the Louver," as in "Afternoon of a Cow," Faulkner vocalized his deep-seated uncertainty about the legitimacy of his vocation.

Soon after Faulkner returned from Europe to Mississippi, he began his second novel by pulling a Prufrockian character named Herb out of an unpublished short story, "Don Giovanni" (BL, 514–15; US, 480–88), and renaming him . . . Ernest. If Ernest Simms represents Faulkner's projection of himself as a fake rube, Ernest Talliaferro in *Mosquitoes* (1927) is one of the *other* false Faulkners, one of the effete rather than the rustic Truebloods. Talliaferro is a fastidious dilettante and an inept seducer, through whom Faulkner evidently wished to satirize a type of pseudo-intellectual he encountered in New Orleans. But Faulkner was among his own targets. As the Count had occasionally carried a cane, so does Talliaferro. Like Faulkner, Talliaferro has "done" Europe in a few weeks' time, gaining "a smattering of esthetics and a precious accent." As the author had affected exaggeratedly genteel speech and manners from time to time, despite his American-Boy upbringing, so does his character, despite an even more undistinguished rearing. As Faulkner had been born Falkner, so Talliaferro (pronounced "Tolliver"?) "had been born Tarver." Each changed his name to elevate its tone (MOS, 12–13, 31–33).[33] Thus, the one novel Faulkner explicitly devoted to the subject of the artistic vocation begins with a Truebloodian self-portrait of a Faulkner unsure of his claim upon genuine artistry. Talliaferro only *visits* a true artist—the sculptor, Gordon.

Mosquitoes may be the only novel into which Faulkner inserted one of his self-parodic Ernests (*and* one of his self-parodic "Mr. Faulkners" [MOS, 144–45]). But Talliaferro anticipates two more seriously drawn characters who serve similar functions in his later fiction. Both Horace Benbow during the late 1920s and early 1930s and Gavin Stevens during the late 1930s and afterward derive partially from the writer's need to include his own replica in the world he creates. Neither is quite so ridiculous as any of Faulkner's Ernests, but both do provide the author with vehicles of self-criticism. In Stevens, particularly, we shall see a personification of Faulkner's doubts about the fruitfulness of a literary vocation.

The anxiety that produced "Afternoon of a Cow" in the mid-1930s thus spanned Faulkner's career. It flared now and then into illuminating manifestations, then subsided; but it was never absent. It originated in the same genesis that produced the vocation it called into question: the same childhood and adolescent experience that made young Billy decide to become a writer made him also doubt his decision; the same cultural traditions that nourished his voice would also tempt him toward silence.

CHAPTER TWO

THE PSYCHOPATHOLOGY OF VOCATION

I don't see what my private life has to do with my writing.

William Faulkner, 1950

Of Children in Swaddling Clothes
    O cities of the sea, I behold in you your citizens, women as well
as men tightly bound with stout bonds around their arms and legs
by folk who will not understand your language; and you will only be
able to give vent to your griefs and sense of loss of liberty by making
tearful complaints, and sighs, and lamentations one to another; for
those who bind you will not understand your language nor will you
understand them.

Leonardo da Vinci, *Codex Atlanticus*

Maud's Corset

Why did Faulkner limp? Why did he lie about nonexistent wounds all of
his life? Why did he assert false identities so aggressively? And why did *this*
Mississippi adolescent choose to become a writer, while his chums were
growing up to farm cotton or sell insurance? If he had to write, why in
ways guaranteed to alienate his neighbors? Once he had written, why did
he have to mock himself in print? After he earned success, what compelled him to court failure?

Faulkner's literary vocation was fatally rooted in deception and fraudulence. Ernest Trueblood was neither earnest nor true. Faulkner's
awareness of the artificiality of his calling—paradoxical in so "natural" a
writer—would affect the whole course of his career. In the late thirties and
throughout the forties, this self-consciousness climaxed in a series of

books that are partially about their own liabilities as books. In highly literate ways, they confess doubts about the value of literacy.

Faulkner's mid-life questioning of his vocation originated in the psychological and social conditions that had influenced him to become a writer in the first place. That decision was far from inevitable: few children growing up in Mississippi between the turn of the century and the First World War entertained the wish to become writers. Yet Faulkner's choice, over-determined, had a superfluity of causes. In poems and stories that he wrote in the late teens and the twenties, he defined his vocation through a matrix of images he drew from childhood experiences. He related his writing to the primal histories of his family and of his body. His ambivalence about family and body consequently insured that his literary identity would rest on shaky ground.

Freudian critics, naturally, have traced Faulkner's vocation to his infancy. Jay Martin, for example, has examined the available evidence of baby William's relation to his mother, Maud. When the child had colic, she had to rock him in a straight chair every night during his first year to stop his otherwise incessant crying. Such devotion, Martin argues, endowed Faulkner with "oral optimism, a basic belief in regular feeding." But, says Martin, "[c]olic that is so persistent and so regularly time-specific suggests . . . some disappointment in the feeding relationship which made necessary a prolongation of the holding position." Because Maud Falkner fed her oldest son efficiently but unlovingly, Martin suggests, he became a storyteller in order to win his mother's affection: "He had lost the loved object, the fantasized mother, by oral eroticism. He tried to call her back with his mouth, by speech—and he spent his life trying to express the wound he felt he had received even before speech." His frustrated need for oral gratification "was sublimated into a drive to give gratification by the same organ, through speaking to others or writing."[1]

For Martin, furthermore, Faulkner's "oral ambivalence" dominated his entire "psychosexual development." His "anal stage" was repressed because of his retarded orality: to earn oral pleasure, including food, he had to submit to the strict regimen of his very orderly mother, who "established regulations that never yielded to impulse." Consequently, "[t]he leading feature of his personality during his childhood seems to derive from the sublimation of anal eroticism into character formation." Martin provides plentiful reminders of Faulkner's anal "retentiveness," including his preoccupation with money, his fastidiousness of dress, and his crabbed penmanship.[2]

Moreover, Martin convincingly links these manifestations to the mother's rigidity, which is epitomized by the back brace she required William to wear when she suspected he was becoming stoop-shouldered.[3] Throughout most of his thirteenth and fourteenth years, she laced him into a canvas corset with padded armholes and a whalebone-reinforced back (BL, 140). It temporarily kept him from playing sports, and it produced an erectness of posture that distinguished him the rest of his life. When she tentatively released him from the contraption, he had to maintain a "ramrod straightness" to "evade the torture" of its confinement (BL, 157).[4] That Faulkner stood at attention ever afterward implies that he had internalized his mother's expectations—or that he continued unconsciously to fear that she might strap him back in the corset. That his fear was partly conscious is suggested by one of the gifts she received from him later: "a three-inch statuette of Atlas with the world on his back—actually a small clock set in a round metal case" (BL1, 215). Perhaps he was assuring her that he still tried to straighten himself under the load he bore; perhaps he was accusing her of bowing him beneath the burden of her expectations. To attain freedom, he would always need to accept strict discipline.

Lessons in the futility of rebellious disorder were provided by Faulkner's father, Murry. A small-town good-old-boy, Murry enjoyed masculine companionship and masculine pastimes. In the livery stable which he owned for a time, he would slouch in a tilted chair listening to his cronies talk about livestock, local politics, and hunting exploits. The physical looseness coincided with moral and intellectual relaxation as well. A silent, unambitious man whose reading tended toward Western shoot-'em-ups, he indulged himself periodically in temper tantrums and alcoholic binges. Surrendering the home sphere to his wife, he surrendered his four sons to her as well, never inviting them fully into his confidence or into his world of horses, hardware, and hunting. When William or his brothers tried to enter that world, they not only failed to win his affection but they immediately aroused the maternal censor within themselves as well. William's various imitations of his father—in academic truancy, in alcoholism, in masculine camaraderie—all failed to earn him either a paternal blessing or a respite from the voracious expectations of his mother.[5]

Martin's diagnosis was anticipated in early 1953 by a New York psychiatrist whom Faulkner, in a weak moment, had consented to visit. For a year following a particularly hard fall from his horse Tempy (BL, 1411), he had suffered back pain so severe that it interfered with his work on A *Fable*, which he was then trying desperately to finish. When his misery forced him to seek medical attention in France in May 1952, the Parisian doctors discovered he had broken two vertebrae (BL, 1422). Back home, he controlled his agony by ingesting beer, liquor, and Seconal, and by consummating his long, hopeless affair with the young woman he then loved, Joan Williams. But in August 1952, while sailing on Lake Sardis near Oxford, he fell from his boat into the path of its keel, which struck him across the back (BL, 1431). A month later a convulsive seizure landed him in a hospital, where he actually told doctors that his spinal trouble had started with his plane crash during World War I, an event that had never occurred. They informed him that he had fractured five, not two, vertebrae, probably in a previous fall from a horse several years before, and that he had been walking around since then with a broken back. As he had previously done in Paris, he refused to undergo surgery. After traditional therapy did nothing to allay the pain, he reverted to his own alcoholic remedy (BL, 1433–34). In October, he fell down his stairway at Rowan Oak at least once: a visitor reported that "[h]is body [was] bloated and bruised from his many falls." Soon afterward, he was fitted for a steel back brace. As the therapists strapped him into it, perhaps he remembered his mother's whalebone corset. [6] He would wear the steel brace—or a "polo player's belt" he acquired at about the same time (BL, 1458)—periodically until the week of his death. [7]

In New York during the late autumn of 1953, mental disturbances accompanied the physical ones. After another collapse, a psychoanalyst named Eric Mosse diagnosed his condition as chronic depression and may actually have administered electroshock therapy (BL, 1442). When brief periods of amnesia visited Faulkner, the author guessed that he had hit his head during one of his falls. But the doctors could find no physiological explanation. So, in March and April, he submitted to nine sessions with Dr. S. Bernard Wortis, a distinguished psychiatrist (BL, 1452–54).

Wortis, a *cherchez-la-mère* Freudian, concluded that "Faulkner might not have received enough love from his mother": but, when the doctor probed, the patient "refused to talk." Wortis deemed him extraordinarily sensitive to other people but noted an effort to disguise that sensitivity: "One curious thing was the way his intense responsiveness never seemed to overflow into facial expression—at least in this consulting-room situation. It was as though he always exercised conscious control" (BL, 1453–54).

Dr. Wortis's coincidental association of Faulkner's self-repressive rigidity with a longing for maternal affection supports Martin's thesis. In the context of Wortis's diagnosis, moreover, the accident-proneness (or "punishment-proneness"?)[8] that landed Faulkner in psychiatry can be traced back at least to Maud's corset. The chronic spinal pain he suffered, and caused himself, throughout the last half of his life becomes legible in the light of his mother's proprietary claim on his back. By persistently damaging the part of his body that she had most clearly shaped, perhaps Faulkner was rebelling indirectly against her influence. By bending what she had straightened, perhaps he unconsciously punished her. Or, perhaps, he punished himself for transgressions against her rigid code by progressively depriving himself of the only token of her love that he carried with him, his erectness. Or, remembering that she had attended to him when he slouched, perhaps he battered his back in a subconscious effort to attract her attention again and to resume wearing her brace—or her embrace. Most likely, all these motives together impelled him to continue placing himself in jeopardy.

Our psycho-orthopedic bridge between Faulkner's teens and his twenties makes hypothetical sense of his phony limp as well. This bogus war souvenir was a deliberate lie, designed to incite pity and envy among friends and neighbors. At least once, it served him as a convenient alibi for a mediocre tennis game (CNC, 63). Well into the 1930s, he used it to excuse his alcoholism.[9] But Faulkner's need to limp transcended such "practical" motivations. The false injury represents a case of accident-proneness *manqué*. He needed so much to be broken or twisted that, when he could not make a real accident happen in World War I, he invented an imaginary one. The fact that in 1952 he attributed his actual spinal ailment to the same phantom air mishap that had produced his imaginary leg wound suggests that both the true and the false infirmities gratified the same desire. More important, both the real and the false wounds were necessary to his self-image as an artist. He would fill his works with lame and broken characters like himself.

The Marble Faun

The best evidence that Faulkner fought a lifelong civil war with his body over his mother's affection appears in the poems and stories of his twenties. Further, these works not only record that war but seem almost to have been generated by it. Faulkner's first book, *The Marble Faun*, combines an inquest into poetic vocation with a recurrent imagery of physical paralysis and maternal embrace.

Although the poetry in this volume went unpublished until 1924, Faulkner wrote most of it in the spring of 1919 (BL, 240–48), at the peak of his theatrical lameness and at the outset of his published career. As "L'Après-Midi d'un Faune" is an abbreviated version of Mallarmé's poem, *The Marble Faun* is an expanded version of it. A "pastoral cycle" written from the point of view of a statue in a formal garden, *The Marble Faun* follows the sequence of the hours from morning through night back to day, and the sequence of the seasons from summer through winter to May. The faun expresses a melancholy longing to leave his pedestal and wander through the natural world around him. "If I were free," he pines, "then I would go . . ." (MF, 13)—to answer Pan's musical call and to frolic with nymphs amid the mountains and valleys of an eroticized landscape. The faun alternates between resigning himself to his imprisonment in stone and wishfully escaping toward—or from—the fecund, maternal earth. The earth has given him life and aspiration, but its gravitational pull paralyzes him. "The spreading earth calls to my feet" (MF, 12), he says, but he is crippled by his very love of and identification with "her":

> And my eyes too are cool with tears
> For the stately marching years,
> For old earth dumb and strong and sad
> With life so willy-nilly clad,
> And mute and impotent like me
> Who marble bound must ever be;
> And my carven eyes embrace
> The dark world's dumbly dreaming face,
> For my crooked limbs have pressed
> Her all-wise pain-softened breast
> Until my hungry heart is full
> Of aching bliss unbearable.   (MF, 36)

Unlike the "years," which "march" in a "stately" procession, the faun's "crooked limbs" can only limp across the breast of the land. Moreover, when the "breast" becomes anatomical as well as geographical, the "crooked limbs" change from legs and feet to arms and hands, with which the faun kneads as he nurses. This awkward, but revealing, equation of walking with suckling transforms the poem's imagery of stasis and locomotion into an extended metaphor for filial devotion and rebellion. All the creatures the faun observes or imagines are ambulatory. Poplar trees have "slender graceful feet / Like poised dancers, lithe and fleet" (MF, 11). Pan's "sharp hoofed feet have pressed / His message on the chilly crest" (MF, 13). The "lusty summer" (MF, 26) walks in a brook to cool his knees, while hillside "trees / March skyward on unmoving knees" (MF, 29).10 Even the moon—an "old" "mad woman"—has "white feet" that incongruously "weave a snare about my brain" (MF, 33). But when the faun envisions *himself* running free, "[l]ike a fox before the hounds," his revery can end only in collapse:

. . . My limbs fail
And I plunge panting down to rest
Upon earth's sharp and burning breast.
I lie flat, and feel its cold
Beating heart that's never old.
                    (MF, 39)

In the summer, the faun was able to fill his heart with "aching bliss unbearable" from the earth's breast. In the autumn, that breast is both "burning" and "cold." When winter comes, the "white silence" (MF, 44) of snow surrounds it, making it inaccessible; and the earth becomes an "it" rather than a "she." Then the spring seems to release the faun from his "prisoned woe" (MF, 46) of ice, so that he feels himself "all sun" (MF, 48). The thaw proves illusory, however: despite the flowering of his garden, his "heart knows only winter snow" (MF, 51).

The Marble Faun is the only book Faulkner dedicated to his mother. Its initials are Maud Falkner's, and its name resembles hers inversely. Its governing imagery recreates his experience in her whalebone corset: an uncomfortable and frustrating confinement followed by an illusory release. Just as the faun dreams of descending from his pedestal ("If I were free, then I would go . . ." [MF, 13]), so young William must have resented the immobilization that deprived him of football and the other activities of a normal American boyhood. Just as the faun suffers during his paralysis ("I cry moonward in stiff pain" [MF, 42]; "my back I cannot turn" [MF, 46]), William's back brace must have caused him occasional torture, which his mother expected him to endure stoically. Just as the faun anticipated freedom in the spring ("I am the life that warms the grass" [MF, 49], he foresees), William must have expected a return to normalcy with the brace's removal. And, just as the faun's hopes are dashed ("My heart knows only winter snow" [MF, 51]), so must William have been disappointed when his mother finally desisted from binding him. For, in order to preserve his freedom, he had to maintain the rigidity his imprisonment had produced. He became his own imprisoner, straightening and breaking his body throughout the rest of his life, fleeing from and longing for the captivity of a maternal embrace forever after.

Near the end of *The Marble Faun*, as the protagonist recognizes his heart's imperviousness to springtime warmth, he begins to imagine a different future. One moment feeling that he is "all sun"—or all "son"?— and that he heats the earth and brings forth life, in the next moment he entertains the opposite possibility:

> Or does the earth warm me? I know
> Not, nor do I care to know.
> I am with the flowers one,
> Now that is my bondage done;
> And in the earth I shall sleep
> To never wake, to never weep.
>   (MF, 49)

No true liberation will come until the final relaxation in the grave. In 1924, while *The Marble Faun* was in production, Faulkner wrote himself a precocious epitaph that would conclude a later book of poetry, *A Green Bough* (1933):

> But I shall sleep, for where is any death
> While in these blue hills slumbrous overhead
> I'm rooted like a tree? Though I be dead,
> This earth that holds me fast will find me breath.
>   (GB, 67; BL, 373–74)

The mother that nourishes also kills, but death brings a consummation in its maternal grasp.[11]

One subject of *The Marble Faun*, then, is Faulkner's radical ambivalence toward his mother. A more important, though related, subject is his abortive attempt to declare a vocation.[12] The imagery of locomotion and confinement overlays a similarly polarized imagery of silence and articulate sound. The faun receives a series of audible summons during his incarceration, literal "callings"—vocations—to action. First, the "spreading earth calls" to his "feet" (MF, 12). Elsewhere he hears invocations from poplar trees, from blackbirds (MF, 20–23), from a brook (MF, 25), from "the fecund year" (MF, 27), from rooks, from the "horns of sunset" (MF, 28), and from nightingales (MF, 29, 33). But the most imperative call he hears is that of the great god Pan, whose "shrill pipes" (MF, 15) control all the other sounds of nature.[13]

Faulkner's allusions to Pan are not so incongruous as they may seem now. The pastoral god of nature enjoyed an especially forceful revival during the nineteenth and early twentieth centuries. Two ancient accidents had converted the goat-legged protector of flocks into a complex cultural symbol. First, the identity of his name with the Greek word for *all* made him a convenient means of imputing a cosmic supremacy to rural landscapes and mores. Thus the pantheistic Romantics could pay homage to Pan as the divine principle within universal Nature. Second, the Roman historian Plutarch had recorded an announcement of the death of Pan during the reign of Tiberius—at the same time, Christian explicators would note, as Christ's crucifixion. Thus Pan and Jesus could be equated as shepherd-gods who died simultaneously; or, alternately, Pan could be construed as a pagan demon destroyed by Christ's triumph. Victorian poets debated the merits of classical and Christian culture by either lamenting or celebrating the "death of Pan." Between 1880 and 1914, following decades of accelerating reference to Pan, dozens of authors—including Swinburne, R. L. Stevenson, Nietzsche, Mallarmé, Pater, Wilde, Kipling, Chesterton, Pound, Frost, Saki, and Lawrence—devoted works to the goat-god's complex mythology.[14]

Faulkner may have learned some of the particulars of Pan mythology—and of pastoral literature generally—from his friend the classical scholar, Phil Stone. But the whole Pan complex so permeated literary culture in the 1910s that young William probably did not need special instruction. He might have known the full range of pastoral, pantheistic, Christian, and anti-Christian Pans.[15] The Pan who served him most fully, however, was the simple, Arcadian god of the pastures, whose principal attribute is the music he plays on his pipes. This is the Pan of Theocritus's *Idylls*—a benefactor except at noon, when he terrorizes anyone who disturbs his siesta, and the patron of rural musicians. It is the Pan of Ovid's *Metamorphoses*, whose pursuit of the beautiful nymph Syrinx frightened her into begging the river-god Ladon to disguise her, so that when Pan seized her he

> . . . held a sheaf of reeds,
> Which when he breathed his sighs at losing Syrinx
> Echoed his loss with melancholy cries,
> A tender music of bird-calls that pleased
> His ear.[16]

In short, the Pan of *The Marble Faun* is the Pan who invented music, and by extension poetry, as a compensation for amatory disappointment. Writing in 1919, Faulkner had reason to identify with this Pan, having recently lost his first love, Estelle Oldham, to another man. (She had married Cornell Franklin in April 1918.) The vocation to which Pan "calls" the faun in Faulkner's poem is a means of sublimating sexual frustration into art. But the faun is doubly frustrated, excluded not only from love but also from the musical self-consolation he has been promised.

Early in *The Marble Faun*, the faun imagines following pipe music to the god's lair. In his imagination, he spies a morose, self-pitying Pan brooding upon his own image in a pool and attempting to transcend his melancholy through music (MF, 16). Later, the faun imagines that the god's flute beckons specifically to him: "Come quietly, Faun, to my call." But it is noon, the very hour when Pan himself enforces silence on the landscape and all its denizens. In effect, then, Pan invokes the faun not to action or music but to mute immobility:

> "There is no sound in all the land,
> There is no breath in all the skies;
> Here Warmth and Peace go hand in hand
> 'Neath Silence's inverted eyes.

> "My call, spreading endlessly,
> My mellow call pulses and knocks;
> Come, Faun, and solemnly
> Float shoulderward your autumned locks.

> "Let your fingers, languorous,
> Slightly curl, palm upward rest,
> The silent noon waits over us,
> The feathers stir not on his breast.

> "There is no sound nor shrill of pipe,
> Your feet are noiseless on the ground;

The earth is full and stillily ripe,
In all the land there is no sound."
(MF, 22–23)

Pan does promise that "the noon will cool and pass" (MF, 22), but this assurance only makes his call more paradoxical: he sends his invitation at the one moment when, by his own rule, the faun cannot answer it. He invokes music and silence simultaneously. Whether Pan intends only a temporary disciplinary period of initiation before allowing the faun to assume his new vocation, or whether he is imposing directly contradictory expectations on the faun, the result is the same. The call is to silence; the vocation incapacitates as it enables; the afternoon of the faun is to be as inert as the forenoon. Insofar as Faulkner was recording his own recruitment into the profession of letters, moreover, Pan's instructions are especially ominous: he directs the faun specifically to relax his hand and turn it "palm upward."[17] To write, Faulkner seems to be saying, he must desist from writing.

Just as the faun suffers a tension between his immobility and his need to move, so he must both speak and remain silent. Consequently, his poem can only be an interior monologue—though, of course, we can read it. Similarly, the career Faulkner was declaring for himself would occur in the silent, frozen speech of the written (and, yes, *hand*written) word, "bound" forever between the covers of books.[18] The author who became notorious for his loquacious prose style would earn notoriety too for his taciturnity in person. But *The Marble Faun* seems to locate the literary endeavor in a realm of experience that *precedes* both speaking and writing. The Nobel Laureate who in 1950 would proclaim the power of "[t]he poet's voice" to sustain human life (ESPL, 120) inaugurated his career by consigning his own voice not just to the silence of print but to the silent condition of discovery that precedes putting marks on paper.[19]

"Black Music"

The conjunction of Pan's call with a faun's paralysis and with the influence of a maternal figure reappears in a pair of stories Faulkner wrote in the late twenties, probably soon after his return to Oxford from Europe.[20] In "Black Music," Pan transforms an architect's draughtsman named Wilfred Midgleston into what Wilfred calls a "farn" (CS, 805) in order to frighten a Mrs. Carleton Van Dyming out of her plans to despoil a tract of Virginia meadow and woodland by building a theater, a "Coliseum." and an "Acropolis" on it (CS, 807). After a vision of the bearded, horned face of the god "explode[s]" in his head, Midgleston drinks his first liquor, buys a tin whistle for piping, strips off his clothing, releases a bull from its pen, and chases Mrs. Van Dyming until she faints beside a tree. When she awakens, she decides to return to New York and sell the property, so Pan no longer requires the services of his "farn" (CS, 811–18). But Midgleston's life has been irrevocably changed. Having experienced "[s]ome-thing that ain't in the lot and plan for mortal human man to do" (CS, 805), he leaves his wife and his home in Brooklyn and takes up residence in a Latin American seaport called Rincon. There he lives as a derelict, poor but happy, for twenty-five years without appearing to age. He de-clines to learn "more than ten words of Spanish" (CS, 799). And his bed is "a roll of tarred roofing paper" (CS, 803) in the attic of a cantina owned by the Universal Oil Company, whose manager's wife, Mrs. Widrington, allows him to sleep there. His age when Pan freezes him is fifty-six (CS, 799), twice Faulkner's age when he probably wrote the story.

In "Black Music," Faulkner returned to the concerns of *The Marble Faun*. The faun's vision of Pan paralyzes and silences him; Midgleston's apotheosis results in his exile from the human community and its language. While not turned literally into stone, Midgleston is nonetheless bound agelessly in a tar-paper sheath, in the grip of a dominating woman.[21] By picking a lock to liberate a furious beast (CS, 816), he has escaped one motherly influence (or rather two: Mrs. Van Dyming *and* his own wife) only to find refuge with another. When Faulkner wrote of Mrs. Wid-rington's attic, he was still living intermittently at home—and still limping from time to time. (The man who owns Mrs. Van Dyming's property before she does is forced to sell it when a goat breaks his leg [CS, 806].) And Maud Falkner's husband had once been the local agent for Standard Oil (BL, 150). Like Faulkner, Midgleston "was a powerful reader when [he] was a boy" (CS, 818); he now "look[s] like a book-keeper" (CS, 800), perhaps because Faulkner too was now a "keeper" of books.

"Carcassonne"

Faulkner considered "Carcassonne," the companion or sequel to "Black Music," important enough to honor with the final position in his *Col-lected Stories* (1950).[22] The protagonist, though self-referentially named

David in an early draft (BL1, 254), is clearly a version of Midgleston: he sleeps in Mrs. Widdrington's [sic] husband's attic in Rincon, beneath an "unrolled strip of tarred roofing made of paper" (CS, 895). The cantina now belongs openly to the Standard, not the "Universal," Oil Company (CS, 897). But "Carcassonne," in depicting Midgleston's present dream-life rather than his farcical past, comes closer than "Black Music" to expressing Faulkner's estimation of his own situation—in the aftermath, the "afternoon," of Pan's call. Like the marble faun, this Midgleston is immobile. His "skeleton" remains "motionless" (CS, 896) beneath the tar paper throughout the story. But his imagination soars, like the faun's, in compensatory freedom. Part of him gallops perpetually on a *buckskin pony with eyes like blue electricity and a mane like tangled fire*" toward a "blue precipice never gained" (CS, 895). And, like the faun, he feels drawn to the maternal earth. The last sentence of the story echoes the faun's meditation: "Steed and rider thunder on, thunder punily diminishing: a dying star upon the immensity of darkness and of silence within which, steadfast, fading, deepbreasted and grave of flank, muses the dark and tragic figure of the Earth, his mother" (CS, 900).

The "dark and tragic" mother is an even more forceful presence . 1 "Carcassonne" than in *The Marble Faun* or "Black Music." Midgleston's strange bed, for example, is given an explicitly maternal provenance. Faulkner compares the scroll of tar roofing paper to "those glasses, reading glasses which old ladies used to wear, attached to a cord that rolls onto a spindle in a neat case of unmarked gold; a spindle, a case, attached to the deep bosom of the mother of sleep" (CS, 895).[23] Metaphorically, Faulkner envelopes himself in his mother's vision. He enwraps himself in her reading of his words, which the "tarred paper" contains. As we shall see, Maud Falkner was her son's most avid audience, a fact he knew well. "Carcassonne" suggests that the anticipation of her strict judgment was what enabled—or required—him to write in the first place. Mrs. Widdrington, the only literal matron in this story, seems somehow to hold Midgleston accountable to a literary vocation: "She'd make a poet of you too, if you did not work anywhere. She believed that, if a reason for breathing were not acceptable to her, it was no reason. With her, if you were white and did not work, you were either a tramp or a poet." Mrs. Widdrington expects Midgleston "to pay for using her darkness and silence by writing poetry" (CS, 897–98).

Not only does Mrs. Widdrington impose silence upon Midgleston to make him a poet; she also constrains him—and not just by encasing him in her "tarred paper bedclothing" (CS, 895). "Carcassonne" seems full of secret, probably unconscious, references to Maud Falkner's bondage of her son. The buckskin pony on which Midgleston imaginatively seeks freedom, while actually remaining confined within his paper prison, is itself harnessed so tightly as actually to sever its back:

> . . . the horse still gallops with its tangled welter of tossing flames. Forward and back against the taut roundness of its belly its legs swing, rhythmically reaching and overreaching, each spurning overreach punctuated by a flicking limberness of shod hooves. He can see the saddlegirth and the soles of the rider's feet in the stirrups. The girth cuts the horse in two just back of the withers, yet it still gallops with rhythmic and unflagging fury and without progression, and he thinks of that riderless Norman steed which galloped against the Saracen Emir, who, so keen of eye, so delicate and strong the wrist which swung the blade, severed the galloping beast at a single blow, the several halves thundering on in the sacred dust. (CS, 896)

In the 1950s and 1960s, when Faulkner persisted in riding his horses even after he had fractured *his* back, perhaps he remembered the broken horse of "Carcassonne." Perhaps too he remembered having written there that "somebody always crucified the first-rate riders" (CS, 897). The association of equestrian liberty with vertebral trauma, whether literal or figurative, conformed to his way of thinking about the state of his vocation.[24]

The association of a child's rebelliousness with a severed spine would also recur. Soon after he moved his family to Rowan Oak in 1930, he invented the story of the ghost Judith Shegog, a former inhabitant of the house who had supposedly fallen in love with a Yankee lieutenant during the Civil War. To evade her disapproving father, she and her suitor planned an elopement. As she climbed down a rope ladder from the house's front balcony one dark night, she lost her grip and pitched backwards onto the brick walk, breaking her neck. In another version she jumped, but she still broke her neck. Faulkner perennially entertained his own children and their friends with this cautionary tale about filial disobedience. He revealed his authorship of the fiction only when he was escorting his niece Dean, whom he had virtually adopted, to her wedding, as if the implicit threat against elopement had outlived its usefulness.[25]

"Carcassonne" displays its author's acute awareness of his body and his association of bodily experience with literary power. A "carcass" is buried in its title for a reason. Midgleston communes with his own "skeleton," which lies motionless: his "body consciousness, assuming the office of

vision, shape[s] in his mind's eye his motionless body grown phosphores-
cent with that steady decay which had set up within his body on the day of
his birth" (CS, 896–97). Here are echoes of the faun's lament and, perhaps, of young Billy's discomfort in his mother's brace. Yet this stagnation
results in imaginative power. While his skeleton decomposes within its
strange girdle, Midgleston thinks of "his tarred paper bed as a pair of
spectacles through which he nightly peruse[s] the fabric of dreams" (CS,
896). Thus the paper enhances his eyesight as well as the mother's, uniting them in a mutual vision that results only from his body's *rigor mortis*.
The paper is itself a brace within which the free-ranging imagination can
be disciplined.

In "Carcassonne," Faulkner presents a startlingly physical allegory for
the paradoxical process of literary creation. Imaginative freedom, signified
by the horseback ride, can derive only from extreme confinement, from
muscular self-control, from holding in whatever tries to escape. Likewise,
poetic utterance—represented by the italicized passages in the story—can
arise only in silence. Midgleston's speech in "Black Music" is banal and
ungrammatical; in "Carcassonne," his thoughts become eloquent only
when they remain within the pure realm of his mind: "*I want to perform
something bold and tragical and austere* he repeated, shaping the soundless words in the pattering silence" (CS, 899). The ideal form of expression
is private, silent, unwritten, unpublished.

What "Carcassonne" displays, finally, is Faulkner's meditation on the
physical experience of writing, in which the act of marking words on
paper is repressed. Sitting at one's writing table, one may become
"wrapped up" in the paper one "tars" with ink, and one may perceive the
manuscript as a window on one's dreams. Inventing the words that embody those dreams may seem as exhilarating as a ride on a winged steed.
But Faulkner's Pegasus flies "where no hoof echoed nor left print" (CS,
895).[26] The inner performance that one attempts to record when writing
remains inside, and no "echo" or "print" of it reaches the page. "Writing"
may engender the performance, but the performance itself remains unwritten. The literature that matters—the only literature that can be said
truly to exist—occurs in the "shaping" of "soundless words" in the
"silence."[27]

In 1933, Faulkner would remember *The Sound and the Fury* as the
novel that came closest to fulfilling his ideal, precisely because he had
written it within a solipsistic vacuum: "one day it suddenly seemed as if a
door had clapped silently and forever to between me and all publishers'

addresses and booklists and I said to myself, Now I can write." And the writing that mattered most preceded his "tarring" the virginal paper with words. Faulkner would locate the supreme pinnacle of his career in the silence before the scratching of the pen. Writing Benjy's section of *The Sound and the Fury* gave him, he said, a definite, physical emotion of "ecstasy, that eager and joyous faith and anticipation of surprise which the yet unmarred sheets beneath my hand held inviolate and unfailing."[28] Appropriately, the text that most nearly subsisted for Faulkner in the silence anterior to writing was devoted to an idiot bound within his own inarticulateness.[29] In Benjy, Faulkner found a character he could write about with his "palm upward."

Such "ecstasy," however, necessitates a cruel deprivation. In "Carcassonne," Faulkner acknowledged the discomforting fact that in choosing his vocation he had condemned himself to experiencing life indirectly and vicariously. Seated at his table, any writer finds himself effectively as cut off from the world as Wilfred Midgleston in his garret. In the unaging Midgleston, Faulkner portrayed himself as stranded in a cocoon of silent language, separated from the world in which living creatures struggle and die. In the aftermath of Pan's call, the faun must eternally endure a marble-bound and artificial "afternoon." Faulkner knew that, as a consequence of his vocation, he had exiled himself from normal human intercourse.

Whether Maud Falkner encouraged her son toward a writer's life when she nursed him in his infancy or when she strapped him into a whalebone corset during his adolescence is finally unimportant. What matters is that, for whatever reasons, Faulkner entered his vocation thinking of it as a prison through which he might escape a worse fate outside. He gained the sequestered liberation he sought: his novels attest, however imperfectly, to the magnificence of his aerial-horseback performances. But the prison remained a prison, and in his middle years Faulkner would rattle its bars.

"Afternoon of a Cow" marks a self-parodic return to the themes and images through which he had so paradoxically announced his vocation years before: stasis and flight, silence and garrulity, constraint and release.[30] In *The Marble Faun* he had divided himself between the mute and immobilized faun and the faun's fleet self-projection; so, in "Afternoon," he sent two "violently sedentary" characters—one loquacious, the other taciturn—hurtling across a flaming landscape. In pursuit of a cow and two horses, "Mr. Faulkner" exhibits the same physical recklessness that had marked Wilfred Midgleston's tenure as a "farn," and that Faulkner himself would display on horseback. "Mr. Faulkner" "hurled himself" after the animals with a "palpable disregard of limb" (US, 426). His burial beneath the maternal mass of Beulah, and beneath Beulah's climactic defecation, seems charged with significance in light of Faulkner's frustrated "anality" and the suffocating influence of his mother. When "Mr. Faulkner" runs headlong into a ravine, he follows the marble faun into his—and Midgleston's—final resting place: "the dark and tragic figure of the Earth."

Dark Twin

Obviously, Faulkner did not become a writer only because of the colic or because of his toilet training or because of his mother's strictures. But the character he formed in his childhood predisposed him to being a certain kind of writer once he lifted his pen. And that formation did not stop when he was weaned. John T. Irwin locates the motivating impulse of Faulkner's career in the next psychosexual stage after the oral and the anal: the genital. Without bothering himself with biographical facts, Irwin infers from the novels a pattern of repeated incestuous conflict.

This pattern appears most clearly, for Irwin, in *The Sound and the Fury* (1929) and in *Absalom, Absalom!* (1936), in both of which Quentin Compson suffers guilt because of his neurotic desire for his sister Caddy. Half of him hopes to seduce her, and the other half needs to avenge her seduction. He displaces his love of his unresponsive mother onto the sister, who is a replica of himself save her sex. And he displaces his hatred of his father—who abdicates paternal authority—onto himself, becoming the ineffectual protector of the sister he himself longs to possess. In *Absalom*, according to Irwin, Quentin projects his incestuous impulses onto Charles Bon, who threatens to marry his own half-sister Judith Sutpen; and he projects his paternal, protective impulses onto Henry, her full brother. Bon becomes Quentin's "shadow self," the "dark self that is made to bear the consciously unacceptable desires repudiated by the bright half of the mind." Henry avenges his sister and father by murdering his "dark" brother, but he also eliminates his chief rival for the love he too desires. Both men serve as Quentin's doubles, and Quentin is himself "a surrogate of Faulkner, a double who is fated to retell and reenact the same story throughout his life just as Faulkner seemed fated to retell in different ways the same story again and again and, insofar as narration is action, to reenact that story as well."[31] That retelling occurs in the quasi-incestuous incidents of *Elmer, Sartoris, As I Lay Dying, The Unvanquished,* and half a dozen other texts.

Citing Otto Rank's *The Double,* Irwin attributes the "incestuous doublings" that proliferate in Faulkner to narcissism. The narcissistic ego, according to Rank, attempts to make itself "the sole object of its own love, to merge the subject and the object in an internal love union." The narcissist desires "to return to a state in which subject and object did not yet exist, to a time before that division occurred out of which the ego sprang—in short, to return to the womb." But, of course, this desire equals the desire for incest. And, since "brother-sister incest is a substitute for child-parent incest," Quentin's love for Caddy derives ultimately from his love for himself: she is his mirror, into which he wishes to merge.[32]

To commit incest, however, or even to think of it, would transgress fundamental barriers. The narcissistic ego, seeking the autonomy of its own ideal image, must reject any instinct that violates that image. So it repudiates the incestuous desire that most clearly expresses its deepest need, projecting it outward into a personification, a "double."[33] Through its double, the narcissistic ego can satisfy its repressed desire and at the same time punish it. It can have its forbidden cake and reject it too. But, to purify itself, it must then kill its double; and, since the double is only a projection of the deepest self, killing it involves a displaced suicide. Thus Poe's William Wilson must die at the hand of his "twin." And Henry Sutpen's vengeful murder of the dark, incestuous Bon anticipates the moment when Quentin Compson merges with his "shadow" by drowning himself. In Irwin's clinical terms, "Quentin's narcissism is . . . a fixation in secondary narcissism, a repetition during a later period in life (usually adolescence) of that primary narcissism that occurs between the sixth and the eighteenth months, wherein the child first learns to identify with its image and thus begins the work that will lead to the constitution of the ego."[34]

Faulkner's life offers ample evidence of his narcissistic tendencies—his ambivalence toward his parents, his habitual passivity as a teenager, his idealization of certain young women both real and imaginary. And on at least one occasion, in 1921, he scandalized his friends at the University of Mississippi by asserting that "incest was not the horrible, hideous crime it was thought to be" (CNC, 52). But Irwin does not attend to the Faulkner who lived and breathed. He cares about the incestuous patterns in the fiction only insofar as they lead him further *into* the writing, beyond mere biography and toward the study of narrative itself.

Irwin argues that, by seeking to return to the womb, or at least to the psychological wholeness of the six-month-old, the narcissist seeks vengeance over time. The attempt to defeat time is inherently Oedipal because it involves a rebellion against paternity—against Father Time. If the past has generated the present, then returning into the past and destroying or revising history make one one's own progenitor. In literature one defeats the authority and the priority of one's fathers—both literal and literary—by becoming an author, by creating a progeny to which one is prior. For Quentin Compson, who struggles at times specifically with his father for "control of the narration" in *Absalom*, Irwin argues, "the act of narrating Sutpen's story, of bringing that story under authorial control, becomes a struggle in which he tries to best his father, a struggle to seize 'authority' by achieving temporal priority to his father in the narrative act."[35]

In short, one kills one's fathers by creating a narrative double for oneself—a text into which one can pour the self one creates by writing it. Just as the narcissist destroys himself when he kills his incestuous double, however, the writer kills himself when he creates his textual double. According to Irwin, Faulkner sensed the act of writing as

> a progressive dismemberment of the self in which parts of the living subject are cut off to become objectified in language, to become (from the writer's point of view) detached and deadened, drained, in that specific embodiment, of their obsessive emotional content. In this process of piecemeal self-destruction, the author, the living subject, is gradually transformed into the detached object—his books. And this process of literary self-dismemberment is the author's response to the threat of death; it is a using up, a consuming of the self in the act of writing in order to escape from that annihilation of the self that is the inevitable outcome of physical generation. . . . Clearly, for Faulkner, writing is a kind of doubling in which the author's self is reconstituted within the realm of language as the Other, a narcissistic mirroring of the self to which the author's reaction is at once a fascinated self-love and an equally fascinated self-hatred.[36]

Irwin's exposition of literary narcissism might be a merely theoretical exercise had Faulkner not anticipated it in his fiction. For example, in *Mosquitoes* (1927)—Faulkner's "most extensive examination of the interaction between the artist and his creation," according to Irwin—he put into the mouths of some New Orleans literati a discussion of the "bisexual" foundation of aesthetics.[37] This conversation culminates in the statement, by Julius Wiseman to Dawson Faircloth, that "[a] book is the writer's secret life, the dark twin of a man: you can't reconcile them" (MOS, 251).

That Wiseman is speaking for Faulkner seems certain. For he and Faircloth are examining poems written ostensibly by Wiseman's sister Eva but actually, of course, by Faulkner—and later published as part of *The Green Bough* (1933). The title of one sonnet, which Faircloth reads aloud in full, is "Hermaphroditus." Its speaker inquires of an androgynous listener whether she/he can satisfy her/his own erotic needs: "canst thou bride / Thyself with thee and thine own kissing slake?" Fairchild suggests that narcissistic self-absorption is the poem's mode as well as its subject: all poetry is an effort of the author's "twinned heart" to seek emotional self-sufficiency, "[l]ike a fire that don't need any fuel, that lives on its own heat." The fact that Faulkner was criticizing his own surreptitiously self-quoted text indicates his full awareness of his own narcissism. It also indicates his distrust of it. When "the inevitable clash comes" between a writer and his book, says Wiseman, "the author's actual self is the one that goes down" (MOS, 251–52).

Faulkner thus conceived of his mission as self-destructively narcissistic. Partially through instinct, partially perhaps through having absorbed Freud's ideas from the atmosphere, he psychoanalyzed his writing. And he diagnosed it as an auto-erotic sublimation in which the writer projects himself into a text which then consumes him. All his life he voiced the hope that his writing would immortalize him: after he died, it would serve as his extension, his "Kilroy was here." For this commemoration to take effect, however, he felt he must subordinate his whole being to it. Thus, he generally rebuffed questions about his life by stressing its inconsequence in relation to his books: "The artist is of no importance," he would say. "Only what he creates is important" (LG, 238). And thus he based his vocation on a paradox: to preserve himself, through his textual surrogates, he denied himself. To gain eternal fame, he sought contemporary anonymity.

Ernest Trueblood, in his very small way, confirms this paradox. By creating an explicit double, Faulkner acknowledged the doubling implicit in everything he wrote. On one hand, writing fiction enabled him to create a permanent arena of self-gratification. On the other hand, the fictions he wrote—and those he affected in poses as well—lay disturbingly outside the self. A man's book may be his "dark twin," but he can never "reconcile" it to himself; worse, he cannot finally even recognize himself in it. Looking back upon the texts into which he had poured his being, Faulkner must have noticed that their author was foreign to him, if for no other reason than that he had changed since writing them. Then he was the writer; now he was only the reader, the dispossessed *ex*-proprietor of Yoknapatawpha County. "Kilroy" may have been there once, but "Faulkner" no longer was—if he ever had been.

"The Leg"

While Faulkner was traveling in Europe in 1925, he wrote a story that almost clinically illustrates Rank's treatise on doubling. A putative horror story, "The Leg" exemplifies Irwin's "dismemberment of the self" all too concretely. Overladen with obviously Freudian content, it suggests that Faulkner intended to tap psychoanalytical resources; and it refers so insistently to Faulkner's own obsessions as to imply that the psyche he was consciously analyzing was his own. In it, Faulkner seems not only to acknowledge but quite literally to em*body* the incestuous-narcissistic sources of his vocation.

The first third of the story relates a boating mishap that is both accidental and deliberate (like the spills Faulkner would suffer in later life?). In 1914, an American at Oxford—autobiographically named Davy—and his English friend George are sculling on the upper Thames. Passing through a lock, they pause so that George can court the lockkeeper's daughter, Everbe Corinthia Rust, whom he has wooed similarly for three years. While George recites "Comus' second speech" to the simple country girl, addressing her by pastoral nymph-names like Sabrina and Chloe, a "yawl boat" approaches the lock from downstream and signals for access. Davy tries to warn George that they must move out of the way so that the water level in the lock can be lowered, but accident-prone George clings to the pile "spouting his fine and cadenced folly as though the lock, the Thames, time and all, belonged to him." Everbe Corinthia stands above them "cow-eyed and bridling" with "her hand on the lever," in the same posture she had adopted three years earlier when "she had opened the lock for us for the first time, with George holding us stationary while he apostrophized her in the metaphor of Keats and Spenser" (CS, 823–24). With the yawl's crew shouting at them, Davy finally orders the girl to pull the lever. As she does so, she falls flat on her rear, soiling her dress; Davy "[shoots] through the gates" of the lock in the skiff; and George disappears beneath the surface of the pouring stream. (Faulkner would essentially repeat this scene more than a dozen years later in "Old Man," in which the two convicts are similarly separated by a flood while a young woman awaits them.) In the "slack water" below, the men in the yawl draw Davy's skiff alongside with a boat-hook, and they note Davy's apparent distress at having "lost" George: "Give 'im a turn, seeing 'is mate . . ." (CS, 824–25). Meanwhile, George has been rescued from drowning—also with a boat-hook—by Corinthia's father and brother, Simon and Jotham Rust, who treat the "Oxford young gentlemen" with disdain. When Davy re-joins his drenched friend, George accuses him of envying the impression his gesture has made on Corinthia, who has shed tears. They row back to Oxford through the "green petrification" of the English landscape (CS, 825–28).

The language and imagery of this excessively complicated beginning are "covertly" sexual in an overt way. Already the story fairly bristles with phallic surrogates—oars, levers, boat-hooks—and the title leg has not even made an appearance yet. Everbe Corinthia's soiled dress (a forecast of Caddy Compson's muddy drawers in *The Sound and the Fury?*) insinuates the carnal meaning of her opening "the lock."[38] Davy's orgasmic ride through the "gates" on the flood she releases and George's near-drowning in the same cataract suggest a disguised treatment of the risky attractions of sexual intercourse. In Davy's guilty precipitation of the process—by giving the highly ambiguous order, "Lock, Corinthia!" (CS, 824) that impels her to pull the "lever"—and in George's nearly fatal refusal to acquiesce in it, Faulkner may be dramatizing his own divided response to the power of the opposite sex.

"The Leg" is of only passing interest, however, for what it might tell us about Faulkner's sexual proclivities. Far more important, it presents an-other elaborate metaphor for the writer's condition, which complements the related metaphors in *The Marble Faun*, "Black Music," and "Car-cassonne." For George's principal activity so far in the story has been to recite poetry. Like the faun in Faulkner's poem and like Wilfred Mid-gleston in the two stories, George is immobilized by this literary endeavor.

As the faun is bound in marble and Midgleston is rolled in tar paper, George is seized in the lock, "holding us stationary." As the faun and Midgleston yearn for freedom and gain it through imaginative flights, so George has a partner who rides away on the lock's discharge. In "The Leg" Faulkner meticulously fashioned a device that epitomizes the tension between restraint and escape that pervades his early writing. More graphically than the similar devices in other works, the lock—simultaneously a dam and a flood, and thus a *controlled* flood, a valve—denotes an "anal" articulation between constipation and catharsis.

Whereas the petrified men of *The Marble Faun*, "Black Music," and "Carcassonne" are explicitly mother-fixated, mothers are conspicuously absent from "The Leg"—except insofar as Davy's ride through the lock represents a dreamlike birth.[39] The Rust family inexplicably lacks a mother, and both Davy's and George's parents remain in the background. This story nevertheless constitutes another chapter in Faulkner's secret history of his body, connecting Maud's back brace with his limp and both of these with his vocation. The remainder of the story makes little sense except through the logic of Faulkner's obsessions. By that logic, it seems absurdly but inevitably right.

World War One calls an end to Davy and George's boat rides on the Thames. On the Western Front, George is killed and Davy loses a leg. While surgeons are amputating the wounded limb, George's ghost visits the operating room, and Davy asks it to follow his leg and "be sure it's dead" (CS, 829–30). During Davy's recovery, George's ghost periodically reports its continuing failure to decommission the leg. Davy, feeling a "gaping sensation below my thigh where the nerve- and muscle-ends twitched and jerked," complains that the leg "jeers at me. It's not dead" (CS, 831). And he suspects that it's doing something sinister. Davy is fitted with a wood-and-leather prosthesis, a "new member" to which his thigh becomes "almost reconciled" (CS, 834). But George's ghost revives Davy's worry about his "outcast" leg's "doings" by reporting that, during its nightly searches, it has revisited the lock on the Thames and has seen Davy himself there in the skiff: "I saw you on the river. You saw me and hid, Davy. Pulled up under the bank, in the shadow. There was a girl with you" (CS, 833). During the ghost's last visit to the hospital, Davy can sense the evil presence of the leg. George "stood beside me in the corridor just beyond the corner of which It waited. The sulphur reek was all about me; I felt horror and dread and something unspeakable: delight. I believe I felt what women in labor feel" (CS, 834). The only mother in the story turns out to be Davy himself.

What Davy—or his hallucination—engenders out of his severed leg is a phantom version of himself, a double who executes Davy's guilty impulses, ravishing a forbidden woman and destroying her protectors. In France one night, Corinthia's brother Jotham tries to kill Davy with a knife, but his blow is deflected by the "artificial leg propped on a chair in the dark" (CS, 840). After Jotham is tried and condemned to death, an army chaplain discovers his motive. While home on leave months earlier, Jotham had watched his sister slip away from their house for an hour every dusk. Suspecting a liaison, he "locked" her in her room one evening. When a noise awakened him later that night, he saw the white figure of his sister "flitting along the towpath." Overtaken by him, she first raged at him and then collapsed in his arms. Jotham saw a punt tied to the bank and heard a man's laugh. He locked her again in her room, but by morning she had again escaped. The next morning she lay unconscious in the towpath at their door. When she awoke, she screamed until sunset and then died (CS, 838–40). Shortly afterward, the father died as well (CS, 836).

Jotham has not merely assumed that Davy is the culprit who seduced his sister. He has acted on firm evidence, which the chaplain finds and then shows to Davy: a photograph of Davy, taken at an English fair and dated at an incriminating time—but a time when Davy was still lying, delirious, in a French hospital (CS, 841–42). We are left to conclude that Davy's amputated leg has become a second version of Davy himself, or that Davy has subconsciously willed it to do so, and that Davy-the-leg has set about ruining the woman that legless Davy secretly desires and destroying her male avengers. Confronted with the photograph of his "shadow self," Davy himself becomes a shadow: "I sat holding the picture quietly in my hand while the candle flame stood high and steady above the wick and on the wall my huddled shadow held the motionless photograph" (CS, 842). As the story ends, its protagonist sits locked in horrified contemplation of his own dark anti-image.

"The Leg" deploys the two principal components of Rank's (and Irwin's) theory: the narcissistic pair and the Oedipal triangle. In Davy and George, Faulkner fashioned a double self-portrait. Davy, an "American boy" with

Faulkner's semi-autobiographical name, and George, an English poseur, dimly mirror "Mr. Faulkner" and Ernest V. Trueblood in all their linked permutations. They meet at "Oxford," a locale that conveniently conflates Faulkner's European pretensions with his Mississippi origins, neatly embodying his ambivalence about his home—and about his own identity. Like Faulkner, Davy and George are both "Oxford young gentlemen" who are made to feel shame for that fact. They both go to war, as Faulkner had longed to do. One dies; the other endures—just as John Sartoris would die and his twin brother would live in *Sartoris* (1929). The survivor is wounded in his leg, as Faulkner pretended to have been. And he is equipped with a prosthetic "harness," as Faulkner had been (and would be).

Nowhere else did Faulkner come so close to confronting the fact of his false limp. "The Leg" depicts a fantasy of amputation in which the subject of castration lurks barely beneath the surface.[40] If Maud Falkner's back brace ultimately implied emasculation, the leg that Faulkner stiffened in life and the lost limb that comes back to haunt Davy in fiction both fulfill and violate her discipline reciprocally. The outcast leg in the story embodies uncontrollable carnal impulses; its benign replacement, which shields Davy from murder, is rigid and, like Maud's corsets, equipped with a creaking, snapping harness. Relinquishing his leg, furthermore, feminizes Davy, enabling him to know "what women in labor feel." His symbolic emasculation renders him hermaphroditic, endows him with the female faculty of gestation as well as with a controlled and chastened (and detachable) male instrument of conception. Ominously, however, the only product of Davy's self-propagation is a monster.

If Faulkner's limp and Davy's amputation constitute indirect prolongations of Maud's stringent childrearing, the oblique incestuousness of Davy-the-leg's crime should come as no surprise. The woman who inspires George to recite poetry and incites Davy to lust secretly is no less unavailable for being a sister and a daughter rather than a mother and a wife. She is one of a bevy of female characters in Faulkner's early writing who must escape through windows from the locked rooms of protective— or possessive—fathers, uncles, and brothers. In repeatedly "trying to manufacture the sister which I did not have,"[41] Faulkner wishfully sublimated his actual incestuous predisposition into a different one, inverting a mother-son affinity into the sibling attractions, safer because fictional, of the Rusts, the Compsons, the Sutpens, and others. The figure who dominates "The Leg" is the woman who "locked" Billy Faulkner into the back brace, crippling him in order to straighten him.

"Elmer"

Another story that Faulkner wrote during his European tour in 1925 confirms his association of artistic vocation with lameness and incest. In an unfinished novel he called "Elmer," Faulkner satirically depicted a young American attempting to become a famous painter in Europe without bothering to paint much of anything. Young Elmer Hodge, though more fully characterized than Ernest V. Trueblood, belongs among Faulkner's self-parodic doubles.

Faulkner traces Elmer's artistic pose to several incidents in his youth, including some that fit the pattern established in *The Marble Faun*, "Black Music," "Carcassonne," and "The Leg." When Elmer's family's house had burned during his boyhood, he had stood watching it, "burrowing against his mother's thin nervous leg" until, the heat scorching him, he had to turn his back to the fire. When his back began to swelter as well, he experienced a "definite growing misery, a desire to weep"; and he wrapped himself in the skirt of his mother's nightgown "to shield the tender young skin of his back." Thus he did not see the fire fighters remove "the low chair in which his mother [had] rocked while he knelt in an impossible excruciating rapture with his head in her lap" (ELM, 346–47). Years later, at the approximate time of his mother's death, he ignominiously wounds himself in the back and in a leg with a hand grenade, during Canadian Army training in World War One (ELM, 381). He spends months recuperating in a hospital in Liverpool, his body "consisting of one huge and itching spine" (ELM, 435); and he walks with a limp and a cane afterward (ELM, 384). Faulkner's family house had never burned, but his mother had both exposed his back to pain and "healed" it. From the chair to the cane, the details of Elmer's memory correspond to the history of Faulkner's inner life. The author would scatter similar traces of this history throughout other works. In *As I Lay Dying*, for example, Jewel scorches his back and Cash breaks his leg trying to save their mother, Addie, whose body is confined and rigidified in a wooden box.

If Elmer associates his mother with the afflictions of his back, he attributes his discovery of art to his sister, Jo-*Addie*. Until he is eleven and she sixteen, they share the same bed, where she allows him to caress her body. To escape having to sleep with him, she leaves home one night, presumably through a window in their room. Later, she sends him a box of wax crayons, with which he learns to draw on wrapping paper (ELM, 348–56). Faulkner, of course, had no sister; the woman who encouraged *him* to become a visual artist was Miss Maud.

"A Portrait of Elmer"

In an effort to salvage the "Elmer" materials during the 1930s, Faulkner pulled the least amateurish parts of his typescript together into a story called "A Portrait of Elmer," which he then tried unsuccessfully to sell (US, 710). To the same satirical self-portrait he had enjoyed sketching in 1925, he added a new ending that epitomizes the self-mockery implicit in all of the works he wrote about his vocation. Elmer has reached Paris. Hoping to support himself as an artist, he has painted only one watercolor, spending his time instead at the bars where famous painters congregate. Somewhat more sophisticated than Ernest V. Simms, editor of "Ode to the Louver," he has nevertheless not even located the Louvre during his first three weeks in Paris, let alone written a bad poem about it (US, 635, 638).

Elmer is sitting at a fashionable restaurant on the Left Bank when he is suddenly stricken with tourist's diarrhea. He abruptly pays for his drink and sets out hurriedly for the rooms he rented in the Rue Servandoni (Faulkner's own Left Bank address in 1925) because the landlady reminded him of his mother. Crossing the Luxembourg Gardens, he breaks into a sprint, strangely belying the limp that in the story is very real. He bursts into the toilet of his apartment building; and there, almost before he can lower his trousers, he releases the "life, volition, all, cradled dark and sightless in his pelvic girdle" (like Davy in "The Leg," he has a womb; but his womb is a bowel). Then he sighs with relief and reaches into the niche where scraps of paper are kept. Alas, the niche is empty. Fatalistically, he pulls his single painting from the portfolio he has been lugging about and uses it to wipe himself (US, 638–41).

If this painting is the portrait "of" Elmer in Faulkner's title, the story makes a clear connection between art and excrement. Faulkner frequently spoke of his writing in terms of parturition, but the jokes in "A Portrait of Elmer"—and later in "The Afternoon of a Cow"—demonstrate that he could think of writing, parodically, in terms of defecation as well. Like "Ode to the Louver," the "Elmer" materials constitute a confession of fraudulence. Faulkner did spend hours in the Louvre (BL, 453–65), but he may well have doubted his ability to appreciate or rival its treasures. Striving arduously not to be a mere tourist like his aunt and cousin, he may have worried that his very effort rendered him the worst tourist of all. Traveling about the European homeland of the vocation he guiltily aspired to, he may have suspected that he was actually incapable of writing anything much better than the "Ode to the Louver."

Young Man Faulkner

Whereas Freudian theory emphasizes the determining effect of infantile experience—during "oral," "anal," and "genital" stages of development—on the mature personality, later psychologists have attended more carefully to adolescent and adult experience. Acknowledging that the infantile categories can help to establish susceptibilities, these revisionists nevertheless deny that childhood experience can sufficiently explain the behavior of adults. The post-Freudian psychologist who has most significantly influenced biographical method has been Erik Erikson. Others may have affected therapeutic practices more profoundly; but, in his theoretical writings and in his applications of his ideas to the lives of great men, Erikson has pioneered the discipline of "psychobiography."

Erikson extends the process of ego-formation into and beyond childhood. To the three infantile, or "preconscious," stages—which he redefines—he adds five stages of "conscious" life that complete a normative cycle of human existence: first, a period associated with school attendance, during which a child learns the "simple technologies" (including literacy and play) through which he can enter the world beyond the family; second, the period of adolescence during which the individual must discover his identity—and usually his occupation; third, young-adulthood, when one normally loves a spouse and creates offspring—or else suffers isolation; fourth, middle age, during which one either cares for the products of one's "generativity"—both one's work and one's progeny—or stagnates; and, fifth, old age, when one must either integrate one's whole life cycle and accept it or else despair. Erikson conceives of each stage as a crisis through which every individual must pass, either positively or negatively. The outcome of each crisis affects one's chances during all the succeeding crises, cumulatively.[42]

Whatever may be the merits and defects of Erikson's particular system, Faulkner certainly experienced "stages" similar to Erikson's. For an investigation of Faulkner's sense of vocation, however, two of the stages are more important than the others, organically related though they all may be. The second conscious phase (fifth in the total cycle), during which individuals must undergo an "identity crisis," normally includes the discovery of vocation. And the fourth (or seventh) phase centers on a "crisis of generativity," during which the individual must judge the products of both his vocation and his love, evaluating the worth of his legacy.

During the Eriksonian "identity crisis," adolescents require a "psychosocial moratorium," during which to integrate the experience of previous stages and structure their view of the world according to "ideologies" available in the surrounding culture. They experiment with a variety of roles provided by their society until they find those that fit the persons they have become. The repertoire of available roles always includes some "negative identities"—roles that parents and other authorities proscribe. Because "identity-formation" is a "generational issue," in which young people react against their elders' expectations, the negative identities appear just as attractive as positive models, and the mature identity always "contains [its] opposite." The person who weathers the identity crisis successfully emerges with an "organizational principle"—an "ideology"—whereby he can maintain "a coherent personality." The person who fails will suffer from "role confusion."[43]

Among the failures Erikson includes most of the historical figures whose lives he has analyzed: Luther, Gandhi, Hitler, and others. In fact, aside from his coinage of the term "identity crisis," Erikson's most visible innovation has been his theory that "great men" realize their greatness by first thwarting it. Laden with an ambition that threatens all too surely to supplant a weak father, all of these men (Erikson's attention to female biography has been sketchy and theoretical) set out purposefully to fail in order not to fulfill their guiltiest Oedipal wishes. Specifically, they all prolonged their "moratoriums" well beyond adolescence, declining to pursue any conventional success directly competitive with their fathers and courting short-term failure in order to preserve a long-term destiny. Both to allay guilt over an "excessiveness of . . . ambition" and to "avoid the danger of success unequal to" that ambition, the "young great man" tends to dawdle, to risk "identity confusion" as preferable to any unworthy identity, and to delay committing himself to an occupational role.[44]

Thus, in Erikson's view, Martin Luther entered a monastery to preserve both himself and his father from the successful legal career the elder Luther wished for him. To avoid displacing his father, he assumed the "negative identity" of the monk, which his father specifically loathed. And when, in his thirties, he emerged from his monastic "moratorium," he sublimated his filial ambivalence into a theology of Paternity and Sonhood, emphasizing each individual's need to confront the Father face to face. Likewise, Gandhi ran away from ancestral expectations when he chose to practice law in South Africa rather than in India. He emerged from his "moratorium" propounding an ironic strategy of strength through weakness, success through failure. And Erikson himself—fundamentally an autobiographer as well as a biographer—provided his own first example of the late start that can catapult a man to exceptional achievement. The stepson of a pediatrician, he set out to become an artist, wandering Europe until he fell in with the Freud family in Vienna. He entered psychoanalytical training only in his late twenties and emerged at age thirty-one as a different kind of doctor from both his stepfather and his intellectual father, Freud.[45]

Erikson would not insist that *all* greatness gestates in a period of self-frustrating latency. At least a few charismatic leaders enjoyed no pause whatsoever. But his pattern has proved useful, not only in the identification of charismatic leaders but in the analysis of their leadership. Thus, a study of Lincoln can locate the "crucial period" for the development of his personality in the New Salem years—his twenties—when he fled from "his ambition and guilt over the radical revolt against his father's world to which it had led him"; and it can trace in Lincoln's Civil War speeches an imagery of domestic conflict in which rebellious sons do battle with loyal sons for the legacy of their fathers. Thus, too, a biography of Beethoven can emphasize the failure of the composer's father, the domination of the household by his mother, the compensatory prolongation of the composer's "moratorium," the importance of Enlightenment "ideology" to the development of his heroic style, and the musical embodiment of a complex family drama in his works.[46]

Richard Lebeaux's Eriksonian biography of Henry David Thoreau presents the pattern in a form so applicable to Faulkner's life that these two very different writers can seem suddenly kindred. Thoreau's father, a feckless small businessman, moved his family about New England, working at various trades, before settling permanently in Concord, Massachusetts. Even then, the family moved from house to house, depriving the boy of what Erikson calls "basic trust." While John Thoreau was a silent, passive man, with whom Henry had little in common, his wife Cynthia was vivacious, garrulous, and aggressive. For her children, she voiced ambitions of "greatness" that imposed upon Henry a burden of expectation which, were he to fulfill it, would force him to pass his ineffectual father. Thoreau basked in his mother's attention but recognized the threat she posed, through him, to his father. According to Lebeaux, Henry came "consciously to feel that it would be wrong to outdo" his father. Consequently, to avoid the guilt that would accompany conventional success, he sought a failure that would justify his father but would not destroy his own chance for greatness. Thus he had to excoriate the impure "commercial spirit" of Concord by setting himself against the community that had witnessed his father's incompetence and by adopting the most "negative" identity—in the town's eyes—that he could assume without becoming a criminal.[47]

When Thoreau graduated from Harvard, he faced an "identity crisis" so severe that he required an especially prolonged "psychosocial moratorium" in which to sort it out. He worked at a series of odd jobs, seeming to follow his father's occupational instability but actually preserving himself for a vocation that would transcend mere jobs. He ignored the "identity-choices" that the town of Concord sanctioned. To proclaim his independent self-reliance, he changed his name—from "David Henry" to "Henry David"—while still living in the home of his parents, who never accepted the reversal. He gave the appearance of idling. Suffering acute depression, he wrote vainglorious promises to himself in his journal, justifying his current failure with talk of a future success uncorrupted by mere enterprise.[48]

Faced with his father's "psychological absence," Thoreau sought surrogate fathers—first his older brother John, then Ralph Waldo Emerson. And he transferred to them the repressed hostility and Oedipal guilt he felt toward his real father. In Emerson, he found not only a "great man" he could emulate but also an "ideology"—Transcendentalism—through which he could order both the world and his own "identity." Only after ungraciously rejecting Emerson's assistance, however, could Thoreau create for himself the illusion that he was strong and independent. *Walden* "emerged out of his desperate need to keep away the shadows of identity confusion, shame, and guilt—shadows which continued to hover threateningly over him in the post-Walden years. . . . It [was] . . . imperative for Thoreau to cling to his Walden identity—indeed, to create and believe in a persona who was more independent and purer than the real man who had lived by the pond." Thus, through art, "Henry David" could convince himself that he had replaced "David Henry."[49]

Faulkner's biography resembles Lebeaux's pattern for Thoreau in almost every particular.[50] His father, Murry Falkner, moved his family about northern Mississippi, settling finally in Oxford on the day before William's fifth birthday. Even in Oxford, however, the family had to move from house to house because of Murry's insecurity (BL, 64–233 passim). Like Thoreau, then, the young Faulkner suffered "residential instability."[51] As men, both retained an ambivalence about "home." Thoreau "traveled much in Concord"; Faulkner acquired property in Oxford and fought to keep it, even when escaping from it. Murry provided a model of occupational instability as well. He worked his way up from fireman to treasurer of his father's railroad, before *his* father aborted that career by selling the company. By the time William left home, Murry had owned or managed a drug company, a farm, a hauling business, a livery stable, a cottonseed-processing plant, a theater, an ice plant, a buggy dealership, a coal-oil agency, and a hardware store—all subsidized by William's grandfather. Finally, when Faulkner was twenty-one years old, his grandfather tired of financing Murry's failures. He arranged a bureaucratic sinecure for his son at the University of Mississippi, where Murry worked unhappily until he was forced to resign in 1930 (BL, 53–662 passim).

In short, Faulkner—like Thoreau—grew up knowing his father to lack a coherent sense of vocation and to depend utterly upon *his* father for his livelihood.[52] Insofar as William sympathized with Murry's plight, he blamed the business world for defeating his father as much as he blamed his father for accepting defeat. He early expressed disdain for conventional ways of making a living. When he was nineteen, for example, and working in his grandfather's bank, he allowed that money "was a contemptible thing to work for" (BL, 179)—a judgment that would return to haunt him during the long stretches of potboiling that lay ahead. Such an opinion absolved his father of any shame for having failed financially, but it left him accountable for trying so futilely. Murry, of course, drew only negative inferences.

Just as Thoreau's relationship with his father "was based more on toleration than on enthusiasm,"[53] William and Murry never reached an understanding, despite their similarities. A moody, silent man, alternately affectionate and angry, Murry remained mostly aloof from the family circle (BL, 152–53). His second son wondered in later life at "how little I actually came to know him, and, perhaps, even less to understand him. He was not an easy man to know."[54] His interests tended toward horses and dogs (BL, 65). For reading he relied on Zane Grey and other Western writers (BL, 687), his wife having thwarted his desire to become a cowboy (BL, 68). He allowed no talking at his dinner table (BL, 153). To a young dandy infatuated with Symbolist poetry, he was a "dull man," as William confided to Phil Stone (BL, 178). At least once during his adolescence, William was seen driving a golf ball directly and deliberately at his father (BL1, 51). When he joined the Canadian R.A.F., he listed his next of kin as "Mrs. Maud Faulkner," changing the spelling of her name to agree with his and suggesting by the form that she was a widow.[55]

Conversely, the father had no resources with which to understand his rebellious son. Dressing sometimes shabbily and sometimes foppishly, writing inaccessible poetry, and refusing to take a job or even to help out at the hardware store, William mystified and angered Murry. The father heartily disapproved of his son's trip to Europe. Certainly, Faulkner's decision to become a writer aroused no sympathy in his father. When William signed his first Hollywood contract, Murry expressed surprise that "mere scribbling could earn five hundred dollars a week." When shown the check, "he asked if it was legal" (BL, 768; BLRO, 98). Earlier, according to a younger son, he had "tried to suppress" *Sanctuary* because of its salacious contents. "He said that if Bill was going to write, he should write Western stories" (MBB, 171). If Murry actually did read *Sanctuary*, it was probably the only novel by his son that he read. The older man spent his brief retirement pasting pictures of horses and dogs into an album (BL, 782).

The "psychological absence" of his father constituted one of Faulkner's deepest motives and gave him one of his most powerful themes, from *As I Lay Dying* to *Absalom, Absalom!* to *A Fable*. Yet, contemptuous of the man who had pressured him to take a job, any job, Faulkner could nevertheless remember fondly in 1950 that he "had an extremely patient father," as if fabricating a parent who had never existed (BL, 1355n).[56] The author seemed to embrace his own paternity with less ambivalence, accepting responsibility for the whole "clan" when Murry died and relishing the birth and childhood of his daughter (BL, 783, 803–5). Much as he loved Jill, however, he was capable of hurtful cruelty to her. When she tried to talk him out of a drinking binge in 1946 by begging him to "Think of me," he replied that "[n]obody remembers Shakespeare's children" (BL, 1204). At a time when his dreams of fame were only beginning to come true (Malcolm Cowley was just then putting together the *Portable Faulkner*) he could reveal that the progeny he loved most were his books and reputation, his sublimations of fatherhood. In the early fifties, he chided Jill for being less ambitious than his current young lover. [57] Still he needed to be "generative." One reason Joan Williams and Jean Stein attracted him in the fifties was likely that they enabled him to play the nurturing father he had not sufficiently been. To Joan Williams, he could say, "I think I was—am—the father which you never had" (BL, 1484; BL1, 511).

If Faulkner's father was psychologically absent, his mother was all too present. As Cynthia Thoreau overshadowed John, Maud Butler Falkner dominated Murry. Her own father had failed in business and abandoned his family when she was a teenager, and she carried a deep distrust of men into a marriage that produced four sons (BL, 57). A strict disciplinarian, she not only strapped William into a back brace but also ran her household according to rigorous principles of accountability. She posted a motto of stoic responsibility ("Don't Complain—Don't Explain") on a sign in her kitchen, and she enforced it with iron determination (BL, 79). As Blotner summarizes her function in the family, "it was Maud Falkner who assumed the fundamental responsibility for disciplining the children, inculcating Christian conduct in them, and encouraging them in school when that time came" (BL, 90).

She also disciplined her husband, controlling his alcoholic excesses, humoring his temperamental outbursts, governing his home. When she fell ill one summer, her sons ran loose because "[i]t was not for anyone else, they felt, to make decisions for them," including their father (BL, 178). In their eyes, she was clearly the stronger parent. When her second son was wounded during World War I, the third son recalled, "Dad sort of went to pieces . . . but Mother kept telling him, 'Hush, Buddy. He'll be back'" (BL, 222). And back he came. Her domination made her a central force in each son's life, but it also fostered deep resentment. As an adult, Faulkner would remember mournfully that his mother had sometimes insisted on going hunting with her menfolks in order to monitor her husband's behavior. "What a shame," Faulkner lamented, "that Mr. Murry and the boys couldn't have gone there to hunt by themselves" (BL, 90).

Unquestionably, the mother shaped the son's vocation far more positively than did the father. Maud had learned how to paint and draw from her own artistic mother. Lacking a daughter herself, she tried to pass her talent on to her oldest son, whom she encouraged to become a painter (BL, 58, 142, 164). She also "had an abiding love for literature . . . and that, too, she passed on to all her children." Maud taught her sons to read before they started school, [58] and she introduced them to the great authors of world literature (BL, 92–93). Her second son, Murry, remembered that she "loved literature and could become completely immersed in it. The world really didn't exist when she was reading something."[59] If Faulkner at age nine told his third-grade teacher that he wanted "to be a writer like my great-granddaddy" (BL, 105)—William Clark Falkner, the author of *The White Rose of Memphis*—he chose this patriarchal model in part because it was chosen for him by his mother, who constantly held her weak husband's strong forebear up for comparison. The first words Faulkner's nephew Jimmy remembered hearing, around 1930, were his grandmother's: "You've got a back like the Old Colonel's . . . but you've got to be a better man than he was" (BL, 494). Surely William, the boy whose back she braced, had heard even more pointed admonitions throughout his youth. If he "more or less unconsciously patterned his life after the Old Colonel's," as a brother conjectured (BL, 105), he did so because of his mother's suggestions. Cynthia Thoreau had presented similar ancestral models to "David Henry," inciting him implicitly to ignore her husband as an example.[60]

Despite the patrilineal model, moreover, Faulkner probably knew that his mother thought he "had gotten his genes from her, not from her big, gruff, sincere, lumbering husband" (BL, 295). The Old Colonel may have been his father's, not his mother's grandfather; but the artistic disposition was primarily her legacy. Writing was unmistakably a feminine rather than a masculine pursuit in the Falkner household. By the time he was fifteen, according to a classmate, Faulkner "would do nothing but write and draw—drawings for his stories. He couldn't help it. . . . It was an obsession" (BL, 154–55). Such devotion to activities that were sure to please one parent and to disappoint the other concretely reinforces the Oedipal interpretation of Faulkner's vocation. Maud would keep a hand in her son's career all her long life. She led Phil Stone to William by advertising the fact that "Billy didn't know what to do with his poems" (BL, 161). She stood by her son when Murry and the neighbors disapproved. While most of the townspeople were ridiculing William by calling him "Count," she paid for his outlandish clothing bill at a Memphis men's store by selling her diamond ring, despite her natural frugality (BL, 255). While Murry reacted with shame to *Sanctuary*, Maud defended her son: "Let him alone, Buddy. . . . He writes what he has to" (BL, 687). Some neighbors claimed that she had forced her husband to provide room and board for "Billy" throughout his twenties, despite Murry's fear that they were turning him into a free-loader (BL, 295).

Like Thoreau's mother, she encouraged her son to "feel . . . 'special,' 'chosen' . . . a potentially 'great man.'" Like Thoreau, Faulkner felt himself "put in the unenviable position of 'justifying'" his mother at the expense of his father, whom he would have to surpass in order to fulfill her expectations.[61] Faulkner's ambivalent response to his mother's ambition for him is evident in his juvenilia. We have already seen in "Carcassonne" the Midgleston character's submission to Mrs. Widdrington, who would "make a poet of you" (CS, 897). In late 1924 he composed a Housmanesque poem called "The Gallows" which connects maternal ambition (and rocking) with filial misfortune:

> His mother said: I'll make him
> A lad as ne'er has been
> (And rocked him closely, stroking
> His soft hair's golden sheen)
> His bright youth will be metal
> No alchemist has seen.
>
> His mother said: I'll give him
> A bright and high desire
> 'Till all the dross of living
> Burns clean within his fire.
> > (HEL, 160; BL, 373n)

Instead, the boy becomes a "felon," at least in the version of the poem Faulkner published as part of *A Green Bough* in 1933, and he is hanged for his transgressions (GB, 34–35). A son's failure to fulfill a mother's expectations results first in his confinement and then in the snapping of his spine.

Except for his maternally sponsored identification with his paternal great-grandfather, Faulkner's sense of vocation derived so singularly from his mother that literacy itself became sexually charged for him. His mother taught him how to read and then showed him what to read (BL, 110), while his father seems to have ignored book-learning altogether.[62] In his youth, Faulkner apparently imitated his mother's handwriting.[63] When he left Oxford, he addressed his letters home only to Maud, even when he was in the R.A.F., and she wrote the family replies.[64] While traveling in Europe in 1925, he wrote weekly letters to her, reporting in detail on his writing (BL, 448–76); but he sent only one picture postcard to his father, conceivably his only written communication to him ever. It showed a pack of hounds in a French forest, and his message concerned the horse-racing and hunting at Chantilly (BL, 472). The red-coated aristocrats "ride right over you if you dont dodge" (SL, 26–27), Faulkner wrote his father, perhaps unconsciously supplying a warning. (Years later, riding to the foxes in pink livery with Virginia gentry, the son would fulfill his desire to join the aristocrats on horseback [BL, 1641ff.].) Faulkner dedicated his first book "To My Mother"; Murry never received such a tribute. Shortly before Murry's death, William told an interviewer that Maud "read every line he wrote . . . but his father didn't bother and suspected that his son was wasting his time" (BL, 744). In 1929, soon after he married, Maud gave her son "a frail spindle-legged writing table," which brother John considered so fragile that it "belonged in some lady's parlor." Faulkner would support his writing upon this symbolically feminine surface throughout his life (BL, 631, 663, 1408). She also provided him with "the only writing chair he ever used" (MBB, 245). Conversely, Faulkner seems to have shut his father out of the act of writing. Literature was a gift from his mother, which he returned to *her*.

As with all gifts, aggression helped to motivate this one. Faulkner repaid his mother with his genius, but also with his spite. He recognized that she had made him her instrument of vengeance against her father and her husband, and he must have felt both guilt and fear for the emasculation she could effect. Phil Stone observed "that all the Falkner boys were tied to their mother and resented it. This was probably partly responsible, Stone thought, for an animosity toward women that he saw in Bill" (BL,

631). No woman could excite his misogyny more harshly than his mother, the woman he loved most. For example, when Maud wrote to Faulkner's publishers in 1928 to accuse them of stealing his royalties, he reacted furiously (BL, 587; CNC, 74). Much later, when Faulkner made a famous endorsement of artistic ruthlessness in the *Paris Review* interview (1956)— "If a writer has to rob his mother, he will not hesitate; the *Ode on a Grecian Urn* is worth any number of old ladies" (LG, 239; BL, 1594)—his own eighty-four-year-old mother had suffered a cerebral hemorrhage only weeks before (BL, 1580).

Perhaps the most baffling, and revealing, comment he ever wrote about his mother appeared in a letter to Malcolm Cowley in 1945: "I more or less grew up in my father's livery stable," he lied. "Being the eldest of four boys, I escaped my mother's influence pretty easy, since my father thought it was fine for me to apprentice to the business" (FCF, 67). Cowley was preparing a biographical introduction to *The Portable Faulkner* at the time. The author's attempt to revise his own history so as to exclude his mother reveals his embarrassment about the feminine sources of his vocation, his retroactive wish to compensate his father posthumously for having acquiesced in Maud's wish that he become an artist, and his retaliation against his mother precisely for having influenced him so much.

Faulkner felt pulled by his parents in opposite directions. His mother called him to the rigors of the schoolhouse, the church, and the library; his father pointed to the diffuse pleasures of the world outside. Within his mother's victory lay the seeds of her simultaneous defeat. To compensate for having subscribed so solely to his mother's ambition for him, Faulkner made rebellious gestures on his "absent" father's behalf. To the identities he assumed because they were negative in his father's eyes, he added some that were negative in his mother's. When he was not affecting foppish cultivation, he was pretending to be an unhousebroken rowdy. He dropped out of high school, college, and church. He drank, smoked, drove recklessly, and hunted. He adopted his father's vices while refusing to adopt his father's virtues of plodding industry and provincial conformity, bourgeois virtues that would have placed the two in competition. So easily might he have won his Oedipal struggle that he had to suppress violently his rivalry with his father to avoid simply falling into victory, winning by default. Like Thoreau, he had to seek failure, and his father's displeasure, in order to punish himself. He had to protect his father from his mother's ambitions for himself, but in a way that would not jeopardize his achieving them. Long after Faulkner had "justified" his mother's life, he still carried the burden of his dead father's failure and remoteness. In his sixtieth year, he could reveal that on the few occasions when he painted pictures, he painted "[d]ogs in the woods, that sort of thing, horses" (FU, 259)—as if he were using the talent he inherited from Maud to provide images for Murry's album. Thus the artistic poseur whom the town called "Count" never extirpated the red-blooded "American boy" who had led a scout troop and visited the seamy sections of Memphis. An effete Ernest V. Trueblood would have to coexist with a virile, but vulgar, "William Faulkner."

Faulkner's extreme ambivalence toward his parents culminated in acute "identity confusion" during a "prolonged" adolescence. As a youth, he needed to fail in his father's terms to succeed in his mother's without appearing to conspire with her against her weak husband. He fulfilled this need by granting himself a "moratorium," during which he could cultivate eventual greatness while suffering immediate embarrassment. Thus, he affected the series of "negative identities" specifically calculated to scandalize his father and the town in which his father had failed—the effete Count No 'Count, the British gentleman, the limping veteran, the bohemian vagabond, the doomed aristocrat, Ernest V. Trueblood. Like Thoreau, he set out to disappoint the expectations of his elders, and he succeeded, refusing to work steadily at any employment in which he might outshine his lackluster father and achieving a reputation for idling instead. Like Thoreau, too, he befuddled his parents and neighbors by changing his name just enough to make a rebellious statement without suffering the consequences of an outright break.

When Faulkner forced his supervisors to fire him from his postmaster's job in October 1924 ("He just *wouldn't* work," his uncle sighed), he was a twenty-seven-year-old drifter without prospects or publications save the forthcoming *Marble Faun*, a vanity book. At about the same time, he was removed from his job as master of the local scout troop because of church leaders' objections to his heavy drinking. Nevertheless, he flaunted a vainglorious self-assurance, as if his very failure were the validation of his superiority. He treated his dismissal from the postmastership, the longest job he ever held voluntarily, as a victory, uttering his famous thanksgiving for the fact that "I won't ever again have to be at the beck and call of every son of a bitch who's got two cents to buy a stamp." Despite his various rejections, he was declaring grandly to his friends, without any real evidence to support him, that "he was a genius" (BL, 364–66).

Such apparently blithe indifference to the world's disapproval surely concealed anxiety about the justice of his arrogant claims. For the "ironic delay"[65] Faulkner granted himself was an exceedingly risky venture. His performance required him to walk (and sometimes limp) for years along a very delicate tightrope between being a ne'er-do-well *now* and being a superman *soon*. He had to succeed *through* failure. Thus, he *might* secure greatness by avoiding mediocrity, or he might—in fact, probably would, almost did—merely achieve a black sheep's local notoriety or a "minor" writer's oblivion. In short, while Faulkner's deliberate postponement of success may have solved some of his psychological problems, it also created others. It exposed him to the possibility that postponement might turn into cancellation. It required him to gamble his life on a vindication that must at times have seemed as unlikely to him as it seemed to everyone else (except perhaps his mother). It committed him to assuming identities that were so blatantly theatrical that even he could not completely suppress an awareness of their falseness. The fact that he ultimately achieved all of the goals of his "moratorium" in no way eliminated the problems it engendered.

During his period of self-imposed latency, Faulkner sought to preserve his genius by entrusting it to guardians. In the "psychological absence" of John Thoreau, Henry David had found a surrogate father in Emerson; Faulkner found his first in Phil Stone and later in Sherwood Anderson. Just as Thoreau turned on Emerson, so Faulkner had to discard Stone and Anderson in order to preserve the illusion of his independence. From Emerson, in the form of Transcendentalist doctrine, Thoreau received "ideological" as well as moral support for his nonconformism. From Stone, Anderson, and others, Faulkner gained not so much a system of ideas as a tradition that justified his truancy. They inducted him into what Lewis Simpson has called "the Great Literary Secession," the Modernist defection from political and commercial society by artists of all sorts. Through them, he became a citizen of the "community . . . of literary alienation"—the international "Republic of Letters"—which sanctioned his abdication of conventional duties and rewards, which valued his eccentricity, and which offered glorious precedents for artistic apotheosis despite worldly obscurity.[66]

From the beginning, the "ideological" foundation of Faulkner's vocation always included the paradoxical principle that true success must originate somehow in failure.[67] Even after he won fame and security—perhaps especially then—he liked to refer to himself as a "failed poet" rather than as a successful novelist. Indeed, he implied that even a successful novelist is primarily a failure: "Maybe every novelist wants to write poetry first, finds he can't and then tries the short story which is the most demanding form after poetry. And failing at that, only then does he take up novel writing" (LG, 238).[68] Similarly, according to a statement that infuriated Ernest Hemingway and that Faulkner often repeated in his final decades, he judged his fellow novelists by a standard of failure rather than of success. He ranked them not by their accomplishments, he often said, but "by the splendor of the failure"—Wolfe first, himself second, and "Hemingway last because Hemingway through good fortune or through good preceptor, had developed a style where he was quite at home, where he did not make mistakes, and that he did not risk as we've risked" (LG, 122).[69] He could acknowledge his own accomplishment only by insisting that it was actually a default. In 1955, he advised young writers not "to think too much about success. . . . Success is feminine. It's like a woman. You treat her with contempt and she'll come after you, all fawning and eager, but chase after her and she'll scorn you" (LG, 219).

Faulkner cultivated a mystique of failure, which still colors his reputation. His pronouncements about his profession and about his colleagues reinforced a legend of victory salvaged miraculously from defeat—a legend that still dominates our myth of him. One of the most gratifying elements in our attraction to this Faulkner is a vicarious triumph of excellence over the conspiracy of silence supposedly arrayed against him, and of genius over the world's contempt for a tramp, a high school drop-out, a Mississippi farmer. At the center of our memory of the mythical Faulkner is his sudden apotheosis in the late forties, when the forces of oblivion were allegedly melting down the plates of his books for scrap metal. We cling to this melodrama even when confronted with contradictory facts. Although Faulkner has now outpolled Hemingway, Melville, Hawthorne, James, and almost everyone else in the popularity contests of academe, we *need* to read his fiction as an act of restitution. We want to believe that we alone have redeemed an unappreciated genius from obscurity, that we alone have recognized the true brilliance behind the unpromising facade. He still wins our admiration by having lost.

Faulkner needed the same redemption before any reader needed it for him. The pastoral structure of his appeal was based upon the pastoral structure of his personality—cosmopolitan sophistication masquerading as rural simplicity (and *vice versa*), incipient genius pretending to folly in order to effect the greatest surprise. At the foundation of his commitment to writing lay a desire not merely for recognition but for a *delayed* recognition, wherein the degree of his merit would be proportionate to the desperateness as well as the length of the delay. Erik Erikson, describing Martin Luther before he nailed his ninety-five theses to the church door in Wittenberg, could have been describing Faulkner (or Thoreau): "I could not conceive of a young great man in the years before he becomes a great young man without assuming that inwardly he harbors a quite inarticulate stubbornness, a secret furious inviolacy, a gathering of impressions for eventual use within some as yet dormant new configuration of thought— that he is tenaciously waiting it out for a day of vengeance when the semideliberate straggler will suddenly be found at the helm, and he who took so much will reveal the whole extent of his potential mastery."[70]

No wonder the word *endurance* is Faulkner's ultimate shibboleth. Before it entered his vocabulary, it defined his psychology. Before it expressed his worldview, it determined his self-image. In the years preceding his public anointment, he played a delicate waiting game, the object of which was to elude immediate approval without sacrificing ultimate esteem. He had to "endure" short-term neglect in order to "prevail" in the long run— to quote the most famous words of the Nobel Prize Acceptance Speech, in which Faulkner indirectly acknowledged his own strategy for achieving his destiny.[71] Like Thoreau, Faulkner had set out to be last in order to be first.

The psychological imperatives behind Faulkner's vocation inevitably produced their own counterreaction. The urge toward immobility, silence, and defeat, in which his sense of himself as a writer originated, would ultimately have to inhibit the career it helped to generate. A career that originates in deliberate failure cannot finally succeed, except paradoxically; and a success that is paradoxical is still at least partially a failure. Nor can a career that originates in false identities permanently dispel the confusion that produced them.

Even when Faulkner had secured his measure of immortality, he could not acknowledge the "Faulkner" who wrote the books as a legitimate version of himself; nor could he completely recognize the books as legitimate extensions—or twins—of himself. In Erikson's terms, the way in which Faulkner resolved his adolescent "identity crisis" insured that he would suffer a middle-age "crisis of generativity." His expert impersonation of a writer enabled him to write some of America's best novels, but it did not protect him from the necessity that he some day confront what he himself saw as his fraudulence. Throughout the late thirties and the forties, Faulkner persistently exposed the halfheartedness of his authorial self-image. In the books—not novels so much as assemblages—that he constructed in those years, he displayed the divisions within his heart.

Faulkner's Southern Honor

If Faulkner rescued his identity from the small town and the middle class by embracing an "ideology" of art, he also "contained" his "opposite."[72] He may have rebelled against the norms that prevailed in north-central Mississippi during the early twentieth century, but he internalized them as well; and the values that he absorbed from the air of Oxford would contribute centrally to the history of his vocation.

In a pioneering book, *Southern Honor*, Bertram Wyatt-Brown has elucidated the communal "ideology" in which Faulkner was educated during his youth. Among the many reasons for which Faulkner and Thoreau became different writers, the most obvious is cultural geography. While both authors were psychologically predisposed to seek careers that would negate community standards, the standards of Massachusetts in the 1830s differed markedly from those of Mississippi in the 1910s. Though Wyatt-Brown focuses on antebellum Southerners, his analysis is valid, at least residually, for several succeeding generations as well.

The "keystone" of Southern culture, well into the twentieth century according to Wyatt-Brown, has been the concept of honor, a "harsh code" which he traces back to "the Indo-European tribes that created Homeric Greece" and which he identifies with "pre-modern" Western culture generally. Whereas in New England, already by Thoreau's time, an "ethic of conscience" had mostly replaced the earlier and more widespread "ethic of honor," Southern culture maintained its central commitment to honor for another hundred years. Conscience, a "modern" development fostered by Christianity, represents an internalization of the voice of God, whereas honor represents an internalization of a community's values. Individual identity based on conscience is private; individual identity based on honor is determined by one's external appearance and public behavior.[73]

Wyatt-Brown defines honor as a "cluster of ethical rules . . . by which judgments of behavior are ratified by community consensus." At the heart of this cluster "lies the evaluation of the public." Any inner conviction of self-worth can be validated only through communal assessment. "In other words," says Wyatt-Brown, "honor is reputation. Honor resides in the individual as his understanding of who he is and where he belongs in the ordered ranks of society." Under the dispensation of conscience, a person *is* what he knows himself to be; under that of honor, he is what his *neighbors* know him to be. Violations of conscience result in guilt, which occurs inside the guilty party; violations of honor result in shame, which occurs in a public arena through enforcement by a community. Wyatt-Brown devotes much of his book to the sanctions through which traditional Southern society controlled deviations from its norms: the legal code, dueling, charivari, lynching. The dictates of honor "required the rejection of the lowly, the alien, and the shamed."[74]

The applicability of Wyatt-Brown's thesis to the youthful Faulkner's case is pervasive. To achieve self-worth, Faulkner frustrated the expectations of his family and his community, adopting poses and costumes that were certain to arouse their condemnation. For the sake of a long-deferred honor, he deliberately incurred a deep and persistent shamefulness, inviting ostracism to vouchsafe eventual acceptance. Indeed, he provoked a nonviolent and informal charivari at the hands of his university classmates. Throughout this ordeal, both he and his community abided by rules that each side understood clearly. Whereas Thoreau rebelled against the conventions of Concord on grounds of principle, Faulkner engaged in a ritual of rejection that had everything to do with honor and shame and little to do with conscience and guilt.

Within the context of Southern honor, Wyatt-Brown says, "inner virtue" is congruent with "outward, public action."[75] People are honorable to the extent that they conform to the attributions of their social status. As a member of a family in decline, Faulkner constructed an identity by denying his inherited and all too precarious place in Mississippi society. To avoid belonging to the middle class, he pretended to be alternately a peasant or an aristocrat. Frustrated in his effort to earn an honorable and visible war record, he invented one. Dissatisfied with the vocations available in his community, he pursued one which the community despised. He fabricated an identity out of lies, within an ethos that equated one's word with one's character.

The psychogenesis of Faulkner's various impostures deserves close attention for the light it will surely shed on his discovery and maintenance of his vocation, and the impostures undoubtedly originated at least partially in an infantile and adolescent libido to which Southern honor was irrelevant. But Faulkner's fraudulence had social origins and consequences also. In a culture in which one *is* what one says and does, a person who turns himself into a series of public fictions is risking existential trouble as well as a bad reputation. In a culture in which what the public says about one is incorporated into one's self-definition, a chronic prevaricator and pretender is courting psychic disaster. Behind Faulkner's boastful confession that "[a]ll writers are congenital liars, or they wouldn't be writers in the first place"[76] lurks his serious recognition of his own dishonorable estate.

For Faulkner entered a vocation that, in the context of Southern honor, was shameful. According to Wyatt-Brown, the spoken word is more honorable, because more public, than the written word, which records merely internal thought and which is committed to paper in private, antisocially.[77] Poetry and fiction are suspect insofar as they are counterfactual explorations of merely internal states of mind. Although Thoreau may have lacked a large readership, he could at least write in the confidence that his neighbors respected written discourse. But Faulkner, like most Southern writers until very recently, had to struggle against the knowledge that his community ignored or even scorned him.

Writers in the antebellum South—Poe most famously—suffered isolation and shame. According to Thomas Nelson Page "[o]ne of Phillip Pendleton Cooke's neighbors said to him after he became known as the author of 'Florence Vane,' 'I wouldn't waste time on a damned thing like poetry: you might make yourself, with all your sense and judgment, a useful man in settling neighborhood disputes and difficulties.'"[78] In 1831, Edward W. Johnston happily asserted that Southerners felt a general "aversion to authorship" in proportion to their "good education and cultivated taste." In 1858, William Gilmore Simms complained that the people of Charleston had "always treated me rather as a public enemy, to be sneered at, than as a dutiful son doing her honor." For Henry Timrod in 1859, the Southern writer was so "constrained by the indifference of the public amid which he lived" as to deserve to be called "the Pariah of modern literature."[79]

Southern writers have characteristically reacted to their *dis*honor either by finally repudiating literature or by attempting to harness their literary talents to the needs of their communities. Augustus Baldwin Longstreet, the inventor of one of the region's few original modes of expression, Southwestern humor, typifies the first reaction. According to Page, he "was so ashamed of having been beguiled into writing what is one of the raciest books of sketches yet produced, a book by which alone his name is now preserved, that he made a strenuous effort to secure and suppress the work after its publication."[80] Similarly, Johnson Jones Hooper regretted that he had established the unsavory Simon Suggs in the public mind, and he felt the "depressing influence" of that character "whenever he desired, or aimed, to soar above it, to a higher rank before the public."[81]

Through the example of William Gilmore Simms and his circle, Drew Gilpin Faust has illustrated the second reaction. Frustrated by the prevailing anti-intellectualism of the South, by the absence of a Southern audience for literature and social criticism, and by the scarcity of public roles available to writers, Simms, James H. Hammond, Edmund Ruffin, Nathaniel Beverly Tucker, and George Frederick Holmes enlisted in the campaign to defend slavery during the 1850s. For Faust, these men typified their generation of Southern intellectuals because of their "social marginality" (all occupied similarly problematic positions within their communities) and because they struggled, fruitlessly, to "establish a recognized place for mind in their society." Like other Southern authors, according to Faust, Simms and his friends faced the difficult task of reconciling thought and action within a culture that valued action and denigrated thought. Thoreau might assume a unity between intellect and labor; in "The American Scholar," Emerson had declared that "[t]he mind now thinks, now acts, and each fit reproduces the other." But Simms and his colleagues found themselves "continually torn between involvement in the real world of affairs and periodic withdrawal into a more ideal, more elevated—and less demanding—realm."[82]

The situation of the Southern writer was only mildly less constrained during Faulkner's era. Throughout the twenties and thirties, literary conferences in the South were devoted largely to rehearsing the same lament that Timrod and others had sounded seventy years before: no publishers, no magazines, no readers. At the Conference on Literature and Reading in the South and Southwest in Baton Rouge in 1935, for example, one speaker after another bemoaned the isolation of Southern writers from the Southern community. John Peale Bishop specifically cited Faulkner as a writer who turned to "obscurity, eccentricity, perversity, and self-indulgence" because he had no audience to restrain him, and Allen Tate agreed: "The position of the Southern writer is seen in Mr. Faulkner—in his appeal to sensation, etc. He has no public of his peers." The writer in the South "has no public at home."[83]

In one of the introductions to *The Sound and the Fury* that Faulkner wrote in 1933, he anticipated these dire appraisals of the Southern writer's situation and confirmed his own isolation. "Art is no part of southern life," he began. In New York and Chicago, bourgeois youths can choose conventional careers in "editorial rooms and art galleries" without fearing for their reputations. In the South, however, such vocations are socially "marginal," to use Faust's word for Simms's coterie. Art, "to become visible at all, must become a ceremony, a spectacle," and artists—"alien mummers"—must "waste themselves in protest and active self-defense until there is nothing left with which to speak." Nevertheless, Faulkner wrote, some Southerners deliberately choose to be artists within this hostile environment.[84] New incarnations of Count No 'Count, exorcising private demons, will always step forward to shame themselves spectacularly.

But then Faulkner added an important qualification. Those Southerners who choose artistic vocations do so without surrendering their honor, without being "forced to choose, lady and tiger fashion, between being an artist and being a man." Indeed, "[o]nly Southerners" are known to "have taken horsewhips and pistols to editors about the treatment or maltreatment of their manuscript." The artist, Faulkner might have said, must be twice as honorable and act twice as forcefully as anyone else, in order to overcome the community's natural prejudice against him. A typically Faulknerian paradox underlies his argument: the artist is the truly honorable man in Southern society, because only the artist struggles against so mighty a presumption of shame. Writers resorted to "actual pistols" only in "the old days," he continued, and "we no longer succumb to the impulse," but that impulse "is still there, still within us."[85] Thus, Faulkner introduced the novel upon which he felt his artistic *reputation* most solidly rested with a justification of his manhood and with a defense of his honor.

Almost a dozen years later, in a letter to Malcolm Cowley, he described the history of Southern attitudes toward art in terms similarly drawn from the vocabulary of honor and manhood. The South was both too busy and too lazy to make literature and music, he wrote: "When they were not doing anything—not hunting or superintending farming or riding 10 and 20 miles to visit, they really did nothing: they slept or talked. They talked too much, I think. Oratory was the first art; Confederate generals would hold up attacks while they made speeches to their troops. Apart from that, 'art' was really no manly business. It was a polite painting of china by gentlewomen" (SL, 216).

Thus, while Faulkner's association of art with femininity may have resulted largely from his mother's powerful sponsorship of his vocation, it was consequentially reinforced by the prevailing "ethic of honor" in which he was reared. As Louis Rubin has written, Faulkner's commitment to his artistry coincided with (and was intensified by) a feeling "that there was something undignified and even unmanly in pursuing such an occupation rather than being a red-blooded, stalwart man of affairs." Rubin traces throughout Faulkner's work "a dichotomy between the man of sensibility and the man of action: Horace Benbow and Bayard Sartoris in *Flags in the Dust*, Quentin Compson and Dalton Ames in *The Sound and the Fury*, Quentin and Thomas Sutpen in *Absalom, Absalom!*, Darl and Jewel Bundren in *As I Lay Dying*, and so on."[86]

Acknowledging that the compulsion of male writers "to demonstrate their masculinity" is not limited to the American South, Rubin nevertheless marshals a convincing argument that Southern writers feel the need more urgently than writers from most other regions. For, in Wyatt-Brown's terms, masculine honor is public and forceful for Southerners, while feminine honor is private and submissive. To secure reputation, the male Southerner must adopt a public role; since the South does not attribute any active function to writing, the writer must either deny or transcend his vocation in order to achieve respect—including self-respect, insofar as he has accepted the "ethic." Thus, Faulkner insisted that he was "no literary man but merely a plain dirt farmer" as a protest "against an identity that his artistic talents and achievements . . . tended to force upon him: that of someone who is no longer part of the community." For

Rubin, Faulkner's "gestures" toward "emphasizing his community identity constituted a means of assuring not only others but himself as well that he was still a part of the community."[87]

Thus, Ernest V. Trueblood's futile attempt to persuade "Mr. Faulkner's" stepson and nephew that his "position in the household is in no sense menial, since I have been writing Mr. Faulkner's novels and short stories for years" (US, 424), echoes the perennial efforts of Southern authors to justify their existence to an indifferent society. And Faulkner's claim that he "grew up in [his] father's livery stable" (FCF, 67) indicates his need to occupy a niche his neighbors could understand and respect. Within Faulkner's pastoral personality raged a conflict between the competing attractions of alienation from, and of integration into, his community.

Until the late 1930s, Faulkner controlled this tension and used it to create great fiction. Out of a double fraudulence, he wrested a singular authenticity. Then, beset by doubts about the worth of his vocation, doubts which he had mostly suppressed since the twenties, he began to scrutinize his own authority, addressing it as one of his principal subjects. Whereas, theoretically at least, he had been able to write *The Sound and the Fury* without thinking about publication, now he could not ignore his relationship to the public that still mostly refused to read his books. Although he did not pursue an active social role for his writing—unlike William Gilmore Simms in the 1850s and unlike the Agrarians in the 1930s—until the Swedish Academy thrust it upon him in 1950, he had been struggling for a dozen years before he won the Nobel Prize to make his books responsive to a public reality. In *Absalom, Absalom!* the Southern tragedies of class and race are registered in the private consciousness of Quentin Compson, who is incapable of disposing of Thomas Sutpen's legacy in a way that extends beyond himself. In *The Hamlet* and *Go Down, Moses*, Faulkner would represent the same realities as communal.

Beginning with *The Wild Palms*, Faulkner launched an exploration of the *public* foundation of his vocation. He had been recruited into the literary life because of deeply personal, even unconscious, needs. Once established as a writer in Wyatt-Brown's honor-ridden South, however, he would necessarily define his identity through his complex relationship to the community he had rebelled against by becoming a writer. His "identity crisis" during his teens and twenties may have originated in a traumatic privacy, but his "crisis of generativity" would necessarily be a crisis of *social* identity.[88] Examining Faulkner in 1953, Dr. Wortis discerned not only that his patient might have received too little "love from his mother" but also that "he suffered with problems of the South which were somehow related to his own tensions" (BL, 1454).

When Faulkner dramatized his struggle to achieve a vocation during the 1920s, he relied primarily on the imagery of his body and his family: crippled limbs, wounded backs, designing mothers. Fifteen years later when he dramatized his struggle to maintain that vocation, he relied primarily on the complex image of the Southern community—on the "ordered ranks of society" which he had incorporated into his literary self-image. In the fractured books of the late thirties and the forties, he analyzed the constituents of his authorial identity by describing the boundaries of, and the divisions within, Yoknapatawpha County. In divided texts that embodied a divided society, he diagnosed his divided imagination.

PART TWO

IKE'S COW

THE DECAY OF FAULKNER'S SENSE OF VOCATION

CHAPTER THREE

THE WILD PALMS

It is the custom on the stage, in all good, murderous melodra-
mas, to present the tragic and the comic scenes, in as regular
alternation, as the layers of red and white in a side of streaky, well-
cured bacon. The hero sinks upon his straw bed, weighed down by
fetters and misfortunes; in the next scene, his faithful but unconscious squire regales the audience with a comic song.

Charles Dickens, Oliver Twist

. . . Much the same thing happened with "Pudd'nhead Wilson." I
had a sufficiently hard time with that tale, because it changed itself
from a farce to a tragedy while I was going along with it,—a most
embarrassing circumstance. But what was a great deal worse was,
that it was not one story, but two stories tangled together; and they
obstructed and interrupted each other at every turn and created no
end of confusion and annoyance. I could not offer the book for
publication, for I was afraid it would unseat the reader's reason, I
did not know what was the matter with it, for I had not noticed, as
yet, that it was two stories in one.

Samuel Langhorne Clemens, "Those Extraordinary Twins"

"If I Forget Thee, Jerusalem"

In "Afternoon of a Cow," Faulkner defined his vocation as a collaboration
between two versions of himself: an uncultivated rustic and a sophisticated
aesthete. He thus based his authorship on an internalization of a division
in society—between people who work the soil and live in direct contact
with their senses, and people who dwell among abstractions, at one remove from their own experience. To maintain his vocation, Faulkner
needed to preserve the distinction between the inner partners who together produced his books. To keep Ernest Trueblood and "William

Faulkner" distinct, in turn, he needed his society to remain double. In *The Wild Palms*, he imposed a drastic division upon the world, as a means of reinforcing his own threatened self-image.

Soon after he gave "Afternoon" to Coindreau in June 1937, he learned that his contract with Twentieth Century-Fox would expire in August, releasing him to Mississippi—and Estelle. He reacted to the mixed news with a drinking bout so extreme that his brother Murry drove from Texas to Hollywood to see him through it. After drying out, William worked until late July on a story called "An Odor of Verbena," which was to serve as the finale to the series of *Saturday Evening Post* stories that Random House would publish as *The Unvanquished* in 1938. He drove home in August (BL, 964–68). He stayed in Oxford for only two months, renewing old pursuits and thinking about an idea for a new novel that he had been contemplating at least since Meta Carpenter's engagement to another man in late 1936. Apparently, he began to write it in mid-September 1937.[1] Three weeks after celebrating his fortieth birthday on September 25, he traveled to New York to see *The Unvanquished* through the finishing stages at Random House (BL, 969–72).

· A business trip, yes. But Faulkner had an even more important reason for being in the city. He knew, somehow, that his former lover and her new husband were living there, having fled Nazi Germany.[2] He called her after he arrived, and the couple met briefly with him in a restaurant. During the following night, he drank himself into a stupor and fell, unconscious, against a steam pipe in the toilet of his room at the Algonquin Hotel. When he failed to keep appointments the next day, a worried friend gained entry to the room, to find him insensible, face down on the toilet floor, clad only in undershorts and suffering a third-degree burn in the small of his back. The wound, which penetrated nearly to his spine, caused him excruciating pain for months. At the outset of his slow recovery, he told Meta Carpenter Rebner that seeing her with "someone else" had precipitated the accident. Before leaving New York in the second week of November, he quoted to her a character he was only beginning to invent. "Between grief and nothing," he told her, anticipating the final words of "Wild Palms," "I will take grief."[3]

Asked why he committed such a self-destructive act, Faulkner replied pettishly, "Because I like to" (BL, 975). This accident provided him unambiguously with the wound he had neglected to receive in World War One, and he took this opportunity to retell his lies about European combat. It also set the pattern for future accidents he managed to suffer whenever the pain from this one subsided temporarily. Throughout his composition of the new novel, which he resumed as soon as he returned to Oxford, his back pain served as an objective correlative for the sorrow he was trying to express. That sorrow resulted not just from his loss of Meta—nor only from his memory of Helen Baird, a previously lost love[4]—but also from a failed marriage, a jeopardized paternity, and a vocation on trial.

In the new book Faulkner reiterated systematically, if unconsciously, the paradoxical terms of his early definition of vocation: identity through double impersonation, liberty through confinement, stasis within furious motion, speech within silence. He embodied these paradoxes within a context of financial concerns that linked the novel both to his bank book and to the national economy. He incarnated this matrix of paradoxes in images that were simultaneously so private as to be obscure and so topical as to be public property: floods, chain gangs, transcontinental travel, and other icons of the Depression during which he wrote.

He called the new novel "If I Forget Thee, Jerusalem," in an intricately personal allusion to Psalm 137:

> By the rivers of Babylon, there we sat down, yea, we wept, when we remembered Zion.

Faulkner had just escaped temporary captivity in the Babylon of Hollywood. Returning to the Zion of Mississippi, however, he discovered himself imprisoned in a hopeless marriage, exiled from the woman who had made him briefly happy.

> We hanged our harps upon the willows in the midst thereof.

In California he had compromised his talent, his "harp," by delaying his novels for the sake of income from screenwriting.

> For there they that carried us away captive required of us a song; and they that wasted us required of us mirth, saying, Sing us one of the songs of Zion.
> How shall we sing the Lord's song in a strange land?

Writing for the movies, Faulkner had had to apply his "wasted" talent to popularization. He had tried to translate the "Lord's song" of his genius into the foreign tongue of commercial art.

> If I forget thee, O Jerusalem, let my right hand forget her cunning.

Faulkner wrote with his right hand. His holy capital was the city of art.

> If I do not remember thee, let my tongue cleave to the roof of my mouth; if I prefer not Jerusalem above my chief joy.

Perhaps Faulkner too was trying to negotiate a contract with himself: failure to fulfill the strict obligations of his craft should result in self-imposed silence. If he could not write without succumbing to commercial pressures, perhaps he should not write at all.

> Remember, O Lord, the children of Edom in the day of Jerusalem; who said, Rase it, rase it, even to the foundation thereof.

If he could not reassert the primacy of art even above his "chief joy" (Meta? enough money?), then the foundation of his art needed shoring—or leveling.

> O daughter of Babylon, who art to be destroyed; happy shall he be, that rewardeth thee as thou hast served us.

Faulkner loved Meta, but she had deserted him. Perhaps he intended to punish her as well as celebrate her in the new book. He would certainly be punishing himself.

> Happy shall he be, that taketh and dasheth thy little ones against the stones.

Faulkner, himself a parent for only four years, was about to create a fictional father who aborts his own child. Embattled in a "crisis of generativity," furthermore, he was considering at least half-heartedly the possibility of repudiating his career. His "little ones" included his novels as well as his daughter. [5]

As he worked on the book from November 1937 through June 1938, his emotional and physical condition may have been negative, but his financial condition improved significantly, if only temporarily. He started with a surplus, the remainder of his Hollywood wages plus a one-thousand-dollar advance from Random House (BL, 968–72). In February, an even bigger windfall arrived. Metro-Goldwyn-Mayer paid $25,000 for the right to film *The Unvanquished*. With his share, $19,000, Faulkner was able to pay all his outstanding debts and to invest in two pieces of property: Bailey's Woods, behind his home at Rowan Oak; and a 320-acre farm in the northeastern corner of Lafayette County (BL, 983–86). The money eased his worries temporarily, allowing him to "write in leisure, when and what I want to write, as I have always . . . dreamed" (SL, 104). Thus, while writing in early 1938, he could, if he wished, mostly ignore the need to attract or accommodate an audience. More than any book since *The Sound and the Fury*, he could write this one without appeasing popular appetites. It would consequently come as close as any novel he ever published to being autobiographical. In 1952 he would tell Joan Williams that he wrote it "in order to try to stave off what I thought was heart-break" (SL, 338).

To write autobiographically in 1938, however, Faulkner had to write about popular appetites despite his freedom. In 1928 he may have been able to close "a door . . . silently and forever to between me and all publishers' addresses and booklists,"6 but by 1938 that door had swung open many times. Insofar as the new novel contains his reassessment of his vocation, it sets that vocation in relation to an audience. It analyzes his relationship to his community. Or, rather, it registers his lack of an audience and records his alienation from his community. Whether Faulkner acted consciously or not, his new novel would investigate the imagination of his public more deliberately than any other book he wrote, not because he wished to adapt himself to it but because he could not.

Ironically, just as he was liberating himself temporarily from the need to please an audience, and just as he was beginning to write a book about his failure to connect with the American public, the American public reached tentatively out to him. The *New Republic* published an article about him by Stark Young in January 1938, and *Time* magazine began preparing a cover story about him at around the same time. Tourists began to invade his privacy for the purpose of staring at him. The most important segment of his public, Oxford, began to pay attention as well. The community whose rejection he had sought through writing, at the outset of his career, now seemed ready to begin accepting him. An article in the Oxford *Eagle* noted that the townspeople who had jeered at Count No 'Count twenty years before "are beginning to admit that Bill Faulkner . . . is a writer of major importance." Though this judgment must have been based on his film work and magazine fiction more than on his novels, the evidence of a reversal must have pleased him. It must also have disconcerted him, however, for he had postulated his identity as a writer on the disapproval of this very community. Faulkner was failing his way into success, whether he wanted to or not (BL, 970, 980, 985).

The most visible sign of his success proved to be a trap as well as a vindication. At Greenfield Farm, his new property out in the county, he determined to breed mules; and he installed his brother John there as manager. The farm gave him an outlet and refuge from his writing and his marriage; it allowed him to enact the "farmer" pose he had already perfected years before; and it provided him with valuable raw material for his next several books. But it proved a liability as well. It tied him down to a location for which he may have pined when he was away but which quickly made him restless when he was there. It connected him concretely to an agrarian tradition of Southern literature that, as we shall see when we come to *The Hamlet* and *Go Down, Moses,* inhibited honest writing while seeming to enhance it. The farm put him in a daily working relationship with the peasant class of northern Mississippi, about which he had previously written from a loftier perspective; now he had to evaluate the literary consequences of that relationship in ways that would further threaten his self-confidence as a novelist. Most ominously, the farm dragged him back into debt rather than insuring him against it. Less a profitable enterprise than a literary gesture, mule-breeding drained rather than augmented his income. By the time he finished his current manuscript, wages, taxes, and other expenses had already forced him to consider another screenwriting contract and to write more stories for the popular magazines. Rather than sell any of his property, however, he risked separation from it in order to keep it. To save Zion, he would return to Babylon. He needed the land in part because it gave him an excuse to leave Mississippi. His possession entitled him to exile; his captivity justified his escape (BL, 986, 988–89, 1002).

The book Faulkner wrote, mostly during the first half of 1938 between ministrations to his back and outings to Greenfield Farm, is a diptych. It consists of two opposite distillations, grounded in opposite social realms, of Faulkner's recent predicaments with women, with writing, and with Hollywood.

The first of the novel's two narratives, "Wild Palms," is the tale of a medical intern in New Orleans, Harry Wilbourne, who in 1937 falls in love with Charlotte Rittenmeyer, the impulsive wife of a businessman there, and absconds with her to Chicago, then successively to a woods camp by a lake in Wisconsin, a mining camp in Utah, and finally back south to a summer cottage on the Gulf coast. Together, they seek that freedom from work and respectability which they come to regard as necessary for the pure pursuit of their love affair. This freedom is finally circumscribed by Charlotte's accidental pregnancy, the abortion of which (performed by Harry) leads to her death and his imprisonment.

The second narrative, "Old Man," relates the trial-by-water of a Mississippi convict who, when drafted into rescue service during the Great Flood of 1927, is swept away by the Mississippi River with the pregnant woman he was sent to deliver from it. The surging waters propel him toward a freedom of which he wants no part and to which he cannot adapt. After weeks of hardship and frustration, including a stay in a "Cajan" alligator camp, he succeeds in returning to the prison farm at Parchman. There he surrenders the woman, the baby he midwived on a flooded and animal-infested Indian mound, the state's rowboat, and himself back into the hands of the law, which had already pronounced him drowned and therefore legally free. The authorities add ten years to his sentence, an imposition he seems relieved to suffer.

Neither of these stories, although each is intriguing in its own way, arouses as much interest as their curious combination. Faulkner confused the matter, of course, not merely by juxtaposing them but also by composing their chapters in alternation and then insisting that the intermingled result is not just a book but a novel. Almost twenty years later, he recalled his discovery of the book's duality in musical terms: "When I reached the end of what is now the first section [of 'Wild Palms'], I realized suddenly that something was missing, it needed emphasis, something to lift it like counterpoint in music. So I wrote on the 'Old Man' story until the 'Wild Palms' story rose back to pitch. Then I stopped the 'Old Man' story at . . . its first section, and took up the 'Wild Palms' story until it began to sag. Then I raised it to pitch again with another section of its antithesis, which is the story of a man who got his love and spent the rest of the book fleeing from it, even to the extent of voluntarily going back to jail where he would be safe" (LG, 247–48).[7]

Closer to the actual time of composition, Faulkner did not sound so sure of himself. In a letter he wrote to his editor, Robert Haas, on July 8, 1938, he described the feeling of disorientation that writing the book had caused: "I have lived for the last six months in such a peculiar state of family complications and back complications that I still am not able to tell if the novel is all right or absolute drivel. To me, it was written just as if I had sat on the one side of a wall and the paper was on the other and my hand with the pen thrust through the wall and writing not only on invisible paper but in pitch darkness too, so that I could not even know if the pen still wrote on paper or not" (SL, 106). His graphic description of alienation from the act of writing can be interpreted in two ways. Either he meant that he had lost his narrative instincts, or he meant that in this book his instincts had led him toward uncharted territory. Of course, he may have meant both: that, having exhausted the known world of his talent, he found himself forced to invent a new world to explore, in which his familiar tools would no longer work. Indeed, the book he described seems to have resulted, at least partially, from his need to redefine what can constitute a novel and to stretch himself beyond his capabilities. The letter about writing through a wall, then, may contain a boast as well as a complaint.

In the same letter, Faulkner defended his title, "If I Forget Thee, Jerusalem," against Haas's fear that it might arouse anti-Semitism (SL, 106). When Faulkner visited New York in October to read galley proofs (and to visit Meta), he acquiesced, and the book became *The Wild Palms* (BL, 1002).

The Double Structure of *The Wild Palms*

From the book's earliest reception, the question of its coherence figured as the central issue critics would address. Most often, their judgment of Faulkner's success or failure corresponded with their indulgence of, or aversion to, the alternation device. All the reviewers seem to have recognized what Faulkner was attempting; the publisher's blurb on the dust jacket had alerted them to the thematic orchestration of "flight and refuge" in "two parallel stories." But few of them approved the attempt, and even those who praised the book qualified their acceptance of its structure. Ben Ray Redman, in a largely sympathetic review, voiced a common reaction: "Some readers may find it an exhilarating game to straddle the backs of two stories simultaneously; others may feel that the exercise is merely annoying and unnecessary. For my part, I am convinced that neither story gains anything from the enforced union, and I am fairly sure that both are losers."[8]

Those who took the structure seriously—a steadily growing contingent—sought to demonstrate the *concordia* within its *discors*. Since the book's first reception, some readers have accepted Faulkner's own opinion that the two stories complement each other contrapuntally. For example,

Alfred Kazin found that although "[t]here are two stories in 'The Wild Palms,' . . . they form a single narrative in theme." Wallace Stegner reluctantly concurred: "Even if one does not agree that the two utterly separate stories are sufficiently orchestrated, one can still see reason for the thematic juxtaposition and the alternation of chapters."[9]

But the most nearly complete immediate acceptance of the book's form came from an unlikely source. Soon after the publication of *The Wild Palms*, the *New Masses*—organ of the American Communist Party—printed a highly favorable review by Edwin Berry Burgum. Although Faulkner generally evoked the automatic disdain of Marxist critics during the thirties, Burgum succeeded in adapting *The Wild Palms* to his dialectical ideology; his chastisement of less approving critics is instructive. The "real relationship between the two stories," according to Burgum, lies in the fact that both Harry Wilbourne and the convict "end within the 'security' of prison walls. The pursuit of freedom, the escape from the conventional, has in neither instance been satisfactory. This is the basic ironic theme which both stories hold in common: in a demoralized age the prison affords the illiterate hillbilly and the educated neurotic doctor alike the only possible framework of social compulsions within which they can exist."[10] Uniquely among the book's reviewers, Burgum recognized the double-narrative device as an instrument of *sociological* perception. His Marxist premises may have blinded him to Faulkner's actual intentions, but they at least enabled him to see that one of the book's subjects is a community divided by class.

In sharp contrast to the initial reviewers, academic critics of *The Wild Palms* tend to assume that the novel is a success and then set out to justify Faulkner's claim of contrapuntal unity for it. In a variety of ways, they have confirmed Hyatt Waggoner's feeling that "the deepest meaning of each story emerges only as it is thought of in connection with the other."[11] They have elucidated correspondences between images in one story and images in the other—between Charlotte's "yellow" eyes and the "yellow" flood upon which the convict navigates, for example.[12] And they have traced structural parallels between the two plots. W. T. Jewkes, for example, has argued "that the author manages, *chapter for chapter*, to make the plot and the central thematic issues of the one story echo and complement the particular emphases and details of the other story."[13]

Most critics have assumed that Faulkner joined the plots together for the purpose of drawing an invidious comparison between the two protagonists. No consensus has emerged, however, about which of them the comparison favors. One reader, defining the stories as opposite versions of a "conflict between freedom . . . and the demands of a restrictive moral framework," can propose that Faulkner is in "apparent sympathy with the convict rather than Wilbourne."[14] Another can condemn the tall convict as "the ideal soldier for a fascist army,"[15] or praise Wilbourne for emerging, "in comparison with the convict, with his dignity as a man."[16] Such judgments illuminate the readers more than the novel. Critics who prefer Harry seem to value nonconformism and personal rebellion; those who favor the convict seem to value discipline and social responsibility.[17] Thus, the partisans of Harry can be described as ideologically more "liberal"; those of the convict, as more "conservative" (with the exception of Burgum, the *New Masses* reviewer, who naturally prefers the "proletarian" convict to the "middle-class" Wilbourne).[18]

But where does Faulkner stand? While the novel itself expresses no clear preference for one character or the other, the author did state his intentions unambiguously outside the text. One month after finishing *The Wild Palms*, he informed his editor that "the convict story" is only "counterpoint to sharpen" the theme of the other story, which he had stated as one of Harry's thoughts: "Between grief and nothing I will take grief" (SL, 106). In 1946, when Faulkner proposed a one-volume publication of *The Sound and the Fury* and the "part" of *The Wild Palms* "about the doctor who performed the abortion on his own sweetheart," he indicated his uncharacteristic readiness to dismantle a novel. The part he was temporarily willing to jettison was the convict's (SL, 228).[19] When he adapted "Old Man" for television in 1953, he was able, without apparent reluctance, to give it a happy ending for a popular audience.[20] And in the *Paris Review* interview of 1956, which he composed with Jean Stein (BL, 1594), he asserted unmistakably that "Wild Palms" is the dominant narrative: "That was one story—the story of Charlotte Rittenmeyer and Harry Wilbourne, who sacrificed everything for love, and then lost that. I did not know it would be two separate stories until after I had started the book. . . . The story is that of Charlotte and Wilbourne" (LG, 247–48).

At the University of Virginia later in the fifties, Faulkner directed most of his comments about *The Wild Palms* toward defending its unity, but some of his observations also suggest that he viewed the unity as asymmetrical. He consistently subordinated the convict's tale to that of Harry and Charlotte; and this subordination reflects his attitudes toward the people *in* the stories. For example, when asked why the characters of "Old Man" were left nameless, Faulkner replied, "To me the story was simply for background effect and they didn't need names, they just needed to be people in motion doing the exact opposite thing to the tragedy of Harry and Charlotte in the other story. To me they didn't need names . . . they were not too important" (FU, 171).

While the main event is a "tragedy" in Faulkner's view, the secondary plot is comic. When asked at Virginia why he had burdened the convict not merely with a woman but with a pregnant woman, he said, "I thought that made it funnier. To me all this is funny. A little more comical to show this man who meant well to get involved in all sorts of things that would have made a weaker or less centered man blench and falter, but not him. It was because he was just stupid and ignorant enough to bull right on through this" (FU, 176–77). Faulkner seems to have intended "Old Man" as comic relief from the intense suffering of "Wild Palms." This fact ought necessarily to shape any comparison of the two stories or of their protagonists. For, fundamentally, the weather-beaten convict and the adulterous intern are different kinds of heroes; and—at least for Faulkner—their stories belong to different literary genres, in which different expectations inhere. Perhaps Faulkner placed them side by side not to compare them but to demonstrate their incomparability.

When asked about the characters of *The Wild Palms*, Faulkner often resorted to a vaguely sociological vocabulary. When he was reminded, for instance, that the characters of "Old Man" were not all anonymous and was asked to explain the "significance" of the names of the Cajuns Tine, Toto, and Theule, he replied that theirs were names "indigenous to that almost unhuman class of people which live between the Mississippi River and the levee. They belong to no state, they belong to no nation. They—they're not citizens of anything, and sometimes they behave like they don't even belong to the human race" (FU, 172). Although he obviously admired this "class" of people in a way, Faulkner did not regard them as serious enough to warrant thematically significant names like Wilbourne's (will-bourne; will-burn; will-born; will-borne; well-born).

Although the convict does not belong strictly to the "race" of Tine and Toto and Theule and the convict's nameless host, he is certainly akin to them. The convict recognizes the form and function of the Cajun host's "little lost spider-legged house" and of his tools—not "by association, ratiocination or even memory of any picture out of his dead youth," but "through pure rapport of kind for kind, hill-billy and bayou-rat, the two one and identical because of the same grudged dispensation and niggard fate of hard and unceasing travail not to gain future security, a balance in the bank or even in a buried soda can for slothful and easy old age, but just permission to endure and endure to buy air to feel and sun to drink for each's little while" (WP, 255–56). Their kinship, then, is defined in the economic terms of labor and leisure. They belong to that recognizable "class" who toil for sheer subsistence. Often in Faulkner, "endurance" is a euphemism for some very harsh realities—especially when applied to "farmers." Asked whether the convict resented the injustice of the ten-year addition to his sentence, Faulkner replied, no: "That additional ten years was simply another quantity in fate just like the flood that he ran into. Once he was in it he had to accept the extra ten years just as he accepted the flood and worked through it and survived it. There was no more injustice than there was to the flood. It was just something that was in the culture, the economy of the land he lived in, just like that flood was inherent in the geography and the climate, and he was a man that said, Well, if this is what it is I'll do the best I can to cut through it" (FU, 176).

Faulkner thus conceived of this character—at least in May 1957—as a *type*, drawn broadly to represent a socioeconomic category. The convict's "philosophy" originates less in an individual personality than in "the culture" and "the economy of the land." The character of his passenger, his comic leading lady, likewise derives from basically sociological perceptions. She "stemmed at some point from the same dim hill-bred Abraham" (WP, 255) as the convict, who "did not even bother to examine" her, "since [his] first startled glance had been ample to reveal to him all the generations of her life and background, who could have been his sister if he had a sister, his wife if he had not entered the penitentiary at an age scarcely out of adolescence and some years younger than that at which even his prolific and monogamous kind married" (WP, 148). She belongs to the same anonymous class of those who "endure" which he represents.

In comparing the values and behavior of Wilbourne and the convict, readers tend to overlook that their value *systems* and behavioral *patterns* differ from each other, that their cultural and economic backgrounds differ. Reviewers and critics have too readily assumed that the values of one must be superior to those of the other. But these characters belong to vastly different worlds, and the behavior of one would be quite inappropriate in the world of the other. Admiration for the convict's capacity to endure and sympathy with Harry and Charlotte's urge to escape need not be contradictory or mutually exclusive responses to the book.

Indeed, to elevate one above the other is to violate the radical breadth of the novel. Faulkner gave the book its peculiar form because Harry and Charlotte's story was inadequate to his own autobiographical imperatives. If he projected onto Harry his desire to escape toward meaningful (artistic) leisure with a beautiful young woman, he projected onto the convict not only his misogyny but *his* capacity for endurance, *his* flirtation with anonymity,[21] and *his* fear of freedom. Afflicted with a pastoral personality, he naturally projected the opposite versions of himself onto opposite segments of his community, segments which in his imagination were not *supposed* to behave similarly. He embodied his need for failure and for paralysis in the farmer-convict; he embodied his ambitious bohemianism in Wilbourne.

The doubleness of *The Wild Palms* derives ultimately from the doubleness of William Faulkner, which in turn reflects divisions in Southern society. The novel's structure sublimates and elaborates, in a serious context, the split identity that had resulted much more facetiously in "Ode to the Louver" and "Afternoon of a Cow." "Old Man"—masterful though it is—stands in a relationship of parody (in the etymological sense of "sidetext" or "counter-text") to "Wild Palms," just as Ernest V. Trueblood, whether as rube or as aesthete, stands in parodic relationship to William Faulkner. The pastoral sources of Faulkner's vocation find perfect expression in *The Wild Palms*, which also reveals the self-inhibiting or self-cancelling effects of pastoralism upon that vocation.

Empson's Double Plots

In *Some Versions of Pastoral*, William Empson provides a conceptual framework for the analysis of counterpoint in *The Wild Palms*. According to Empson's usage, the term "pastoral" refers less to a literary mode or genre than to a habit, often unconscious, of social perception. He devotes one long chapter to the dramatic device of the "double plot," derived from the comic interlude of the Miracle Plays and developed in English drama by Robert Greene, Shakespeare, Dryden, and others. In Empson's pastoral "version," the double plot serves a quasi-sociological function. "An account of the double plot," he writes, "is needed for a general view of pastoral because the interaction of the two plots gives a particularly clear setting for, or machine for imposing, the social and metaphysical ideas on which pastoral depends. What is displayed on the tragi-comic stage is a sort of marriage of the myths of heroic and pastoral, a thing felt as fundamental to both and necessary to the health of society." It unites on one stage, or in one text, characters and situations that belong to divergent social spheres. In the pastoral "sub-plot," humorous commoners incongruously replicate the heroic actions of an aristocratic or royal "main plot." Even when the two plots apparently "have nothing to do with each other," as in Greene's *Friar Bacon and Friar Bungay*, by Empson's pastoral dispensation they can yet "form a unity by being juxtaposed." Such a device, says Empson, enables a dramatist to "fill out a play, and has an obvious effect in the Elizabethans of making you feel the play deals with life as a whole." Secondarily, the two plots "make a mutual comparison that illuminates both parties."[22]

Above all else, the double plot provides its author with an excellent vehicle for indirectly voicing his ideas and feelings about the social structure he inhabits. It allows him inconspicuously to articulate an attitude toward the relations between two classes—by comparing their respective virtues and vices, by harmonizing their differences, by reinforcing or subverting a hierarchy of which they make part. Whether consciously or unconsciously, in *The Wild Palms* Faulkner presented his attitude toward the social structure in which he grew up.

The Wild Palms does not compare a "tragic king" with "comic people" like Shakespeare's 1 *Henry IV*, nor even high society with low society like Middleton and Rowley's *The Changeling*.[23] Rather, like them, *The Wild Palms* reflects the composition of the particular society which engendered it—one without royalty or a true aristocracy. The "Wild Palms" plot portrays characters who belong to, but revolt against, the dominant bourgeois stratum of modern America—the white-collar world of businessmen, professionals, intellectuals; the "Old Man" subplot draws its characters from the lowest social level of the same society—the milieu of redneck dirt-farmers and illiterate hayseeds. The world of "Wild Palms" happens to correspond to Faulkner the writer, engaged in his own lifelong rebellion against the middle-class; the world of "Old Man" corresponds to Faulkner the farmer, immersed in the everyday realities of concrete experience.

The combination of the two worlds in *The Wild Palms* creates the illusion of a total social background, and it effects an apparent fusion of the two halves of an authorial personality. Faulkner's vocational self-image involved a fruitful symbiosis between opposite elements of his personality, a "farmer" and an "aesthete." To collaborate, however, these inner twins had to remain carefully differentiated; were they to become confused, they would no longer be twins, and the symbiosis would die—along with its fruits. Ernest Trueblood and "William Faulkner" may switch roles as often as they please, but they must never become alike. And the social division they mirror must remain stable, or else chaos will ensue in Faulkner's literary practice as well as in the divided community he internalized to become a writer.

If Faulkner's double novel expresses a political attitude, surely its first principle is distance. The unignorable fact about the book's fusion of varied materials is that those materials are originally remote from each other. Faulkner may have had to insist in interviews that the two stories were one, but they were *two* first. Indeed, while he was building literary correspondences of theme and imagery into the counterpoint between Harry and the convict, he also removed an explicit narrative connection between them, as if to emphasize that the correspondences are artificial. According to Thomas L. McHaney, "there is good evidence that both stories were originally set in 1927, though 'Wild Palms' was later changed by a decade."[24] The only substantial connection that remains is the fact that the heroes of both stories conclude their travels at the Mississippi State Penal Farm in Parchman. After 1938, conceivably, the two inmates could meet and compare their histories; Faulkner often said that his characters' lives continued outside the books in which he partially described them. Indeed, the double plot might easily have been fastened to some such frame tale of mutual retrospection. But Faulkner reserved that possibility for his readers' extratextual speculation. The two narrative lines, if they converge, do so only off the page, and only if forcibly extended to an imaginary intersection. Communication between these two totally different men is difficult to envision. They belong to worlds so separate that they could never have understood each other. In his synecdochical, miniaturized reproduction of his community, Faulkner gratuitously segregated his two heroes and their "classes."

At the same time, of course, he gratuitously integrated them by combining them in the same book in the first place. Although Wilbourne and the convict conspicuously never meet, Faulkner did provide some vicarious contacts between them by interjecting substitutes for each protagonist into the plot of the other. Thus, the Polish miners in Utah act as the convict's class surrogates within "Wild Palms." In "Old Man," similarly, the mild-mannered doctor on the steamboat, who intercedes to have the convict placed ashore at Carnarvon, is a member of "the Medical race" (WP, 249), like Harry. Neither of these encounters results in real interaction. Instead, by demonstrating the inability of any party to communicate with another, they reinforce the segregation. In both cases, the "classes" hardly even speak the same language. Harry and Charlotte share only one word with the miners, "ron," and they do not understand its meaning. The Red Cross doctor manages to abandon the convict at the precise place where the levee will be broken next, by misconstruing—mistranslating—the convict's pronunciation of "Parchman" as "Carnarvon."

Another such encounter, in "Wild Palms," epitomizes the perspective from which Faulkner wrote the novel. From his jail cell in the Mississippi coastal town where he is tried, Harry Wilbourne sees a domestic arrangement, in the mudflat of a river mouth, that resembles the one he had attempted to establish with Charlotte. On the mudflat lies the concrete hull of a World War I "emergency ship," stranded there since 1918. Aboard it, Wilbourne sees "a thin line of drying garments" tended by "a tiny figure which he knew to be a woman" (WP, 314), who shares this shelter with a man who appears to be a fisherman. Through the weeks of his incarceration and trial, Harry watches this couple as they make a living for themselves and cope with the elements. As he watches, the tail of a hurricane strikes the coast, and the fisherman and his woman must weather a ten-foot tide that "did not fall for twenty hours" (WP, 315)—a rough replica of the flood in "Old Man." The Parchman convict and *his* woman never, in that story, are driven to the mouth of the Pascagoula River, nor do they ever set up housekeeping in a deserted hull. Their adventure precedes Harry's by ten years anyway, so the couple he watches cannot be the same two people. But they do, apparently, belong to the same social station: like the convict's hill-bred "race," like the Cajun alligator hunter, and like the Polish miners, the fisherman and his mate extract their living from the natural environment by the labor of their bodies. They belong to Faulkner's anonymous, "enduring" class, whereas Harry belongs to the same self-pauperized "leisure" class that Faulkner ordinarily perceived as his own. Thus, when Harry looks out through his cell window and "beyond the flat one-storey border of the river, across the river and toward the sea" (WP, 314), he views the fisherman and the woman from across more than just water and mud. The greater distance between them is social. Such a distancing is crucial to the meaning of the book's structure.

Eisenstein's Double Plots

Faulkner described the entrance to the Utah mine in "Wild Palms" as "a scene like something out of an Eisenstein Dante" (WP, 186–87). What he knew of the films, writings, or theories of the great Soviet director cannot be fully known. Eisenstein was expelled from Hollywood a few months before Faulkner arrived there in 1932.[25] But the Russian's films were widely distributed in American cities, and Faulkner may have heard his theories discussed in New York and California. What he meant by using the name in this context, and why he changed it from "Demille" in his typescript,[26] is not clear. But it does provide an excuse for introducing, as a "perspective by incongruity," Eisenstein's commentary on the "structural meaning" of the double-plot device in both film and fiction.[27]

In the early history of the cinema, Sergei Eisenstein was among the chief exponents and practitioners of what he called "montage thinking"— derived, he said, from D. W. Griffith's "method of parallel action," which Griffith had discovered in the novels of Charles Dickens. "The idea," according to a quotation from Griffith in Eisenstein's important essay on this intellectual genealogy, "is merely that of a 'break' in the narrative, a shifting of the story from one group of characters to another group." In his application of a novelistic convention to the theory and practice of film editing, Eisenstein envisioned the "possibilities of a profound, intelligent, class-directed use of this wonderful tool"—possibilities unrealized before the Russian Revolution. To demonstrate the method used by both his predecessors "of a *montage progression of parallel scenes, intercut into each other*," he cited Dickens's "parallel interlocking" in *Oliver Twist* of London slum life with scenes at the Brownlows' country estate as an example of "parallel montage of two story lines, where one (the waiting gentlemen) emotionally heightens the tension and drama of the other (the capture of Oliver)." Whereas this method was for Dickens and Griffith a narrative and emotional tool, for Eisenstein it became primarily a political tool ("a means before all else of revealing [an] *ideological conception*") and an instrument of social theory and didactic precept. From the perspective of Marxist theory, he described the shortcomings of his masters:

The structure that is reflected in the concept of Griffith montage is the structure of bourgeois society. And he actually resembles Dickens's "side of streaky, well-cured bacon" [the metaphor in *Oliver Twist* for melodrama or tragicomedy]; in actuality (and this is no joke), he is woven of irreconcilably alternating layers of "white" and "red" [the colors of the Russian Civil War]— rich and poor. (This is the eternal theme of Dickens's novels, nor does he move beyond these divisions. His mature work, *Little Dorrit*, is so divided into two books: "Poverty" and "Riches."). And this society, perceived *only as a contrast between the haves and the have-nots*, is reflected in the consciousness of Griffith no deeper than the image of an intricate race between two parallel lines.

. . . .

And, naturally, the montage concept of Griffith, as a primarily parallel montage, appears to be a copy of his dualistic picture of the world, running in two parallel lines of poor and rich towards some hypothetical "reconciliation" where . . . the parallel lines would cross, that is, in that infinity, just as inaccessible as that "reconciliation."[28]

The double plot in *The Wild Palms* strongly resembles the "primarily parallel montage" of Dickens and Griffith. Eisenstein would concoct a *dialectic* of montage to replace their dualism, a dialectic in which "the microcosm of montage had to be understood as a unity, which in the inner stress of contradictions is halved, in order to be re-assembled in a new unity on a new plane, qualitatively higher, its imagery newly perceived." His purpose would be "to create *a new quality of the whole from a juxtaposition of the separate parts.*" This idea he linked naturally to the creation of a "new social structure," which would arise out of a correspondent social fusion.[29]

Faulkner's novel, of course, leads to no such resolution nor to any new social structure. If Eisenstein's assumption is correct that "the final order" of an art work "is inevitably determined . . . by the social premises of the maker,"[30] Faulkner's social premises are revealed as "dualistic" and conservative. E. B. Burgum, the *New Masses* reviewer of *The Wild Palms*, correctly recognized the book as a social microcosm. But he oversimplified the tensions within it: as we shall see, *The Wild Palms* is anything but the incipient "proletarian novel" he suggested. Faulkner assigned to his "enduring" classes not revolutionary zeal but a long, patient submission in life, for which they are compensated only intangibly. A fundamental social discontinuity bisected Faulkner's world, and he liked it that way.[31]

Southern Double Plots

Yet that discontinuity operates across an imposed *continuity*. The social and psychological forces the book embodies are in precarious balance, and cohesive energies are as important as disruptive ones. For, having separated his community into incompatible halves, Faulkner still needed to hold them together. Having divided himself into opposite halves, he still depended on cooperation between the halves. The process of "filling out" that each plot accomplishes for the other effects a mysterious satisfaction that many other Southern writers have also sought. The interaction between the two plots can produce a sense of reciprocation between segments of society, and between segments of self, that Southerners have normally had trouble integrating.

Louis Rubin has identified as a dominant motive in Southern storytelling the teller's need to participate in a unified social community and to integrate the roots of his own personality. Rubin recounts witnessing the bewilderment of a Northern friend confronted with the conversational recreation of Southern intellectuals. In the company of John Donald Wade, a distinguished historian and biographer at the University of Georgia, and some of Wade's equally reputable colleagues, the Yankee noticed their quickness to revert to a disturbingly nonacademic style of discourse:

> Mr. Wade and his companions were good raconteurs. They kept telling stories to each other, one after the other, and laughing uproariously at every opportunity, slapping their sides and the like at each quip and sally. Their stories were about people around home. They told them in good southern fashion, with lots of drawling and contracting of syllables—"Well, by Gawd, ah jes said to ole Bill . . ." and "Man, lemme tell you bout what old Charlie Jones said when . . ." and "well if that don't beat anything I ever heard tell . . ." and so on—and if you hadn't known that the story-tellers consisted of a distinguished literary scholar and editor, a distinguished historian, and a distinguished economist, you might have thought that they were members of the local farming community thereabouts. . . .
> . . . What dear old John Wade and his two distinguished academic colleagues were doing was demonstrating to each other, but most of all to themselves, that they were still southern boys.[32]

"Southern boys" they were indeed, one way or another, before they became learned scholars. Wade and his friends were impersonating, as fraudulently as Faulkner playing farmer, the men they might have become had they not entered the world of letters and ideas. Wade himself suggested, in his contribution to the symposium *Culture in the South* in 1934, that the survival of old-boy characteristics in Southern intellectuals demonstrated the homogeneity of Southern culture, the integration of its mind with its body. [33] But Rubin proposes the opposite idea—that the intellectual's intermittent assumption of the down-home style symptomizes a split in Southern culture. Within the Southern writer, Rubin implies, two voices speak: the voice of a scholarly and sophisticated community, and the voice of the town market and the stable. Neither one really speaks to the other. In truth, the writer feels a disconnection between his vocational and his communal identities, and his reversion to the vernacular voice originates in an attempt both to regain something that is lost or tenuous and to nourish the work of his mind with that lost experience. James Cox, an expert on Southern schizophrenia in the person of Clemens/Twain, spells out the flaw in this strategy: "[F]or all the modern southern writers' capacity to remain socially at home in the southern community, for all their almost militant assertion of their southernness, their identity as writers is separate from the community. They may indeed feel at home around the old family dinner table, but the writer in them is not recognized or really acknowledged by the community in anything more than a perfunctory way. In order to be 'at home' in the community, the writer has to come down into it; it does not rise up to acknowledge his imagination." [34]

A ritualized condescension is endemic in Southern culture, and it has been expressed throughout the literary history of the region—often in forms very similar to that of *The Wild Palms*. For a minor example, John Fox, Jr. (a popular regionalist at the turn of the twentieth century who depicted the mountain folk of eastern Kentucky) published a collection of stories in 1897 in which the chapters alternate between tales told in standard English by an educated observer and tales told in mountain dialect by a "good old boy." Thus, the narrator of the title story, "On Hell-fer-Sartain Creek," exudes the down-home conviviality of a neighborly backslapper: "Thar was a dancin'-party Christmas night on 'Hell fer Sartain.' Jes tu'n up the fust crick beyond the bend thar, an' climb onto a stump, an' holler about *once*, an' you'll see how the name come." The lyrical mode of the next story contrasts sharply: "When thistles go adrift, the sun sets down the valley between the hills; when snow comes, it goes down behind the Cumberland and streams through a great fissure that people call the Gap." [35] The deepest gap in the book occurs within the author, between his two narrative voices—one vernacular, immediate, and social; the other literary, distant, and reflective. Such a schism underlies many other Southern books.

For a later, somewhat less obscure example, the chapters of Robert Penn Warren's *At Heaven's Gate* (1943) alternate between the standard authorial voice of the principal narrator and the rustic drawl of Ashby Wyndham, whose "Statement" interrupts the action of the main plot in precisely the way "Old Man" interrupts "Wild Palms." Indeed, Wyndham's association with the Tennessee River, upon which he enters Nashville in a shanty boat, suggests that Warren may have derived the idea of alternating the chapters of two mostly independent stories about separate social spheres from *The Wild Palms* itself, which was published at about the time he began writing *At Heaven's Gate*. Of course, Warren need not have borrowed the device from Faulkner. It resulted naturally from the cultural inheritance both men shared: the Southern intellectual's legacy of alienation from his community.

The Wild Palms alternates between the two voices of the Southern writer and between two literary personae. "Wild Palms" represents a self-consciously professional performance, the writer speaking *as writer* about an introspective experience. "Old Man" represents a compensatory reversion to the hyperbolic manner of vernacular discourse, the writer as *teller* (or at least re-teller, telling a *told* story over the convict's shoulder) of an experience basically physical, photographable, tangible. This alternation is only partial, however, because Faulkner has short-circuited it. In "Wild Palms" the voice is literate, even to the point of self-parody, and it belongs to the profession of writing. In "Old Man" the voice *translates* the tale the convict tells his fellow prisoners ("up yonder in that bunkhouse . . . lying his head off probly," [WP, 326]), as if trying to imitate in a writer's language the spontaneous fluency of a nonliterate speaker. But it remains the translation of a *vernacular* experience, like Trueblood's translation of his employer's experience with Beulah the cow.

The narrative voice that predominates in *The Wild Palms* is polysyllabic, hypotactic, and grandiloquent—in a word, "Faulknerian." With this Truebloodian voice, that of the title story's hero is continuous. In Wilbourne's colloquy with McCord in the Chicago train station, for example, Faulkner provides his hero with the narrator's own idiosyncratic diction and syntax: "It was the mausoleum of love," Harry can say, "it was the stinking catafalque of the dead corpse borne between the olfactoryless walking shapes of the immortal unsentient demanding ancient meat" (WP, 139). But, when the hero of "Old Man" opens his mouth—he *is*, supposedly, telling the story—he cannot speak quickly or articulately enough for the circumlocutory narrator, who impatiently breaks in to translate: "'The water was still high. It was running pretty hard still. I never made much speed for the first week or two. After that it got better.' Then, suddenly and quietly, something—the inarticulateness, the innate and inherited reluctance for speech, dissolved and he found himself, listened to himself, telling it quietly, the words coming not fast but easily to the tongue as he required them: How he paddled on . . ." (WP, 332).

When the narrator allows the convict to continue speaking, he does so for the purpose of demonstrating his "drawling and contracting of syllables."[36] Here is an anticipation of Faulkner's great vernacular narrator Ratliff, whose more successful competition with Faulkner's professional narrative voice makes the texture of *The Hamlet* perhaps the richest of any novel's in the Faulkner canon. The seed is here of a *linguistic* pastoralism, more fully developed in *The Hamlet*, which resolves itself in a harmony between two very distinct personae: one in frayed collar and necktie, derived from books; the other in denim overalls, derived from old-boy taletelling.

Behind the vernacular voice is a vernacular world, a world apparently unamenable to literary treatment. Faulkner attached "Old Man" to "Wild Palms" as a gesture toward the literary assimilation of that world. For it is a world that a writer risks losing as soon as he recognizes his vocation, and consequently one that some writers—especially Southerners—devote that vocation to regaining. Thus John Donald Wade and his friends told stories to link themselves to a community otherwise receding from their participation. And thus the pastoral motive manifests itself in Faulkner.

Perhaps an apt paradigm for what happens in *The Wild Palms* is the scene in which Harry Wilbourne, from his prison window in the coastal town, watches the fisherman and the fisherman's woman across the mudflat in the river mouth. Harry is something of an author himself, if a parody of one, and he watches the couple in the concrete hull with a particular fascination, for they remind him of his own recent past with Charlotte. From them, he seems to absorb a capacity for his own brand of "endurance." Out of the same concentrated gaze and across a similar distance, Faulkner watched the pastoral denizens of his world and absorbed them into his fiction.

Thus, the main distance between "Wild Palms" and "Old Man" is a distance in perception. The primary discontinuity at work in *The Wild Palms* is the one between art and reality, between the words on Faulkner's page and anything they might remotely refer to in the real world. The double-plot device, as Faulkner purveyed it, above all else forces a reader to acknowledge that both stories are *only* stories.[37] It focuses attention upon the book as a *literary* phenomenon: with every shift from one chapter to the next, the reader must repeal his suspension of disbelief and rejustify the act of reading in which he is engaged. One of the book's subjects is the very phenomenon of narration. In a way *The Wild Palms* is an elaborate joke—a serious joke, but a joke nonetheless. And the butt of the joke is Faulkner himself, or any man who tries, as Faulkner did, to "reduce the world" onto the tip of his pen.

For Love or Money

At about the time that young Count No 'Count told his future wife that money is "a contemptible thing to work for" (BL, 179), William Faulkner began preparing himself for a vocation that would not require him to work for money. Yet, of course, he had to make a living. From his early thirties onward, he boiled various pots in the editorial offices of popular magazines and in Hollywood. In 1938, however, he thought momentarily that the periodic necessity of compromising his amateur status might have ended. With his money from MGM and Twentieth Century-Fox, he hoped to be able to "write in leisure" (SL, 104). To the extent that he would work for money, he would farm, pursuing an occupation with which he had ironically identified since the beginning of his literary career. In the book he wrote during those bright months of financial optimism, consequently, he directly addressed the subjects of leisure, idleness, and several kinds of work. In *The Wild Palms* he investigated the commercial status of his artistic vocation. Inevitably, this investigation led him to explore his place within his community.[38]

Faulkner laid out the terms of his relationship to work through his two protagonists. Harry Wilbourne and the tall convict have entirely different understandings of the nature of labor. Faulkner never said much about Harry's economic situation, but he talked enough about the convict's to suggest a primarily economic basis for his characterization. For the convict, according to Faulkner in 1957, labor "meant the orderly work of following a mule in a furrow. . . . When he was in the prison, or even at home . . . he got a new pair of overalls whenever the other ones wore out, he got something to eat every night or a pallet to sleep on, but the work was ordered, began at sunup and went on to sundown" (FU, 179–80). The "work" from which Harry flees is not remotely similar to the work toward which the convict strives to return. It serves a different function, and he does it for different reasons—not for subsistence, certainly. When he abandons it, he does so to follow a new vocation—love, which in this novel will stand for art as well—whereas the convict remembers a sense of vocation only after his journey begins and he is separated from his daily toil. When the hero of "Old Man" finds momentary relief from his ordeal, he spends it earning a living for himself and his two charges. At the Cajun alligator-hunting camp, he enjoys an idyll of labor, during which "he was temporarily lost in peace and hope . . . and he thought quietly, with a kind of bemused amazement, *Yes. I reckon I had done forgot how good making money was. Being let to make it*" (WP, 261–62, Faulkner's italics).

In "Wild Palms," however, Harry and Charlotte's idyllic moments come *between* their periods of work for department stores and mining companies. At the lake in Wisconsin and again in the Utah mining camp, after the miners desert it and Harry's paid function ceases along with his pay, they temporarily find the conditions of economic inactivity for which they search throughout the book. With their livelihood momentarily guaranteed by limited supplies of food and shelter, at both places they fill their time with activities that ideally are noneconomic and purely without any end beyond themselves—love and art. For the convict, as for Faulkner the farmer, freedom is being able to earn money; for Harry, as for Faulkner the artist, it is not having to.

The problem of having to make money pervades "Wild Palms." Faulkner's economic trials and windfalls entered his composition of the book forcibly. Some access to, or lack of, money lies at almost every turn in the story's plot, affecting every move the lovers make. Harry's predicament is predetermined by his father's bequest to him, when he is only two years old, of two thousand dollars earmarked for a medical education—and of an appreciation for the "intrinsic value of money" (WP, 31). His cash inheritance proves grossly insufficient, however, and he must supplement it by drawing on the moral capital in his father's ethical estate of industry, frugality, and continence. Harry's pursuit of an education, frustrated by inflation and unemployment, is even more arduous than his father's had been: "beneath the apparent serenity of his monastic life he waged a constant battle as ruthless as any in a Wall Street skyscraper as he balanced his dwindling bank account against the turned pages of his text books" (WP, 32). Similarly, Faulkner had to balance his own dwindling bank account against the turning pages of his current novel.

During the remainder of the story the competition between time and money continues, as Harry tries to finance a love affair instead of an education. When Charlotte first meets Harry, he is an intern in a New Orleans hospital, living in respectable poverty without private means. Having "repudiated money and hence love" (WP, 34), he works toward something besides financial security, the identity of which he cannot quite determine: to fulfill his father's will or gain social status and respectability or recompense his sister. Charlotte begins to break down his rigid financial probity as soon as they declare their mutual love: she tries, unsuccessfully, to buy him a cab ride. Because he refuses to accept her money, their affair seems doomed by his lack of resources. He succumbs to her influence only when he finds a wallet containing precisely $1,278 in a trash bin and keeps it—enough money to get them to Chicago.

Henceforth, in Chicago and afterwards, Harry progressively transfers his probity from the husbanding of his finances to the husbanding of their love; both he and Charlotte begin to describe that love to each other in the language of economics. *"The value of love,"* Charlotte says, for example, "is *the sum* of what you have *to pay* for it and any time you *get it cheap* you have cheated yourself" (WP, 48, my italics). The remainder of their story tells, figuratively, of the successive payments they must make on that love: family, respectability, freedom, and life itself. Their trouble is that love pays those who invest in it only in its own nonnegotiable currency. As Charlotte says, "You live *in* sin; you cant live on it" (WP, 83, Faulkner's italics).

Charlotte finds work in Chicago, selling her papier-mâché sculptures to department stores for window dressing. But she then feels even more strongly the priority of love over mere economic endurance. When she offers Harry the proceeds of her first sale, his old pride makes him resist it until she refutes him with an economic argument:

"You dont like the idea of your woman helping to support you, is that it? Listen. Dont you like what we've got?"

"You know I do."

"Then what does it matter what it *cost* us, what we *pay* for it? or how? You stole the money we've got now; wouldn't you do it again? Isn't it *worth* it, even if it all busts tomorrow and we have to *spend* the rest of our lives *paying interest?*" (WP, 87–88, my italics)

Harry relents, but his puritan conscience does not. After he loses a job testing blood for syphilis in a medical laboratory, and after they have spent all their money on provisions for the lake camp, he suggests they separate so that she will not have to support him when she returns to Chicago. Again Charlotte reasserts the primacy of their love, again in economic terms: "No! No! Jesus God, no! Hold me! Hold me hard, Harry! This is what it's for, what it all was for, *what we were paying for:* so we could be together, sleep together every night: not just to eat and evacuate and sleep warm so we can get up and eat and evacuate in order to sleep warm again!" (WP, 118–19, my italics). By contrast, sleeping, eating, and evacuating are exactly what the convict in "Old Man" pays for with his freedom.

Love and money prove incompatible for Harry and Charlotte, who follow a course that alternates between the two. They always prefer love; but, in the world as it exists, they inevitably fail to secure it. Love, Harry says, "cant last. There is no place for it in the world today, not even in Utah. We have eliminated it. . . . We have radio in the place of God's voice and instead of having *to save emotional currency* for months and years to deserve one chance [to] *spend it all for love* we can now *spread it thin into coppers* and titillate ourselves at any newsstand" (WP, 136, my italics). [39] Unlike the convict, for whom work (when he can do it) is part of the order of his universe, Harry finds that work rewards him only with "coppers" and not with "emotional currency." The convict's kind of work, however, compensates him not only with money (as he would have gained at the alligator camp had the flood not followed him there, and as he did gain in several jobs along the return route) but with overalls, something to eat, a pallet to sleep on, and a firm identity.

These attitudes toward work reveal something of the economic roots of characterization in *The Wild Palms*. A further revelation occurs through Faulkner's treatment of leisure, and especially of art, its highest activity. During the course of their adulterous escapade, Harry and Charlotte take a number of "jobs" to finance their love when they run out of "coppers." Significantly, the only ones that are even minimally fruitful are exercises in commercial art—the bastard offspring of labor out of leisure. After she realizes that "you cant live on" sin, Charlotte's first gainful employment is to make decorative figures for a Chicago department store. Then she collaborates with a photographer on magazine covers and advertisements, using the same wire-and-paper statuary. She is, after all, an artist.

Her first conversation with Harry, in fact, concerns some modern paintings hanging in the apartment of Crowe, the New Orleans socialite at whose party they first meet. "I paint too," she tells him, "I *can afford* to say. I *can afford* to say I can beat that, too" (WP, 39, my italics). Just as when they discuss their love, their talk of art also relies naturally on economic language. Charlotte constantly calculates the "value" of both love and art: how much they can "afford," how much it is "worth," and how much they should be willing to "spend" on it.

Harry's first reaction to Crowe's paintings is an economic one—a yokel's wonder and a Protestant's outrage at the mercantile viability of useless things: "Wilbourne stood before the paintings in complete absorption. It was not at what they portrayed, the method or the coloring; they meant nothing to him. It was in a bemusement without heat or envy at a condition which could supply a man with *the obvious leisure and means to spend his days* painting such as this and his evenings playing the piano and feeding liquor to people whom he ignored" (WP, 38, my italics). Such a mode of life, founded on a "condition" of "leisure," runs contrary to Harry's (and the convict's) inherited work ethic. But Charlotte persuades him to strive with her toward a similar "condition of leisure"—toward the freedom to "spend their days" "affording" love.

The picture in front of which Charlotte introduces herself to Harry comes to symbolize for them their commitment to a love that is free of economic or domestic motives. In Wisconsin, where they retreat—ironically on Labor Day—after Charlotte's work plays out, Harry reminds her of their first encounter. When their only neighbor leaves for the winter, Charlotte suggests that they are like Adam and Eve; and Harry replies that they have *always* been alone: "Ever since that first night. That picture. We couldn't be any more alone, no matter who went away" (WP, 109). They have gone to Wisconsin to seek a leisure like the one that produced the picture. Their love belongs, ideally, to that same condition which produces art and bohemian parties, for it must be their primary activity, with priority over the demands of the stomach or of respectability. A mere job distracts from that full-time vocation.

Once they attain that leisure, their problem becomes how most "profitably" to "spend" it. Crowe, an artist, spent his partying and painting. But Harry is no artist; nor does he at first really approve of the luxury represented by Crowe's party. The work ethic willed him by his father reasserts itself at the lake, and he has not yet learned the value of leisure. "*I am bored,*" he concludes after most of their stay there. "*I am bored to extinction. There is nothing here that I am needed for. Not even by her. I have already cut enough wood to last until Christmas and there is nothing else for me to do*" (WP, 112, Faulkner's italics). He tries his hand at Charlotte's sketchpad; although several months later he tells his Gulf Coast landlord that he is "trying to be a painter" (WP, 18), he finds here that he is color-blind, so he makes a calendar instead of sketches. When he recognizes from this calendar that the time has come for them to leave the lake, he becomes ecstatic. "I never saw you look so happy," Charlotte tells him. "Have you painted a picture or have you discovered at last that the human race really doesn't have to even try to produce art[?]" (WP, 115). Charlotte would be content to fill their idleness with nothing but their love; after their next stay in the city, Harry too is ready for leisure.

Back in Chicago, they *both* become commercial artists. Charlotte works as a window dresser in a department store. Harry supplements her income by contributing semipornographic stories to confession magazines. Faulkner himself usually wrote for a higher class of periodical, but he must have poured his disgust for his own potboiling into his description of Harry's "writing": "he wrote and sold to the confession magazines the stories beginning 'I had the body and desires of a woman yet in knowledge and experience of the world I was but a child' or 'If I had only had a mother's love to guard me on that fatal day'—stories which he wrote complete from the first capital to the last period in one sustained frenzied agonising rush" (WP, 121).[40]

Faulkner did not like to work that way himself, even on potboilers. He said many times that he always tried to quit writing before he exhausted whatever ideas were in his mind: "I have heard of people that can set aside so many hours a day . . . but that has never been for me. I like to write when it's hot [the creative power, not the weather] and then I quit and rest and then I get at it again. And sometimes, fourteen or sixteen hours a day, and then sometimes I won't write a word for fourteen or sixteen days" (FU,

49). One should write, he often advised, only "when it's hot," and not to meet a deadline or a quota, nor to force oneself to finish an unpleasant task, and certainly never to make money.

Nevertheless, Faulkner certainly did his share of writing for money. Harry and Charlotte's excursions into commercial art represent a specter that haunted their creator during much of his career—his own inability to make a sufficient living from the sale of his novels, and the consequent necessity that he prostitute his skills. Their escape to the lake and to the mountain mine reflects his own effort to establish the right "condition of leisure" for himself. Their failure forecasts his. At the lake, when Harry counts the cans of food in their stockpile to see "how many days more they would have left" (WP, 112) in which to do nothing but love each other, surely Faulkner was counting his own remaining days of "leisure" before he would have to sell a story or scrounge another job in Hollywood.

In 1957, when financial insecurity was only a powerful memory and when his fond dream of leisure was permanently realized, Faulkner could still speak very positively against any admixture of economics and art of the kind he had been forced to perform himself. When asked at the University of Virginia to confirm that "a true author isn't one who sculpts his material toward the commercial side," Faulkner replied by elaborating the idea of a "true author" into a statement of his calling as a writer: "That's right. Yes, if what he wants is money, then there are probably easier ways to make money than being an author. I think that the young man or young woman that wants to write will have to make that choice. He has got to decide, Do I want to do this because I have a demon that won't let me alone or do I want to make some money at this? I think in the case of the men and women who have been the good writers, that choice never occurred to them" (FU, 184). The writer's vocation, in this version of the dream, should rise above and beyond the problem of having to make money. It should be economically pure, the occupation of the writer's *idle* hours.

In a way, "Wild Palms" represents Faulkner's version of a Hollywood novel.[41] If one of the recurrent subjects of that genre is the artist's temptation to compromise his art for the sake of money, fame, or power, Faulkner's story can be said to sublimate his own artistic frustration into the frustration of an equally "pure," equally idealistic vocation—that of love. His bouts with Hollywood and with his magazine market were diversions from his true vocation, just as Harry and Charlotte's sojourns in

Chicago are diversions from theirs—for him, the writing of uncompromised novels; for them, the enjoyment of their love. Harry as pornographer might be the indirect portrait of some of the writers Faulkner met in the movie studios, who deluded themselves that they were doing what they wanted. Ultimately, however, Harry awakens to the truth that the vocation he has chosen for himself is Charlotte's love, and that his mere "job" keeps him from it. Then they seek the new condition of leisure that will free them for each other—an economically pure activity that pays for itself in its own currency. "It's not avocation that elects our vocations," Harry complains. "[I]t's respectability that makes chiropractors and clerks and bill posters and motormen and pulp writers of us" (WP, 135). The constant motive of the lovers in "Wild Palms" is to avoid the dictates of respectability and to elect their own vocation, regardless of its expense. With *The Wild Palms*, Faulkner reminded himself that Count No 'Count had chosen to become a writer to avoid the respectable success his father, and Oxford, wanted for him. He used his brief period of financial independence in 1937 and 1938 to utter a lament for the periods of Babylonian captivity he had temporarily left behind.

Faulkner's and his lovers' "vocations" are functionally identical. His account in the 1950s of how he discovered his calling resembles significantly the description of the New Orleans party where Harry and Charlotte first meet. In response to the question "When did you first realize that you wanted to write?" Faulkner looked back to his first acquaintance with Sherwood Anderson in New Orleans in 1925: "I met Sherwood Anderson. . . . I liked him right off, and we . . . got along fine together. We would meet in the evening, in the afternoons we'd walk and he'd talk and I'd listen, we'd meet in the evenings and we'd go to a drinking place and we'd sit around till one or two o'clock drinking, and still me listening to him talking. Then in the morning he would be in seclusion working. . . . And I thought then if that was the life it took to be a writer, that was the life for me. So I wrote a book and when I started I found that writing was fun" (FU, 21–22).

Of course, Faulkner had decided to be a writer well before he met Anderson. But his misleading anecdote bears a kernel of truth: he entered his vocation because it provided a kind of labor that would not violate the idleness his constitution required. The bourgeois world from which Harry and Charlotte escape and the bohemian existence toward which they flee were Faulkner's bane and refuge as well.

Floods, Chain Gangs, and Strikes

Writing in 1937 and 1938, Faulkner remembered his discovery of the writer's life in the 1920s. In recollecting Sherwood Anderson and Helen Baird (the woman he loved and lost in 1927, and who provided the most direct model for Charlotte Rittenmeyer),[42] Faulkner also recollected himself a dozen years earlier. Or else, worried in the late thirties about the direction of his vocation, he contemplated its origins in his posturings of the mid-twenties and thereby reminded himself of his bohemian acquaintances. In either case, *The Wild Palms* embodies his revivification of the images through which he had defined his vocation in *The Marble Faun*, "The Leg," and other youthful esoterica: captivity and escape, restraint and release, stasis and motion, speech and silence.

By 1937, however, Faulkner could not write about his writing as if it existed in a vacuum. He could no longer imagine himself as Wilfred Midgleston, a solipsist rolled within his own manuscript. He had been forced too often into the marketplace. When he returned to the subject of his vocation in 1937, then, he had to include the literary taste of the American public as part of his subject. In *The Wild Palms*, he constructed his double allegory of love and art out of the materials of contemporary popular culture. More than any of his previous books except perhaps *Sanctuary*, which he aimed partially toward commercial success, *The Wild Palms* drew its substance from the films, the journalism, and the best-sellers of the day. For his private vocabulary of paradoxical images, he found public equivalents among the subjects that obsessed America during the thirties. Of course, what obsessed America primarily during the thirties was the Great Depression.

We seldom think of Faulkner in connection with the Depression. Literary history usually consigns him to the generation that matured during the frivolous twenties. In the *Literary History of the United States* (1948), for example, Maxwell Geismar treats him as an anachronistic vestige of the Jazz Age surviving incongruously into the thirties: while other writers turned toward social issues, "Faulkner marked the final full expression of the aesthetic nihilism that evolved out of the American twenties." Similarly, in 1962 William Phillips cited Faulkner as an exception to the rule that American literature underwent "a major shift of sensibility" between the earlier decade and the later: Faulkner wrote in "detachment . . . as though nothing had changed." And Granville Hicks, reappraising the literature of the thirties in 1967, excluded Faulkner from consideration: "There is only one great name of the thirties—I would now say the greatest—that I have not mentioned, William Faulkner. Although there is evidence that he was affected by the depression, he scarcely alluded to it in his fiction."[43]

Faulkner did not contribute articles to radical journals, as Hemingway did. Nor did he ever, during the thirties, travel from town to town "looking for America," as did Dreiser, Anderson, Caldwell, and many other writers. But he did not ignore the national upheaval. His reaction to the Depression may have been delayed; it may have been indirect, even ironic; but it was not blithe. In several ways, his novels of the period reflect the imagery of apocalypse.[44]

Indeed, Faulkner filled *The Wild Palms* with motifs that were already distinctly identifiable with the Depression—floods, chain gangs, sharecroppers, strikes, a special kind of travel. He alluded to them not because he wished to address economic problems or spur social reform, but because he was momentarily interested in the audience that would not read his books; and the Depression was naturally on that audience's mind. A primary subject of this novel is *what sells*. What sold in 1937 and 1938— and what made reputations—were vicarious descents into, and vicarious escapes from, hardship and deprivation. Faulkner saturated *The Wild Palms* with the representational conventions of the Depression for the purpose of subverting them, as a deliberate affront to a public that allowed current events to mould its imagination. He borrowed Depression tropes from the popular entertainment as well as from the serious literature of the day, and—violating the conventional expectations he aroused—wove them into an extended metaphor for his own private hardships and deprivations.

Floods

In late October and early November 1937, two films about floods were released within a few days of Faulkner's serious accident at the Algonquin Hotel.[45] *The River,* directed by Pare Lorentz, was a critical success; *The Hurricane,* directed by John Ford, was popular at box offices. If Faulkner saw one or both of them, he probably did so not in New York, where he was too incapacitated by his burn to attend the cinema, but in Mississippi after he returned there or in Memphis, which he felt well enough to visit as early as November 16 (BL, 976). I like to imagine that Faulkner began writing "Old Man" after watching one or both of these movies, and that the structure of *The Wild Palms* resulted from his ironic appropriation of the double-feature convention. Even if he did not see either of them, however, they provide convincing evidence that the novel, and especially "Old Man," derived from Faulkner's fretful attunement to the American public's appetite for artful, and thus safe, disasters.

The River was produced by the Farm Security Administration to publicize the New Deal's restoration programs in the South. It records a century of land abuse in the Mississippi Valley, Nature's revenge on the people who live there, and the Roosevelt administration's efforts to repair the damage. Lorentz and his camera crew had traveled through the Mississippi watershed between October 1936 and January 1937, filming its people and concentrating on the rural poor, for the final product would include a "sharecropper sequence." Just as they finished shooting their script, the winter flood of 1937 struck. They remained in the area through February of that year, exposing thousands of feet of film. The resulting half-hour movie climaxed in these flood sequences and concluded with admiring attention to the TVA dams that had been built to control the river. Not only an effective political statement, it is also a moving visual poem about energy and its containment. Among its scenes are many possible sources for Faulkner's descriptions in "Old Man": a farmer plowing with mules along a levee, the rise of the waters, islanded houses and hills, cascades through widening crevasses, rescue operations. [46]

The other flood movie of late 1937, though set far from Mississippi, provides even more extensive analogies with *The Wild Palms* than Lorentz's hymn to soil erosion and hydraulic engineering. *The Hurricane* is a faithful adaptation of the novel by Nordhoff and Hall, published in 1935. Far from a documentary, Ford's movie appears to offer mere escapism; its spectacular storm and flood were created by technicians in a Hollywood back lot. [47] To the extent that a theme rides the special-effects tempest, it is the destructiveness of law untempered by mercy.

On the South Sea island of Manukura, a native seaman named Terangi marries his childhood sweetheart, Marama. In Tahiti soon afterward, Terangi hits a "white man" who offends him. (In the novel, the culprit calls him "nigger.") [48] A French colonial judge sentences him to six months' hard labor on a "road gang." Terangi escapes. When he is recaptured, a year is added to his sentence. Again Terangi escapes; again he is recaptured; again his sentence is lengthened. After several repetitions of this cycle, he has served eight years in prison and owes sixteen years more. During his final escape he accidentally kills a guard; so the French governor of Manukura, Eugene de Laage, commits himself sternly to hunting the fugitive down. De Laage's vindictiveness almost literally raises the wind. A hurricane soon floods the island with sea swells and torrential rain, destroying everything and almost everyone. Terangi and Marama survive, with their daughter, by binding themselves to a palm tree. They manage to save de Laage's sympathetic wife as well, an act for which the softened governor allows them to sail off into the sunset toward Fenua Ino, the "forbidden island." There, presumably, the deserving family will live happily ever after. All that remains of Manukura is a mound of sand upon which stands the ruin of a church.

If Faulkner saw *The Hurricane* while he was conceiving *The Wild Palms*, he saw not only an exciting, well-constructed film but also images and situations that would soon inhabit his novel. He saw a visualization of one of his titles: palm trees, first swaying and then thrashing, constitute a master symbol in the movie. He saw "civilized" gentlemen converse about the simple, silent "races." He saw some of those simple people survive a flood by climbing into trees. He saw a chain gang. He saw, amid the hurricane's devastation, the delivery of a baby within a beleaguered boat. Most of all, he saw a primitive couple asserting their passion against the representatives of civilized morality. At the end of the final reel, if he watched it, he saw a hackneyed fulfillment of his own deepest wish for escape: to sail into the sunset with the woman (Meta Carpenter?) and the daughter he loved.[49] At the end of "Wild Palms," Harry Wilbourne watches, as if at a movie, similar survivors of a hurricane—minus the daughter—through his prison window.

Faulkner saw in both *The River* and *The Hurricane*, if he attended them, a subject of obvious interest to the American public. Readers as well as moviegoers consumed flood fantasies. In addition to the Nordhoff-Hall novel of 1935, for example, E. P. O'Donnell's *Green Margins* of 1936 mixed rebellious lovers with a hurricane in the Mississippi Delta, and the Joad family's final tribulation in *The Grapes of Wrath* (1939) is a flood. Faulkner alone may have yearned to escape with Meta Carpenter or Helen Baird to some forbidden solitude, and Faulkner alone may have been relieved that each woman had closed the escape route. But for millions of Americans the cinematic and novelistic disasters must have looked the way their economic disaster had felt.[50] Indeed, *The River* implicitly presented its flood as a synecdoche for all the problems of the decade, which Roosevelt's programs would solve. Millions of the same people must occasionally have fantasized about a liberating cataclysm, which would wash away their plight.

The flood of "Old Man" also embodies the Depression, for it turns the countryside into an emblematic disaster-scape, a human environment traumatized and paralyzed by circumstance. In the second chapter, especially, the flood's meaning transcends its physical existence. The farmland lies submerged beneath a "steel-colored" and "concrete" surface, as if the urban wasteland has seeped out into the country. The landscape seems deceptively tranquil until the truckload of convicts reaches a bridge where a stream had flowed: "Here they both saw and heard movement—the slow profound eastward and upstream ('It's running backward,' one convict said quietly.) set of the still rigid surface, from beneath which came a deep faint subaquean rumble which . . . sounded like a subway train passing far beneath the street and which inferred a terrific and secret speed" (WP, 62).

The real damage of the flood hides below the surface and results from a regressive, mechanical motion. But even the surface appearance of the disaster seems strangely metaphorical, as if it objectifies a less visible devastation. A town through which the convicts pass, though "amputated" by water, appears unaffected by the occurrence of the flood. "[O]rdered and pageant-like and without motion, upon the limitless liquid plain beneath the thick gray sky" (WP, 67), it seems to have been paralyzed regardless of the flood, which simply makes manifest a condition that had already turned the rural South into a Depression-scape.

Faulkner knew floods before 1937; the swollen river that impedes the Bundrens in *As I Lay Dying* testifies to that fact. He seems to have paid attention to a serious flood of the Tallahatchie River in January 1932 (BL, 758n). But his exposure to devastation and displacement on the scale of "Old Man" seems to have been vicarious. During April and May 1927, he had worked on the manuscript of *Flags in the Dust*, from which the Great Flood apparently did not distract him (BL, 547–48).[51] In January and February 1937, while Pare Lorentz filmed his flood sequences, Faulkner was in Hollywood, preoccupied by movie scripts, by the construction of *The Unvanquished*, and by Meta Carpenter's imminent marriage.[52] Although he did not view these major floods personally, he did receive other forms of intelligence. *The River* may have become one of these in 1937, but long before then his impressions had been shaped by newspaper reports and eyewitness accounts.

For example, his friend Lyle Saxon, who spent the spring of 1927 assisting refugees from the Great Flood, wrote a series of articles about the event which he incorporated into a book about the river's history and legendry, *Father Mississippi*, a copy of which Faulkner possessed.[53] *Father Mississippi* anticipated specific scenes in "Old Man." Just as "Old Man" opens with the short convict reading to his companions from the Memphis newspaper, whose headlines Faulkner quotes (WP, 29–30), so Saxon had punctuated two chapters of his narrative with headlines from the New Orleans papers. Among the thirty photographs of the flood scattered through Saxon's book are many that could serve as illustrations for "Old Man," including an aerial photograph of isolated Indian mounds housing "as strange a gathering as the celebrated collection in Noah's ark." Saxon described climbing into a tree from a sinking motorboat and waiting there two hours before rescuers took him to a levee, where he compared his anxious reaction to dispossession with the graceful "resignation" of his "simpler brothers." Stranded on the levee, he conversed with a civil engineer who advocated a flood control project for the Atchafalaya River basin, where Faulkner chose to locate *his* Indian mound. During their discussion, a baby was born near them. Faulkner's scene on the mound neatly conflates Saxon's levee episode with his Ark-like island. Faulkner's "Cajans" may also owe some of their characteristics to Saxon's "stolid, quiet . . . race."[54] *Father Mississippi* may have supplied "Old Man" with particular scenes of action. But the elements from Saxon's book did not coalesce as a story until 1937. Conceivably, seeing *The River* or *The Hurricane* activated his memory of the flood scenes in *Father Mississippi* and perhaps even prompted him to reexamine them in his library. Once he decided to write about the 1927 flood, he might naturally have consulted his friend's book to gain a concrete feel for the subject.

He chose in late 1937 to write about a flood because it was then a topical, and proven, subject for melodrama. He chose it, however, not because he assumed it might lead to popular success but because it *had led* to a kind of success, from which he still wanted to save himself. What he did with his flood, once he decided to write about it, contradicts both his documentary and his escapist examples. Unlike *The River*, "Old Man" dramatizes no sociological or engineering problem to be solved. Unlike *The Hurricane*, Faulkner's tale ends with reincarceration, not a sail into the sunset. In effect, Faulkner chose a flood as his subject so that he could invert a theme that seemed marketable. He chose to frustrate his audience's expectations, and his adversarial relationship with his readers is part of his subject.

He also chose then to write about a flood because he was increasingly concerned with the subject of his literary vocation, and flooding was evolving for him into an apt image of writing. In "The Leg," a dozen years earlier, he had already depicted the opening and closing of the Thames lock as an occult correlative for writing. In 1940, only three years after he began "Old Man," floods, dams, and Indian mounds would serve as an extended metaphor for his career. Departing even further from the popular meaning of the floods in *The River* and *The Hurricane*, Faulkner in *Go Down, Moses* would turn the Mississippi Delta into a mirror for himself.

Chain Gangs and Sharecroppers

One of the principal documentary subjects of the thirties was the Southern chain gang. National interest in this institution appeared early in the decade, when it emerged as a public symbol for a whole citizenry in economic shackles. In 1932 John Spivak, an investigative reporter, exposed the cruelties of a Georgia chain gang to a public whose appetite had been whetted the previous year by the ghostwritten "first-hand account" of Robert E. Burns. Burns's sensationalized story, *I Am a Fugitive from a Georgia Chain Gang!*, became an award-winning motion picture directed by Mervyn LeRoy; this film version initiated a cinematic and literary genre which "Old Man" parodically exploited.[55] LeRoy's movie not only presented a case for penal reform in the South but also expressed a longing for escape which millions of Americans shared. By 1937, the conventions of chain-gang melodrama were so overworked that Faulkner need not have been conscious of the original to draw upon its power in *The Wild Palms*. Even *The Hurricane*, for example, with its French chain gang for Polynesian prisoners, recognizably tapped the genre's specific masochistic pleasures. Like *The Wild Palms*, too, it combined the iconography of prison-and-escape with the iconography of flood-and-refuge, demonstrating their emotional congruence. Similar "quotations" of the chain-gang mythology were frequent and diverse.

Yet *I Am a Fugitive* contains elements not normally associated with the genre, elements that appear in Faulkner's novel also, in "Wild Palms" as well as in "Old Man." When the Burns character, called James Allen in the film, first escapes to Chicago (Harry and Charlotte's initial refuge also), his landlady discovers his real identity and blackmails him into marriage. He falls in love with another woman, however, and asks his wife for a divorce. When she not only refuses to divorce him but also threatens to send him back into bondage if he persists in his affair, his reply suggests a hidden source of the film's success: "It'd be no worse," he tells her, "than serving my time out with you."

This equation of wedlock with imprisonment must have enhanced some viewers' subliminal identification with the escapee. It certainly complements Faulkner's juxtaposition of the convict's "escape" in "Old Man" with Harry and Charlotte's flight from marriage in "Wild Palms." Faulkner simply bisected the two halves of the chain-gang fantasy's appeal: pity for the prisoner's unjust plight, and the wish to be in *his* exciting prison rather than in the dungeon of domesticity most people inhabit. Bound to his own wife who would not divorce him, Faulkner would have been especially sensitive to the marital subtext of the chain-gang genre. He clearly exploited it in *The Wild Palms*.

The genre came to signify social injustice rather than marital discord, however. By mid-decade, moreover, it explicitly provided a way of thinking about the Depression. In several of its incarnations, it served rather obviously as a microcosm for the whole collapsed society. For example, the chain gang in *Hell's Highway*, a movie directed by Roland West, actually seems preferable to the difficult world (including wives) outside. Andrew Bergman summarizes the film's conclusion:

> After a revolt of the chain gang, most of the prisoners are brought back. The Governor, a just man in a white suit, arrives to declare that conditions on the gang will be ameliorated. The prisoners seem pleased and the film winds up with some banter from a Mormon jailbird concerning the advantages of chain gang life to having three wives awaiting one's release. A mild chuckle, and all are glad to be back.
>
> Between Allen's anomie [in *I Am a Fugitive*] and the chain gang as home [in *Hell's Highway*] lay no real distance. Both spoke to the paralysis of the world outside; neither related to a society of possibilities. . . . The national landscape seemed like an empty lot.[56]

At the end of *The Wild Palms*, Faulkner's tall convict echoes the Mormon's preference for the security of prison. Although the Governor does not come in a white suit to rectify the prisoner's conditions but sends his "emissary" to compound an injustice instead, the convict still regards the prison as his home and is relieved to return to it. The escape motive—deadly serious in many films—becomes elaborately comic in "Old Man," a parody in which the convict "escapes" only against his will and makes every effort to return to the law's embrace. The parodic element in *The Wild Palms* may be partially responsible for the confused reaction to it. Readers in the thirties, confronted by "Old Man's" chain-gang accoutrements—the "sudden glare of the electric bulbs and the guards' voices" (WP, 30) waking the prisoners in their barracks; the shackled coffle "herded" by sadistic trusties (WP, 68); the corruption of the prison bureaucracy (WP, 80)—would have formed generic expectations that Faulkner purposefully confounded. Thus, a reader like *New Masses* reviewer Edwin Burgum could see the tall convict as a "prototype of the underprivileged,"[57] a proletarian Paul Muni. But "underprivileged," an awkward term in any context, is especially inappropriate to Faulkner, who repeatedly deflated the type of sentimentality it expresses.

A related, even more widespread documentary subject was the rural poverty that chain-gang conditions epitomized. The fact that Pare Lorentz felt obliged to include a "sharecropper sequence" in *The River* suggests the strength of the subject's grip upon contemporary representations of the American South. Indeed, the life of the sharecropper became during the thirties an important component of the national self-image, offering as it did a symbol of the Depression's consequences. It produced a noteworthy literary and cinematic genre, inspired in part by the popularity of Caldwell's *Tobacco Road* (1932). More serious "sharecropper novels" included *Cabin in the Cotton* (1931) and *I Was a Sharecropper* (1937) by H. H. Kroll, who *was* a sharecropper, and Charlie May Simon's *The Share-Cropper* (1937). Two masterpieces evolved out of the genre, though neither belonged to it fully: Steinbeck's *The Grapes of Wrath* (1939) and Agee and Evans's *Let Us Now Praise Famous Men* (1940).[58]

The effect of the sharecropper literature as a whole was to portray the farm as a kind of prison, a prison of the spirit. Agee, for example, applied the prison metaphor to a description of the birth of a sharecropper's child: ". . . in this instant already his globe is rounded upon him and is his prison, which might have been his kingdom."[59] Faulkner simply reversed the common metaphor. The farm may be prison-like, as Agee, Steinbeck, and others implied; Faulkner turned their implication into symbolic fact.

For Parchman is specifically a prison *farm*, "a cotton plantation which the convicts work under the rifles and shotguns of guards and trusties" (WP, 23–24). It is a pauperized avatar of the plantation economy of the Old South. The labor conditions of the convicts are virtually identical with those of cotton tenancy: "the land they farmed and the substance they produced from it belonged neither to them who worked it nor to those who forced them at guns' point to do so" (WP, 30). Substitute for guns a less blatant coercion, and the setting of "Old Man" accurately captures the rampant dispossession and oppressive peonage that afflicted the South in the 1930s. Although set in 1927, the story works as a symbolic, parodic documentary of Depression Mississippi.

The tall convict's involuntary escape is thus an ironic product of the thirties—and of Faulkner's self-incarceration on his farm. But confinement and escape have been central themes in Southern literature since the early nineteenth century, an inevitable consequence of slavery. The most direct literary reactions to slavery (plantation exposés like *Uncle Tom's Cabin*, and the fugitive-slave narratives of Douglass and others) are direct forerunners of the sharecropper novel and the chain-gang movie, appealing to the same reformist impulses and to the same melodramatic fantasies. Even the idealizations of plantation life, Kennedy's *Swallow Barn* and its ilk, suppressed a secret fascination with the same subjects, as we shall see when we look at *Go Down, Moses*. And Edgar Allan Poe, the least political of antebellum Southern authors, adopted confinement-and-escape as a primary subject, whether in "The Premature Burial," "The Cask of Amontillado," or "The Pit and the Pendulum."

Like Poe, Faulkner brought a more personal than political commitment to bear on the South's original Gothic theme. In turning to the sharecropper and chain-gang genres popular in the 1930s, he might have contemplated their ideological contents, if only for the purpose of subverting them. But his real attraction to the imagery of shackles and leg irons may relate equally to the artificial limp he affected after World War I and to the corset in which his mother bound him when he was a boy. In *The Marble Faun* and "Carcassonne," he had depicted his literary calling as a state of simultaneous captivity and flight. In *The Wild Palms*, he updated the portrait.[60]

Depression Picaresque

If the convict travels amid a symbolic Depression-scape, Harry and Charlotte's travels participate in a Depression cliché in and of themselves. Faulkner's most ambulatory novel was written during an intensive period of travel literature, when writers of every kind and reputation took to the railroads and highways, "looking for America" and reporting the Depression's effects. Edmund Wilson in *The American Jitters* (1932), Sherwood Anderson in *Puzzled America* (1935), Erskine Caldwell in *Some American People* (1935), James Rorty in *Where Life is Better: An Unsentimental American Journey* (1936), Nathan Asch in *The Road: In Search of America* (1937), and Louis Adamic in *My America* (1938) all helped to establish the genre. Between 1938 and 1941, according to one historian of the phenomenon, "[t]he 'I've seen America' book, a novelty in 1935, became the dominant nonfiction mode. Writer after writer told how, when, and where he 'discovered' America, how 'knowing' the country (that is, traveling it) provided his most vital education, and what America meant to him."[61]

Taking America's pulse did not occupy nonfiction alone. Many a novel, too, displayed a "cult of experience," whereby a writer's authority was enhanced proportionately as he was able to demonstrate not just a traveler's familiarity, but an unsentimental (that is to say, "underprivileged") traveler's familiarity with Depression America. For example, a preface to Edward Anderson's *Hungry Men* (1935), a novel about peripatetic unemployment, informs its readers that "Mr. Anderson himself rode the blinds of crack passenger trains, freight manifests and slow locals, in gondolas and cattle cars; slept in welfare flops, ten-cent hotels, parks and darkened churches."[62] Nathan Asch says in *The Road* that he undertook his round-trip coast-to-coast bus tour to "find the flesh, the blood, the living spirit to animate the skeleton of a novel."[63] He never published such a novel, but many others did. The supreme expression of the picaresque motive in thirties literature, *The Grapes of Wrath*, belongs to the same vintage (1939) as *The Wild Palms*.

The motive sought expression outside literature also. In *I Am a Fugitive from a Chain Gang* (1932), *Wild Boys of the Road* (1933), *It Happened One Night* (1934),[64] and the film version of *The Grapes of Wrath* (1940), it reached motion picture screens. By 1941 at least, it was familiar enough to serve as a recognizable object of parody. In Preston Sturges's *Sullivan's*

Travels (1941), a young film director rebels against the triviality of Holly-wood entertainment (his own hits include *So Long, Sarong; Hey Hey in the Hayloft;* and *Ants in Your Pants of 1939*) and decides to make a "so-cially significant" documentary film to be called *Oh Brother, Where Art Thou?* Sullivan disguises himself as a hobo, eludes his press agents, and sets out to "discover America" by hopping freights and hitchhiking. Just as he is completing his experiment, however, he contracts amnesia during a railyard brawl. For allegedly assaulting a railroad official, he is sentenced to . . . (what else?) a chain gang. Sturges displays all the by-now-tired chain-gang conventions: manacles, dogs, sadistic guards, an isolation box. The convicts' only prison-breaks, however, occur on "Picture Show Sun-days," when they are herded into a Negro church to attend a movie (while, incidentally, the church congregation sings "Go Down, Moses"). Here, watching the other prisoners roar with laughter at a Mickey Mouse cartoon, Sullivan discovers that what people really want is to be enter-tained. Having learned that the best charity he can provide for the poor is humor, he returns to Hollywood to manufacture it.[65]

Much less consciously than Sturges, Faulkner also burlesqued the chain-gang and "I've-seen-America" genres. Beneath the superficially se-rious tone of "Old Man" lurks a joke aimed at readers whose expectations had been shaped by automatic treatments of hackneyed subjects. Faulkner also aimed the joke at himself. As *Sullivan's Travels* is a movie "about" movie-making, so *The Wild Palms* is "about" writing books. As Sturges explored the relationship between high-minded artists and low-minded audiences, so Faulkner was treating the gap between himself and the read-ing public. While Sturges's Sullivan finished by condescending to his viewers, however, Faulkner reconfirmed his aloofness—and mocked it.

Connected to the picaresque motive in Depression literature was an impulse toward varied resumés. A writer's dust-jacket blurb tended to ben-efit from a reference to many kinds of jobs, as well as to footloose unem-ployment between them. The biographical sketch introducing Clara Weatherwax's *Marching! Marching!* (1935), for example, certifies that, "[s]ince high-school days Miss Weatherwax has had a variety of jobs—both white-collar and proletarian, mostly for fifty dollars a month or less, and the kind of work mentioned or described in this book she knows through experience or close contact." The ideal definition of the writer's vocation became colored, in the thirties, by the romance of the road and an infatuation with lower-class labor. The proletarian novel—the "characteristic fiction" of the thirties—purveyed both the romance and the infatuation.[66]

The Wild Palms participates in the "unsentimental" travel literature of its day. Harry and Charlotte's northward and westward excursion shares certain traits of the contemporary picaresque mode. It combines "fitful employment at many jobs," although none of them is truly menial, with "prolonged wandering about."[67] It includes visits to an urban park-bench milieu, to a rural (though nonagricultural) homestead, and to an industrial, labor-embroiled-mine—all of which were obligatory stops on the road-book tour. Like Asch and Anderson and Caldwell, Harry and Charlotte investigate a variety of economic environments in their search for an equilibrium in which to survive permanently. As in the travel-book mode of the period, one of the central subjects of *The Wild Palms* is domestic economy, the mechanics of acquiring food, shelter, and clothing.

The motive behind the travel, both in Faulkner's novel and in the road books, differs from the motive for conventional travel books. Unlike most of the classics of travel literature, the road book in the thirties was devoted not to the conspicuous consumption of landscape and architecture, but to an inventory of economic alternatives. Henry James sought a "sense of place"; Wilson and Caldwell and Anderson sought a sense of ecology. Landscape occurs not as an array of psychological stimuli, but as the ground from which a living is extracted. Edmund Wilson, for example, prefaces many of the chapters of *The American Jitters* with brief evocations of landscape or architecture: New York City, Kentucky's Cumberland Mountains, industrial Detroit, the Bluegrass region of Tennessee, the "enchanted forest" of New Mexico, Hoover Dam in Nevada, Los Angeles, San Diego, and the textile cities of Massachusetts. But, for Wilson, these places are important primarily as economic environments. The landscapes in *The Wild Palms*—the Mississippi Gulf Coast, the prison farm at Parchman, New Orleans, Chicago, the Wisconsin lake camp, the alligator country in the lower Delta, the mine in Utah, San Antonio, even the floodscape in "Old Man"—constitute a similar assortment of environments from which the characters must wrest a tenuous living.

Again, however, Faulkner frustrated the expectations he must have aroused in many readers. Harry and Charlotte's motive for traveling is incongruous within the context of Depression picaresque, for they are seeking creative *un*employment at a time when most travelers were chasing after jobs. Their travel ends in disaster because their goal is utopian:

no place exists such as they are seeking, free of economic restraints. They never find a locale where they can establish a viable ecology of leisure. They are gratuitously "underprivileged," sacrificing a steady income to pursue idleness and poverty. Their rejection of security gains added meaning because it happens during the midst of the Depression.

Insofar as Harry and Charlotte's travel is linked to a quest for "vocation," whether erotic or occupational, it reenacts an old metaphor from Faulkner's past. In *The Marble Faun*, the "bound" protagonist equates his "calling" with locomotion. In "Carcassonne," the hero must imprison himself in his roll of tar paper so that he may fly across the sky. By contrasting the homebody convict with the peregrinating lovers, Faulkner dramatized one of the tensions in himself that made him a writer.

Proletarian Literature

Probably the most popular stop of all in Depression travel books was any scene of conflict between industry and organized labor. Wilson visited the West Virginia coal mines and the textile mills of Lawrence, Massachusetts, during strikes; Rorty, the Imperial Valley of Southern California during a lettuce workers' strike; Anderson, strike-ridden cotton and rayon plants in the Atlantic Piedmont and in Elizabethton, Tennessee; Asch, the Southern Tenant Farmers' Union in Marked Tree, Arkansas; Adamic, strikes by steelworkers in Pittsburgh and by dockworkers in San Francisco. Strikes were an important subject for fiction as well—not only in the "proletarian novel" of which it was the central device but in more traditional books too, such as Caldwell's *God's Little Acre* (1933) and Steinbeck's *In Dubious Battle* (1936).

Although a scholarly study of "The Strike in the American Novel" includes no reference to Faulkner,[68] he did in fact write about a strike or two. In *Pylon*, the aviators who are to compete in the flying meet at Feinman Airport threaten to withhold their services in a labor dispute with the management, a dispute that results in a scene "exactly that of the conventional conference between the millowners and the delegation from the shops" (PY, 149). In "Wild Palms," Harry and Charlotte witness a truncated labor confrontation in the Utah mine where Harry has taken a job as company doctor.

When he accepts this job, Harry assumes duties that clearly ally him to management rather than to the workers (WP, 128). When he and Charlotte reach Utah in January 1937, they find that Callaghan Mines is failing, that "[t]here hasn't been a payroll . . . since September," and that the mine workers have reacted in three different ways. The Chinese simply left in October, having "smelled" the lack of money. The Italians "made a little more noise. They struck, all proper. Threw down their picks and shovels and walked out." Through a "deputation," they negotiated with Buckner, the company manager, and departed with a woolen shirt and a can of beans apiece. This labor dispute—the closest Faulkner ever came to describing a real strike—occupies only one paragraph. Faulkner was much less interested in the imaginative possibilities it offered than he was in the third group of laborers, the Poles. For they have simply stayed, oblivious to their exploitation and unaware "that a man could let folks keep on working without intending to pay them," doing all the work of the mine in the belief that they are "making overtime" (WP, 187–88).

When Faulkner came to the business of the proletarian novel, he did not tap its emotional or intellectual sources. *The Wild Palms* presents nobody's conversion to political radicalism. No one's class-consciousness is aroused. Even though the novel is concerned with human justice, it does not take sides in a class conflict that is scarcely recognized by its victims, let alone by Harry and Charlotte, who are seeking a separate peace. The situation of the Poles represents a parody of the traditional strike novel. Instead of confronting their employers with demands or grievances, they must be informed by their surrogate boss, Wilbourne, through his ostensible labor-relations secretary, Charlotte, that they even have grievances. She explains their situation to them by drawing cartoons in which a caricature of a fat capitalist withholds sacks of money from caricatures of miners (WP, 200–201).

Charlotte behaves as a parodic representation of the "proletarian novelist"—or, at least, of the artist who enters the service of propaganda. As she awakens her "proletarian" audience to their victimization, however, she also awakens them to the hopelessness of their situation. She is an instrument of accommodation and acceptance. For, after her mute pronouncements, the Poles submit to the injustice without trying to rectify it. Following this "proletarian" climax, nothing happens: not victory, nor hope of victory; not even a true understanding of their fate; only *endurance* in the immutable conditions of their lives, one of which is and always will be (as for the farmer-prisoner) to labor in the earth and to receive compensation only from the earth, not from other men.

Where does Faulkner stand in relation to the "proletariat" in this "strike novel" *manqué?* He chose to insert his protagonists into the mining camp during the third phase of its labor troubles, *after* the genuine strike. He found his story value in the Poles, who *accept* circumstances, including unjust ones; who must be told that they have been mistreated, because they are too innocent to know; and who make no positive effort to achieve fairness for themselves, because they are too innocent to hope. In Charlotte's cartoons, they appear compositely as "every man who ever labored in the bowels of earth" (WP, 202). This description includes the convict of "Old Man." Like the alligator hunter, the Poles are his kin. The word *endurance*, which applies to all of them, carries with it inherent political (as well as psychological) implications that Faulkner never thought to articulate. He applied it, almost exclusively, to that virtue of the lower classes that allows them to accept injustices without trying to remedy them. It implies a satisfaction with one's status and an indifference to social mobility. Having internalized the peasantry's worldly failure, he projected his own radical patience onto the peasantry. Meanwhile, Count No 'Count's rebelliousness was a virtue he reserved for members of the bourgeoisie like Harry and Charlotte.

On the surface, Faulkner's treatment of the miners implies a sweet sentimentalization of the poor. But, in effect, it denies them any logic or method for improving their lot. If endurance is one's primary virtue and therefore one's primary moral asset, one sacrifices dearly to protest one's condition. In most of Faulkner's work, aspiration to social mobility is among the ugliest of characteristics. In his conservative vision of justice, vague intangibles compensate for a lack of wherewithal.

The most remarkable fact about the Depression provenance of *The Wild Palms* is that Harry and Charlotte, although they are beneficiaries of a relatively privileged social dispensation, experience an even harsher, more desperate fate than the convict. According to the fashion of the thirties, the sharecropper and the worker should suffer a constant burden of hardship and exploitation; their bourgeois foils should enjoy an easy and frivolous living, compared to the struggle for survival of the proletariat.

In *To Have and Have Not* (1937), for a relatively mild example, Hemingway provides a more conventional double plot, in which Harry Morgan (although not exactly a prole) is dignified by juxtaposition with Richard Gordon, a middle-class writer apparently rebellious against social privilege but actually corrupted by it. Gordon survives with his pretensions, if not his manhood, intact while writing "a novel about a strike in a textile factory."[69] Morgan does not even endure, but he possesses intangible compensations that suggest a reversal of the title. To paraphrase Carlos Baker, Harry Morgan *has* virtues that the leisure-class ne'er-do-wells around him *have not*.[70]

The relationship between Harry Wilbourne and the convict is far more complex than that between Morgan and Gordon; but similarly compensatory "possessions" accrue to the convict, just as the land, by enduring a flood, is compensated by the fertility it gains. Hemingway's juxtaposition is clearly invidious; Faulkner's is much less so. For Wilbourne also *has* a certain dignity, which *differs* from the convict's. The double plot here does not function chiefly to compare, any more than a still life compares apples and oranges. It functions more to fill out, to complement, like the murals of a WPA diptych. Harry and the convict behave according to incompatible perceptions of the world. Their worlds are *different*. And the words that apply to one world apply differently to the other: *labor* and *leisure*, *duty* and *vocation*, even *endurance*. For Harry finishes his story totally committed to his own kind of endurance, enunciated in the last words of "Wild Palms," but a very different kind from that of the convict. Harry's is tragic; the convict's is comic.

Though the social structure it portrays is itself a fiction, *The Wild Palms* is inevitably a political utterance. A "sharecropper" documentary that is not ameliorative, a travel book that subordinates economics to romance, and a strike novel that is defeatist all suggest an aggressive conservatism. The plot discontinuity acts prescriptively as well as descriptively to separate the social levels it treats, and thus to preserve class distinctions.

The Wild Palms is a product not only of William Faulkner's fortieth year but also of Franklin Roosevelt's second administration. Faulkner could have written it without ever having witnessed the Mississippi in flood, a Southern prison farm, or a labor confrontation; for these phenomena were common images in the public symbology of the Depression years. Even if he were unaware of the "major shift of sensibility" in American literature in the thirties and intended no allusion to it in his novel, his references to the "proletarian novel," to the "see-America book," to sharecroppers, to fugitives from chain gangs, and to floods draw *The Wild Palms*, if only negatively, into a fragile participation in that new sensibility. More likely, however, he understood the tendency that Caldwell, Steinbeck, even Hemingway, and others evinced, and he was aware of the more extreme manifestations of the decade as well. Perhaps he meant for *The Wild Palms* to express his disapproval of politically motivated art, just as it expresses his distaste for commercially motivated art. Whether intentionally or not, he stands in instructive contrast with most of the literature of the thirties' second lustrum, a holdout from the deliberate harnessing of literature to leftist ideology.[71] In an era of "proletarian" writing, he remained a confirmed "pastoralist."[72]

At the University of Virginia in the fifties, Faulkner would deny that he had ever attempted to sell political or economic ideas: "Not at all. I was trying to talk about people, using the only tool I knew, which was the country that I knew. No, I wasn't trying to—wasn't writing sociology at all. I was just trying to write about people, which to me are the important thing. Just the human heart, it's not ideas. I don't know anything about ideas, don't have much confidence in them" (FU, 10). But ideas are also a part of the human experience that any artist "would like to reduce . . . onto the head of a pin" (FWP, 95); and ideas, including ideas about "sociology," necessarily contributed to the shape of Faulkner's fiction, whether he wished them to or not. Because Faulkner's identity as a writer was deeply rooted in his society, moreover, his "sociological" perception inevitably reflected his perception of his own vocation.

CHAPTER FOUR

THE HAMLET

It's a question of language, for one thing—this business of saying a word and having it understood. Down there—in Macedon, I mean—there's a different vocabulary. I don't mean to say it is an inferior vocabulary. Words like weevil and bale are just as honorable as publisher and best-seller, and words like covey and quail are a hell of a lot better than Fascist-subconscious and liquidate, but there is a limitation. There is a limitation here too. The thing I'm after is a place where there is an unlimited vocabulary—where you can speak almost any word and have it touch the immediate experience of other people. That's out, of course, so now my problem is one of selection; of choosing between the vocabulary of the province and the vocabulary of the metropolis.

Hamilton Basso, Courthouse Square

. . . I would think how words go straight up in a thin line, quick and harmless, and how terribly doing goes along the earth, clinging to it, so that after a while the two lines are too far apart for the same person to straddle from one to the other.

William Faulkner, As I Lay Dying

"The Peasants"

In the farcical "Afternoon of a Cow," Faulkner articulated his literary vocation as a collaboration between two versions of himself that corresponded to opposite segments of his community. He gave *The Wild Palms* its double structure to separate as well as to unify the two selves, for his vocation depended on their clear differentiation no less than on their simultaneity. The extremity of the book's structure testifies to his anxiety about that differentiation. His next novel, *The Hamlet*, demonstrates even more fully the consequences of disorderliness in the structure of Faulkner's pastoral personality. If writing is metaphorically equivalent to the translation of "low" subjects into "high" language, what happens when Ernest V. Trueblood buys a mule farm? Worse, what happens when subliterate vulgarians like "Mr. Faulkner" move into town and become bankers? What happens to a vocation founded on social distinction when society becomes indistinct? What happens? *The Hamlet.*

Faulkner sent *The Wild Palms* to Random House on June 25, 1938. He spent the rest of the summer overseeing his employees at Greenfield Farm and recuperating from his still-painful back wound. In late September, he went to New York to read galleys for the new novel. While there, he visited Meta Rebner, attended the theater, flew a plane in New Jersey, and finished a short story he called "Barn Burning."[1]

In this now-classic narrative, Faulkner returned to a project he had begun over a decade before. In late 1926 or early 1927, he had conceived a work about an upwardly mobile family of Yoknapatawpha County rednecks, named Snopes. He had written then the manuscript entitled "Father Abraham," which contains a substantial germ of the Snopes saga (FA, 3–4). In a style that was sometimes coarsely vernacular and sometimes lyrically poetic, it recounted one episode—a horse auction—in the career of Flem Snopes, a redneck who is rising from sharecropping in Frenchman's Bend to the presidency of a bank in Jefferson. At the same time, Faulkner had composed the novel he called *Flags in the Dust*, which his publisher later renamed *Sartoris* after the "aristocratic" family at its center. According to Blotner, Faulkner worked on these two projects "alternately" (BL, 526–31).

If Faulkner was indeed "writing at them alternately" in the twenties, his procedure dimly augured his method for *The Wild Palms* ten years later. In effect, the Snopes saga originated as one half—the lower-class, "comic" half—of a pastoral double plot, of which the aristocratic and tragic half was published as *Sartoris* eight years before he wrote "Barn Burning." During the interval, he drew upon the Snopeses for comic relief in *Sanctuary* (1931), and he made one concerted but aborted effort between 1930 and 1933 (BL, 656–827 passim) to write a novel about their ascent into middle-class respectability. Out of this effort came several published stories: "Lizards in Jamshyd's Courtyard," in which Flem Snopes fools some of his neighbors into buying a worthless old house by planting gold coins on its grounds; "Spotted Horses," a reworking of "Father Abraham" in which Flem sells worthless wild livestock to the citizens of Frenchman's

Bend and then evades responsibility for the violence that results; "Centaur in Brass," in which Flem, having connived his way into the supervisor's job at the power plant in Jefferson, systematically steals the brass valves and fittings from the boilers until his two black laborers foil him; and "Mule in the Yard," in which Flem's cousin, I. O. Snopes, causes a widow's house to burn and is forced by her to make an ironic reparation. Each of these stories is basically humorous, though Flem's exploits result in harm. Each experiments with vernacular speech, and the second and third rely on vernacular narrators. If Faulkner had finished his Snopes saga in the early thirties, it might have been a relatively simple series of consistently comic sketches. But in 1934 he decided to defer the Snopes work until after he finished *Absalom, Absalom!* (BL, 828). Then, following *Absalom, The Wild Palms* had proved more urgent.

By the time he returned to his Snopes project in 1938, his perspective on his "redneck" material had changed drastically. When he first invented the Snopeses, he was still a would-be poet for whom they provided party anecdotes; now he was a farmer himself, in the poorest section of Lafayette County. When he wrote "Father Abraham," he was struggling to establish a career; now he was reassessing a career fully, if problematically, in progress. Consequently, a work that might have been a series of entertaining tall tales became instead a variegated matrix of styles and tones.

"Barn Burning" is far from comic. Its subject is the divided loyalties of Colonel Sartoris Snopes, the young son of an embittered sharecropper who burns the barns of several successive landlords. "Sarty" must decide whether to protect his father, Ab, by lying or to heed his newly formed conscience. In the end he warns their current employer, Major de Spain, about Ab's intentions and then runs away from home the night Ab sets fire to de Spain's barn. Faulkner's clear sympathy with the character and his satisfaction with "Barn Burning"—which he liked well enough to place at the beginning of his *Collected Stories* in 1948—may have derived from the story's twisted embodiment of his own arcane family history. As with the Bundren family in *As I Lay Dying*, however, the elements of that history are confusingly displaced across family roles. Sarty's father suffers from fraudulent war wounds that superficially resemble Faulkner's: Ab's "stiff back" and his "stiff and ruthless limp" (CS, 8) are quite real, but he received them as a horsethief rather than as a soldier. Like his creator, Sarty has a ne'er-do-well father and a heroic namesake. Like Maud Falkner, Sarty's mother, Lennie, takes her son's part in family disputes;

but, unlike Murry, Ab dominates his wife. When Ab leaves their cabin to set de Spain's barn afire, he orders Lennie to "hold" Sarty, and she does so, as Faulkner's mother had held him in various ways; but the boy manages to break her grip. Sarty's association of honor and freedom (and exile) with horseback riding (CS, 22–24) echoes "Carcassonne." Faulkner may have projected his own "limp," his own ineffectual father, and his own overly solicitous mother into Sarty's situation. The tone of the story is grim, and its style is highly literate. Just as the narrator of "Old Man" "interprets" the tall convict's narrative, so the narrator of "Barn Burning" "translates" Sarty's inarticulate thoughts and Ab's "unprintable" words into language that is not just "respectable" but poetic.

When Faulkner returned home from New York in October 1938, he was preoccupied by his harvest at Greenfield Farm. By December, however, he had found time to produce a detailed synopsis for the Snopes project, which he included in a letter to Robert Haas, his editor at Random House (BL, 1003–6). This letter documents Faulkner's intentions for the Snopes trilogy more clearly and more immediately than any other source. It is certainly more authoritative than Faulkner's several retrospective accounts of the trilogy's history during the forties and fifties. In 1957, for example, he recalled conceiving the full trilogy in detail during the mid-twenties: "I thought of the whole story at once like a bolt of lightning lights up a landscape and you see everything but it takes time to write it, and this story I had in my mind for about thirty years, and [each of the volumes] . . . happened at that same moment, thirty years ago when I thought of it" (FU, 90). Yet the scheme he devised in 1938 differed significantly from the books he actually wrote. Spurred by his composition of "Barn Burning," Faulkner in his synopsis paradoxically outlined a work so consistently comic that he had to drop that somber story very early in the composition of the trilogy. By the time he finished the first volume in December 1939, however, he had modulated its tone so variously that the dark mood of "Barn Burning" seems to have presaged what followed.

In the letter to Haas, the projected trilogy included "The Peasants," in which Flem Snopes would "consume" a small village in the country and gain a foothold in the town of Jefferson; "Rus in Urbe," in which Flem would rise from half-ownership of a back-street restaurant to the bank presidency by blackmailing his wife's lover; and "Ilium Falling," in which the Snopeses would "eat up" Jefferson through corrupt politics and shoddy real-estate developments (SL, 107–8).

This outline describes the skeletal structure of the finished trilogy fairly accurately. But the letter goes on to provide a considerably more detailed account of his plan, which differs from the published novels substantially. Before Flem marries his pregnant bride, protecting her good name for a price, his "youngest brother"—obviously Sarty—runs away after trying to keep his father from burning a barn. Out west, this brother has a son about whom the other Snopeses remain ignorant. Flem moves his family to town. His wife's daughter recognizes "what a sorry lot" Snopeses are and escapes first to New York, then overseas during "the War." Serving in the ambulance corps, she meets Flem's brother's son, whose father "has tried to eradicate the Snopes from him." After the War, she introduces Flem's nephew to a similarly purified female Snopes. He marries this "remote cousin," and they have a son, who they hope will "raise the family out of the muck." This youth, however, turns out to have all the Snopes vices with none of Flem's shrewdness or firmness. In the end, Flem's final joke on Jefferson, and on his own kin, is to bequeath all his property to this syphilitic scoundrel. Unaware of his good fortune, the worthless heir spends the day of Flem's funeral breaking into Flem's house, attempting to blackmail Flem's virtuous daughter, and flirting with black wenches (SL, 108–9).

Faulkner's statements about his writing were never very reliable. Furthermore, he wrote to Haas not only to inform him of his writing schedule but also to request a loan, for which the projected novels would be the collateral. He was therefore likely to exaggerate the maturity of his conception; and, indeed, the outline seems somewhat improvisatory, as if he were bluffing his way through it. The single "bolt of lightning," which in 1957 Faulkner said had illuminated the Snopes landscape thirty years before, had not yet run its course in December 1938. The basic shape of Flem's career *had* been clear to Faulkner since the twenties, but he had not yet worked out all the details of event and character by which it would be achieved. His remark in the fifties that "you see everything but it takes time to write it" implies that he fashioned the Snopes stories according to some comprehensive, preconceived story plan that had come to him with the "bolt of lightning." More likely, as lightning normally does, it exposed only a sharp profile—the profile he had already sketched in "Father Abraham" and in *Sartoris* (SAR, 172)—and each Snopes story was part of an experimental groping toward a full contour.

The letter to Haas is important not only because it reveals the incompleteness of the Snopes scheme even after Faulkner began to compose *The Hamlet* but also because of the particular ways in which it varies from the final trilogy. First, the central character for Faulkner was clearly Flem Snopes—not V. K. Ratliff, Gavin Stevens, Mink Snopes, or Chick Mallison, all of whom have been advanced as "thematic" protagonists of the trilogy but none of whom appears in the letter. Likewise, the action was confined to Snopeses, with a major part assigned to Sarty, the hero of "Barn Burning." Just possibly, Faulkner preserved this scenario through 1939, with Sarty as the indirect instrument of Snopesian nemesis: he is retained very briefly in the final version of *The Hamlet*, and he might still have turned up in the concluding volumes of the trilogy. Far more likely, however, Faulkner abandoned Sarty when he virtually abandoned "Barn Burning."[2] As the book grew, he found a more efficient and credible device for closing the trilogy in "The Hound," which he had written in 1930 (BL, 672). In this story, a poor-white farmer named Ernest Cotton murders his more affluent neighbor over a trivial dispute, attempts to conceal the victim's body, and is apprehended because the victim's dog howls near its master's corpse. Although a Snopes appears briefly in "The Hound," his role is insignificant. In 1939, Faulkner turned Ernest Cotton into Mink Snopes, Flem's cousin; he created a grievance for Mink against Flem; and he adopted Mink as his new agent of poetic justice. Whether through Sarty's hereditary line or through Mink's vengeance, however, the defeat of Snopesism would still come from within the Snopes family itself. At this stage in Faulkner's thinking, then, his plot derived not from an opposition between Snopesism and anti-Snopesism, such as preoccupies the novels, but from a playing out of the self-destructive forces within Snopesism itself.

The central subject for the projected trilogy, more clearly than for the completed one, was the negative consequences of upward social mobility. This fundamental concern is unobscured in the outline because Faulkner did not there extend his criticism to the entire community, as he did in the novels themselves. The story he proposed here is Flem's, not Frenchman's Bend's or Jefferson's; and Flem's story is a rags-to-riches parody of Horatio Alger.[3] The outline projects a much more unified work than the final trilogy provides, and its unifying subject is Flem's social mobility.

Faulkner's working design for the first volume of the Snopes trilogy must have been loose and impromptu. At the time he wrote to Haas, it probably included "Spotted Horses," "Lizards in Jamshyd's Courtyard," and "Barn Burning," with "Centaur in Brass" and "Mule in the Yard" reserved for the second volume. As he began writing in late 1938 or early

1939, he recognized that "Barn Burning" violated the genial mood, the vernacular idiom, and the common subject matter (business transactions at the level of the "folk") of the other stories. So he reduced it to its few comic elements by putting only an abbreviated summary of it into V. K. Ratliff's ironic cheek and Jody Varner's outraged ears, and by removing the pathos that the original story had gained from Sarty Snopes's point of view. To replace "Barn Burning," he drew upon a story he had written in 1935, "Fool About a Horse," in which a vernacular narrator from Frenchman's Bend recounts his father's hilarious misadventures in horse-trading. Now he turned that protagonist into Ab Snopes and the narrator into V. K. Ratliff and inserted the tale near the beginning of the manuscript he was starting to write.

These stories—"Spotted Horses," "Lizards in Jamshyd's Courtyard," "Fool About a Horse," and the stripped-down version of "Barn Burn-ing"—constituted the comic core-plot of Faulkner's Snopes epic. They could easily have evolved into an anthology of homogeneous tales similar in structure to *The Unvanquished*. Instead, they became the bottom layer of a palimpsest, whose evolution resembled that of *The Wild Palms* more than that of *The Unvanquished*. Whereas a comic subplot attached itself to the serious main plot in *The Wild Palms*, however, in *The Hamlet* Faulkner supplemented his essentially comic main plot with an infusion of serious material that was not sufficiently coherent to constitute a plot of any kind.

The first segment of the novel (Book One) conforms with the comic plan. To the "Barn Burning" summary and "Fool About a Horse," Faulkner added an account—the seed of which appears in "Lizards"—of an intricate transaction in goats between Flem and Ratliff. Beginning with Book Two, however, he added materials that bore little apparent relation to the rise of the Snopeses. In lengthy digressions, and in an increasingly literary style that diverges sharply from the rural idiom of the core stories, Faulkner wrote about a school teacher named Labove who falls in love with the woman-child Eula Varner, and about Hoake McCarron, the outsider Eula favors over all her local suitors. In Book Three, he rein-vented "Afternoon of a Cow" by replacing "Mr. Faulkner" with an idiot named Ike Snopes and by translating the episode of the burning pasture into language that out-Trueblooded Trueblood; and he adapted "The Hound" both to the Snopes plot and to the stylistic complexity the novel had attained. In Book Four, he reverted to his core plot: "Spotted Horses" and "Lizards in Jamshyd's Courtyard" finally came to rest here, but Faulkner now rendered them in the highly literary language that had come to dominate the whole novel.

When Faulkner finished this first volume of the Snopes trilogy in December 1939, he had renamed it *The Hamlet*. (He would not complete the second and third volumes, *The Town* and *The Mansion*, until the late fifties.) While writing it, he had been diverted by the operation of his farm, by a lawsuit for which he was called as a witness in Washington, D.C., and increasingly by financial worries. He had been forced several times to lay the book aside so that he could crank out commercial stories to sell (BL, 1008–34). Though he could still summon up enough self-confidence to assert to Robert Haas that "I am the best in America, by God" (SL, 113), his slide back into insolvency stirred all the old doubts.

The Hamlet became a complex rather than a simple synthesis of discrete tales both because Faulkner's perception of the society it described was becoming confused and because his perception of his descriptive talent was becoming confused as well. In fact, the two confusions were interrelated. A vocation founded on pastoralism would necessarily register shifts in the structure of society. And a pastoral writer undergoing a crisis of vocation would naturally project his private perturbations onto his community. The Snopeses were an outward and visible sign of an inward and spiritual disjunction.

Faulkner and the Southern Dialogue

Critical recognition of that disjunction has waxed and waned over time. When *The Hamlet* was published on April Fool's Day, 1940 (BL1, 750), most reviewers complained that it was incoherent. Wallace Stegner, for example, noted its "lack of continuity." Paula Snelling deplored its division "into four parts which have little to do with one another." Robert Littell called it "a book which one not only . . . cannot put down, but *must* not. For then one is lost."[4] For almost half a century, criticism of *The Hamlet* has been devoted primarily to refuting these ancient first impressions. Faulkner's exegetes have fought a battle on behalf of *The Hamlet's* coherence that was won during the opening volleys.

The history of this one-sided debate is epitomized in two reviews by

Robert Penn Warren. Evaluting *The Hamlet* in early 1941, he noted its departure from Faulkner's previous, Jamesian concern with organization. After comparing the "loose and casual" effect of *The Hamlet* with the structural tightness of *Light in August*, Warren expressed a "hope that the author will not cease to concern himself with the formal problems which have apparently engaged him in earlier work." Five years later, however, in his review of Malcolm Cowley's *Portable Faulkner*, Warren revised his estimation of the book's unity. Cowley had erred, Warren wrote, in dismissing the structure of *The Hamlet* as merely episodic: "I think that in that novel we have a type of organization in which the thematic rather than the narrative emphasis is the basic principle, and once we grasp that fact the unity of the individual work may come clear." Partially because of the New Critical movement which Warren was then helping to lead, his call for an investigation into Faulkner's "thematic organization"[5] was amply answered. A generation of critics sharing his faith in Faulkner's innate orderliness have elucidated thematic structures in competitive profusion, replacing any alleged disjointedness with the "real" coherence that exists below the confusing surface.

In 1941, Warren defined the subject that holds *The Hamlet* together as an opposition "between the non-aristocratic Frenchman's Bend world, unconscious of its past, and the Snopes world, which Ratliff, the characteristic Faulkner commentator, recognizes as the enemy." Most later explicators of the book's unity have offered variations on this scheme. Warren Beck and James Watson both provided book-length discussions of the opposition between humanism and amoral materialism throughout the Snopes trilogy. For Florence Leaver, the structure of *The Hamlet* resolved itself into a twofold "hierarchy of minds"—Snopeses and opponents to Snopesism. Peter Lisca located the book's unifying principle in its love stories. Viola Hopkins suggested a thematic "patterning" based upon "escape-and-return" motifs. For T. Y. Greet, the structure was governed by a contrast between reason, championed by Flem, and sensation, whose goddess Eula is sacrificed to rational opportunism. For Olga Vickery, "the meaning of the book [was] established not by the plot but in and through the successive tales of barter and stories of love."[6]

Only recently have some critics reasserted the earliest reviewers' skepticism. Arthur Kinney, for example, calls *The Hamlet* an "uneven" work that "we cannot integrate," and he blames its shapelessness on the "slackened, confused, and uninspired poetics" of Faulkner's later years. Joseph Reed refers to the "mystery" of "a world in which all the events seem relevant to the narrative but never reach a point of synthesis or imposed meaning." John Matthews celebrates the novel's "noncentered-ness." And Donald Kartiganer asserts that "Faulkner has built an anarchy, indeed a madness, into the structure of Frenchman's Bend."[7]

But Matthews's opposition of Snopesian "centeredness" to anti-Snopesian "playfulness" ironically echoes the "unifying principles" of previous Faulkner criticism. And even Kartiganer, in a book devoted to explicating "[t]he fragmentariness of Faulkner's novels," begins his chapter on *The Hamlet* with a disavowal of the falsely confused readings of the past: "To many readers the novel has seemed without structure, merely a composite of previously published stories. . . . Yet I will argue . . . [that] structure is not only present in this novel; it is raised to the level of mythic force, controlling and defining the characters who live within it."[8]

The argument for *The Hamlet's* unity was clinched long ago. The scholars' structures provide helpful perspectives on Faulkner's novel. As one returns to the book, however, one's experience remains much fuller than they can account for. One appreciates the bravura of Faulkner's various performances more than the *ex post facto* perception of their unity. Next to the exhilaration produced simply by reading the prose of "The Long Summer," an awareness that idiot Ike fits into a moral or mythic pattern or that Jack Houston's brief biography "complements and contrasts with the story of Mink Snopes and his wife"[9] brings only a limited satisfaction. Mere comprehension of the novel requires that one combine the diverse narrative components into some scheme. But this necessary centripetal endeavor can progress only so far before the reading experience collapses into a reductive black hole. The book's difficulty lies in perceiving its coherence, a job that has largely been accomplished. But what is attractive about the book, and valuable, is its implicit invitation to chaos.

The need for toleration of *The Hamlet's* disorderliness has not gone unnoticed. Irving Howe, after repeating the obligatory acknowledgment that "*The Hamlet* is a unified piece of work," qualified that statement: "I doubt that the true values of *The Hamlet* can finally be apprehended through discussions of structural unity. For this is a novel that needs most of all to be appreciated as a performance or a series of performances."[10] Carey Wall, twenty years ago, summarized a situation that still basically prevails:

Most criticism of *The Hamlet* has been concerned with its unity and its themes, and the general opinion now seems to be that the book's episodes are firmly unified by means of its themes, most of which are identified in accordance with various descriptions of "Snopesism." But persuasive as these discussions are, they fail to illuminate the book as a whole. They do not explain why Faulkner has used a chain of episodes rather than a tightly woven plot, nor why he has colored the episodes with such a variety of moods, nor why he has chosen to evoke these particular moods, nor why he presents Ike Snopes' love for the cow in language that celebrates, that evokes beauty and splendor. [11]

What is needed is a combination of the centripetal criticism that has already proved indispensable, though incomplete, with a centrifugal criticism (only slowly emerging within Faulkner studies in the work of Kartiganer, Matthews, and others) that would describe the expansive as well as the concentric energies of Faulkner's art. We need to remember that *The Hamlet's* digressions remain digressive even after they have been systematized, and that the novel remains episodic even after its episodes have been arranged into an organic artistic whole.

For Kartiganer, "[t]he unity of the book emerges from the coherence of all the strands of Frenchman's Bend into the renewed sense of its identity: an entire community . . . committing itself once again to the structure and the mythos of the hamlet." [12] But the converse is also true: the *dis*unity of the book emerges from the *in*coherence of the community. For *The Hamlet* originated in Faulkner's anxious observations of class conflict in early twentieth-century Mississippi. It is formally inchoate because it describes a society in turbulent transition; it is stylistically and tonally volatile because Faulkner's attitude toward that turbulence was complex.

He was not unique. Scores of Southern writers during the twenties and thirties responded to shifts in the structure of their society, whether to encourage or to resist them. Throughout the decade-long evolution of *The Hamlet,* indeed, the South witnessed a vehement public debate about the status of the rural poor. The terms of the debate, while superficially economic and political, were imaginative as well. For many writers, the sharecropper and the tenant farmer were not only figures in an agricultural landscape but also characters in a private drama: the public debate originated in countless inner struggles between sympathy and revulsion. For Faulkner, increasingly obsessed by the relationship between his books and their subjects, the debate about real peasants naturally conformed with his frustrated effort to define a vocation that he always partially, incongruously identified with peasant labor. Furthermore, the first critics of Faulkner's novels evaluated them in the context of the debate: for his earliest readers, including Warren, *The Hamlet* was one among many books about Southern farmers.

Literary historians normally attribute the Southern Renaissance to the reaction of conservative intellectuals against social changes in the South during the first quarter of the twentieth century. Yet the so-called Renaissance also included many Southern intellectuals who were enthusiastic about the changes and who also produced a significant literature, albeit one neglected by critics and historians. Twenty years ago, John Bradbury defined a need to "redress the critical balance" between two opposite factions: while the reputations of "new traditionists" flourished, a "strong and wide-spread liberal wing, covering both urban and rural subjects, has been largely ignored."[13]

One way of "redressing the critical balance" is to see the literature of the Southern Renaissance as part of a dialogue between two intellectual camps—one loosely defined as conservative, the other as liberal. Within this dialogue much variety obtained: individual writers moved from position to position along a spectrum of opinion, or even occupied more than one position at a time. Such a critical framework offers a useful representation of the intellectual atmosphere in which Faulkner conceived and executed his trilogy of the Snopeses. For the dialogue centered on just those forces of social change that comprise the core of his Snopes material. Even though Faulkner himself may not have been consciously aware of a "debate," it provides a valuable perspective on the particular form into which he shaped this material and on the politics of his critical reputation.

By "dialogue," I mean to follow R. W. B. Lewis's usage of the word in reference to nineteenth-century American intellectual history: "Every culture seems, as it advances toward maturity, to produce its own determining debate over the ideas that preoccupy it: salvation, the order of nature, money, power, sex, the machine, and the like. The debate, indeed, may be said to *be* the culture, at least on its loftiest levels; for a culture achieves identity not so much through the ascendancy of one particular set of convictions as through the emergence of its peculiar and distinctive dialogue."[14]

The twentieth-century Southern dialogue differed substantially from the New England-based dialogue Lewis examines, but it exhibited the same relationship with its culture. Its full anatomy remains only partially documented, [15] but the "parties" to the dialogue, as Lewis calls them, are roughly identifiable; and we can distinguish, within individual literary performances, what he calls the "coloration or discoloration of ideas received from the sometimes bruising contact of opposites."[16] Viewed from within the dialogue, even apparently noncontroversial events and actions can assume meanings and relationships they otherwise lack.

The dialogue has a long history, having crystallized during the "New South" movement enunciated by Henry Grady and others;[17] but it did not foster great literature until the 1920s. During the last half of that decade, and especially during the Great Depression, the poles of the debate gravitated toward two academic communities—Vanderbilt University in Nashville, Tennessee, and the University of North Carolina at Chapel Hill. [18] In Vanderbilt's humanities departments, a circle of poets gathered around John Crowe Ransom and called themselves "Fugitives." They were mostly uninterested in social issues until the late twenties, when they metamorphosed into a different group with an overlapping membership. In 1930, this group, the "Agrarians," published *I'll Take My Stand*, a manifesto of reaction against the "capitalist-industrial" reformation of the South. Ultimately, their influence was not political or economic but literary and pedagogical. Meanwhile, the University of North Carolina nurtured a liberal leadership in its School of Public Welfare and its Department of Sociology, both of which were chaired by Howard W. Odum. A distinguishing characteristic of "liberal" fiction has been its vaguely sociological nature, a characteristic the Fugitive-Agrarians were quick to denounce. One of the tenets of conservative criticism was that art should be self-contained, should not concern itself with social issues for their own sake, whereas liberal Southern writers more frequently felt a responsibility to articulate social problems and solutions. Fittingly, the liberal camp, while shaping literary opinion hardly at all, influenced governmental policies widely. [19]

The Chapel Hill group initiated a Southern tradition of social analysis and programmatic reform. In a series of meticulously documented books—including Odum's *magnum opus*, *Southern Regions of the United States* (1936)—they shaped the concept of regional planning for the South and then extended it to the nation. They welcomed social change, or at least they despaired of preventing it; and they proposed to control it only in such a way as to bring the most benefit to each region of the country through a centrally administered federalism. Necessarily in the case of the South, that benefit would be initially economic; and the regionalists were pragmatically willing to consider any means of raising the standard of living or improving the material welfare of the populace, whether through new industry, agricultural technology, or public ownership of power facilities. Their problem-solving orientation and the force of their diligent research made them persuasive with private foundations and governmental agencies.[20]

Odum's ideas did not inspire writers as they did bureaucrats. No literary school grew up around him, although he himself wrote three novels. Instead, the primary literature of the liberal wing of the dialogue was sociological in the pure sense. Social scientists and journalists produced an abundance of analyses of the South: John Dollard, Hortense Powdermaker, Allison Davis, Arthur Raper, and Gunnar Myrdal among the former; Clarence Cason, Jonathan Daniels, Virginius Dabney, W. J. Cash, and James Agee among the latter.[21]

Consonant with the spirit behind this body of inquiry, however, creative fiction in the South also turned toward social problems. The "liberal" novel of the Renaissance period showed a marked tendency toward satire and didacticism. Among the "liberal" authors, T. S. Stribling, Erskine Caldwell, Hamilton Basso, Grace Lumpkin, Paul Green, Olive Dargan, and others shared a concern with contemporary social conditions. In *The Wild Palms*, as we have seen, such concern even gained an entrance, if only an ironic one, into the writing of William Faulkner. So many of the forgotten literati of the Renaissance addressed these problems that theirs might be considered the majority opinion.

From their consensus, the Agrarians "seceded." The Agrarians were less pragmatic and more idealistic than Odum, who regarded their concern for the South as merely literary. The primary impetus for their activism, in fact, originated in philosophical and aesthetic concerns. Although they railed against Northern "abstraction," they were never so interested in the actual conditions of tenant farmers or mill workers as they were in the abstract evil of monopoly capitalism, in the *idea* of having an "organic" relation to the soil, or in the intellectual beauty of a "homogeneous" culture. Insofar as they surveyed the actual scene about them, they did so to deplore the growing evidence that the culture of the South was being diluted by Northern economic pressures; to condemn the displacement of a supposedly "agrarian" economic order by industrial capitalism; and to extol, by comparison, the halcyon virtues of a mythical Old South in which people lived in right relation with nature, with history, and with one another. They expressed these views, first, in a series of essays and biographies during the late twenties; then, definitively, in the symposium *I'll Take My Stand* in 1930; and later, with a gradually dissipating focus, in books, symposia, and articles throughout the thirties.[22]

The Agrarians exerted an influence not on the Farm Bureau or any New Deal agencies, but on other men and women of letters. The principal Agrarians—John Crowe Ransom, Allen Tate, Donald Davidson, Robert Penn Warren, Cleanth Brooks, John Gould Fletcher, Andrew Nelson Lytle—were poets, novelists, and critics first and sociologists, political scientists, and economists only secondarily and nonprofessionally. Agrarian ideology extended into their fiction and poetry and affected their critical standards, often fixing the terms of acceptance for new work—including Faulkner's.

In contrast to the liberals, the Agrarians were interested primarily in the literary ramifications of the issues they argued. Indeed, the first aim of their social criticism was to create an environment congenial to the creation of poetry. They became social critics because of literary frustrations. Liberal authors, by contrast, became novelists because of *social* frustrations; for them fiction was a meliorative instrument. Grace Lumpkin, Lillian Smith, and Hamilton Basso intended their novels to unfold specific problems of race, labor, and class relations that manifestly existed in the outside world. For conservatives, art was its own end. This divergence of purposes led naturally to a wide gap between the values and the standards of the two parties.

Perhaps the best way to define this gap is through the Agrarians' dislike for scientific method, upon which the Chapel Hill sociologists naturally relied. The Agrarians' distrust of abstraction stands as the foundation of their thought. The literary application of this posture went under several rubrics, among which the simplest was "poetry as a way of knowing." Poetry, in other words, is a more satisfactory and accurate form of knowledge than science, because it is more concrete. Through imagery and meter, it furnishes the detailed sensual experience that composes the flesh of "the world's body"—not just its statistical skeleton.[23] Conversely, the liberal aesthetic, although it was never formulated so explicitly as the conservative one, valued art not as a means of knowledge but as a means of action.

The language in which the Agrarians couched their doctrine of literature as knowledge was loaded with the same conservatism that filled their social and historical arguments. According to Ransom, this aesthetic knowledge happens when "we are able to contemplate *things as they are* in their rich and contingent materiality." According to Warren, the knowledge of a literary work is not the knowledge by "report" or the knowledge by "symptom" that science confers; it is rather "knowledge by form. No, knowledge *of* form."[24] "Things as they *are*"—such is the proper content of literature, not things as they *should* be; and this content is in itself a knowledge of *form*, concretely filled out. Poetry should replicate the ritualistic structures of traditional society. At the end of the knowledge that art brings comes an *acceptance* of the factual inevitabilities of human existence, against which no correction can succeed.

In 1935, John Crowe Ransom distinguished between novels he admired and novels he disliked according to the degree to which they displayed the "concrete formalism" he valued. He praised Faulkner as a truly "Southern" writer, whose work embodied "a sense, the opposite of revolutionary, of *society as a fixed order* which goes on though private persons err and suffer." He described in less flattering terms a rival tradition of the Southern novel: "The Liberal in fiction attacks the formal societies, which seem to rest on a cruel class distinction and to be conservative rather than progressive in principle; naturally he finds material to his hand in the Southern scene. His weapon is the case-history of the persecuted hero; it is satire, and caricature. Certainly the Liberal may make out his case, but he should argue it openly as Mr. Mencken does, and not under the form of fiction." In short, fiction should be reserved for more exclusive purposes, such as "knowledge of the conditions of life." As an art form, it should refer to society only through society's "formal" manifestations, not through response to political controversies or as the solution to a "problem." Writers to whom Ransom objected on these grounds included Erskine Caldwell, the early Ellen Glasgow, and T. S. Stribling.[25]

Thomas Sigismund Stribling's reputation provides a convenient example for discussing the dialectical reception of novelists during the Southern Renaissance, both because conservatives considered him representative enough of liberal practice to devote more than passing attention to him and because he offers an instructive contrast with the work and reputation of William Faulkner. Stribling lived most of his life (1881–1965) in south-central Tennessee and northern Alabama, the principal settings of his fiction. In a series of novels during the twenties, he satirized the Southern way of life. But his reputation, if any remains, rests on his novelistic trilogy about Lauderdale County, Alabama, a trilogy that follows the fortunes of the middle-class Vaiden family from just before the Civil War until 1931. These books—*The Forge* (1931), *The Store* (1932), and *Unfinished Cathedral* (1934)—achieved popular success, despite the crudity of Stribling's prose style, and *The Store* won a Pulitzer Prize. His later novels did not fare so well, however, and today he is relegated to scholarly neglect and popular oblivion.[26] The course of Faulkner's career was symmetrically opposite. Stribling's books probably deserve the neglect they have recently suffered, but worse writers have sustained critical interest for a longer time. The credit for his literary misfortune belongs partly to a bundle of negative reviews written by the Agrarians; and the present state of Stribling studies is a tribute to their abiding influence. Tate, Warren, Davidson, and Wade all disapproved of him strongly enough to commit their objections to print.[27]

In a twenty-page article in 1934, for example, Warren reduced Stribling's place in literature to "a Paragraph in the History of Critical Realism" and compared him invidiously with Faulkner. By "critical realism," he meant "an extension of the naturalistic premise: the naturalistic novelist took science as the source of his method and his philosophy." According to Warren, Stribling's novels fail "because he is infatuated with some system of abstractions. . . . His interest in the special persons and the special incidents of his stories is essentially an interest in illustration." In Stribling's novels, "[c]haracter appears as a long-hand for a social proposition. Event appears as a sort of allegory, a morality play of 'social forces.' The whole is a documentation in dramatic form of a social proposition which, presumably, the author wants to see realized in actuality." By contrast, Warren asserted, Faulkner was "too much of an artist" to allow his opinions about poverty and other public issues to contaminate his fiction. While Stribling regarded the novel as a "device for communication," Faulkner "and a considerable group of the younger Southern novelists" are "more conservative": they "conceive of the novel as *itself* the communication."[28]

Not everyone appreciated this difference. Among Stribling's defenders, Byrom Dickens published a response to Warren's negative essay, praising Stribling's trilogy as "one of the sanest pictures of the South to be presented by a Southern novelist." Dickens did not refute Warren's objections so much as demonstrate that they had no meaning for him. He admired the liberal's "realistic" handling of various "problems"—those of race and class in particular. And he threw Warren's propaganda charge back in his face: Stribling "offers no remedy, presents no solution for the evils portrayed. He merely presents characters and conditions as he sees them, glozing over nothing." The Agrarians themselves were the propagandists, "with their economic obscurantism and nostalgic yearnings for the past"; and Warren's disapproval of Stribling arose from political rather than artistic motives: "After all, that which seems to irk Mr. Warren most is Stribling's Liberalism; presumably Stribling would be a better novelist were he an Agrarian." In large measure, Dickens was right: the artistic differences between the liberals and the Agrarians were inextricable from their political differences. [29]

The liberals did not know so much about literature as the Agrarians, but they knew as well what they liked. They liked fiction that served as a "medium of regional criticism," in Howard Odum's words, "protesting against the older decadence and the current immaturity" of the South. They did not like what they perceived as a "determined reassertion of the validity of the legend of the Old South, an attempt to revive and fully restore the identification of that Old South with Cloud-Cuckoo Town, or at any rate to render it as a Theocritean idyl," which is how W. J. Cash described the work of the Agrarians. Cash parodied conservative fiction in a purported review of a new novel "of the Agrarian school," whose author he called "Mr. John Jacob Neanderthal." At about the same time, Thomas Wolfe incorporated a less facetious satire of the Agrarian movement into one of his manuscripts: "So the refined young gentlemen of the New Confederacy shook off their degrading shackles, caught the last cobwebs of illusion from their awakened vision, and retired haughtily into the South, to the academic security of a teaching appointment at one of the universities, from which they could issue in quarterly installments very small and very precious magazines which celebrated the advantages of an agrarian society." Wolfe's thinly fictionalized version of himself, George Webber, found these dilettantes "puzzling and astonishing." Having "derived from generations of mountain farmers who had struggled year by year to make a patch of corn grow in the hill erosions of a mountain flank," Webber rejected the opinion of "lily-handed intellectuals . . . that what he needed most of all was a return to the earthly and benevolent virtues of the society which had produced him."[30]

Wolfe's affected dirt-farmer resentment of the Agrarians' agricultural pretensions typifies the real differences that lay between the parties. The liberals' reformism often derived from a personal experience or family heritage of poverty. Howard Odum, for example, commuted to the Classics Department at the University of Mississippi on muleback from a nearby community where he taught school to earn tuition—a Labove without a Eula. W. J. Cash was a scion of South Carolina cotton-mill functionaries and North Carolina small farmers. Erskine Caldwell was the son of an itinerant Presbyterian minister whose origins resembled those of the Lesters and the Waldens. [31] For these children of the New South, "dwelling on the soil" meant hookworm and chopping cotton, and they welcomed the escape from drudgery that industry seemed to promise.

By contrast, the Agrarians derived from a remarkably uniform background of established, though modest, social advantage. [32] While they did not live so far from the realities of farm life as Thomas Wolfe would suggest, they did experience them vicariously. For example, John Crowe Ransom's claim to agricultural expertise rested partially on the fact that he "had a garden." [33] Generally lacking a family memory of subsistence economics themselves, they were nevertheless ready to prescribe "dwelling on the soil" for others. Between the liberals' pressure toward upward social mobility and the conservatives' refusal to recognize the tangible benefits of social change lay differences that reflected both their political sympathies and their literary intentions. Those differences also affected the way in which they received each other critically.

Faulkner's reputation, like Stribling's, was substantially shaped within the partisan atmosphere of the Southern dialogue. His place in the dialogue remains more ambiguous, however, because he was a writer of such comprehensive genius that he exerted a wide appeal within both parties. Each party praised him for different reasons, and each found fault with him on different grounds. [34]

W. J. Cash's opinion of Faulkner typified the generous liberal view of him during the thirties and forties. Cash admired him more than any other Southern novelist. But Cash's indifference to the aesthetic preoccupations of the Agrarians extended to his perception of Faulkner, which was essentially political. While he appreciated him as a *critic* of the South, he disapproved of what he felt to be Faulkner's reluctance to entertain "any consideration of social forces." Although he could, as he said, "dispose with the much touted performance of T. S. Stribling without too great a pang, on the plain and obvious ground that Stribling is more interested in his background than in his figures," nevertheless he asserted that the novelist's proper concern *should be* with his characters' position in "the social fabric and the social inheritance."[35] That Cash missed such a "background" in Faulkner testified to the wide difference between them.

Other liberals voiced similar reservations about Faulkner. For example, Paula Snelling, Lillian Smith's co-editor at the *North Georgia Review*, admitted that "the man has truly remarkable powers" but wondered whether he had yet put them to any constructive use. She accused him of being symptomatic rather than diagnostic of the ills that afflicted the South. She would have been more comfortable with problems that have solutions than with Faulkner's perpetual questions. She would prefer, she said, that Faulkner restrict himself to depicting characters for whom sociological categories were at least relevant: "If Faulkner were able to employ his tremendous talent toward showing to us depravity, greed, amorality as they exist in the hidden recesses of those beings who are sufficiently amenable to civilization's mould to function as respected units of our culture he would do unique service both to literature and to humanity. But he is lured by the bizarre, the decadent, the awe-ful as is a moth to a flame."[36] Admire him as it might, liberal thought on the whole was simply unprepared to assess Faulkner's achievement.

It was up to the conservatives, and specifically the Agrarians, to appreciate Faulkner and to explain their appreciation to everyone else. When his critical fortunes turned in the late thirties and early forties, the people who did most of the turning were men who had been associated with Agrarianism. By then their interest had shifted from social polemic back to literature, and Faulkner's reputation matured contemporaneously with the growth of the New Criticism they helped foster. As their influence spread, it carried with it the respectability of "Faulkner studies." Until recently, most Faulkner scholarship has followed the methodology inherent in the cognitive theory of literature proffered by Ransom.

According to the New Criticism of Tate, Warren, Ransom, and Brooks, the fundamental value of a literary work resides in the work itself, which is its own "ontology" rather than a "symptom" of some other reality. The proper study of an artwork, therefore, should concentrate not on its author, its historical context, or other external factors, but upon the work itself. It should focus on the "structural properties" of literature and should submit each work to formal analysis or "explication," paying special atten-

tion to image, symbol, theme, and narrative point of view. The subliminal political motives inherent in the methodology of Agrarian New
Criticism itself made it blind to the same motives when they appeared in a
work of art; politically inoffensive works were naturally selected for praise
as apolitical. Consequently, the canon of the New Criticism—as established in Brooks and Warren's *Understanding Fiction*, Tate and Gordon's
The House of Fiction, and the mass of academic criticism such texts inspired—came to reflect incidentally the political biases of its founders.
Whole categories of Southern writing were thus excluded: the romantic
formlessness of Wolfe, the "sociologism" of Caldwell, and the "disordered
liberalism" of Stribling. [37]

Faulkner's reputation flourished under the New Critical dispensation.
As early as 1935, John Crowe Ransom praised him as "the most exciting
figure in our contemporary literature just now."[38] Four years later, George
Marion O'Donnell's essay on "Faulkner's Mythology" initiated a long and
mutually beneficial symbiosis between the neglected author and the fledg-
ling apparatus of the New Criticism. O'Donnell was a second-generation
Agrarian, and his Faulkner essay participated in the Southern dialogue as
fully as did his essays on tenant farming a few years before.[39] O'Donnell
challenged the view of Paula Snelling, for one, that Faulkner was absorbed in irrational cruelty and nihilism. He was, instead, "really a traditional moralist, in the best sense." The principle unifying his work was
"the Southern social-economic-ethical tradition which Mr. Faulkner possesses naturally, as a part of his sensibility"—in other words, the principle
of Agrarianism. O'Donnell conceded that Faulkner inhabited a reconstructed South: "All around him the antitraditional forces are at work";
consequently, his novels embody "a series of related myths (or aspects of a
single myth) built around the conflict between traditionalism and the antitraditional world in which it is immersed." Accordingly, O'Donnell
divided Faulkner's world between "two kinds of characters; they are Sartorises or Snopeses, whatever the family names may be. And in the spiritual geography of Mr. Faulkner's work there are two worlds: the Sartoris
world and the Snopes world." The conflict between them is "universal"—
fundamentally, a "struggle between humanism and naturalism."[40]

The conflict may be universal; but it is also local. In fact, it is precisely
the Southern dialogue. The effect, if not the intention, of O'Donnell's
essay was to make a partisan claim for the affinity of Faulkner's work with
Agrarian ideology. O'Donnell connected Faulkner unambiguously with

the conservative side of the dialogue, both politically and artistically. His assessment was persuasive enough to fuel hundreds of concordant thematic exegeses of Faulkner's work. Malcolm Cowley relied heavily on O'Donnell's essay in his "Introduction" to the *Portable Faulkner* in 1946. During the same year, Robert Penn Warren—though more cautiously than O'Donnell—restated his own assertion that Faulkner was a traditionalist.[41]

Like O'Donnell, Warren was writing about himself as much as about Faulkner. This Warren had mellowed from the young polemicist who wrote "The Briar Patch" for *I'll Take My Stand*; but he was basically the same critic who, in 1966, could agree with Norman Podhoretz that "Faulkner is an a-political writer. It is really strange that in his vast panorama of society in a state where politics is the blood, bone, sinew, and passion of life, and the most popular sport, Faulkner has almost entirely omitted, not only a treatment of the subject, but references to it."[42] That Warren could see Faulkner as apolitical and, at the same time, place him squarely within the dialogue between the "old order" and the "new order" is a significant contradiction. Warren has been a "political" novelist himself; but he must have known that a writer need not treat expressly political figures and political events (Huey Long or the Black Patch Tobacco War) to be political. By condemning the naïveté of Faulkner's quasi-political exercises in *A Fable* and *Intruder in the Dust*, he avoided having to account for the less obvious but far more accomplished treatment of politics at the very heart of *The Hamlet*. By "a-political," Warren really meant "political in the right way"; and it was because Faulkner was political (as well as artistic) in the right way—according to Warren's lights—that he could fit into *Understanding Fiction*, whereas Stribling, Caldwell, and even Wolfe clearly could not. Warren was as blind to the political Faulkner as Byrom Dickens had been to the political Stribling: after all, one's political ally is not a politician but a statesman. The New Criticism has always discouraged discussion of the political context of art, without recognizing that an emphasis on form can be politically expressive in itself.[43]

Thanks to the New Criticism, Faulkner's works have been thoroughly ground in the mills of formal analysis. *The Hamlet* has been rendered coherent. The emphasis properly has been placed on the works themselves, as they are; comparatively little attention has been paid the subordinate questions of how and why Faulkner wrote them in the peculiar way he did. This neglect is due substantially to the fact that Faulkner's works were first perceived, and were most persuasively explicated, within the context of the Southern literary dialogue. But the dialogue is important not only as the context in which he was initially received and in which his critical identity was largely established. It also provided the working environment in which he composed his fiction and from which, however unwillingly, he drew some of his ideas. His response to that context was neither simple nor one-sided: the dialogue occurred within him as well as around him. *The Hamlet* expresses both—no, more than two—of his inner voices.

Faulkner and Class Mobility

The "Southern dialogue" shaped literary documents as well as the discourse about them. When an author created a character who moves from farm to factory, for example, he was participating in the dialogue, whether consciously or unconsciously. When Byron Bunch goes to work in a sawmill in *Light in August* (1932); when Grace Lumpkin's mountain people move to her fictionalized version of Gastonia, North Carolina, in *To Make My Bread* (1932) and Will Thompson moves to Caldwell's "Scottsville," South Carolina, in *God's Little Acre* (1933) to work in textile mills; when Otho Mortimer returns to sharecropping in Tennessee after three years in a Detroit automobile factory in Caroline Gordon's *The Garden of Adonis* (1937); when Texas sharecropper Sam Tucker narrowly escapes being forced off the land and into a factory in George Sessions Perry's *Hold Autumn in Your Hand* (1941); when James Agee drives George Gudger, one of the family heads of *Let Us Now Praise Famous Men* (1941), to the sawmill where he earns a dollar and a quarter a day[44]—when similar events occupy crucial positions throughout the pages of Southern Renaissance fiction, the image of the farmer in the factory becomes more than merely topical. It must have been emotionally powerful. When frequent repetition of the image coincides with a simultaneous controversy at the level of public debate, in which ideologues exchanged verbal blows over "the man from the farm [going] in the factory door,"[45] the fact becomes obvious that industrialization commanded imaginative as well as political attention.

Seemingly trivial narrative elements can thus gain significance from the context of the dialogue in which they participated. They can become rhetorical despite their authors' intentions. When Uncle Buck and Uncle Buddy institute a cooperative land-distribution system for the slaves and poor whites of their neighborhood, their action gains meaning from the glut of proposals for land distribution that filled the thirties.[46] When Faulkner's most rapacious and immoral character is Flem Snopes, that name gains meaning from the name of John Scopes, whose "Monkey Trial" in 1925 was one of the catalysts that brought the dialogue to expression. When Lucas Beauchamp declines "to use improved implements, refusing to let a tractor so much as cross [his] land" (GDM, 116), his prejudice invites juxtaposition with H. C. Nixon's *Forty Acres and Steel Mules*, which espoused the industrial improvement of agriculture.[47] When Gavin Stevens praises a literary magazine sponsored by Governor Huey Long as "one of the best . . . anywhere" (KG, 229), his opinion locates him within the dialogue: Long's magazine was the conservative *Southern Review,* and its editors included Brooks and Warren. Such apparently minor details can provide useful clues toward reconstructing the forces that worked on Faulkner's imagination during the composition of his books.

One of the perennial issues in the Southern dialogue, and a ubiquitous preoccupation of its imaginative literature, was vertical mobility in Southern society, which is also the central concern of Faulkner's core-plot for *The Hamlet.* R. W. B. Lewis's nineteenth-century dialogue in New England was expressed primarily in theological terms—innocence, sin, evil, hope, redemption. The dialogue that accompanied the Southern Renaissance emphasized political and economic terms instead. One principal issue was the question of class structure. Some of the sociologists, though not the Odumites,[48] set about anatomizing class and caste in communities they called "Southerntown" or "Cottonville," with the purpose of diagnosing social disorders. The Agrarians and their allies attributed those disorders to outside forces such as "Northern industrialism." Asserting the "organic unity" of the ideal agrarian society about which they dreamed, they denied the applicability of the class concept to a Southern model.

Agrarians generally referred to the word "class" only to disprove its usefulness for talking about the South. The authors of *I'll Take My Stand* embraced the old idea of cultural "homogeneity," according to which no classes existed, because the people who would belong to them had no awareness of their membership in separate groups. They all derived from the same stock; they believed in the same values; they shared the same mores; as often as not, they were one another's in-laws or cousins. Ransom called the social order of the Old South "loosely graduated," "not fixed as in Europe. . . . It was a kindly society, yet a realistic one; for it was a failure if it could not be said that people were for the most part in their right places."[49] Southern society was "not fixed," yet most people were "in their right places"; this contradiction lies at the heart of the Agrarian perception of society. No hierarchy existed, but if it did it was all right because it was just. Society was homogeneous because the bonds among the classes were greater than the differences. Even if they were natural economic enemies, Edd Parks wrote in 1938, "the small farmer and the large planter, the yeoman and the slaveholder, were eventually forced into the same position because their philosophies possessed definite elements of kinship, and were at complete variance with the philosophy of industrialism."[50]

John Wade simply attributed the consensus to Southern hospitality and to the humanism he associated with the soil: "in the South, because it was a sparsely settled, farming region, people in the various classes, white and black, knew one another personally, intimately. Most often, as a result— one can risk saying so—they had a sort of affection for one another; but even if they had instead a sort of hatred, no one sinned so pointedly as to mistake people for mechanisms." In the North, Wade wrote, "industrialism" has turned people into "specialists" unable to conceive of one another except as abstractions. Marxism might, then, address its class analyses to Paterson, New Jersey, or Lowell, Massachusetts, but not to Nashville, Tennessee, or Marshallville, Georgia. There, the "classes" sat at the same Christmas table and told stories that everybody could enjoy together.[51]

To talk about class unity is one thing; to watch it disintegrate is another. In the face of the "redneck revolt" and other manifestations of class animosity, the Agrarians retreated to the assertion that these signs of heterogeneity had simply followed industry out of the mechanical North. Meanwhile, liberal sociologists and anthropologists were amassing evidence that the social divisions of the South were indigenous. The studies of John Dollard, Hortense Powdermaker, Gunnar Myrdal, and others testified to a deep stratification of Southern society along class lines, within both racial groups. In "Southerntown," "Cottonville," and "Old City," these researchers found an intensely hierarchical society, which—by "interview-observation" and "life-history" techniques—they analyzed into at least three class divisions. Among these groups great differences prevailed, not only in living conditions and behavioral patterns but also in value systems and personality types.[52]

To refute the sociological studies, the Agrarians were sometimes forced to rely on evasions. In a review of Dollard's book, for example, Lyle Lanier simply rejected the applicability of "scientific knowledge" to social complexities. He submitted Dollard's "general method" to a "logical analysis" and found it totally subjective and *un*scientific. He needed only to cite Dollard's admission that "he had the typical sectional bias of the Northerner" in order to invalidate Dollard's whole project. Insofar as he refuted Dollard's specific observations, furthermore, he attended not to class but to racial caste.[53]

Donald Davidson, however, found what he called "The Class Approach to Southern Problems" obnoxious enough to address it directly in an essay that was provoked by C. Vann Woodward's favorable review of *Forty Acres and Steel Mules*, by H. C. Nixon, an apostate Agrarian. Davidson objected to Woodward's approval of Nixon's "class approach," as opposed to the "sectional approach" Nixon had once espoused: "He likes Mr. Nixon's book because it holds that the exploitation of the South as a colonial dependency of the North is now less important than the exploitation of three overlapping classes: farmers, laborers, Negroes." Against Woodward's theory that Southern history has shifted "from an emphasis on section-consciousness to an emphasis on class-consciousness," Davidson advanced the democratic ideals of "Jeffersonian" agrarianism, which he said the South more than other sections had converted into fact. He illustrated his argument with the subject of a Woodward biography: "Distinctions in Tom Watson's day were not very sharp, and were not based on economics. Family, or perhaps clan, mattered; not 'class.'" Agrarianism, Davidson maintained, "rejects the 'class approach' on principle," for "Jeffersonian politics and economics planted deeply in America," or at least in the South, "a conception of what the Marxians claim to be striving for—the so-called 'classless society.'"[54]

Davidson saved for the end of his essay an observation that he seemed to add only for good measure, but which Dollard might have argued was the real ground of his objection. The difficulty of considering the "class approach" is "enormously increased," he said, if it "means, as it generally seems to mean nowadays, the obliteration of the color line in the South. Southern experience shows that the introduction of the race issue into general problems inevitably confuses all issues, postpones the solution of general problems, and renders any solution of the Negro problem more difficult than ever." He added that "[t]his alone is a solid and sufficient reason for the traditional Southern insistence that the Negro be put in a separate category and that his problems be treated separately."[55]

Davidson's final argument anticipated one of W. J. Cash's themes in *The Mind of the South*, which appeared two years later in 1941. Cash maintained that, throughout Southern history, racism has discouraged class consciousness. In the "Southern mind," white solidarity has been so necessary for subduing the Negro threat that disputation within the caste has been effectively suppressed. Furthermore, whatever emotional needs a class identity ordinarily fulfills have been more amply satisfied by a compensatory racial identity. In effect, Cash's insight mediated between the perception of the anthropologists, who saw class differentials in the behavior, the ideology, and even the personality of each citizen of "Southerntown," and the Agrarians, who saw the Southern community as "homogeneous." Although objectively the South may be highly stratified, it is also validly perceived as fluid and democratic by many of its inhabitants. Thus the "mind of the South" has simultaneously and illogically "been nearly innocent of the notion of class in any rigid and complete sense" *and* has held to "the conviction that God . . . called one man to be rich and master, another to be poor and servant, and that men did well to accept what had been given them, instead of trusting to their own strength and stirring up strife."[56] Not only does the Southern class system not exist; it is ordained by divine providence. Without the consciousness of class affiliation and thus without recourse to collective action, saddled with the weight of God's judgment and ever ready to sublimate class ambition into caste hostility, the lower-class Southerner, according to Cash's theory, has had neither the opportunity nor the motive to seek to improve his status. The class system of the South has perpetuated itself simply by refusing to be recognized.

The focus of the dialogue about social mobility was the group of people at the lowest level of society, the sharecroppers and tenant farmers whose upward ascent Faulkner personified in the Snopeses. Their plight caught the attention of the Chapel Hill sociologists especially, who directed many practical proposals toward improving the sharecroppers' lot. Conversely, the Agrarians defended the ideals of subsistence farming, from which the tenant system, they said, was merely an unfortunate deviation. Sharecropping attracted the interest of many novelists and journalists, whose treatment of it ranged from shocked outrage to complacency, from the intense involvement of Steinbeck and Agee to the detachment of John Crowe Ransom, formulating his "Aesthetic of Regionalism" as he watched poor farmers through the window of his passing railroad compartment.[57] An extreme expression of the latter attitude appeared in an article on "The Tenant Farmer in the South" by Richmond Croom Beatty and Faulkner's mythographer George Marion O'Donnell, in which they momentarily dispensed with the fiction of class harmony and exposed a different view of the lower orders:

> . . . there exists one class of people which the sociologists—because of their major premise: faith in universal human improvement—have never been able to understand. This is the class sometimes referred to as the "po' whites." These people are poor indeed, and many of them are tenant-farmers. They live, as if by choice, in squalor and indolence. Before the sterner varieties of religion went out of fashion, it was customary to explain them by saying that they were depraved. We believe that, if Sociology is to mature, it must come first to the realization that this loosely defined but easily recognizable class is, generally, beyond salvation. The sociologists of the future, in other words, will have to make their truce with the Problem of Evil—as every other man has had to do, and every science, and every art.
>
> What would probably happen with respect to this class, if sent in numbers to the model village [proposed by W. T. Couch], would be that the homes in such villages would, in many cases be burned piecemeal by the "peasants" themselves for firewood, the rotating gardens by midsummer would be weed-ridden, the radios torn to pieces (no frightful loss), the bookcases tobacco-spattered, and the schoolhouse befouled.[58]

Thus, fundamentally, the economic terminology of the Southern dialogue disguised the same theological issues that exercised the participants in Lewis's nineteenth-century New England dialogue.

The fear of what would happen when the "po' whites" entered the village also controlled the core-plot of Faulkner's Snopes trilogy. *The Hamlet* opens with the very image Beatty and O'Donnell used to ridicule the idea of lower-class improvement: the dismantling of a home by a "depraved" peasantry (HAM, 3–4). This opening epitomizes the whole trilogy, for when Flem Snopes enters Jefferson he consumes that "model village" just as thoroughly as the firewood vandals have consumed the Old Frenchman place. Both the Beatty-O'Donnell essay and the Faulkner trilogy express deep-seated anxieties about the egalitarian forces at work in the South during the first half of the twentieth century.

Faulkner grew up during the so-called "rise of the rednecks," when poor-white electorates throughout the South transferred political power from aristocratic to plebeian hands. In Mississippi, where the populist trend lasted longer than anywhere else, the first decades of the century saw a shift in leadership from the gentlemanly, oratorical figures of traditional Southern politics to the iconoclastic, demagogic "New Men" who wore galluses and cultivated the idiom of the farmer's market—men like James K. Vardaman and Theodore G. ("The Man") Bilbo. Lafayette County boasted its full share of New Men, including one who succeeded Bilbo as governor. This was Lee M. Russell, a self-made lawyer from a poor farm family in a place called Dallas, a hamlet like Frenchman's Bend in the red-clay hills of its county's southeastern corner. The formative event in Russell's life occurred at the University of Mississippi, when the college fraternity to which he aspired (whose members were the sons of professional and plantation families) blackballed him and then doused him with water from a third-floor window. Like Thomas Sutpen, rejected from the front door of the "Big House," Russell set about avenging his pride. Eventually he succeeded in persuading the university's board of trustees to outlaw fraternities at "Ole Miss" (BL, 81).

William Faulkner was familiar with Russell. One of the trustees he persuaded was the author's grandfather, J. W. T. Falkner, Sr., who was so impressed by the young man that he took him into his law firm as a third partner with himself and his son, J. W. T. Falkner, Jr. Faulkner observed Russell's success in gaining a political following among the impoverished and inarticulate farmers out in the county, who saw in him a fellow redneck who had risen despite his—and their—handicaps. Faulkner must have taken to heart the results of the Election of 1912: Vardaman won a U.S. Senate seat; Russell won a state senate seat; the supervisory offices for a majority of the Lafayette County beats, or precincts, went to representatives of the small farmer and the sharecropper—men named Bundren, Lovelady, Carothers, and Joe Parks; but his uncle, Falkner, Jr., who headed a Vardaman club that year, was defeated two-to-one in a race for county attorney. Eight years later the same uncle managed Russell's gubernatorial campaign in Lafayette County. The cost of the Falkners' collaboration with the rising rednecks would soon become increasingly apparent, and that cost made an impression on the incipient writer (BL, 81–82, 116, 143–45, 244).

In 1920, Joe Parks, whom Faulkner's neighbors have identified as the main prototype for Flem Snopes, led some like-minded opportunists in engineering the forced retirement of Faulkner's grandfather from his bank presidency, to advance a fraudulent speculation in nonexistent oil. Parks assumed the bank presidency during the very month when he moved his family in from the country to occupy the house in which Faulkner had grown up and which Parks had bought when Faulkner's father took a minor administrative job at the university (BL, 257–59). Soon afterward, when Parks's colleague in upward mobility, Governor Russell, was shaking up the university to eradicate the last vestiges of the fraternities, one of those vestiges was William Faulkner, who resigned from the school (BL, 284–88). A decade later Russell's sometime ally, Bilbo, succeeded in carrying these educational reforms even further. The highest achievement of Bilbo's scandal-ridden second administration was to incorporate the state universities into his patronage system by firing dozens of teachers and administrators in 1930. One of the victims was Faulkner's father (BL, 661–62, 674).

Such was Faulkner's exposure to "reform" politics. Had Faulkner read Beatty and O'Donnell's essay in 1935, he might have disapproved of their dogmatic acerbity, but he would probably have agreed with their thesis. Years later, in 1953, when he was beginning to sound like a liberal on the question of race relations, he could still criticize *The Grapes of Wrath* on the ground "that the idea that man was improvable, that society could be improved, was a fallacy that softened Steinbeck's view and made him a sentimental liberal" (BL, 1470).

The Hamlet was published the year after *The Grapes of Wrath*. Both books treat the efforts of sharecropper families to improve their living conditions. Paradoxically, the Snopeses succeed in "improving" themselves as grandly as Lee Russell or Joe Parks did, while the Joads only *endure* their destitution. Faulkner admired the unthreatening, sedentary virtues of "endurance" as much as Steinbeck, and he distributed them sympathetically throughout the peasantry of his fiction. As long as the poor stayed in their place, as the Joads did *despite* themselves, they earned his deep respect; when they exchanged virtuous endurance for unscrupulous prosperity, however—resorting to bank coups, demagoguery, and shady business dealings and displacing the Falkner family from its rung on the social ladder in the process—they became Snopeses. The poor we may always have with us, Faulkner might have said, but the discontented poor we have with us to a fault.

Out of this nexus, literature evolved. *The Hamlet* was born in Faulkner's observation of local and state politics during his adolescence and young manhood. While his own family underwent a series of social demotions, the New Men from the hinterlands were filling the centers of power and wealth, with results that were sometimes disastrous, sometimes ridiculous. The ideas that evolved into the Snopes narrative were first rehearsed between Faulkner and his literary mentor, Phil Stone, the trilogy's dedicatee. Both young men were in positions to feel threatened. Even before World War I, when Faulkner was yet in his teens, they discussed together the process of democratic usurpation they saw happening around them. On long walks into the countryside then and later, they surveyed the cultural damage and formulated a legendry to record their own experience of it. According to Blotner, Stone did most of the talking: "He knew the stories of country people who were painfully pulling themselves up by their bootstraps. . . . For some of these strivers, the two privileged young men had a kind of admiration. Others among the 'rednecks' seemed monsters of acquisitiveness and boorishness. For them they felt contempt and a kind of wonder" (BL, 173, 566n). To alleviate the discomfort this social transformation caused them, they did not react with angry indignation (as some of the Agrarians did) or with insults (as Beatty and O'Donnell did). Rather, they found excuses to laugh, and those excuses engendered *The Hamlet*.

The Snopes material, as it was conceived during these walks and as it grew over the next two decades, derived from Faulkner's experience of the Mississippi *res publica*. The various episodes of Snopes chicanery originated in incidents in the public history of lower-class hegemony—incidents that Faulkner witnessed or heard about. For example, John Faulkner asserted that his older brother had come upon the germ of "Spotted Horses" while helping their uncle, J. W. T. Falkner, Jr., campaign for election to a district judgeship (MBB, 158–59). More than any other of Faulkner's books before *Intruder in the Dust, The Hamlet* seems to capture public rather than private experience, functioning more clearly on a social than on a personal level of expression. Its core-plot derived strictly from public events—political campaigns, business transactions, crimes of calculation rather than of passion. Crimes of passion did enter the book, but only late in its evolution. The original mode of the book was satire, which was directed at the rising New Men.

Despite his vantage point of a threatened, *déclassé* aristocrat, however, Faulkner viewed his subject with an ambiguous sympathy that complicated his vision and diluted his satire. The events of *The Hamlet* may be communal, but so was Faulkner's pastoral personality; and the "rise of the rednecks" consequently had a private meaning for Faulkner as well. He admired the Mississippi peasantry very much, and he understood well why they might struggle to rise from poverty and ignorance. But he abhorred the actual results of their struggle. He sympathized fully, even identified, with them when they were subservient to the soil; but, if they succeeded in entering the middle class, they became Snopeses. This ambivalence toward the "plain folk" of Yoknapatawpha begot the emotional and stylistic complexity of *The Hamlet*.

The Hamlet is a product of the pastoral gaze turned by cultured intellectuals upon their soil-stained neighbors which animated dozens of works during the Southern Renaissance. That scrutiny might, in fact, be called the characteristic posture of the whole literary movement. In *The Hamlet*, Faulkner's pastoral attention is directed primarily at the gross effects of upward mobility: at Bilbo's governmental abuses, at Joe Parks's manipulation of the Oxford business community, at the general triumph of a vulgar ethic over the genteel one. Consequently, the dominant emotion of the book, from which it nevertheless frequently departs, is a blend of contempt and amusement expressing itself in ridicule; the central object of that ridicule is the behavior associated with redneck ascendancy. Faulkner's central target, Flem Snopes, stands for all those New Men who pushed their way out of the dirt and into the corridors of power. Around that bull's-eye are secondary, easier targets: I. O., Wesley, Lump, Montgomery Ward, Clarence, Byron, Virgil, and other Snopeses. Around them all, and serving as their background, are a mass of farmers and croppers who lack the gumption or the "sourness" or the ambition to improve their status by any available means—people who display the virtues of "endurance." Yet these are also the people, according to Gavin Stevens in *The Town*, who constitute Flem's "one tool, weapon, implement—that nethermost stratum of unfutured, barely solvent one-bale tenant farmers which pervaded, covered thinly the whole county" (TN, 280). *The Hamlet* is emotionally complex because these people (the "Peasants" of Faulkner's original title, for whom he felt a deep, pastoral sympathy; and the Snopeses who arose from among them and gained power through them, for whom he felt a horrified repulsion) were in sociological fact identical.

More than in any other Faulkner novel before *Intruder in the Dust*, *The Hamlet* achieves its meaning in the context of the Southern dialogue. Its defining imagery articulates communal experience. When Mink and Ike Snopes both reject money—money given Mink by his wife, who earned it irreputably, and given Ike by Jack Houston as a bribe to protect his cow—the gesture seems to express Faulkner's own ambivalence about acquiring money in ways that compromised his art and his integrity. [59] But the image also has a public dimension. Certainly, the money that Ratliff unearths with Armstid and Bookwright at the Old Frenchman's place is significant in relation to the contemporary debate. Through Flem's guile and Ratliff's greed, Faulkner turned that property into a perfect figure for the metamorphosis of the land from fertility to profitability, from subsistence farming to cash farming, which Agrarians opposed as an abuse and which liberals supported as a reform. [60] The buried treasure is a money crop of the most direct—and most specious—kind. Faulkner employed it again in *Go Down, Moses*, to similarly comic effect, and other writers used the same image (Erskine Caldwell in *God's Little Acre*, for example) with an equal allusiveness to the public debate about land and money.

The closing image of the book contains a literal reminder of the public arguments about sharecropper mobility: when Flem, on his way into Jefferson, utters the last line of the volume—"Come up," as if to command the fulfillment of his ambitions by fiat—he places himself in the company of a wide assortment of other Southern literary characters of the thirties, all trying in various ways to "come up" themselves. He also places himself in an old tradition of Southern literature, in the context of which much of *The Hamlet's* confusion becomes clear.

Faulkner and Southwestern Humor

An important precedent for the Agrarians' fear of class mobility and an essential source of Faulkner's narrative style in *The Hamlet* is Southwestern humor, the comic literature associated with the Southern frontier in the early nineteenth century. Scholars[61] have traced Flem Snopes's literary ancestry back to A. B. Longstreet's Ransy Sniffle, to Johnson J. Hooper's Simon Suggs, and to George Washington Harris's Sut Lovingood. They have demonstrated the kinship of subject between *The Hamlet* and the Southwestern sketches, and they have compared Faulkner's hyperbolic imagery to that of the antebellum authors. But they have mostly emphasized sources and influences rather than the cultural forces that led Faulkner to produce Southwestern effects many decades after Southwestern humor had declined as a literary movement.

Kenneth Lynn, in a controversial book, has traced the origins of the genre back into the eighteenth century. The first Southwestern humorist of accomplishment, in Lynn's estimation, was William Byrd II, whose *History of the Dividing Line* (written in the 1720s but unpublished until 1841) inaugurated a tradition of invidious comparison between upper-class (Virginian) and lower-class (North Carolinian) behavior. Until the time of Mark Twain, according to Lynn's thesis, works of Southwestern humor were almost invariably critical representations by genteel authors of an illiterate, vulgar populace they scorned and feared. Except for George Washington Harris, the best-known Southwestern humorists of the thirty years before the Civil War (Longstreet, Thompson, Kennedy, Noland, Pike, Cobb, Thorpe, Baldwin, Hooper, even Davy Crockett in part) were uniformly men of property and position, conservative in literary taste and identifiable "either with the aristocratic faction in state politics, or with the banker-oriented Whig party in national politics, or with both." Threatened by the egalitarian energies of Jacksonian Democracy, the Whigs stood for stability, moderation, and reason, and they undertook to "fight against economic and social mobility by means of ideas." Concordantly, "the literary hero developed by the Southwestern humorists was a Self-controlled Gentleman—the very model of Whiggery's ideals" and "the American cousin of Addison's Man of Reason." Such a figure, according to Lynn, appears as either the narrator or a vocal observer in virtually all the sketches of Southwestern humor before the war. This gentleman's moderation and correct prose stand as cultural norms. The humorists deployed these norms through the device of the "frame," whereby the literate narrator's voice encloses and controls the voices of vernacular speakers: "For Longstreet and his successors found that the frame was a convenient way of keeping their first-person narrators outside and above the comic action, thereby drawing a *cordon sanitaire*, so to speak, between the morally irreproachable Gentleman and the tainted life he described."[62]

A typical Southwestern sketch such as Longstreet's "The Fight" opens in the measured prose of an eighteenth-century essay, then introduces a scene of grotesque provincial violence conveyed in the substandard language of the backwoods, and closes with a reflection that, "[t]hanks to the Christian religion, to schools, colleges, and benevolent associations, such scenes of barbarism and cruelty as that which I have been just describing are now of rare occurrence."[63] Thus the author could portray his social values without having to declare them explicitly. This formula, in Lynn's version, prevailed until Twain opened up the frame and allowed the vernacular content to tell itself without the mediation of a genteel commentary. *Huckleberry Finn*, because it was democratic, marked both the apotheosis and the obsolescence of the Southwestern tradition.

Lynn exaggerates his argument for the Whiggishness of Southwestern humor.[64] A more accurate statement of the case might be that Southwestern humor provided a literary forum for the resolution of tensions between folk culture and official culture, between oral experience and literary experience, and that it accommodated partisan expression by either side (though in its earliest manifestations the genteel "party" predominated). It was, in short, an instrument of "dialogue"—often within a single author. In its classical utterances from Byrd to Longstreet to Twain, Southwestern humor has been one of the most direct literary results of the "pastoral gaze" that has frequently occupied the vision of American writers. It has provided a sensitive gauge of American society's perception of and feelings about the "nethermost stratum" (TN, 280) within it. Although it has disappeared as a literary movement, the "nethermost stratum" it depicted remains, and tensions remain between that and other segments of society. Consequently, the strategies and structures of Southwestern humor continue to furnish means for articulating such tensions.

The arena in which the opposed forces in Southwestern humor contended was linguistic. For example, "Georgia Theatrics," the first sketch in Longstreet's *Georgia Scenes*, begins in the language of genteel, professional discourse and encloses within its "frame" the language of rural, uneducated, poor-white Georgia. The contrast between the two idioms is more than decorative: it constitutes the essential business of the piece:

If my memory fail me not, the 10th of June, 1809 found me, at about 11 o'clock in the forenoon, ascending a long and gentle slope in what was called "The Dark Corner" of Lincoln. I believe it took its name from the moral darkness which reigned over that portion of the county at the time of which I am speaking.

. . . .

"You kin, kin you?"

"Yes, I kin, and am able to do it! Boo-oo-oo! Oh, wake snakes, and walk your chalks! Brimstone and——fire! Don't hold me, Nick Stoval! The fight's made up, and let's go at it. ——my soul if I don't jump down his throat, and gallop every chitterling out of him before you can say 'quit!' "65

The linguistic juxtaposition points to an implicit moral contrast. The narrator's patient rationality acts as an obvious antidote to the barbaric yawp of the yokel whose hallucinatory kick-and-gouge fight with himself the narrator has overheard. According to Lynn, "Georgia Theatrics" contains a political allegory, which was recognized by conservatives at the time of its publication in 1835 as a parable of what they regarded as Andrew Jackson's reckless and ridiculous assault on Nicholas Biddle's National Bank. Longstreet intended to demonstrate the dangers of Jacksonian Democracy by dramatizing the moral superiority of the narrator's orderliness and elegance.66 The same moral perspective controlled, though often more ambiguously, the narrative strategies of Hooper, Thorpe, and most of the contributors to William Trotter Porter's *Spirit of the Times*. The same juxtaposition of idioms (of "the English" and "the Georgia language," in Longstreet's words)67 is what defines their work as Southwestern. Thus, Southwestern humor is a divided form, which came into existence because of a divided society. Contrary to Charlotte Renner's suggestion that in *The Hamlet* "Yoknapatawpha County is about to lose its oral tradition and hence its coherence,"68 the particular "oral" tradition Faulkner found most useful was divided from the beginning.

When Mark Twain came to use the same device, however, he turned it inside out. "[I]n literary terms," Lynn says, "the 'Jumping Frog' marks a historic reversal. The narrator, it turns out, is telling a joke on himself, not on the Clown. In the 'Jumping Frog,' it is the vernacular, not the polite style, which 'teaches the lesson.' "69 Thus, the linguistic conflict in the Southwestern frame tale could be applied to the advantage of either party or even to a nonpartisan rehearsal of the conflict, depending on what ventriloquist was throwing his voice. Like Empson's double plot, the frame-tale device is a neutral instrument for the articulation of all kinds of ideas and feelings about social class. Faulkner's *Hamlet* demonstrates just how subtle this articulation can become and just how complex can be the feelings. This complexity determined the corresponding complexity of the book as it finally appeared.

The narrative juxtaposition of vernacular and literary voices might be called "linguistic pastoral."[70] This discontinuity, invaluable to the critical representation of a divided community, is the chief legacy of Southwestern humor, which is in turn Faulkner's most vital inheritance from the Southern literature of the past. By extension, the device also aids in the resolution of two incongruent realms of experience: the routine, concrete, vernacular experience of everyday life and the more abstract experience of intellectual concepts, usually derived from books and sometimes relevant to the other realm but usually divorced from it. With Faulkner, as with most Southerners, ordinary observation took in a group of people whose experience seemed totally *un*sophisticated. At the same time, he was fluent in the languages of artistic, legal, military, and sporting establishments with which those people were completely unfamiliar. Between these two realms (that of "Mr. Faulkner" and that of Ernest Trueblood) only a tenuous imaginative commerce was possible. The Southwestern device provided a means of violently yoking them together.

Ike's Cow

Southwestern humor happens to be the most direct and most consistent American manifestation of "linguistic pastoral," but of course it is not the only example of it. Part of Faulkner's literary heritage was an English tradition of the novel that included a developing recourse to "linguistic pastoral." Raymond Williams's treatment of the pastoral novel in Britain has a general bearing on Faulkner as well:

> A knowable community can be, as in Jane Austen, socially selected; what it then lacks in full social reference it gains in an available unity of language in all its main uses. But we have only to read a George Eliot novel to see the difficulty of the coexistence, within one form, of an analytically conscious observer of conduct with a developed analytic vocabulary, and of people represented as living and speaking in mainly customary ways. . . . There is a

new kind of break in the texture of the novel, an evident failure of continuity between the necessary language of the novelist and the recorded language of many of the characters.[71]

In a way this "failure of continuity," which has been one of the great resources of the novel at least since George Eliot's time, is what *The Hamlet* is all about. Few novels have so violently embodied the social discontinuity Williams describes. The book literally fits Richard Poirier's definition of the novel form as "a medley of voices competing for attention, each with its social or psychological or theological support," and all "competing for predominance within a structure which is at the same time urgently working toward order and harmony." Out of this parliament of idioms the meaning of *The Hamlet* legislates itself. Its two principal voices are those of Ratliff and the omniscient narrator, close relatives of "Mr. Faulkner" and Ernest V. Trueblood. But Ratliff's vernacular voice is only the most voluble among many vulgar organs that are heard in the novel. I. O. Snopes's parody of erudition and Ratliff's parody of I. O. are among the wittiest of the others. Likewise, the omniscient narrator is subject to unpredictable vocal changes from page to page. The texture of even the purely "written" sections of the book is unstable, varying from the discursive exposition of the book's opening to the gorgeous euphuism of Ike's bovine idyll. Few uninterrupted stretches of prose occur in any one voice; many pages contain several radically different ones. The resulting polyphony is both delicate and robust; it both captivates aesthetically and convinces sociologically. As Poirier says of Norman Mailer, another writer given to rhetorical extravagance, Faulkner's "engagements with language" are political as well as literary: "they are a way of discovering how to hold together elements that perhaps by nature would tend to destroy one another, both in a political and in a literary structure."[72]

Furthermore, all the voices are contained within Faulkner himself. Like his character Gavin Stevens, he was someone "who could discuss Einstein with college professors and who spent whole afternoons among the squatting men against the walls of country stores, talking to them in their idiom" (KG, 16). But Faulkner, who did more listening than talking to both such groups, was able to accommodate more than just two patterns and to impose some kind of order upon their multiple interferences with one another. Since they all dwelt within him, *The Hamlet* expresses internal tensions among antagonistic components of his identity, as well as the social conflict that accompanied the "rise of the rednecks." Most of his adult life, as we have seen, he performed simultaneously the two contradictory roles of confident literary genius (who knew that he deserved the Nobel Prize) and simple farmer (who "don't know much about writing")—the cultivated sophisticate and the shrewd rube, "Faulkner" and Trueblood (or Gavin Stevens and V. K. Ratliff). Critics sometimes play Faulkner's game by "exposing" his rustic mask as a ploy; but both roles were vital to his sense of himself, both grew out of his immediate experience, and both sought realization in his work. His amphibious intelligence, which he shared with many another Southerner, was thus perfectly suited to pastoral expression, for his gaze at the "nethermost stratum" was directed partially inward at his own personality.[73]

The Hamlet began as a series of Southwestern frame tales, appropriate to the containment of an upwardly mobile peasantry. Some of the early stories in the core-plot, however—"Spotted Horses" and "Fool About a Horse" in particular—were narrated not by self-controlled gentlemen but by V. K. Ratliff, a *mostly* self-controlled redneck sewing-machine agent. Yet *The Hamlet* does not, like Twain's "Jumping Frog," reverse the moral perspective of the frame device. A comparison of the early short-story texts with the text of *The Hamlet* reveals that most of Faulkner's revisions involved changes from provincial speech to literary English.[74] Ratliff's narrative role was curtailed in the process of revision and confined to the first section of the novel. Later sections became progressively less vernacular. Nevertheless, Ratliff's narrative presence is substantial enough to provide a folk perspective on the Snopeses, just as the omniscient narrative voice provides a genteel perspective on them. Although Ratliff is upwardly mobile in a modest way, he is Faulkner's spokesman for the "enduring" classes. In effect, Snopesism is condemned both from above, by the aristocracy it threatens, and from below, by the peasantry it exploits. Through Faulkner's manipulation, both ends of the social hierarchy combine to form a stylistic alliance—Lynn's *cordon sanitaire*—that is united by victimization against any movement across the hierarchy. Though the novel's parliament of voices reaches a conservative consensus, however, it remains unable to enforce that consensus. *The Hamlet* is a series of narrative frames (frames within frames, sometimes) in a variety of styles, each one contrived as a new perspective on, and as a new entrapment of, the yahooism it encloses, and each one broken open by its contact with the other styles with which it must contend.

Stylistically, the plot of *The Hamlet* consists of an attempt to assimilate a polished literary idiom into a vernacular context. Book One opens sounding very much like Southwestern humor and sounds even more like it before many pages go by. The manner in which it juxtaposes vernacular and genteel narrative voices bears exact comparison with the sketches of Longstreet:

> Frenchman's Bend was a section of rich river-bottom country lying twenty miles southeast of Jefferson. Hill-cradled and remote, definite yet without boundaries, straddling into two counties and owning allegiance to neither, it had been the original grant and site of a tremendous pre–Civil War plantation, the ruins of which—the gutted shell of an enormous house with its fallen stables and slave quarters and overgrown gardens and brick terraces and promenades—were still known as the Old Frenchman's place, although the original boundaries now existed only on old faded records in the Chancery Clerk's office in the county courthouse in Jefferson, and even some of the once-fertile fields had long since reverted to the cane-and-cypress jungle from which their first master had hewed them. (HAM, 3)

. . . .

> "All right," Ratliff said. "So they went up the road, leaving Miz Snopes and the widow wrastling at the cookstove and them two gals standing there now holding a wire rat-trap and a chamber pot, and went up to Major de Spain's and walked up the private road where that pile of fresh horse manure was and the nigger said Ab stepped in it on deliberate purpose." (HAM, 14–15)

The contrast here is obvious. Ratliff's voice, which dominates Book One, gave Faulkner a chance to demonstrate his command of the verbal and moral resources of the vernacular. These assets are different from those of Faulkner's "own" characteristically circumlocutory rhetoric, and they are more limited. Profane, ungrammatical, and often monosyllabic, Ratliff's idiom refers primarily to a mundane reality—to a strictly visual physical nature and a strictly political community, to a world of livestock, real estate, contracts, and lawsuits. His reaction to Ike Snopes differs from that of his cronies, but his *vision* of Ike is the same as theirs. The language of Book Three could not possibly be Ratliff's, and the vision that accompanies that language is beyond his ken. Ratliff maintains the matter-of-fact tone of a rustic journalist. From him, one learns that Will Varner is the beat supervisor, that the Old Frenchman place was acquired through foreclosure, that Ratliff grew up sharecropping on the same farm that Ab cropped, that Pat Stamper threatened the removal of money from the county. He can make statements of moral judgment only by means of irony or understatement: "I dont know as I would go on record as saying he set ere a one of them afire. I would put it that they both taken fire while he was more or less associated with them" (HAM, 12); "Old man Ab aint naturally mean. He's just soured" (HAM, 29). These are less moral judgments than overtures to stories. When he does rise to an expression of indignation—"Aint none of you folks out there done nothing about it?" (HAM, 71)—it is eloquently simple, and the action that accompanies the indignation is as effective in combating Snopesism as anything in the novel. Nonetheless, his language is descriptively and analytically inadequate to the purposes Faulkner required of it. Faulkner's own feelings were much more complicated than Ratliff was prepared to communicate.

Book Two centers on an institution of major importance to *The Hamlet* particularly and to Southern culture generally—the country schoolhouse. Between Ratliff's oral gymnastics in "Flem" and the literary aerobatics of "The Long Hot Summer," the schoolhouse in "Eula" stands as a necessary transition. It provides an educational bridge between rough-hewn Ratliff and the highly allusive narrator of Ike's epithalamium. It invites the special attention of the pastoralist, for it encapsulates the cultural encounter between a native, vernacular heritage and an imposed, literary one. Labove, the schoolmaster, is an apparent victim of just such a collision. He has been accurately connected with Irving's Ichabod Crane,[75] but he also follows in a strictly Southern tradition of battling schoolteachers who defend book learning with their fists: from Longstreet's "The Turn Out" (1835) through Richard M. Johnston's *Dukesborough Tales* (1871) to Jesse Stuart's *The Thread That Runs So True* (1949). Labove also belongs to another archetype of Southern humor, or of any folk humor: the hayseed who goes to college—or to the city, or to the army, or to court. Twenty years ago, Andy Griffith incarnated the type; one of his recordings included a comedy routine in which a rural clown described his first exposure to a football game. Labove's experience with the Ole Miss football team participates in the same peasant's joke, invented and enjoyed only by nonpeasants, on the rituals of official culture. His grandmother in her cleated football shoes, his coach trying to explain the game to him, and his obtuse response to it ("But how can I carry the ball to that line if I let them catch me and pull me down?" [HAM, 108])—these are the stuff of pastoral farce. But Labove is not entirely comic; he wants to be governor some day, which—as Will Varner knows (HAM, 105)—is no laughing matter. Like Lee Russell, his ambitions lead him to the university and into a new realm of experience, a world of power accessible only through polysyllabic words. The rest of his story is Faulkner's joke on the New Men, and Labove is his comic butt.

The narrator of Book One describes Will Varner as "Rabelaisian" (HAM, 5) and Ike Snopes as having a "Gorgon-face" (HAM, 85). Otherwise, the sources of his erudition are quite nonliterary. Book Two, however, hardly begins before Eula Varner's appearance suggests "some symbology out of the old Dionysic times—honey in sunlight and bursting grapes, the writhen bleeding of the crushed fecundated vine beneath the hard rapacious trampling goat-hoof" (HAM, 95). A new stylistic element has entered the prose—not new to Faulkner, that is, but new to this novel. Eula's early childhood walks are "like a bizarre and chaperoned Sabine rape" (HAM, 96). Taking her to school, her brother Jody is Phaeton, "transporting not only across the village's horizon but across the embracing proscenium of the entire inhabited world like the sun itself, a kaleidoscopic convolution of mammalian ellipses" (HAM, 100). Labove's classroom "had become a kind of bucolic Roman holiday" (HAM, 102), and he himself looks "like a composite photograph of Voltaire and an Elizabethan pirate" (HAM, 110).

Faulkner's heightened allusiveness, his euphemistic diction, and his compulsive syntax enter *The Hamlet* when Labove enters Frenchman's Bend. The teacher, after all, is a classics scholar as well as a law student. He brings with him "a Coke, a Blackstone, a volume of Mississippi Reports, an original Horace and a Thucydides" (HAM, 110) along with a "cheap reproduction of an Alma-Tadema picture which the classics professor had given him" (HAM, 112). Out of such books and images come the allusions that now fill Faulkner's prose, instilling it with the naïve vigor of a rural classicist trying to reconcile Mississippi with Homeric Greece. Sitting "on the schoolhouse steps at recess and eating a cold potato," the eleven-year-old Eula Varner reminds Labove of "the very goddesses in his Homer and Thucydides" (HAM, 113). Much of the mock-heroic incongruity of Book Two, which overflows with it, derives from Labove's confused perspective. He demonstrates what happens when a foreign erudition is imposed upon a vernacular intelligence. When he finally assaults Eula in the schoolroom, he whispers to her "his jumble of fragmentary Greek and Latin verse and American-Mississippi obscenity" (HAM, 121). Such is also the macaronic amalgam of *The Hamlet* itself: not Greek and Latin verse, perhaps, but a book-learned rhetoric nonetheless; not obscenity, but a vulgar Mississippi patois all the same.

Labove's circulation between the university and the cotton-and-coon culture in which he had been raised fits another pastoral paradigm. Faulkner himself followed it, returning from sojourns in academia, Europe, and bohemia to an exile-in-residence in his "little postage stamp of native soil" (LG, 255). For other Southern writers who did not return so literally as Faulkner did to the places they would write about, the school would still represent a significant transition. John Crowe Ransom, for example, in one of his earliest published poems, appropriately entitled "The School," asked a question to which many Southern writers would seek an answer: "Equipped with Grecian thoughts, how could I live / Among my father's folk?"[76] Faulkner's "father's folk" were not "folk" at all, except metaphorically; but among the intentions of *The Hamlet* was his attempt to frame that same question, if not to provide the answer. Labove's befuddlement results from that attempt.

Of course, this question does not embody an exclusively Southern predicament. Raymond Williams has presented the same dilemma in regard to the British novel: "It is a question of the relation between education—not the marks or degrees but the substance of a developed intelligence—and the actual lives of a continuing majority of our people: people who are not, by any formula, objects of record or study or concern, but who are specifically, literally, our own families."[77] This discontinuity, which perhaps most intellectuals feel, between one's cerebral vocation and one's trivial, historical life (which is to say between one's ideas and the world) is intensified in the South by the acute linguistic differentiation that accompanies it there. It is politicized in the South in a way that does not happen elsewhere in America, because in the South the internal division between one's intellect and one's everyday life can be linked more clearly through language to an external division between classes.

Dixie politicians like Gavin Stevens have known the electoral benefit of bilingualism ever since (in the 1830s) they became accountable to vernacular as well as standard-English constituencies. Indeed, the poor-white voter needs to identify with someone who speaks not only like himself but also like the powerful and wealthy people he dreams of joining—or of displacing. Huey Long's people, for example, appreciated his mastery of *both* idioms. "They liked the fact that Huey talked like them, that he was so obviously one of them," T. Harry Williams has written; but they "also wanted their leader to be different from them, to be in some ways superior, to talk sometimes in a language they but dimly understood. When he talked in the cultured cadences of a planter-statesman, they could believe that here indeed was a man who was fitted to lead them, a man who was of the people and who yet knew the smooth ways of the lordly ones, a man who could defeat the planter masters at their own game."[78]

Novelists must perform similarly agile rhetorical feats, not for audiences of rednecks but for portions of themselves. "Writers have their constituencies much as do politicians," as Poirier says, though the constituencies may be internalized. "A writer feels some obligation, however perverse it might be in the individual case, to certain realities and to the proportionate weights among them."[79] For Faulkner, as for George Eliot, meeting those obligations, which are really obligations to one's own identity, involved other problems, problems of character and action:

> George Eliot's connections with the farmers and craftsmen—her connections as Mary Ann Evans—can be heard again and again in their language. Characteristically, she presents them mainly through speech. But while they are present audibly as a community, they have only to emerge in significant action to change in quality. What Adam or Dinah or Hetty say, when they are acting as individuals, is not particularly convincing. Into a novel still predicated on the analysis of individual conduct, the farmers and craftsmen can be included as 'country people' but much less significantly as the active bearers of personal experience.[80]

Faulkner's farmers emerge more fully into "significant action" than George Eliot's, but they also remain "country people" whose "personal experience" finally defies penetration. One also hears *his* "personal connections" in the language of his characters. One feels the presence of a sophisticated analytical intelligence brooding upon simple, instinctual lives. No matter how sympathetically Faulkner views his rustics, no matter how successfully he imagines himself into his country identity, the constitutional incompatibility of the two modes of experience inhibits his characterization. In a way, *this* is what *The Hamlet* is about: the inhospitality of the novel, as a form, to its own subject matter.[81] Book Three, especially, explores this fundamental incongruity between the resources of the novel and the intentions of pastoral representation.

The Ike Snopes episode in "The Long Hot Summer" marks the fulfill-ment of a self-parodic impulse which developed parallel to the initial anti-Snopes impulse that culminated in the basically Southwestern core-plot. At the time of Lee Russell's gubernatorial campaign in the spring of 1919, when Faulkner and Stone were already incubating a satire on the red-necks, Faulkner was hard at work on the allusive, stylized, bookish poems he would begin publishing later that year in the *Mississippian*. Among the several parodic responses Count No 'Count provoked, as we have seen, one—"Une Ballade d'une Vache Perdue," by "Lord Greyson"—"de-scribed the heifer, Betsy, lost and wandering far from home." According to Blotner, the perpetrator had lavished incongruously romantic diction upon the cow's "rounded curves" and "waving tresses" (BL, 240, 271).

Faulkner's Pastoral War taught him, if he had not already known, that the conventional poetic machinery of pastoralism looks ridiculous if it comes too near the real machinery of farm life. It prepared him to recog-nize the discontinuity between literary convention and actuality and to undertake his own self-parodies in "Ode to the Louver" and, much later, "Afternoon of a Cow." Nevertheless, he persevered in his pastoral exer-cises. Some of his earliest "characters" were fauns, or faun-like rustics such as the "tieless casual" of "The Hill" (1922), a laborer who inhabits a "hamlet" and whose mind is "untroubled by moral quibbles and prin-ciples" (EPP, 92). At the same time, however, the Snopes saga was gestating: Faulkner was entertaining both sentimental and satiric attitudes toward the "nethermost stratum" of his society, simultaneously praising the "plain folk" for their "endurance" and deriding any social advancement by up-wardly mobile "rednecks." The same doubled-edged feeling deeply af-fected *The Hamlet* twenty years later.

When he came to incorporating "Afternoon of a Cow" into *The Hamlet*, he again allowed his erudite *alter ego*, Ernest V. Trueblood, to write for him; but he pointedly transformed "Mr. Faulkner" into the idiot Ike Snopes. Consequently, Ike's section represents the application of one of the most celebrated purple patches in a notoriously purple career to the rendering of an utterly inarticulate soul. In Ike, Faulkner presents an epit-ome of the pastoral subject. A peasant, a laborer, illiterate and "enduring" in an absolute sense, Ike embodies the impenetrable consciousness—instinctual, *non*intellectual, not only inhospitable but irrelevant to literate intelligence. He undergoes, to an extreme degree, what William Empson calls "the pastoral process of putting the complex into the simple."[82]

Insofar as Ike facilitates "[t]he essential trick of the old pastoral," which was "to make simple people express strong feelings . . . in learned and fashionable language,"[83] he gratifies Faulkner's most sentimental feelings about the "enduring" classes, and he is endowed with tragic overtones. However, insofar as he reincarnates Faulkner himself, and Faulkner's *Doppelgänger* Trueblood, he brings with him all the comedy of the self-parodic "Afternoon." The climax of both stories, after all, is the punch line of a joke about manure, delivered in the same language in each. To that *The Hamlet* adds a joke about cow-humping, the *reductio ad absurdum* of all pastoral romance. Ike is both tragic victim and comic target, both empty-headed idiot and mock-divinity, and he arouses both pathos and laughter.

This ambivalence signifies Faulkner's own awareness of his dilemma as a pastoralist, which is the inapplicability of his art to his subject. The very lushness of his prose makes a continual concession to that fact:

> Then he would hear her, coming down the creekside in the mist. It would not be after one hour, two hours, three; the dawn would be empty, the moment and she would not be, then he would hear her and he would lie drenched in the wet grass, serene and one and indivisible in joy, listening to her approach. He would smell her; the whole mist reeked with her; the same malleate hands of mist which drew along his prone drenched flanks palped her pearled barrel too and shaped them both somewhere in immediate time, already married. He would not move. He would lie amid the waking instant of earth's teeming minute life, the motionless fronds of water-heavy grasses stooping into the mist before his face in black, fixed curves, along each parabola of which the marching drops held in minute magnification the dawn's rosy miniatures, smelling and even tasting the rich, slow, warm barn-reek milk-reek, the flowing immemorial female, hearing the slow planting and the plopping suck of each deliberate cloven mud-spreading hoof, invisible still in the mist loud with its hymeneal choristers. (HAM, 165)

Perhaps the best way to explain why Faulkner directs his verbal heavy artillery at so defenseless a target is to compare it with the even greater megatonnage of a nearly contemporary work by a younger writer, James

Agee. *The Hamlet* and *Let Us Now Praise Famous Men* are both products of a tradition of rhetorical extravagance that is identifiable, in American literature, with the South. The stylistic extremism of both books derives partly, if not mostly, from their struggle to articulate purely oral experience. The instability of Faulkner's text reflects the variability of his attitude toward the rural lower class he was depicting, as the violence of Agee's expresses his astronomical distance from the people whose lives he sought to describe. Although Agee's book shows that an author need not actually bring the *lingua communis* into his text for it to fertilize his prose, both books are crucially shaped by contact between literate and vernacular speech.

Agee's work, first published in September 1941, was the result of a journalistic assignment from *Fortune* five years earlier to "do an article on cotton tenancy" for the magazine's "Life and Circumstances" series, a documentary feature on poor and lower-middle-class Americans. He and his photographic collaborator, Walker Evans, spent the summer of 1936 in Hale County, Alabama, living with three tenant families and attempting to record their lives. The "Life and Circumstances" series, according to William Stott, "treated its subjects in a tone of breezy condescension, probably because the magazine's editors feared their readers—well-off, hard-headed businessmen—would be bored by the lives of average folk were they not made quaint and amusing." Agee tailored his article to abuse just such complacency, worked to dignify the tenants and their customs and possessions, and insisted that they were "in all important respects, as worthy and precious as any *Fortune* reader." Consequently, the manuscript, ten times longer than assigned and provocatively eccentric, was refused by the magazine and did not attain publication until the eve of Pearl Harbor, when it was ignored.[84]

Let Us Now Praise Famous Men focuses more upon Agee's incapacity to feel and to imagine the inner lives of the tenants than upon the tenants themselves. As much a confession as a documentary, it aggressively concedes the insufficiency of Agee's language, the insincerity of the moral vision that subsists in that language, and the inability of his words to touch the people toward whom he directed his (and his readers') attention. The result is a meditation upon the whole process of pastoral expression, which seems to him "curious, obscene, terrifying, and unfathomably mysterious":

I realize that, with even so much involvement in explanations as this, I am liable seriously, and perhaps irretrievably, to obscure what would at best be hard enough to give its appropriate clarity and intensity; and what seems to me most important of all: namely, that these I will write of are human beings, living in this world, innocent of such twistings as these which are taking place over their heads; and that they were dwelt among, investigated, spied on, revered, and loved, by other quite monstrously alien human beings, in the employment of still others still more alien; and that they are now being looked into by still others, who have picked up their living as casually as if it were a book, and who were actuated toward this reading by various possible reflexes of sympathy, curiosity, idleness, et cetera, and almost certainly in a lack of consciousness, and conscience, remotely appropriate to the enormity of what they are doing. [85]

Agee's sense of "the enormity of what he is doing" pervades the book and invests his prose with a thoroughgoing hyperbole. Not only his introductory "Preamble" but also the sections describing the "Money," "Clothing," "Education," and "Work" of the three families—which comprise the bulk of his text—are written in a heightened style that calls continual attention to itself. Furthermore, by directing the reader's reflection to the "enormity" of the reader's own action, Agee underlined *his* repeated failure to touch the reality toward which he was reaching. In conventional pastoral, one is encouraged to believe that one has entered the shepherd's realm oneself and is congratulated for one's own simplicity; in Agee's book, one is constantly reminded that the impersonation is illusory and that the intelligence the author is applying to his subject, and summoning his reader to apply, is "alien" to the objects before it. The only way Agee could convey his feeling for the Gudgers' house, for example, was to translate it into his own emotional prose poetry. Inevitably, a reader's perception of the house stops short with Agee's perception, or rather with the *act* of his perceiving, with the chemistry of his vision. While one comes to know that chemistry embarrassingly well, the actual objects ultimately prove to be beyond reach, just as Agee intended them; he insured their elusiveness with his rhetoric: "a house of simple people which stands empty and silent in the vast Southern country morning sunlight, and everything which on this morning in eternal space it by chance contains, all thus left open and defenseless to a reverent and cold-laboring spy, shines quietly forth such grandeur, such sorrowful holiness of its exactitudes in existence, as no human consciousness shall ever rightly perceive, far less impart to another."[86]

In a book that bulges with documentary catalogues, with detailed descriptions of trivial gestures, and with verbal rhapsodies upon the tenants' artifacts, the linguistic record of these people is conspicuously absent. According to Stott, Agee experimented with a much simpler prose style, "'writing the book in such language that anyone who can read and is seriously interested can understand,' because he felt 'the lives of these families belong first (if to any one) to people like them and only secondarily to the "educated" such as myself.' He gave up the effort, finding that he couldn't contrive a 'credible language' and that the naïve tone made 'perfectly defenseless children' of the tenants."[87] Only fragmentary vestiges of that experiment remain in the published text. The tenants' language is reported only a few times: in Agee's record of Emma Wood's farewell (". . . I want you and Mr. Walker to know how much we all like you, because you make us feel easy with you; we don't have to act any different from what it comes natural to act, and we don't have to worry what you're thinking about us, it's just like you was our own people and had always lived here with us, you all are so kind, and nice, and quiet, and easygoing, and we wisht you wasn't never going to go away but stay on here with us, and I just want to tell you how much we all keer about you"); in his description of a sign in the Gudgers' house that reads "PLEAS! be QUITE."[88] Otherwise, linguistically, Agee was not an amphibian but a diving bird, whose sharecroppers were as much a pretext for demonstrating his own virtuosity as they were creatures in their own right. Of this fact, he was painfully, guiltily aware, and his primary concern in the book is less to survey cotton tenancy than to examine his own motives for trying. The same statement cannot *quite* be made about Faulkner's novel, but some of the same self-doubt that congests *Let Us Now Praise Famous Men* also complicates *The Hamlet.*

"I respect dialects too deeply," Agee says, "when they are used by those who have a right to them," to risk corrupting them with frequent imitation. "The tenant's idiom has been used ad nauseam by the more unspeakable of the northern journalists."[89] Faulkner does imitate the tenant's idiom; but the only idiom the Yoknapatawpha novelist shares with the Hale County correspondent for *Fortune* is the hyperbolic literary one, which calls attention to itself and to the whole process of imposing polysyllabic words upon monosyllabic sensibilities. The prose in Ike's section of "The Long Summer" is as incongruent with its subject as Agee's; and, though Faulkner's pastoral conscience was not so melodramatic as Agee's, the nature of Ike's Trueblooded lineage shows clearly enough that Faulkner was capable of questioning his own intentions.

The ambivalence that governs Ike's section is a token of that questioning. To each grandiloquent verbal flight, Faulkner appended a burlesque pratfall—a deflation not so much for Ike, who "endures" it, as for his own virtuosity. A long midsummer *aubade*, for example, concludes with a Southwestern gesture toward the barnyard:

> Dawn is now over. It is now bald and forthright day. The sun is well up the sky. The air is still loud with birds, but the cries are no longer the mystery's choral strophe and antistrophe rising vertical among the leafed altars, but are earth-parallel, streaking the lateral air in prosaic busy accompaniment to the prosaic business of feeding. . . . he lays the plucked grass before her, then out of the clumsy fumbling of the hands there emerges, already in dissolution, the abortive diadem. In the act of garlanding, it disintegrates, rains down the slant of brow and chewing head; fodder and flowers become one inexhaustible rumination. From the sliding rhythm of the jaws depends one final blossom. (HAM, 183–84)

One remembers the conclusion of Jiggitts and Lester's "Pastoral Poem": "She chews her cud with dainty jaw, / As now I milk her, 'saw cow, saw' " (BL, 266). The natural fate of Faulkner's pastoralism is self-parody. The Ike Snopes episode, which originated in a stag-party joke and before that in a college prank, not only contains some of Faulkner's most characteristically Faulknerian prose; it is also *anti*-Faulknerian. It is simultaneously pastoral and mock-pastoral.

A final irony of Faulkner's Truebloodian self-parody lies in the fact that Ike's section is "framed" by vernacular subchapters, in which Ratliff acts to terminate the exploitation of the idiot by his cousins. Ordinarily in Southwestern humor the vernacular voice provides the extravagance, while the genteel voice reclines calmly, content simply to comment through its own rationality on the verbal pyrotechnics with which it must contend. In *The Hamlet*, however, Ratliff's understated irony seems serene compared with the rifeness of the Truebloodian voice in Ike's section. The narrator's language seems as dangerously volatile and uncontrolled as the peasantry to which it refers. If *The Hamlet* stands synecdochically for a social structure, in the way that Lynn asserts for Southwestern humor, it stands for a very unstable hierarchy in which the upper orders, addled by their insecurity, are more frenzied than the lower. The narrative confusion relates to a social confusion that the Whigs never had to face. Faulkner's narrative persona does not resemble here the "Self-controlled Gentleman" of Longstreet, whose moral didacticism was menaced by vernacular destructiveness. The "frame device" in *The Hamlet* has been blasted open by its upwardly mobile contents: Flem Snopes is too powerful a force for the self-indulgent narrator of Book Three to check. After Flem seizes the last line of the book for himself, Faulkner will require two more novels, and nearly twenty more years, to repair the frame and contain the energy Flem represents.

The structure of *The Hamlet* owes more to the ongoing tension within Faulkner between the divided components of his identity—and between his torn responses to the segments of his stratified community—than it does to any imposed thematic form or plot device. The primary unity of the book is the unity (disunity, really) of the performance which expresses that tension. The parts of the book arrange themselves according to a syntax almost more of feeling than of meaning. A similar principle orders *Let Us Now Praise Famous Men*, where a like discontinuity obtains among segments of the exposition, as if Agee had to keep breaking off his efforts to touch the tenant families when he saw that each effort, in turn, would fail, and as if he had to keep starting again because he was compelled to try. One of Agee's chapters is called simply "Colon";[90] all of them seem to fulfill functions of an emotional grammar. The same is true of *The Hamlet*, where the narrative breaks seem to articulate shifts in attitude rather than developments of theme.

It would be easy here to suggest that Book Four effects a balancing or a blending of the vernacular voice, ascendant in Book One, with the genteel voice which dominates Book Three—a blending of Ratliff's idiom with Trueblood's. Such a resolution would offer a social and psychological integration, a neat synthesis for the dialectic that animates Books One through Three, and a convenient conclusion to this discussion. But it would also partake too narrowly of the centripetal, New-Critical forces that have too often threatened to squeeze Faulkner's books into various prefabricated molds. Regardless of whatever superficial patterning

Faulkner may have imposed upon *The Hamlet,* the motivating force that shaped the original Snopes material into the final achievement of the novel lay deeper down, in his struggle to repair a pastoralist vocation rent by social change. Recognizing that disruptive force is the most direct avenue toward understanding and enjoying Faulkner's comic masterpiece.

CHAPTER FIVE

KNIGHT'S GAMBIT

It was not the sitting down which was peculiar. Mr. Faulkner did this often—steadily perhaps is a better word—if not in the house, then (in summer) well down in a large chair on the veranda just outside the library window where I would be working, his feet on the railing, reading a detective magazine.

—Ernest V. Trueblood, "Afternoon of a Cow"

When Bill received word he had won the Nobel Prize, I fully believe he was about written out. He had said years ago that if that happened, he'd turn to writing mystery stories. One thing about them, he said, was that once you found a formula that worked, you could keep on using it over and over, by simply changing names and places.

—John Faulkner, *My Brother Bill*

Crops and Robbers

In the structure of *The Wild Palms* and in the style (or styles) of *The Hamlet*, Faulkner embodied divisions *within* his community and *within* himself. The detective stories in *Knight's Gambit*, most of which he wrote for cash during respites in the composition of *The Hamlet* and *Go Down, Moses*, predicate a division *between* his community and the outside world. In the spirit of Agrarian sectionalism, the first five of these stories contrast a homogeneous, rural "us" with an invasive, destructive, Northern-and-industrial "them." In the final story of the collection, however, he acknowledged that his seeming Agrarianism represented only half of an internal debate. There he countered his own defense of Southern agriculture—and of the Southern "farmer" within him—with a readiness to accept changes in the South's social structure and an implicit confession of his own urbanity. In revising this, the title story, during the 1940s, moreover, he turned it into a virtual repudiation of the commercial origins of the first five stories. Embarrassed by having cultivated a popular audience, which he identified with the citizens of Oxford who had labeled him "Count No 'Count," he tried to redeem these stories for more discerning readers. Having indulged the taste of "Mr. Faulkner," who liked to sit "on the veranda just outside the library window . . . his feet on the railing, reading a detective magazine" (US, 431), he handed the project to Ernest V. Trueblood for completion. In effect, he turned *Knight's Gambit* into a self-parodic text at war with its own formulaic plotting, at war with the readers for whom he had first intended it, and at war with one version of himself. By the time he published it in 1949, the book's principal subject had become his own struggle to define—and salvage—his vocation.

The six stories ("Smoke," "Monk," "Hand Upon the Waters," "Tomorrow," "An Error in Chemistry," and "Knight's Gambit") all present episodes in the amateur-detective career of Gavin Stevens, the county attorney of Yoknapatawpha. Except for the first and third stories, they also share the narrative point of view of Stevens's nephew Charles Mallison, who plays Watson to his uncle's Holmes. In the first five, all published in magazines during the thirties and early forties, Stevens solves murders; in the title story, by far the longest, he prevents a murder and poses a mystery of his own. The resolution of this mystery also resolves the pattern of the whole book—by violating it.

Faulkner first attempted popular crime fiction in the late twenties, when he wrote "The Big Shot" and *Sanctuary* (BL, 492–93, 604–5). He wrote "Smoke," the opening story in *Knight's Gambit*, as early as 1930, between the first and second versions of *Sanctuary*; and it bears an imprint of that proximity (BL, 644–45). Gavin Stevens seems to have originated as a relative of Gowan Stevens, the ineffectual college boy of *Sanctuary*. Also, a character resembling Popeye makes his way into "Smoke": a small man wearing city clothes, "with a face like a shaved wax doll, and eyes with a still way of looking and a voice with a still way of talking" (KG, 27), who carries a pistol with a silencer and runs down a child with his roadster on his way back to Memphis. No other story in *Knight's Gambit* even indirectly involves the underworld milieu of *Sanctuary*, although Memphis crouches malignantly just beyond the horizon in most of them and although characters occasionally travel to and from that city.[1] While the dominant setting for Faulkner's mysteries is agricultural, however, each of the stories postulates a struggle between urban vice and rural virtue similar to the one that *Sanctuary* enacts.

That struggle occurred within Faulkner before it shaped *Knight's Gambit*. In his intermittent quest for money and fame, he felt both an attraction to cities and a betrayal of his small-town roots. In the cities were publishers and an intelligentsia who could at least read his fiction if not always appreciate it. In the hinterland were relatively uneducated peasants and townspeople who bought very few of his books and could not understand him even when he was writing about themselves. Yet he knew that the country—and country people—provided him with his primary subjects. *Knight's Gambit* articulates his contradictory feelings about those pastoral subjects, about his limited public, and about his commitment to the very act of communicating himself to either the city or the country.

As with *Sanctuary*, Faulkner composed "Smoke" and the other stories of *Knight's Gambit* out of his need for cash and public recognition. He frequently stated that he wrote *Sanctuary* for money. Throughout the rest of his life, he repeated the assertion—half confession and half boast—which he had made in his "Introduction" to the Modern Library edition of 1932, that his invention of *Sanctuary* was deliberately crass. "I began to think of books in terms of possible money," he said. "I decided I might just as well make some of it myself. I took a little time out, and speculated what a person in Mississippi would believe to be current trends, chose what I thought was the right answer and invented the most horrific tale I could imagine and wrote it in about three weeks." He added less emphatically that, to redeem the novel, he had rewritten it—had actually "had to pay for the privilege of rewriting it," because the galleys had already been set up for the first version—"to make out of it something which would not shame *The Sound and the Fury* and *As I Lay Dying* too much" (SY, vi, vii–viii). Twenty-five years later, he could still assert that *Sanctuary* was "basely conceived" (FU, 90); his guilt for having sacrificed the purity of his vocation by pandering to public taste still lingered. The stories of *Knight's Gambit* grew out of motives and imaginative resources similar to those that produced *Sanctuary*, and they created a similar embarrassment in need of redemption.

During the thirties and forties, Faulkner found relief from his chronic financial difficulties in the markets for popular entertainment: Hollywood and the national magazines. Like the film studios, the magazines that paid most—especially the *Saturday Evening Post*, *Collier's*, and *Cosmo-*

politan—required formulaic plots, sentimental resolutions, and language accessible to the least common denominator in their mass audience. The acme among these was the *Saturday Evening Post*, edited until 1936 by George Horace Lorimer. Frank Luther Mott has described the *Post*'s influence on short fiction and the principal criticism the magazine invited: "Perhaps the fault oftenest alleged against Lorimer's *Post* was that it was largely devoted to a 'crass materialism.' Moreover, we have been told, this was commonly mixed with romance that was often more 'crass' than the materialism. Thus business success, romance, sports, humor, and public affairs were said to constitute the *Post* pattern; and short stories, serials, and articles were alleged to be created and repeated according to a few variants of a successful formula, thus killing originality, new ideas, and the art impulse in general."[2] Whether such objections were justified, the *Post* certainly became for William Faulkner a personal symbol of bad writing and corrupted talent. In 1930, he could expect $750 a story from the *Post*; by 1940, the average payment was $1,000. From publications with greater prestige and lower circulation, he could expect only half or one-fourth as much (BL, 648–1088 passim). He aimed each of the six detective stories in *Knight's Gambit* at the premium prices of the *Post*, to which he initially submitted at least five of the stories.

In "Smoke," Faulkner first introduced Gavin Stevens, a character upon whom for thirty years he would increasingly rely: "a Harvard graduate: a loose-jointed man with a mop of untidy iron-gray hair," who could communicate equally well with college professors and illiterate farmers (KG, 16). This bilinguist solves the hired killing of a county judge by a Memphis thug. Stevens reveals that the man who hired the murderer, Granby Dodge, did so to cover his own slaying of his cousin—which he disguised first as an accidental fall from a horse and then as the deed of the victim's own son—in order to claim the cousin's land. Faulkner sent the story to the *Post* three times during 1930 and 1931. After three rejections, he submitted it unsuccessfully to *Scribner's* and finally to *Harper's*, which accepted it in January 1932 for $400 (BL, 644–758 passim). Hans Skei concludes from Faulkner's unusual persistence with the *Post* that "Smoke" was "a deliberate attempt on Faulkner's part to write a story that catered to the *Post*'s taste."[3]

Blotner does not record the submission history of "Monk," except for the fact that *Scribner's* bought it in January 1937 (BL, 952). Faulkner probably wrote it in the midst of money problems, however, soon after suggesting that he might "get hold of one of the magazines and take a story that they will buy and change locale and names, etc." (SL, 95–96). This proposal, in June 1936, reflects the level of his desperation at about the time he must have written "Monk." In this story, Stevens solves the mystery of "a moron, perhaps even a cretin" (KG, 39), who has murdered the prison warden who befriended him. At a meeting of the State Pardon Board, Stevens discovers that Monk—since executed—was incited to his crime by a fellow prisoner named Terrel. A second villain, the state governor (who resembles Theodore Bilbo), suppresses Stevens's information and allows Terrel to go free.

Another "feeb" is victimized in "Hand Upon the Waters," which Faulkner wrote in May or June 1939, taking time out from *The Hamlet* to placate his creditors. Lonnie Grinnup, the idiot scion of one of the founding families of Yoknapatawpha County, is discovered drowned and hooked on his own trotline at the fishing camp he inhabits with a deaf-and-dumb companion named Joe. Stevens learns that Boyd Ballenbaugh has killed the idiot in order to collect the indemnity from an insurance policy that his brother Tyler helped Lonnie to buy. Stevens recognizes that Lonnie's death was not accidental when he deduces that the paddle in Lonnie's boat was put there by someone else, because he knows that Lonnie never used one in running his trotline. In a nighttime confrontation with Ballenbaugh at the fishing camp, Stevens himself is saved from death by the last-minute intervention of Joe. The *Post* editors bought the yarn for $1,000 (BL, 1024).

In August 1940, they paid the same price for "Tomorrow" (BL, 1056), in which Chick Mallison relates a case from the early years of his uncle's law practice. Jackson Fentry, a poor farmer on jury duty, stalemates the murder trial of a man named Bookwright who has committed a homicide the rest of Yoknapatawpha County considers justifiable. When Stevens, as the defense lawyer, investigates, he discovers that Fentry has declined to acquit Bookwright because the man he killed was Fentry's long-separated foster son. Soon after he sent "Tomorrow" to the *Post*, Faulkner reported to Bennett Cerf that he was "[s]till writing short stories. Some of them are bound to sell soon. If I can get one for top price, it will get me through to October, which will give me two months to write and sell another" (BL, 1055).

His reason for writing "An Error in Chemistry" was no less mercenary. In autumn 1940, he wrote to Robert Haas that "I am doing no writing save pot-boilers. [Harold] Ober [my new agent] sells just enough of them to keep my head above water." (SL, 136). That November, Faulkner appropriated a county-fair carnival then in Oxford for the setting of this ingenious tale of disguise (BL, 1061). Joel Flint, a carnival performer, marries the spinster daughter of a prosperous farmer and settles down in the community. When he kills his wife two years later, he turns himself in but then disappears mysteriously from prison. Later Stevens discovers that Flint, actually an escape artist and illusionist called Signor Canova, has been masquerading as his own father-in-law, whom he has killed in order to acquire and sell his property. Flint betrays himself when he attempts to dissolve sugar into raw whiskey, a procedure that any Yoknapatawpha native knows is the wrong way to make a toddy (KG, 127). Faulkner hoped this story would be attractive enough to earn more from the *Post* editors than their standard $1,000, but he also told his agent that he would "as usual . . . take the quickest sale before the highest" (SL, 137). The sale was neither quick nor high. "An Error in Chemistry" was rejected by the *Post*, by *Collier's*, and by six other magazines before *Ellery Queen's Mystery Magazine* bought it for $300 in 1945. Though it won an additional $250 in a prize contest that December, Faulkner had become thoroughly dissatisfied with his market (BL, 1062, 1085, 1189, 1201). "What a commentary," he wrote to Harold Ober. "In France, I am the father of a literary movement. In Europe I am considered the best modern American and among the first of all writers. In America, I eke out a hack's motion picture wages by winning second prize in a manufactured mystery story contest" (SL, 217–18).

In January 1942, he sent the final story of the group to Ober, along with an admonition to "get the check to me as soon as you can" if it sold (SL, 148). In "Knight's Gambit," Stevens prevents an aristocratic youth, Max Harriss, from murdering—by luring into the stable of a spirited horse— the Argentine cavalry captain who threatens to marry either his widowed mother or his sister and thereby deny him his inheritance. In the process, Stevens reveals that in his youth he himself had courted the mother, before she became Mrs. Harriss. *He* marries her at the end and becomes the stepfather of Max and of Max's sister, who marries the Argentine. At the conclusion of this improbably Oedipal sequence, Max, the Argentine, and Chick Mallison have all joined the army, in response to the Japanese attack on Pearl Harbor. This narrative understandably proved too complicated for the *Post*, and Faulkner offered to revise it accordingly: "I can take a lot of matter out of KNIGHT'S GAMBIT though, simplify it to primer class" (SL, 149).

When he actually rewrote it, however, he elaborated rather than compressed its basic situation. The story seemed to attract his attention exceptionally, as if he recognized in this piece of what he habitually called "trash" the ingredients of a serious work. Over the next six years, he rewrote it at least three times, each time complicating it further, until in the final version it filled more than 110 pages—almost half of the published book (BL, 1105–1282 passim).

The final revision occurred during his preparation of the *Collected Stories* (1950). In November 1948, he informed Malcolm Cowley that he hoped to provide that volume with a careful organization: "[E]ven to a collection of short stories," he wrote, "form, integration, is as important as to a novel—an entity of its own, single, set for one pitch, contrapuntal in integration, toward one end, one finale." He was excited about the idea, and included a proposal for the table of contents. It did not include any of his six detective stories (FCF, 115–17), though they had appeared in a similar list two months earlier (SL, 274–75). Later in November, he had decided that these very stories deserved separate publication before he compiled the large anthology. He outlined his plan to Saxe Commins, his new editor at Random House: "I am thinking of a 'Gavin Stevens' volume, more or less detective stories. I have four or five short pieces, averaging 20 pages, in which Stevens solves or prevents crime to protect the weak, right injustice, or punish evil. There is one more which no one has bought. The reason is, it is a novel which I tried to compress into short story length. It is a love story, in which Stevens prevents a crime (murder) not for justice but to gain (he is now fifty plus) the childhood sweetheart which he lost 20 years ago" (SL, 280). He spent the next five months accomplishing this plan, rewriting the short "novel" at least twice more; and by the beginning of June 1949 *Knight's Gambit* was ready for publication (BL, 1275–87).

Faulkner's motivation for transforming these six mere entertainments into a volume on his authorial shelf and delaying the culminating achievement represented by the *Collected Stories* to do so must have been complex. Undeniably, he must have enjoyed them at some level, for he had long appreciated the detective genre as a reader. Yet he had always denigrated his own contributions to it as incidental potboilers that distracted him from his serious writing. Always economical with narrative properties, he may have relished the prospect of boiling these pots twice, through the double sale the book would achieve for the first five of them. Further, he may have hoped to exploit the recent success of *Intruder in the Dust* (1948), a novel in which Chick assumes Stevens's detective role and which bears obvious affinities to the *Knight's Gambit* group. But that very success had eased the financial pressure that would suggest such a motive: in July 1948, Random House had sold the motion-picture rights for *Intruder* to Metro-Goldwyn-Mayer for $50,000, eighty percent of which accrued to the author (BL, 1257). Although this good fortune did not end Faulkner's financial problems forever, it did insure his relative security at the time he declared to Commins his wish to defer the *Collected Stories* until after assembling the Stevens anthology. Thus, his revision of "Knight's Gambit" was not hastened by penury.

A different purpose primarily motivated Faulkner. He had revised *Sanctuary* partially to salvage his literary integrity from the shame of crass commerce. Likewise, he had revised the stories of *The Unvanquished* and added "An Odor of Verbena" to make that group a volume, because he hoped "to transform them from ephemeral magazine stories into a unified work that might last" (BL, 951). When he considered the body of his short fiction in 1948, therefore, and noticed one other group that made "an entity of its own," he may have welcomed the opportunity to wipe that slate clean also—to reclaim those stories and the imaginative effort he had invested in them, by a similar transmutation. As he had been willing to "pay for the privilege" of revising *Sanctuary* in 1930, deferring the *Collected Stories* may have been a price he was willing to pay in 1949 for the privilege of salvaging another part of his career.

Faulkner composed *The Unvanquished* and *Go Down, Moses* by combining and revising previously published short stories, and then by adding a final piece of writing to tie them together. But he composed *Knight's Gambit* by leaving five stories intact and even in chronological order, and then by revising, several times over, the final capstone narrative. Consequently, the latter book provides a uniquely clear example of a phenomenon that affected much of Faulkner's writing: the revision of formulaic magazine fiction into serious literature. *Knight's Gambit* displays an exact demarcation between its commercial past and Faulkner's efforts to redeem it from that past, whereas in the former two books that past is overlaid with redemptive efforts.

Furthermore, because of the movie sale in 1948, the demarcation is underscored by Faulkner's sudden emergence from immediate financial need. The attempt to redeem the early work was unimpeded, for instance, by the debts that had first suggested the *Unvanquished* volume. As he had done in *The Wild Palms*, the last book before *Knight's Gambit* that he wrote under only minimal financial constraint, he turned his attention in 1949 to the state of his vocation; and the revision of the title story incorporates an involved reflection upon the necessity of ever having had to write detective fiction at all. While *The Unvanquished* remains stylistically uniform, therefore, *Knight's Gambit* is strikingly discontinuous. The final story not only attempts to redeem the first five; it also comments on them, rejects them, and moves beyond them. The resulting division is probably the most important fact the book presents, for it articulates other discontinuities in Faulkner—between his crass and his artistic intentions, between urban and rural identities, between "low" and "high" audiences, between himself and his own writing.

When Faulkner wrote the first version of "Knight's Gambit" in 1942, he intended merely to integrate the previous stories, as well as to earn some money by using a formula that had twice before interested the *Post*. But when he revised it in 1949, he intended not only to draw all six stories into the compass of his artistry, elevating and shaping them with this capstone, but also to allay his own embarrassment for having had to write them. Thus, his revision fulfilled contradictory impulses. It was an act of integration but also of neutralization; it was a way of publicly acknowledging his illegitimate issue and fostering them toward worthiness, but at the same time of publicly—if perhaps unconsciously—dispossessing himself of them. Both the unities and the divisions of *Knight's Gambit* derive from its genesis in a particular formula for commercial success.

Uncle Abner

What formula did Faulkner repudiate by revising "Knight's Gambit"? The *general* sources of Faulkner's detective formula are not obscure.[4] In 1929, "thinking of books in terms of possible money," he had turned naturally to the crime novel and the mystery story. They were part of his literary blood, as they are for anyone growing up in the twentieth century who is not isolated from popular culture. Blotner describes brief periods throughout Faulkner's life when he read detective stories in quantity (BL, 605). A. I. Bezzerides recalls accompanying Faulkner to a drugstore in Oxford in the late forties to exchange one stack of mysteries for another and hearing Faulkner remark that, "no matter what you write, it's a mystery of one kind or another."[5] His library contained volumes by Rex Stout, Georges Simenon, John Dickson Carr, Dashiell Hammett, Ellery Queen, Mary Roberts Rinehart, and Dorothy Sayers.[6]

One author his library lacked, however, offers a more probable source for the Gavin Stevens stories, or at least a more specific analogue. This was Melville Davisson Post (1871–1930), a lawyer from Clarksburg, West Virginia, who turned to writing for his living in 1896.[7] He experimented with several kinds of fiction, but his primary talent was for mysteries. Chronicling the adventures of half a dozen detective heroes, he became one of the most successful popular writers in America during the early decades of the century. His most lasting creation was Uncle Abner, an antebellum Southern squire whose authority as a detective derives from his Calvinistic sensitivity to God's justice. Post wrote nearly two dozen Uncle Abner stories; between 1911 and 1928, they were printed and reprinted in many popular magazines, including the *Saturday Evening Post*. In 1918, he gathered eighteen of them into a collection called *Uncle Abner: Master of Mysteries*, which achieved an immense success. In 1942, while the plates for Faulkner's masterpieces were being melted into armaments, Stanley Kunitz and Howard Haycraft reported that *Uncle Abner* had "never been out of print." Their description of Post's literary method is pertinent here:

> Post's stories always appeared in magazines first (editors paid record prices for his work) and were then collected into book form. He proclaimed himself the champion of plot-technique in the short story; and, indeed, he is probably the most creditable exponent of what has come to be looked down upon as the formularized, or "machine-made," magazine story. . . . Be that as it may, Post himself, in his preoccupation with formula, underestimated some of his greatest literary gifts. The Abner stories are still read and re-read not so much for their intensive plots—highly original in their time but hackneyed by imitation today—as for the author's cogent realization of character, place, and mood.[8]

Faulkner undoubtedly knew about Post when he conceived of Gavin Stevens in about 1930: Post's stories were ubiquitous in the national magazines of Faulkner's childhood and youth, and their author enjoyed wide fame. The Uncle Abner stories might very plausibly have attracted the attention, if not necessarily the admiration, of a Southern adolescent with a weakness for detective fiction, especially since they were set in a rural milieu with which a small-town Mississippian could identify. Melville Davisson Post would have been a logical model for him to emulate. If, in 1936, he could propose to imitate "a story that [the magazines] will buy" and "change locale and names" to conform with Yoknapatawpha, Post's stories offered locales Faulkner would not have needed to change very much. Furthermore, if he wrote *Sanctuary* because he thought it approximated "what a person in Mississippi would believe to be current trends," Uncle Abner was one reason many people in Mississippi subscribed to the *Saturday Evening Post*.

Although a West Virginia community, Post's Clarksburg is an agricultural rather than a mountainous setting. It is, moreover, the native home of Stonewall Jackson, and Post considered himself a Southerner. Uncle Abner is a distinctively rural detective—not just a country gentleman but a cattleman who is actively involved in the life of his community on all its levels. The rural milieu of Post's detective series makes the most compelling argument for an affinity with Faulkner's. Both Gavin Stevens and Uncle Abner concern themselves with rural matters: the disposition of real estate, the alliance of families through marriage, the intrusion of outsiders into an otherwise closed society—matters of less urgency for a less cohesive society.

The structure of rural societies affects the structure of both men's narratives. The action in *Knight's Gambit* is observed by a community, for which either Chick Mallison or an unnamed narrator acts as a spokesman, sometimes relating collective experience in the first-person plural. Chick's counterpart in *Uncle Abner* is Abner's nephew Martin, a young adolescent who, like Chick, narrates his uncle's exploits—into which he sometimes enters—and frequently serves him as an interlocutor. Like Chick, Martin speaks from a common knowledge of his community's history and behavior, a knowledge that Abner often transcends. Abner and Stevens are both figures of moral authority among their neighbors, whom they frequently entertain with phenomenal displays of observation and deduction. Coincidentally, each is a bachelor whose past includes a mysterious, failed romance.[9]

Besides milieu and character, the two books share a variety of similar incidents and devices. For example, "An Act of God" concerns a county-fair mountebank who murders the seducer of his daughter; Faulkner's illusionist in "An Error in Chemistry" murders the father of the woman he has seduced. Chess sets enter both "The Adopted Daughter" and "Knight's Gambit." In "The Angel of the Lord," a broken stirrup-leather leads Abner to the discovery of a murder; in "Smoke," a murdered man is found with his foot fast in the unbroken stirrup of his horse's saddle. In both books, horsemanship, woodcraft, and familiarity with purely local customs often provide the detectives with their clues. Both books culminate in a climate of impending war—the Civil War in one and World War II in the other—into which both young narrators will be swept. [10]

A more significant resemblance between the books inheres in the conditions of evil which they postulate. Evil enters the community, usually from the outside, whenever the hereditary transmission of property is interrupted. A society linked to the land requires a clear order of possession, and efforts to transgress that order disrupt the social fabric. Each detective is committed above all to preserving this order, and both volumes are filled with crimes of covetousness, in which interlopers dispossess rightful owners by murder, theft, or legal trickery. Likewise, rightful owners jeopardize the legitimacy of their tenure when they neglect or abuse their land or when they threaten its future stewardship. Thus Abner rebukes the villain of "The Wrong Hand": "You have no heirs. Your brother's son is now a man; he should marry a wife and rear up children to possess these lands. And, as he is thus called upon to do what you cannot do, Gaul, he should have the things you have, to use."[11] Thus, also, the community in "Smoke" knows that trouble impends when Anse Holland, an "outlander" who has married "the only daughter of a man who owned two thousand acres of some of the best land in the county" (KG, 3), not only fails to farm it but also "mistreats" it (KG, 6).

In these stories, two kinds of people endanger society: brotherless daughters, who defeat patrilineality; and "outlanders," foreigners who marry these daughters to usurp their fathers' property. The heiress is dangerous because she attracts strangers, and the strangers are dangerous because, in a closed, "homogeneous" society, their assimilation requires violent adjustments. Among Post's characters, for example, a man named Doomdorf attracts immediate suspicion when Martin relates that "there was no Southern blood in him." Another villain, Dix, in "The Angel of the Lord," is revealed as an obvious scoundrel when Martin points out that he had come from "over the mountain," that he "had married a remote cousin of ours," and that he "had always lived on her lands, adjoining those of my Uncle Abner."[12] The malefactors in Faulkner's detective stories follow a similar pattern. Whereas in *The Hamlet* the Snopeses are at least Southern farmers from communities *like* Frenchman's Bend, the villains of *Knight's Gambit* represent external threats.

A final similarity between Abner and Stevens rests in their attitudes toward justice. Both distinguish between an inferior, human level of justice and a higher, transcendent level. Uncle Abner, although inconsistent on the point, frequently declares this distinction. "In the law court," he says, "that procedure would be considered sound sense; but we are in God's court and things are managed there in a somewhat stranger way."[13] Stevens expresses a similar philosophy. For example, in a conversation with his friend the sheriff—who corresponds in function to Abner's friend Squire Randolph, a dull-witted magistrate—he draws a related distinction:

> "I'm interested in truth," the sheriff said.
> "So am I," Uncle Gavin said. "It's so rare. But I am more interested in justice and human beings."
> "Ain't truth and justice the same thing?" the sheriff said.
> "Since when?" Uncle Gavin said. "In my time I have seen truth that was anything under the sun but just, and I have seen justice using tools and instruments I wouldn't want to touch with a ten-foot fence rail." (KG, 111)[14]

Both detectives sometimes overlook merely legal truths in order to accomplish a higher justice—Abner in "An Act of God," for example, and Stevens in "Knight's Gambit," when he allows a murder attempt to go unprosecuted.

The higher justice in both books, as in *The Hamlet*, resides ultimately in the rightful distribution of real property. Abner, to whom Martin refers as the "right hand of the land,"[15] disposes his cases according to the legitimacy of human stewardship over God's earth. A thorough Biblical scholar, Abner chooses as his favorite texts the Tenth Commandment, against covetousness, and 1 Kings 21, in which the Lord sends Elijah to chastise Ahab for usurping Naboth's vineyard. Stevens does not defend his judgments by quoting Scripture, as Abner does, but he does seem to base them on a similar authority. Chick portrays him against "the broad, heat-miraged land, between the cotton and the corn of God's long-fecund, remorseless acres, which would outlast any corruption and injustice" (KG, 60); and Stevens, like Antaeus, derives his strength from this holy soil.

Whether or not Faulkner borrowed his detective formula from Melville Post's pattern, the analogies between the two are instructive. Both authors wrote from a similar social position in a similar milieu. Both were committed to certain "agrarian" principles. Faulkner's remote, partial sympathy for the Southern Agrarian movement of the 1930s may have influenced the shape of his detective stories as much as his reliance on actual models in the *Saturday Evening Post*. His revision of them in the 1940s registered a growth beyond that movement.

Formula: Naboth's Vineyard

In an essay conveniently entitled "Naboth's Vineyard," Renato Poggioli has described literary pastoralism—or at least one type of pastoralism—in language that elucidates *Knight's Gambit*:

> In the pastoral dispensation the humble and the poor lead a life that is almost safe from internal disorder; yet their harmless happiness is all too often threatened by the encroachments of the proud and the powerful, by the incursions of those who roam the wild, or by the oppressions of those who dwell within city walls. Thus, for no fault of its own, the bucolic community is forced to taste the bitter fruits of that insecurity which should curse only those who by living within the great world accept the struggle for life as the condition of man. It is also for this reason that many a "pastoral oasis" comes to an untimely end. The idyllic imagination is aware of such a challenge, and its response is one of protest, if not of revolt. The bucolic reaction to might and violence is primarily sentimental; the consciousness of its own innocence, merging with the awareness that the precariousness of its happiness is due to acts of men rather than to "acts of God," produces in the pastoral soul a sense of outraged justice.

Through a series of kindred literary dispossessions (in 1 Kings 21, in Virgil's First Eclogue, in *Don Quixote*, in Goethe's *Faust*) Poggioli traces a tradition of pastoral rebellion against the encroachments of the mighty. This strain of pastoralism—unlike the traditional bucolic vision, which "is after all fundamentally static, and as such alien to the notion of social and political change"—has registered periodic protests against "the wicked and the mighty" who "covet the property of the meek and the weak and . . . by means fair or foul succeed in satisfying their evil greed."[16] The first five stories of *Knight's Gambit* voice just such a protest.

The protest is leveled not at the hierarchical social structure of the community, but at outside threats to that structure. It is aimed at defending the agrarian South against the forces of change from which so many literary Southerners of the twenties and thirties tried to secede: the modern city, capitalism, central government, and the mass market epitomized by the *Saturday Evening Post*. *Knight's Gambit* illustrates the trespasses of what Poggioli calls the "great world" upon the "pastoral oasis" of Yoknapatawpha.

Two contradictory pastoral visions order Faulkner's world, then. In *The Wild Palms* and *The Hamlet*, a conservative sense of justice applies to affairs *within* the community: sharecroppers and doctors do not mix; Snopeses should not rise. In *Knight's Gambit*, a reactionary sense of justice applies to relationships *between* the community and the outside world. The first adjudicates injuries by contriving "compensations" for the victims; the other, by expelling or destroying the injurious party. Each dispensation preserves the status quo.

The murders in the first five stories conform to a pattern. They are crimes against the orderly transmission of property from one generation to the next, and thus against the land, against agriculture, against patriarchy. Such transmission is most orderly through male rather than female heirs, because fathers can control their own sons more effectively than they can control other men's sons who might marry their daughters. Sons occasionally leave for the city or factory and bring back urban and industrial values if they return; but more often they either stay on the land or return from the seductive city chastened and purged. Daughters, however, even when they themselves remain faithful to the land, may marry men who will betray it; and the community may consequently lose control over vital parts of its territory. Endogamy, or marriage within the community, safeguards the social welfare; exogamy, or marriage outside, jeopardizes it. Whether by a son or by a daughter, exogamy in Faulkner's stories constitutes a sin that breeds crimes.[17]

The victims of these crimes include proprietors whose lands are usurped and inheritors dispossessed of their patrimonies. The criminals are men either foreign to or alienated from the traditions of the community. Their *modus operandi* frequently involves marrying into the closed society, to which they nevertheless remain strangers. (Thomas Sutpen provided an earlier example of the evils of exogamy in *Absalom, Absalom!*) Gavin Stevens uncovers their misdeeds not like Sherlock Holmes through esoteric knowledge of arcane disciplines, but precisely through his intimate familiarity with his neighbors and his county. The clues he detects have significance within a local, rural context; and the malefactors who leave them either stand outside that context or have fallen so far from its traditions that their ignorance of it betrays them—ignorance of how to run a trotline, of how to make cold toddies, of the idiosyncratic behavior of a particular horse. In Faulkner's formula, the social good is located within the boundary of a closed community; evil occurs when that boundary is penetrated. The first five stories in *Knight's Gambit* conform to such a pattern; the sixth breaks it.

The very first paragraph of "Smoke" sets forth a paradigm that recurs throughout the book. When a "foreigner" marries a landowner's daughter and gains control of the land, trouble ensues:

> Anselm Holland came to Jefferson many years ago. Where from, no one knew. But he was young then and a man of parts, or of presence at least, because within three years he had married the only daughter of a man who owned two thousand acres of some of the best land in the county, and he went to live in his father-in-law's house, where two years later his wife bore him twin sons and where a few years later still the father-in-law died and left Holland in full possession of the property, which was now in his wife's name. But even before that event, we in Jefferson had already listened to him talking a trifle more than loudly of "my land, my crops"; and those of us whose fathers and grandfathers had been bred here looked upon him a little coldly and a little askance for a ruthless man and (from tales told about him by both white and negro tenants and by others with whom he had dealings) for a violent one. (KG, 3)

Old Anse disturbs the people of Yoknapatawpha because, as they say, "wherever he came from and whatever he was bred to be, it was not a farmer" (KG, 5). Not only does he fail to "[do] justice to" (KG, 5) "some of the best land in the county" (KG, 3), he also refuses to pay taxes on it, thus threatening his heirs with dispossession. Of his twin sons, the younger, Anselm Junior, resembles him most. He runs away from home while in his teens, returns to demand half the estate—threatening thereby to divide it—and abandons it permanently when his father obstinately refuses to give it up. The older twin, Virginius, remains on the land farming it and leaves only when forced. When his father accuses him of coveting the whole farm, Virginius replies, "I'd rather take a little of it and farm it right than to see it all in the shape it's in now" (KG, 6). When he leaves, he goes only a few miles away to stay with a maternal cousin on a "good farm" (KG, 7), which he then disencumbers of debt.

Granby Dodge, the cousin, is "no farmer either" (KG, 7). He borrows from Virginius enough money to pay taxes on the Holland farm, but only because he considers it a capital investment. He negotiates with his bene-factor a mutual deed-of-trust will and inserts himself into the line of inher-itance. He then conspires with urban forces to execute his crime, hiring a Memphis hoodlum to assassinate Judge Dukinfield, the arbiter of Old Anse's will whose very name ("Duke in field") signifies agrarian legit-imacy. Dodge's treachery miscarries because of his choice of instruments: Old Anse's horse is too well known by the community, while the hood-lum—with his fast car, conspicuous manner, and city tobacco—is too foreign to it. The clues that Faulkner's detective notices, then, are of two types: those that distinguish the inside from the outside, and those that distinguish the outside from the inside. Stevens bases his criminology upon a sure knowledge of the community's boundaries.

In the end, Virginius inherits the land for himself and, in stewardship, for his brother. The resolution of the mystery leaves the land "intact" and in the control of the man best prepared to "do it justice" (KG, 5). Thus the justice that prevails in "Smoke" applies as much to the land as to the men who have contested it. To emphasize the importance of inheritance, Ste-vens advises Virginius to "[m]ake Anse your heir, if you have to have a will" (KG, 34). Clear, unambiguous lines of descent are necessary to pre-vent such assaults on property as Dodge has made, and the most secure line follows the path of greatest consanguinity.

"Monk" is concerned less with a weakness in the process of inheritance than with the consequences of a disinheritance already accomplished and with the miraculous perseverance of the agrarian heritage despite it. Like the Holland twins, Monk is the product of an exogamous union. His father had returned to the county, after ten years in the "great world," with a woman companion: "a woman with hard, bright, metallic, city hair and a hard, blonde, city face," wearing an expression that is deadly "as a snake is deadly" (KG, 41). The metallic serpent from the city, who intrudes upon the "green solitude" of the agrarian garden, appears elsewhere in Faulkner. But this woman is less dangerous than she might be, because the man she tempts from the community is a liability to it, having already betrayed his heritage. He further betrays it by abandoning Monk to be raised by his grandmother, who dies before she can even teach him that his real name is Stonewall Jackson Odlethrop. Monk is adopted first by a moonshiner and then by the owner of a filling station. When he grows up, he is convicted of a murder he did not commit. Listening to his indictment, he inexplicably objects to the reading of his name: "My name ain't Monk; it's Stonewall Jackson Odlethrop" (KG, 45). Five years into his life sentence, a trouble-making convict named Terrel persuades him to murder the prison warden. Stevens later discovers that Terrel incited Monk by somehow instilling in him a desire "to go out into the free world, and farm" (KG, 52). Like his betrayer Terrel, Monk has never worked on a farm: "He had seen it, of course, the cotton and the corn in the fields, and men working it. But he could not have wanted to do it himself before, or he would have, since he could have found chances enough" (KG, 49). Yet he is willing to kill and die for the idea of farming.

Why was Monk moved by Terrel's agrarian appeal? How did he re-member his namesake Stonewall Jackson, the defender of the agrarian community? Stevens "solves" the who-done-it questions, purely by acci-dent, at a meeting of the parole board. But these real mysteries remain; indeed, Faulkner turned them into the point of his story—the only "veri-similitude and credibility" that narrator Charles Mallison renders from the "mutually negativing anecdotes" of Monk's tale (KG, 39).[18] Chick offers only a gesture toward explaining Monk's agrarianism rationally; then he resolves the mystery with another mystery. The power of the land, he says, the perdurability of the agrarian ideal, is ineffable. All we know is that it persists. "[T]here it was," Chick says, "inherited from the earth, the soil, transmitted to him through a self-pariahed people—something of bitter pride and indomitable undefeat of a soil and the men and women who trod upon it and slept within it" (KG, 46).

Like the tall convict in "Old Man," Monk belongs to the patient "en-during classes" of whom Faulkner approved. Terrel and the state governor represent rebellious elements of the same class, and each is therefore a villain. Like Monk, Terrel had worked in a filling station. He too was jailed for murder, and his own explanation of the crime is significant within the context of Knight's Gambit: "he said that the deceased had seduced his (Terrel's) daughter and that his (Terrel's) son had killed the man, and he was merely trying to avert suspicion from his son" (KG, 56). The patrimony threatened by the seduction was only a filling station—a business, not a tradition—and Terrel's defense therefore proved a sham. So, obviously, does his pretense to agrarian sentiments.

Chick describes the Governor as "a man without ancestry and with but little more divulged background than Monk had; a politician, a shrewd man who (some of us feared, Uncle Gavin and others about the state) would go far if he lived" (KG, 50–51). Actually, the Governor does have a "background," though not the kind Chick means. He even tells Stevens about it: "Mr. Stevens, you are what my grandpap would have called a gentleman. He would have snarled it at you, hating you and your kind; he might very probably have shot your horse from under you someday from behind a fence—for a principle" (KG, 54). Like Flem Snopes, the Governor is a little man who has become big; and his hegemony, from Stevens's point of view, amounts to a perilous inversion of the social hierarchy. Monk, Terrel, and the Governor all derive from a similar social "background." But Faulkner sentimentalizes Monk, who mysteriously carries on the agrarian tradition, while he condemns Terrel and the Governor, who rebel against it. Thus a "conservative," "bucolic" vision of the community intersects with a "reactionary" defense of it against outside forces.[19]

"Tomorrow" also resolves *its* murder mystery with another mystery. It presents the facts of the case from the beginning. The "well-to-do farmer" Bookwright has committed the same crime in which Terrel had tried to implicate his son in "Monk," the murder of a daughter's seducer. The community apparently considers this an acceptable action for a farmer to take, though not for the owner of a filling station. Bookwright has avenged his daughter and, more important, saved her inheritance—the prosperous farm itself—from the claim of the "outlander" Buck Thorpe, a "kinless" man "who had appeared overnight from nowhere, a brawler, a gambler, known to be a distiller of illicit whiskey and caught once on the road to Memphis with a small drove of stolen cattle, which the owner promptly identified" (KG, 86). After Thorpe's death, the community learns that he had a Memphis wife, confirming their approval of his elimination.

But the jury includes Jackson Fentry, and Fentry hangs the jury. Why? The mystery in this story pertains again to a motive rather than to the particulars of a crime. Still, the solution illuminates the crime as well: Fentry's obstructionism derives from the same original sin that Bookwright prevents—liaison with an outsider. In his youth, Fentry left the land to earn some money in a sawmill, "risking a year or two to earn a little extra money, against the life his grandpa led until he died between the plow handles one day, and that his pa would lead until he died in a corn furrow, and then it would be his turn, and not even no son to come and pick him up out of the dirt" (KG, 92). He met a woman, an outsider, whose companion he became and whose child he adopted. He returned to his grandfather's farm, not with the corrupt values of industry, but with a recommitment to the life of the soil and a dedication to raising his new ward within the farming heritage he received from his own father and grandfather. He named him Jackson and Longstreet Fentry and raised him to be a farmer.

From an agrarian education, however, the child was abducted by his dead mother's wealthy relations and by their ally, the law. This separation disinherits the boy from the land, corrupting him beyond repair. It disrupts the transmission of property and of the agricultural tradition from one generation to the next. The result is the useless, dangerous Buck Thorpe, whom Bookwright eliminates before Buck can reenact the sin that ruined *him*. Ultimately, Bookwright murders Thorpe because of Thorpe's removal from farm life at an early age. The true murderers of "Bucksnort" are his own maternal family. Fentry condemns his literal murderer only because he remembers the farm boy who was to have been his heir: "somewhere in that debased and brutalized flesh which Bookwright slew there still remained, not the spirit maybe, but at least the memory, of that little boy, that Jackson and Longstreet Fentry, even though the man the boy had become didn't know it, and only Fentry did" (KG, 105).

The criminal in "Hand Upon the Waters" murders for part of $10,000, the double indemnity on Lonnie Grinnup's life. Boyd Ballenbaugh conforms to one of the patterns for malefactors in *Knight's Gambit*. Like Buck Thorpe and Monk Odlethrop's father, he has been lured away from the land by money, industry, the city; and he has returned with the lessons one learns "on the road to Memphis." He "had gone to Memphis years ago, where it was understood he had been a hired armed guard during a textile strike, but . . . for the last two or three years, [he] had been at his brother's, hiding, it was said, not from the police but from some of his Memphis friends or later business associates." Like Anse Holland and Granby Dodge, he arouses suspicion because he is "not a farmer": "he would brag about his past exploits or curse his present luck and the older brother who made him work about the farm" (KG, 71). Boyd's brother, Tyler, has also left the county and returned to it, but with a difference: he married (presumably a local girl, because Faulkner does not say otherwise) and bought land. Although he still mortgages his crop for money with which to speculate in the cotton market, his agrarian instincts are solid enough that he shares "the country-bred man's inherent, possibly atavistic, faint distrust, perhaps, not of men in white collars but of paving and electricity" (KG, 73). They are solid enough that Stevens can overlook his minor complicity in his brother's scheme.

Lonnie Grinnup fits the pattern for victims in a symbolic way. He owns neither land that anyone wants nor any eligible daughter or wayward son. Nor is he, an orphan, literally the heir of any landed father. But he represents the last link in a line of transmission that has diminished progressively from generation to generation. He has been dispossessed, even before his birth, of the estate created a hundred years ago by his ancestral namesake, Louis Grenier. His meager homestead represents the final residue of a vast patrimony: "Actually his hut and trotline and fish trap were in almost the exact center of the thousand and more acres his ancestors had once owned" (KG, 66). The appropriate heir to his depleted estate is the deaf-and-dumb orphan Joe, to whom Lonnie has been a "father" (KG, 67). By making themselves the beneficiaries of Lonnie's legacy, however, the Ballenbaughs disrupt the proper line of transmission.

"An Error in Chemistry" begins with the same "original sin" that opens "Smoke" and that Bookwright prevents Buck Thorpe from committing in "Tomorrow." The "good though small farm" (KG, 109) of Wesley Pritchel is threatened by the marriage of his only daughter to "the foreigner, the outlander, the Yankee who had come into our county two years ago as the operator of a pitch" (KG, 109). Joel Flint is a "dweller among the cities" (KG, 110), who insinuates his way into the Pritchel property, consciously plotting to appropriate it by an elaborate deception. He fails because he remains foreign—specifically, because he affects "a harsh and contemptuous derogation, sometimes without even provocation or reason or opportunity, of our local southern custom of drinking whiskey by mixing sugar and water with it" (KG, 110). Flint, or Signor Canova, has the worst possible motive for murder. Like Flem Snopes salting the grounds of the Old Frenchman place with coins, he intends to turn the land he usurps almost literally into money. He tries to sell the farm to "three northern men" who would mine the claypit in the middle of it and "manufacture some kind of road material out of the clay" (KG, 115). Flint not only murders for money; he threatens to divert land from agricultural to industrial use. Furthermore, the highway industry is the worst possible one he could attract to the land. Throughout *Knight's Gambit*, roads (especially "good roads") expose Yoknapatawpha County to the depredations of the city, of money, of the North, of exogamy, of the "great world" in general. Roads penetrate the community boundaries; they carry intruders into it and betrayers out of it, the road to Memphis bearing the heaviest traffic of any.

During the early decades of the twentieth century, the slogan "good roads" became an American catchphrase for progress. Especially in the Southeastern states, the proponents of the "New South" fostered the growth of a vigorous "good-roads movement," which encouraged commerce and succeeded in altering the landscape of the region permanently.[20] Thus, when Faulkner wrote that the "pine hill country in the eastern part" of Yoknapatawpha was populated by a clannish people "whom outsiders never saw until a few years back when good roads and automobiles penetrated the green fastnesses" (KG, 40–41), he was alluding to a current political issue. When he repeated the phrase in the next sentence, he drew that issue into the meaning of his mystery. "It was the good roads . . . which . . . brought Monk to Jefferson" (KG, 41), Chick says. They carried him off the land, into the filling station—their adjunct—and ultimately to his imprisonment and death. The "benefits" that George Tindall assigns to "good roads" in his history of the "New South" ("in the breakdown of provincial isolation, in the greater mobility of labor, in farm-to-factory commuting")[21] were not benefits in William Faulkner's view, though he did more than his share of commuting to Memphis, New York, and Hollywood. In the final scene of "Tomorrow," he placed Stevens and Chick on the road from Frenchman's Bend: "we were on the highway now, the gravel; we would be home in an hour and a half, because sometimes we could make thirty and thirty-five miles an hour, and Uncle Gavin said that someday all the main roads in Mississippi would be paved like the streets in Memphis and every family in America would own a car." "We were going fast now" (KG, 104), Chick adds, and the "we" includes all of Mississippi, all of that agrarian community whose well-being depends on stability and permanence—now moving fast, in one way and another, "on the road to Memphis."

The first five stories of *Knight's Gambit* repeat a formula. Crime results from interference, by a league of malicious outsiders and treacherous insiders, with the orderly processes by which land and agrarian values are transmitted from one generation to the next. As George Marion O'Donnell recognized, this pattern informs much of Faulkner's early fiction: the Old South beleaguered by a New South seduced by Progress. In the title story, however, Faulkner broke this pattern. Whereas he exposed sources of evil in the earlier stories, in the last one he indicated some of the community's strengths and inner defenses. He turned the old formula "upside down" (KG, 147), as Stevens keeps noticing, and answered the old problems of exogamy, patrimony, and expropriation with endogamous matrimony and assimilation.

If unwise marriages result in disrupted patrimonies in "Smoke" and "An Error in Chemistry," in the title story a problematic patrimony resolves itself in marriage. The initial situation seems formulaically engineered for disaster: "the old plantation six miles from town . . . had been an old place even in his grandmother's time, not so big in acreage but of good land properly cared for and worked . . . and the widower-owner . . . stayed at home and farmed his heritage . . . and the child, the daughter, the motherless girl . . . at seventeen and without warning to anyone, not to the county anyway, married a man whom nobody in that part of Mississippi had ever heard of before" (KG, 143–44). What follows is predictably disruptive to the community. Harriss, the daughter's new husband, proves to be a New Orleans bootlegger. The name she takes from him is Faulkner's pun on "heiress"; it defines her function in the community. At first, this outsider merely introduces the appurtenances of the city and of "big business" to the county: a big shiny car, a fur coat, a chauffeur, and a nurse. But after his wife's father dies and Harriss assumes control of the plantation, he completely transforms it. Whereas his father-in-law had "stayed at home and farmed his heritage" (KG, 143), Harriss becomes an absentee landlord who increasingly diverts the land from cultivation. He rebuilds the simple old house into an ersatz Hollywood mansion. He rents the farmland to someone who "didn't even live in the county" (KG, 153), then plows under "the old fields once dedicated to simple profit-producing corn and cotton," and sows them to "pasture grass costing more per pound than sugar" (KG, 154). He converts the place into a horse farm and invites his city friends—"strange outlanders" in sport cars—up for weekends of polo and "paper hunts" (KG, 156–58). Then Harriss dies, and his wife leaves for Europe with their two children.

From the beginning of this story, however, Faulkner suggested an alternative pattern—an endogamous one parallel to the exogamous one, mostly hidden from view but constantly emerging. In her youth Mrs. Harriss had experienced a prior romance, culminating in a broken engagement, with an unknown local suitor (KG, 144–45). The real mystery of "Knight's Gambit" pertains not so much to the murder attempt, the facts of which Faulkner did not obscure, as to this shadowy figure, who of course turns out to be Gavin Stevens. Chick Mallison becomes the detective, and Stevens the perpetrator of the intrigue.

Along comes the Argentine, Captain Gualdres, who fits the pattern of villainy in the previous stories and who arouses the immediate suspicion of the spectators of the Harriss drama. In the eyes of the county, he is an opportunistic "foreigner," intent on usurping the Harriss legacy through marriage. But he soon ingratiates himself with the community. On horseback rather than in a fast car, he travels throughout the county to learn the land and befriend its people. As they realize that "horses were his heart's love" (KG, 167), he grows in their esteem; finally, they see in him a fulfillment of "all the tenets of [their] agrarian and equestrian land" (KG, 168). Unlike the previous "foreigners" in *Knight's Gambit*, Captain Gualdres is gradually assimilated by the community. A prime suspect at the outset of the story, in the end he becomes the potential victim. This process of reversal culminates in his marriage with the Harriss girl, who loves him, rather than with her mother, who controls the money. When he enlists in the army, his assimilation is final: the foreign interloper finds *himself* seduced by the country he had intended to exploit.

Meanwhile, Max Harriss, who fits the pattern of victimization (as an heir threatened with dispossession), becomes the villain. Stevens prevents him from committing murder in defense of his birthright, a crime like the one for which the community actually congratulates Bookwright in "Tomorrow." In "Knight's Gambit," the would-be protector of the agrarian community himself requires the same assimilation as his victim, and Stevens provides it by forcing him into the army.

By the end of the story, Mrs. Harriss's endogamous romance surfaces. Stevens's marriage with her provides the agrarian formula with the happy resolution it lacks in all the previous stories. It restores local proprietorship over the "small but good" farm; and it imposes domestic control over both the daughter and the son of the house, insuring a safe transmission for at least one more generation. The insecurities latent in property are at least temporarily voided, and the community's boundaries are repaired—but with a difference. They now extend beyond Yoknapatawpha County.

Faulkner first composed "Knight's Gambit" shortly after the United States's entry into the Second World War. Suddenly, a series of stories that had been predominantly concerned with the preservation of distance between one community—a "pastoral oasis"—and the "great world" became attuned to the needs of the whole nation. An element of patriotic chauvinism entered "Knight's Gambit": Faulkner wrote two other stories about the regional response to the national defense, "Two Soldiers" and "Shall Not Perish," within a few months (BL, 1097–1101). The first typescript version of the Stevens story ends with Chick's promise to bring back a Japanese war souvenir for his uncle's wedding present.22 Perhaps Faulkner saw in the war a portent of social change in the South, a historical moment after which the old isolation would be impossible. Perhaps he chose to resolve the older, closed pattern of his crime stories at the very time when that pattern was becoming obsolete—when regional boundaries were dissolving and male heirs were leaving home *en masse*. Perhaps, too, he recognized that a community must either accommodate inevitabilities or die. "Knight's Gambit" expresses Faulkner's hope, if not his belief, that the Southern community would be able, like Mrs. Harriss in Europe, to travel through the "great world" without betraying itself: "she had the power or capacity, whatever it was, or maybe the gift, the fortune, to have spent ten years among what his great-aunt would have called the crowned heads of Europe, without ever really knowing she had left Yoknapatawpha County" (KG, 161).

Here is the aristocratic equivalent of "endurance," and it ironically unites Mrs. Harriss with Jackson Fentry and Monk Odlethrop. The strength that enables the county to survive even the impact of Harriss and his friends offers hope that it can assimilate almost any change. In fact, Harriss has left the county, and particularly his indirect heir Gavin Stevens, with a property far more valuable than it had been when he indirectly inherited it himself. This precedent creates the possibility that the community can withstand all the forces of progress—even when they are focused upon it by so powerful a figure as Huey Long, the great "good-road" builder of Louisiana,23 with whom Faulkner explicitly compares Harriss. Harriss's vice, conspicuous consumption, can become the county's asset, if only he can learn to control it. He has not built a "good road" from Jefferson to his estate, but he would have if he had only thought of it, "just as Huey Long in Louisiana had made himself founder owner and supporter of what his uncle said was one of the best literary magazines anywhere, without ever once looking inside it probably nor even caring what the people who wrote and edited it thought of him" (KG, 229–30).

Faulkner's allusion to the *Southern Review,* the principal organ of the Southern Agrarians after 1935, is appropriate in *Knight's Gambit.* It suggests another context in which the reversal of his pattern may have meaning. The Agrarians had mostly dispersed by 1942, or regrouped in Northern universities. Their interest had shifted from sociological topics to literary ones, for which they had always been more competent anyway. Their softening on political subjects coincided with a similar softening in Faulkner. Faulkner never *stopped* enunciating agrarian ideas (just as he never stopped pretending to be a farmer). The Christ-like corporal in *A Fable* (1954), for example, is specifically a peasant whose land is wrecked by bombardments directed from cities. Gavin Stevens voices a states'-rights philosophy in *Intruder in the Dust* (1948). But the symbolic expropriation in *A Fable* is no longer specifically Southern, and the locus of guilt in *Intruder* lies within the community rather than without. By mentioning the *Southern Review* in "Knight's Gambit," and especially by suggesting the cooperation between its editors and their redneck adversary (he was familiar with Warren's *All the King's Men* [BL, 1214]), perhaps Faulkner was signaling his assent to their seeming acquiescence.

One last context—a formal one—helps to explain the discontinuity between "Knight's Gambit" and the earlier stories. The title story serves the collection as a capstone narrative. Like the comparable capstones he wrote to transform *The Unvanquished* (1938) and *Go Down, Moses* (1942) from collections into novels, it effects a reversal that reorganizes the book it concludes. In Part Four of "The Bear," Ike McCaslin attempts to break with the past, to dispossess himself of his heritage, to step outside history by refusing to repeat it. His act, though unsuccessful, transforms the meaning of every other story in *Go Down, Moses* and crystallizes them in a matrix. *The Unvanquished* did not lack continuity when Faulkner wrote "An Odor of Verbena" to complete it, but Bayard Sartoris's refusal to avenge his father's murder transforms that book in the same way that Ike's decision shapes *Go Down, Moses.* The previous acts of violence in the book—from Bayard and Ringo's childish ambush attempt in "Ambuscade" to their brutal retaliation against Grumby for murdering Bayard's grandmother in "Vendee"—gain a mutual direction from their ultimate reversal. "An Odor of Verbena" resolves the previous stories by breaking their pattern of violence and reprisal. [24]

The title story of *Knight's Gambit* resolves that book, perhaps less effectively, in a similar way. It revises, or reverses, the formula in the previous stories. Its purpose is to defeat repetition by negating the further replication of a particular pattern. When restatement becomes redundant, the imagination requires deviation; and "Knight's Gambit" provided Faulkner with a welcome opportunity for variation, regardless of its wartime or Agrarian contexts. Paradoxically, the story written to unify and "integrate" the volume, to round it off and give it form, does so by means of a violent disruption of its design.

Revision: Embarrassment and Redemption

The revisionary force of "Knight's Gambit" is already present in the twenty-three-page typescript of 1942. The foreigner, named Gualdes rather than Gualdres, is already the target rather than the perpetrator of the murder attempt; at the end, he is already assimilated into the community by his enlistment. Gavin Stevens is already the shadow lover of Mrs. Harriss, and their marriage provides a resolution, if barely. Indeed, the basic plot of the final version of the story is fully present in its initial form, and much of the language of the typescript was incorporated into the published text of 1949. That language resembles the language of the other stories, with which the typescript version is generally compatible in style and tone.[25]

In revising "Knight's Gambit," Faulkner made the story "more complete and very plottified," as he told Harold Ober (BL, 1105; SL, 153), by adding incidents and correcting motivation. He filled out the characterizations of both Stevens and Chick considerably, making the development of each a matter of central concern in the final version. Other changes were tactical. In the first version, for example, Max Harriss threatens Gualdes because he needs the legacy Gualdes jeopardizes in order to pay gambling debts. In the published story, he threatens him because he falsely believes that Gualdes has been philandering with his fiancée, a farmer's daughter named Cayley, and that the foreigner has thereby insulted his mother and sister—the proper objects of Gualdes's attention. Thus Faulkner purified the Harriss boy's motives, making them more firmly agrarian. His criminal is now defending not just one but two households of women against the predation of the Latin lover who, presumably, covets their property. The change domesticated Max some-what—despite his fast car and European education—and clarified Faulkner's departure from his previous pattern. 26

But revisions such as these amounted to no more than minor adjust-ments. Faulkner contrived others that purposefully disrupted the book's coherence, that denied it an "entity of its own" except as a gesture of repudiation or exorcism. Among these was the addition of an extended bibliographical metaphor, through which Faulkner commented upon the whole enterprise of writing popular literature in which he had unwillingly engaged. For example, when Faulkner in his revision of "Knight's Gam-bit" recounted the history of the Harriss family, he began by comparing the four current players in its drama—Mrs. Harriss, her two children, and the Argentine—to the "stock characters in the slick magazine serial, even to the foreign fortune-hunter" (KG, 142). Thus he inserted a pejorative reference to magazine serial fiction into a book of stories that he had written, more or less as a series, for the slickest magazine of all—stories, moreover, in which he had created his *own* set of stock characters: the seduced heiress, the "outlander," the threatened heir. He was writing here about his own commercial ventures; and in case anyone might miss the point, he repeated it: "the county had been watching" the drama "as the subscribers read and wait and watch for the serial's next installment" (KG, 142). And again: "[F]or the next five years what [Chick's] uncle called that whole broad generation of spinster aunts who, still alive seventy-five years after the Civil War, are the backbone of the South's social and political and economic solidarity too, watched it as you watch the unfolding story in the magazine installments" (KG, 148–49). What this community watches, in the version of 1949, is a dramatization of the story Faulkner wrote for the *Saturday Evening Post* in 1942. In their reactions to it, they represent Faulkner's conception of what happened to his stories once they were published by the *Post*.

Faulkner often expressed disdain for his potboilers and for the publica-tions in which they appeared. As early as 1924, hoping more for mere acceptance than for a lucrative sale, he sent manuscripts to various East-ern magazines. When one of them was returned, as all of them were in those years, he told his mother, "This one is back from *The Saturday Evening Post*, but the day will come when they'll be glad to buy anything I write, and these too, without changing a word" (BL, 378). That day never truly came: even in 1954, the editors of the *Post* could regard one of his stories as unsuitable for its readers (BL, 1515). Throughout the thirties and forties, they rejected his writing frequently. To increase his chances of acceptance, Faulkner soon realized, he must write what he felt to be an inferior quality of fiction. He saw that his most successful submissions had followed recognizable formulae. Discerning or inventing these formulae occupied him increasingly, and he came to trust his sense of what the *Post* wanted. He once assured his brother John that the *Post* would buy some stories John had written. When they were rejected, Blotner relates, "Faulkner was irate. . . . He had considered himself an expert judge of the kind of thing the magazine would buy" (BL, 881). This anger was provoked too by the scandalous economic reality that the market for literature was less profitable than the market for entertainment.

From the moment in 1929 when he "began to think of books in terms of possible money" (SY, vi), he perceived two markets, two kinds of writing, and two kinds of motivation. About his short stories, for example, he wrote to his agent Morton Goldman in 1935, "I sell either to Scribners and Harpers for pittances, or to the Post" (SL, 88). Five years later, while struggling to save his land, he reported a familiar dilemma to his editor Robert Haas: "I wrote six short stories by March 15 [1940], trying to write the sort of pot boilers which the Post pays me $1,000.00 each for, because the best I could hope for good stories is 3 or 4 hundred, and the only mag. to buy them is Harper's etc. . . . Actually I would have been better off now if I had written the good ones. Now I have not only wasted the mental effort and concentration which went into the trash," but also the time spent "watching each mail train in hopes of a check" (SL, 121–22). Two months later, he complained that "first class stories fetch no money in America" (SL, 128).

His dilemma was compounded by the fact that writing commercially was not only distasteful to him but difficult as well. He had to make a conscious effort, in writing for the slick magazines, to accommodate their readers. The novelist whose "first class" stories could perplex professional reviewers had to brake his pen with a double drag to communicate with the average magazine subscriber. Even his comparatively accessible stories must have remained baffling to many *Post* readers: some chapters of *Knight's Gambit* can genuinely challenge comprehension. Many of Faulkner's stories were rejected for just this reason. Writing for the *Post*, then, must have required a large imaginative effort to downshift from a highbrow to a lowbrow style, to adjust his vision from one level of intensity to another. According to Blotner, he complained that the average *Post* story took him two weeks to write (BL, 1097). Compared to many other commercial writers, Faulkner boiled his pot very slowly.

His perception of a discontinuity between audience levels has significant implications for his career. From 1930 until 1950, his popular reputation, insofar as it existed, rose or fell in inverse proportion to the quality, as he judged it, of the work he produced. *Sanctuary*, the first book he wrote for money, became a best-seller. The specific public for which he said he designed it, by asking himself "what a person in Mississippi would believe to be current trends" (SY, vi), loathed it when it appeared in February 1931; but they were impressed by its notoriety and by the generous Hollywood contract to which it led (BL, 685–87, 766–68). They had been even more impressed by a publication of a few months before: "The appearance of 'Thrift' in the *Post* for September 6, 1930," writes Blotner, "occasioned comment among [Mississippi] Oxonians. To publish a book or two was one thing, but to appear in a national magazine, a household reading staple like the *Post*, that was real success. The [Oxford] *Eagle* acclaimed its author as one 'who is fast gaining national and international recognition'" (BL, 664–65).

This particular reception suggests a new dimension to Faulkner's pastoral surveillance of the community in which he dwelt. The Mississippi citizenry who might have read Faulkner in the *Post* were in many cases the very people about whom he wrote, and the two discontinuities— between himself and his subject and between himself and his readers— reinforced each other. This fact lends a special poignancy to Faulkner's initial presentation of Gavin Stevens as the man who could "discuss Einstein with college professors" and talk with the countrymen "in their idiom" (KG, 16). The *Saturday Evening Post* did not *quite* exemplify the discourse of countrymen, but it certainly contained no articles about Einstein for college professors either. In a way, Faulkner was doubly bilingual. On one hand, he could impersonate both Ernest V. Trueblood, his rhetorical *alter ego*, and the "squatting men" at Varner's store in order to produce the polyphonic music of *The Hamlet*. On the other, in *Knight's Gambit* he wrote simultaneously for two incompatible audiences—one "popular," one "literary."

Faulkner had already depicted the barrier between these two audiences in *The Wild Palms*. The two protagonists of that novel relate to each other as producer and consumer of popular literature, though they do not deal directly with each other. Harry Wilbourne, who enacts many of Faulkner's insecurities about his own career, spends part of his time in Chicago writing profitable fiction. If his "primer-bald moronic fables" (WP, 123) do not closely resemble Faulkner's own magazine fiction except as parodic exaggerations of it, neither does the tall convict of "Old Man" accurately represent the average "person in Mississippi" (SY, vi) to whom Faulkner claimed in 1932 to have pandered—except as his grotesquely humorous distortion of that being. In the second sentence of "Old Man," Faulkner described the convict's attainments as a reader. The convict nurses an outrage directed at "the writers, the uncorporeal names attached to the stories, the paper novels—the Diamond Dicks and Jesse Jameses and such—whom he believed had led him into his present predicament through their own ignorance and gullibility regarding the medium in which they dealt and took money for, in accepting information on which they placed the stamp of verisimilitude and authenticity" (WP, 23).

Faulkner's ultimate irony here is that the real criminal in these detective stories is the author himself—the man without "good faith" (WP, 23) who writes for money. If the tall convict is Faulkner's joke on his Mississippi readers, the *Detectives' Gazette*, which the convict peddles among his neighbors to earn the money for his robbery-pistol, is his joke on himself. In effect, he accused himself of "[u]sing the mails to defraud" (WP, 24), of writing fiction that bears no commitment to the truth of the human heart. Both writer and reader are guilty of shirking their duties to each other. Between Harry, a producer, and the tall convict, a consumer, gapes a shattered synapse across which communication ceases.

A similar discontinuity holds within *Knight's Gambit*. The first five stories remain substantially as he submitted them to the *Post*. Although their prose is thicker than that of the usual *Post* fare and "they are un-doubtedly more deeply conceived than most crime stories,"27 they remain examples of Faulkner's lowbrow discourse. In translating only the final story from the language of the *Post* into literary discourse, therefore, he was creating a book in which—at least in his own perception—un-salvaged and salvaged materials would rest side by side. The revision of "Knight's Gambit," in a number of ways, expresses Faulkner's awareness of that fact; in some ways, it is the main subject of that revision.

In the final version of the story, the people of Yoknapatawpha "read" the narrative action as though it were a magazine serial. They therefore mis-read it. They are no more capable of understanding the events they watch than Oxford had been able to appreciate Count No 'Count. In 1929, Faulkner had complained from his home town that he lived "in a complete dearth of print save in its most innocent form. The magazine store here carries nothing that has not either a woman in her underclothes or someone shooting someone else with a pistol on the cover" (SL, 43). Now he would incorporate his neighbors' taste into his own narrative. In a long passage describing the community's imperceptiveness, Faulkner referred persistently to various other kinds of fiction, in books, theater, legend, and so forth. The community's reconstruction of the Harriss family's history is not only a fiction but a fiction borrowed from other fictions:

> And there was something else: an appendix or anyway appendage; a legend to or within or behind the actual or original or initial legend; apocryphal's apocrypha. . . . It was something about a previous involvement, prior to the marriage: an engagement, a betrothal in form in fact, with (so the legend said) the father's formal consent. . . . So it—the first, the other one, the true betrothal, worthy of the word for the simple reason that nothing came of it but apocrypha's ephemeral footnote . . . and nothing remained unless perhaps the flower, the rose pressed between the pages of a book . . . —was probably, without doubt, it had to be, the aftermath of some boy-and-girl business of her schooldays. . . .
> . . . even the rumor, legend's baseless legend, was born rather of a chance remark of her father's one day, and now its own part of the legend, to the effect that for a girl of sixteen to be partner in a betrothal was like a blind man being a partner in the ownership of an original Horatian manuscript. (KG, 144–46)

Significantly, Charles Mallison inherits the legend of the apocryphal suitor as part of his mother's and grandmother's library. The books in this collection are sentimental novels, "through which moved with the formal gestures of shades the men and women who were to christian-name a whole generation: the Clarissas and Judiths and Marguerites, the St Elmos and Rolands and Lothairs: women who were always ladies and men who were always brave, moving in a sort of immortal moonlight without anguish and with no pain" (KG, 143). These books are as unfaithful to verisimilitude as the authors of Diamond Dick and the *Detectives' Gazette*. Their plots are formulae. Their characters, like those in the magazine serials, are types. They falsify the truth of the human heart, and so does the legend associated with them. The matrilineal inheritance of which they are part is a false one. Thus, once more, Faulkner repudiated the maternal origins of his vocation. Against the female legacy, he posed a male library, containing "books which his grandfather had chosen or heired in his turn from his father" (KG, 142).

The town's effeminate legend is false because it sentimentalizes what actually happened. [28] Chick and the townspeople misread the facts of the Harriss case because they perceive its principals as romantic types. They believe, for example, that the heiress's father forced her to marry the boot-legger to bring Harriss's money into the farm. As an unannounced expo-nent of Faulkner's *masculine* literary identity, in the face of his apparent surrender to a feminine, "popular" identity, Stevens disputes this assump-tion. Feigning detached curiosity, he explains why he disagrees, in a "voice which talked constantly not because its owner loved talking but because he knew that while it was talking, nobody else could tell what he was not saying" (KG, 148). This sounds so much as if it could be Faulkner's description of his own rhetorical practice that we should pay very close attention to what the author says, or fails to say, in the sentences that follow:

> The whole plot was hind-part-before, his uncle said; all the roles and parts mixed-up and confused: the child acting and reading what should have been the parent's lines and character . . . not the parent but the child putting aside the childhood sweetheart (no matter how thin and ephemeral had been that entanglement, his uncle said, asking, so his, Charles's, mother told, for the second time if anyone had ever learned the sweetheart's name or what had become of him) in order to lift the mortgage on the homestead; the child herself choosing the man twice her age but with the Midas touch whom it should have been the father's role to pick and, if necessary, even bring pressure to bear to the end that the old romance . . . be voided. (KG, 148)

Likewise, Faulkner turned his detective formula "upside-down" and "hind-part-before." He presented stereotyped characters from whom, based on the previous stories, we should expect typical behavior; then he confounded those expectations, breaking down formularized perception and substituting the "truth." Stevens knows that the community's percep-tion is false, because he himself is the secret sweetheart in Mrs. Harriss's past. [29] He occupies a position of privileged information, unavailable to anyone else in the story except as *he* reveals it. This privilege effects a major reversal of the earlier stories, in which the realm of true knowledge is public, though local. In the earlier stories, Stevens can solve crimes because of his superior grasp of local common knowledge. In "Knight's

Gambit," however, he cultivates a mystery of which he is the author and preserves it for as long as it suits his purpose. These two kinds of performance correspond to Faulkner's different methods at the two levels of discourse on which *he* performed.

Stevens's purposeful elusiveness resembles Faulkner's own literary inaccessibility; in "Knight's Gambit," the town of Jefferson understands him no more perfectly than Faulkner's Oxford—and the American public it epitomized—understood him. Like Faulkner, Stevens speaks by indirection and ellipsis; his listeners, including Chick, often lose his meaning. "Say it in English if you can" (KG, 138), Max Harriss tells him when Stevens answers a question with an elliptical question; and Stevens must repeat his meaning, but at a lower level. Like Stevens, Faulkner had to translate his meanings down to a popular idiom: when he first considered revising "Knight's Gambit," still hoping to sell it to the magazines, he planned to "simplify it to primer class"—another version of "saying it in English." When he came to the business of redeeming his primer fictions, however, he had to translate them back into his own language.

Gavin Stevens is a perpetual translator, and translations of various kinds occur throughout the story. Stevens demonstrates his fluency in Spanish, Greek, and German; he is presumably competent in other languages as well. Mrs. Harriss's father reads Ovid, Horace, and Catullus in the original Latin (KG, 152). His daughter, according to Stevens, translated Stevens's letters not only from one language to another but also from one level of discourse to another. Chick attempts to translate Stevens's conversation in Spanish with Gualdres, but must rely on his uncle's later memory of it.

At least since Ernest V. Trueblood had translated the story of his "employer" for Faulkner's translator, Maurice Coindreau, Faulkner had been concerned with impediments to communication. He was deeply aware of the difficulty of successfully transmitting himself to his auditors and of the necessity of doing so on the proper level of discourse. Within "Knight's Gambit," Faulkner demonstrated the discontinuity between democratic accessibility and esoteric inaccessibility, between the shadowy openness of the popular mind and the obscure precision of an elite comprehension. Within the very text of this "fiction," he rehearsed his own chronic effort to reconcile his private needs with the public demand.

The most suggestive translation in the story is Stevens's "Translation," "which the whole family referred to with a capital T—the rendering of the

Old Testament back into the classic Greek into which it had been translated from its lost Hebrew infancy—which [Chick's] uncle had been engaged on for twenty years now . . . retiring to the sittingroom once a week
always . . . shutting the door behind him" (KG, 207). At one level, the
Translation is a ridiculous gesture toward the eccentricity of detective heroes—in a class with Philo Vance's encyclopedic erudition and Nero
Wolfe's collection of orchids. At another, it reflects a project Faulkner
himself was working on at the time he revised "Knight's Gambit": the
translation, in A Fable, of the New Testament into modern language and
incident, and of ostensibly French dialogue into English. At still another,
it epitomizes Faulkner's whole career: in attempting to capture the truth of
"the human heart in conflict with itself" (ESPL, 119), he had been trying
to write a kind of Scripture, with which "magazine serials" interfered. His
revision of "Knight's Gambit" was not divinely inspired, assuredly; but it
did embody an effort to restore a text to the purity of its author's original
intentions, before the distortions of transmission and reception.

"Knight's Gambit" accomplishes a backward movement to recapture
the truth behind the legendary fiction associated with Mrs. Harriss's first
suitor. In the first long digression in the story, Chick presents the popular
legend as it has been transmitted to him from his grandmother and
mother (KG, 143). Stevens immediately begins to criticize that fiction: in
two successive revisions of it near the end of the book, he corrects it
progressively, ultimately revealing himself and marrying Mrs. Harriss. His
corrections are still fictions, however, no matter how accurate they may be
historically, and he revises each fiction in turn, trying to arrive at the most
"truthful" one—truthful, that is, to the heart. This, for Faulkner, is the
proper method of the writer: the process of revision should involve a steady
elaboration of one's meaning, not merely an accommodation of the least
common denominator in the public—not simply "saying it in English."

Certainly, the revisions of "Knight's Gambit" complicate our reading of
the original magazine fiction. Rather than "simplify it to primer class," as
he had first proposed (rather, that is, than translate it into demotic English), he worked to force his readers to work at recapturing his meaning.
As with so much of Faulkner's fiction, we must reread "Knight's Gambit,"
and then the previous stories in the volume, to reconstruct the evidence
we have missed. We must continually revise our reconstruction of his
meaning, moving backward—literally, through the pages of his books—
toward the sources of his meaning. The ultimate object of Stevens's Trans-

lation is not just to regain the Greek Bible. It is to regain the Word at the root of every mere word; to seek the "lost Hebrew infancy" of every intention; to retranslate any text, including detective stories, into what Faulkner called in his Nobel Prize Speech "the old verities and truths of the heart, the old universal truths lacking which any story is ephemeral and doomed" (ESPL, 120). It is to move backward along the distorting line of transmission, toward a unity between utterance and audition. *Knight's Gambit* articulates that desire and its inevitable failing.

The first time Stevens corrects the legend of Mrs. Harriss's lost sweetheart he offers Chick a story about having crossed two letters written in different languages and at different levels of discourse (KG, 236). A confusion like this governs *Knight's Gambit*, but with a purpose. For his second revision, significantly, Stevens recommends that Chick consult a scene from a book. The final resolution of the mystery of Faulkner's own book— and the solution to Faulkner's guilt over its origins—is to be found "[i]n the library. Simply by opening the right page in Conrad" (KG, 244). The nearest advance to the Word behind the word is yet a fiction, the most truthful one Stevens can impose upon the facts as he knows them. It is a book above formula, beyond the common apprehension, like the Bible Stevens translates back into itself.

CHAPTER SIX

GO DOWN, MOSES

Always in August my nature will go its own way and seek its own peace. I roam solitary, but never alone, over this rich pastoral land, crossing farm after farm, and keeping as best I can out of sight of the laboring of loitering negroes. For the sight of them ruins every landscape, and I shall never feel myself free till they are gone.

James Lane Allen, *A Kentucky Cardinal*

We have here a problem in the sociology of sensibility that is obscured by certain psychological attitudes brought to Negro life by whites.

The first is the attitude which compels whites to impute to Negroes sentiments, attitudes and insights which, as a group living under certain definite social conditions, Negroes could not humanly possess. It is the identical mechanism which William Empson identifies in literature as "pastoral." It implies that since Negroes possess the richly human virtues credited to them, then their social position is advantageous and should not be bettered; and, continuing syllogistically, the white individual need feel no guilt over his participation in Negro oppression.

Ralph Ellison, "Richard Wright's Blues," in *Shadow and Act*

"Stories About Niggers"

Go Down, Moses embodies one final version of the pastoral worldview that so thoroughly if variously ordered Faulkner's work at mid-career. First, *The Wild Palms* and *The Hamlet* articulated a pastoralism of class, in which Faulkner defined his unstable relationship to his redneck neighbors—and the unstable relationship between the aristocrat and the peasant within himself—by means of narrative schizophrenia and stylistic excess. Then, the early stories of *Knight's Gambit* articulated a pastoralism of region, in which Faulkner depicted the threat to the Southern "oasis" posed by forces of change in the "great world" outside. Unlike the pastoralism of class, which asserted the immutability of a social structure despite the actual breakdown of that structure, the regional pastoralism alluded readily to serpents in the agrarian garden, which Faulkner ultimately attempted to accommodate. That accommodation required a recognition of historical change that *The Wild Palms* and *The Hamlet* were designed to resist, and it prodded him to reevaluate the economic grounds of his career.

Finally, *Go Down, Moses* articulated a pastoralism of race, which even more insistently than class or region led Faulkner to question his vocation. *The Wild Palms* started as an exercise in separating social levels and ended by calling attention to its own artificiality. *The Hamlet* started as a series of Southwestern frame tales and ended by confounding "William Faulkner" with Ernest V. Trueblood. *Knight's Gambit* started as a "formulaic entertainment" and ended by repudiating both its popular audience and its agrarian premises. *Go Down, Moses* started as a standard literary exploitation of Southern blacks, and it ended not only by reversing its racist formulae and by impelling Faulkner to redeem an embarrassment, but also by forcing him to examine his relationship *as a writer* to the panorama of Southern history. In engaging black people as a literary subject, he launched his fullest, riskiest investigation of his career, and he resurrected the tensions—between confinement and release, between stasis and motion, between silence and speech—that had generated that career. *Go Down, Moses* records a full-blown Eriksonian "crisis of generativity."

He commenced the book as a treatment, at first humorous but then serious, of his literary and social relationship to Negroes. When he wrote "Delta Autumn," however, a new concern diverted the whole volume toward a very different subject. The topic that occupied Faulkner in that story, and for years afterward, was exhaustion. He began to view human history as a process of progressive depletion, against which he would construct the Nobel Prize Acceptance Speech and some other texts as wishful counterstatements. Moreover, his perception of cosmic decline simply reinforced a sense of personal exhaustion: during his early forties, he suffered the onset of a spiritual menopause—a gnawing suspicion that his life was finished and that writing was futile. As abstractions, race and exhaustion are apparently separate subjects. But in Faulkner's experience they became closely related; he attempted to combine them during the revision process that followed "Delta Autumn" and, especially, during the creation of "The Bear." That combination reflects Faulkner's recognition that writing truthfully about Negroes was for him an enterprise doomed to failure, and that his own literary exhaustion originated in the moral exhaustion of the South.

The composition history of *Go Down, Moses* is far more complex than that of any of Faulkner's previous novels. When Random House published it in May 1942, *Go Down, Moses* incorporated at least ten different short stories, eight of which had already been printed in various periodicals. But Faulkner's original conception of the book had been modest. Its germ was a small group of stories about Southern Negroes that he had written for money. When he first broached his idea for the book to his Random House editor, in April 1940, one month after the publication of *The Hamlet*, it was part of an emergency plan to liquidate his mounting debts. To generate immediate income, he was writing "trash stories," he reported, though he had two more lucrative ideas in mind which he lacked the time to pursue: "a blood-and-thunder mystery novel" and a book "in method similar to THE UNVANQUISHED," chapters of which he had tried unsuccessfully to market as short stories (SL, 122).

The further development of the book suggests that the stories he mentioned here must have included "A Point of Law," "Gold Is Not Always," "The Fire on the Hearth," and "Pantaloon in Black." He may also have meant to include "The Old People," which he had also recently written (BL, 1024); but it belongs more plausibly to a different cycle of stories, including "Lion" and "A Justice," in which Quentin Compson relates his experiences hunting with Sam Fathers in the big bottom of the Tallahatchie. The other four stories all portray black characters; and, though Sam Fathers is part Negro, "The Old People" emphasizes his Indian blood. Likely, Faulkner added it only later, after his conception of the collection had expanded beyond the narrow racial perspective of its first four stories. Despite his blanket reference to those stories as "trash," he was actually quite proud of the last of them; moreover, despite his blanket denial of their success, he had sold the first to *Collier's* for $1,000 the previous winter (BL, 1036).

He had written "A Point of Law" in August 1939, during a break in the composition of *The Hamlet* (BL, 1027–28). "I have had to put the [*Hamlet*] mss. aside twice," he had written to Haas, "to write short stories to keep pot boiling, will have to hammer out another one now" (SL, 114). The humorous story he then confected introduced Lucas Beauchamp to his fiction for the first time—as a comical black tenant on the cotton plantation of Roth Edmonds. Written in the mode of dialect humor still popular then, it relates Lucas's attempt to eliminate a young black chucklehead named George Wilkins from the plantation, both as a competitor in the bootlegging business and as a prospective son-in-law of whom he disapproves. His efforts, mostly committed under cover of darkness, are foiled by his daughter Nat, who contrives to place the incriminating moonshine on Lucas's own doorstep and who has secretly married George. The legal point of the title is Nat's surprise immunity, as George's new wife, to testifying against him, a technicality that frustrates Roth Edmonds's attempts to prosecute both Lucas and George (US, 213–25).[1]

The purchase of this story by *Collier's* encouraged Faulkner to repeat the formula that had earned him a thousand dollars. In February 1940, he turned out the next two stories of the group (BL, 1036–37), both of which follow Lucas's efforts to find a buried treasure despite the opposition of both Roth Edmonds and Lucas's wife Molly. In "Gold Is Not Always," Lucas uses the salted-mine trick that Flem Snopes had perpetrated in "Lizards in Jamshyd's Courtyard," to hoodwink the salesman of a metal detector into renting his own machine, which Lucas has "paid for" with one of Roth's mules. His success as an entrepreneur of buried treasures only exasperates the white landlord further (US, 226–37). In "The Fire on the Hearth," Lucas himself spends his nights searching for the treasure with "his" machine. Molly forces him to abandon his moonlight obsession by threatening to divorce him and by risking her own life to show him his folly. Apparently, Faulkner hoped to create a profitable series of "Lucas Beauchamp" stories like the "Bayard-Ringo" series out of which he had formed *The Unvanquished*. As Blotner surmises, Faulkner must have hoped to "use Lucas Beauchamp as a central recurring character—a kind of Uncle Remus who fooled adults instead of telling stories to children" (BL, 1037).

Presumably, however, he found the comic Negro trickster either inadequate to his purpose or incompatible with his taste, for he wrote no more "Lucas Beauchamp" stories. This restraint may have been financially motivated: "Gold Is Not Always" did not find a buyer until September, and then only the *Atlantic Monthly* for $300, while "The Fire on the Hearth" never did sell (BL, 1060). Nevertheless, the next story Faulkner wrote suggests that his principal reason for discontinuing the Lucas series was shame.

With "Pantaloon in Black," which he completed in March 1940, Faulkner dropped Lucas and the comic tone he associated with him (BL, 1038). He did not employ him again until 1948, by which time (in *Intruder in the Dust*) the character had become more serious. "Pantaloon" tells of the mourning of Rider, a powerful black man who works both for a local sawmill and for Roth Edmonds, upon the death of his wife Mannie. Following her funeral, he spurns the consolations of his friends and returns to his cabin, where Mannie's ghost visits him. To escape the pain of remembering her, he attempts but fails to distract himself—first with work, next with alcohol, then with gambling, and finally by murdering a white man who cheats him at dice. Apparently choosing "nothing" rather than "grief," he provokes his own lynching. Afterward, the sheriff's deputy who "had been officially in charge of the business" cites Rider's violent behavior following Mannie's death as proof that "[t]hem damn niggers" lack human feelings. Describing Rider's actions to his own wife, he misreads every manifestation of the black man's lament as a vicious disrespect for Mannie's memory (US, 238–55).

"Pantaloon in Black," a tragedy of stereotyped perception, refers at a basic level to Faulkner himself. It consists of two narrative segments: the main portion of the story, in which an omniscient narrator describes Rider's last day objectively; and an epilogue in which a typical white Southerner discloses his racist vision of the Negro. The story's meaning lies chiefly in the ironic distance between these two accounts.[2] A similar distance separates the three Lucas Beauchamp stories from "Pantaloon": this four-story sequence provides a model for one primary impulse in *Go Down, Moses*—the impulse to resist a stereotype, to break a pattern of perception, to reverse a repeated signal. The same revisionary force that had shaped *The Unvanquished* and that would later shape *Knight's Gambit* affected *Go Down, Moses* early in its creation. "Pantaloon," in the dignified humanity it confers upon Rider, revises the conventional perception of the Negro as clown or buffoon that dominates the Lucas stories. Indeed, coming as it did during the month following the composition of "Gold Is Not Always" and "The Fire on the Hearth," and taking as its subject a gross misreading of black behavior, "Pantaloon in Black" is surely "about" its author's guilty need to revise his own literary misperception of the Negro. That need became one of the defining motives of *Go Down, Moses*. Insofar as "Pantaloon" expresses it, the story is less about a black man named Rider or about race relations in the South than it is about the frustrated ambition of William Faulkner.

Faulkner liked this story better than the previous three. In a cover letter to his agent Harold Ober, he called it a "good story" (SL, 119), to distinguish it from "trash." But its particular reception must have confirmed his positive feeling for it only too well. In March, having just rejected "Gold is Not Always" and "The Fire on the Hearth," *Collier's* rejected "Pantaloon in Black" as well—but on the ground that "there was no place in the magazine for such excellent work" (BL, 1039). When a sale transpired the following August, it was to a "quality" publisher, *Harper's*, for only $400 (BL, 1056).

Faulkner wrote "Pantaloon" in March 1940. He unveiled the idea of a collection to Robert Haas in April (SL, 122). In May he elaborated it: "Ober has four stories about niggers," he wrote. "I can build onto them, write some more, make a book like THE UNVANQUISHED, could get it together in six months, perhaps" (SL, 124). Within two weeks, the project had solidified: on June 7, 1940, the "four stories about niggers" had become "5 short stories already written, two others planned, both of which might sell, one of which is a mystery story, original in that the solver is a negro, himself in jail for the murder and is about to be lynched, solves murder in self defense" (SL, 128). The latter must have been a variation on the "blood-and-thunder mystery novel" (SL, 122) he had mentioned in the earlier letter—the Lucas Beauchamp story he would finally produce eight years later as *Intruder in the Dust*. He was apparently trying to concoct enough stories to justify a volume, as part of a deal with Random House that he was currently negotiating to avoid selling Greenfield Farm. In late June, he threatened to accept a contract from Viking Press, but Bennett Cerf offered a $2,000 advance on the book of short stories if Faulkner would stay with Random House. When Faulkner accepted these terms, *Go Down, Moses* was officially conceived (BL, 1047–50). The seven short stories he spoke of in the letter—all about blacks—are its embryo.

The next two stories he wrote after "Pantaloon" were "Almost" and "Go Down, Moses." Neither of these was a "Lucas Beauchamp" story, but both were about Negroes. Faulkner may have felt he could connect them to

Beauchamp, as indeed he quickly did. He drew the first of them from the passage describing Uncle Buck and Uncle Buddy McCaslin's efforts to reform the slave system which he had inserted into "Retreat" during his revision of *The Unvanquished*. In "Almost," Bayard Sartoris describes Buck's pursuit in 1859 of one of the McCaslin slaves, Tomey's Turl, who habitually runs away to the neighboring plantation where his sweetheart Tennie lives. For years the McCaslins' neighbor, Jason Prim, has been scheming to marry off his spinster sister Sophonsiba to Uncle Buck, and he "almost" succeeds when Buck is trapped in her bedroom that night. Buddy rescues his brother from matrimony by winning a poker game, when Prim forfeits his bet upon realizing that Tomey's Turl has been dealing the cards. Prim recognizes that Turl, whose ownership Buddy has wagered against Buck's marital freedom, has stacked the deck so that he can move closer to Tennie. Faulkner sent "Almost" directly to the *Post*, which had printed most of the other "Bayard" stories; this one, however, the editors rejected (BL, 1050–53).

Faulkner wrote "Go Down, Moses" at about the same time, composing parts of it on the versos of a typescript revision of "Almost." He derived this story too from the material of a previous novel, *Absalom, Absalom!* At first, he named its protagonist Henry Coldfield Sutpen, and made him the grandson of Rosa Sutpen, one of Thomas Sutpen's slaves. While he was still working on the typescript, however, he altered these names (BL, 1054–55). As James Early suggests, Faulkner must have "sensed that in its general tone this story was more akin to the stories of other Negroes he had written earlier in the year than to a novel as powerful as *Absalom, Absalom!*"[3] Henry Coldfield Sutpen became first Carothers Edmonds Beauchamp and then Samuel Worsham Beauchamp; and his grandmother became Aunt Molly[4] Beauchamp, the wife who had brought Lucas into line in "The Fire on the Hearth." As the story opens, the grandson lies in an Illinois death row when Molly calls upon Gavin Stevens, the hero of the detective stories Faulkner was then writing. She has divined that her grandson is in trouble, and she asks Stevens to locate him. Stevens remembers the youth from six years before, when Roth Edmonds had banished him from the Edmonds plantation for some misdemeanor and when he had led a brief criminal career in Jefferson before disappearing. Aunt Molly declares that "Roth Edmonds done sold my Benjamin. Sold him in Egypt. Pharaoh got him—." Stevens discovers that the boy is about to be executed; and, with the local newspaper editor, he helps Molly retrieve his body from Illinois and bury it with dignity (US, 256–66). Faulkner sent "Go Down, Moses" to the *Post*, which rejected it (BL, 1055).

Although this story belongs as logically to *Knight's Gambit* as to the Lucas Beauchamp stories, Faulkner's alteration of the names indicates his determination to connect it primarily to the latter. As with *The Unvanquished*, he hoped to provide a continuity among the stories of the projected volume. While transforming them into a book, he may have become aware of another resemblance it bore to *The Unvanquished*: both collections afforded him an opportunity to salvage work that had been cheaply conceived and crassly executed. When Faulkner compared his new project to *The Unvanquished*, he revealed the meagerness of his ambitions for it. For *The Unvanquished* was the book, after *Sanctuary*, that he most consistently denigrated. He had blatantly concocted its stories as a formulaic series he could sell to the *Post* (BL, 855, 951). In 1934, he referred to them as "orthodox prostitution" (SL, 85). Yet, only two and a half years later as he revised the stories into chapters, according to Blotner, he began to feel that while "[t]his book might not have the weight of *The Sound and the Fury* . . . he could make it into a serious work of art, much as he had rewritten *Sanctuary* so that it would not 'shame' its two immediate predecessors" (BL, 958).

For *Go Down, Moses* he would come to entertain even higher ambitions. By the time he completed it in 1942, he must have hoped not only that he had redeemed the "nigger stories" which formed part of it but also that he had partially justified his complex relationship with the Negro race.

Faulkner probably turned to "stories about niggers" at this time partly because of his recent experiences with blacks. Primary among these was his assumption—through his purchase of Greenfield Farm in 1938—of the role of latter-day plantation master, a role that brought him into the very center of his cultural heritage. He had always wanted a farm, since his great-grandfather, his grandfather, and his father had each owned one. It would also, he wrongly expected, "provide some sort of hedge against the uncertainties of a writer's income." But the strongest appeal must have been "the idea of a link with the land, a more vital one than the proprietorship of Rowan Oak could give" (BL, 984). According to Michael Millgate, "its main importance was that it gave him an opportunity to acquire the kind of knowledge about farming—about the crops, the ani-

mals, the seasons, the weather, the land, and, not least, the tenants—
without which he could scarcely have written such books as *The Hamlet*
and *Go Down, Moses*."[5]

But neither Faulkner nor his brother John, whom he installed at the
farm as its manager, did the actual work of farming. John confessed to
Time that he was "not much of a farmer" and averred that "it would take a
man a lifetime to learn how to plough a straight furrow."[6] He later wrote
that William knew "a lot about farming but it was mostly from the book
side" (MBB, 242). Although "Farmer" William may have taken "a hand
now and then in the affairs of the farm" (BL, 1026), apparently he re-
stricted his labor to entering dates and names in his studbook or transactions in the commissary ledger (BL, 1048–49, 1091). He did buy a "Sears,
Roebuck garden tractor" and numerous attachments for it, with which to
mow his lawn at Rowan Oak (MBB, 202); and his stepson Malcolm
Franklin remembers Faulkner using his pasture at Rowan Oak as an annex
to his writing table: "He would sit at his typewriter for long stretches at a
time, there before the window that looked out across the pasture. Quite
suddenly he would get up, open the door to his office, reach for his hoe
placed conveniently just outside the door beneath the porte-cochère, and
head for the pasture. There he would stay for an hour or more furiously
chopping bitterweed. . . . Then he would return to his typewriter and
begin work" (BLRO, 84). Here, "Mr. Faulkner" and Ernest V. Trueblood
inhabit the same sweaty skin.

The men who worked Greenfield Farm, however, were its tenants, and
they were black. Faulkner entered into a relationship with them that must
have reminded him of the Old South. Perhaps, indeed, his main purpose
in acquiring the land was to solidify the plantation ethos he had already
begun to create by restoring Rowan Oak from dilapidation to inhab-
itability. A few years after be bought the mule farm, he enjoyed represent-
ing himself to an interviewer as a "country squire," who "bosses his cotton
plantation near Oxford, Miss., where he lives with his family in a fine
120-year-old house" (LG, 39). A local friend would characterize him as "a
plantation man. That's what he was. That's what he was trying to do."[7]

The racial implications of this cotton-baron impersonation are graphically displayed in a photograph that Faulkner commissioned in May
1938, two months after buying Greenfield. He had invited about a dozen
friends to attend, in costume, a "hunt breakfast" at Rowan Oak; and he
asked J. R. Cofield, the Oxford photographer, to preserve the occasion on

film. In the center of a group portrait that Cofield snapped on the front steps, Faulkner placed himself and Estelle on either side of Uncle Ned Barnett, the black major domo whom he had "inherited" from his parents and for whose welfare he always assumed responsibility. Dressed in the formal regalia of a butler, with a heavy gold chain looped across his vest, Ned held a silver tray, from which the man he habitually addressed as "Master" had just received a glass of bourbon. Faulkner had turned out in "shining boots and fawn-colored breeches, huntsman's cap, ruffled shirt, . . . velvet jacket, and gray gloves." From a thong about his neck hung a "hunting horn," which he had blown to welcome his guests (BL, 991–93, 998). Such was the ironic image of seigneurial splendor with which Faulkner chose to commemorate his proprietorship of a Mississippi mule farm. First at Rowan Oak and later at Greenfield Farm, he indulged a fantasy of plantation pomp.

Faulkner was as paternalistic with his tenants as he was with Ned, the family retainer. In his memoirs, John, who actually kept the store, re-called with businesslike disapproval his brother's generosity to "the Negroes"—keeping prices low in the farm commissary, for example (MBB, 193–96). For several years, too, William sponsored Fourth of July barbecues to celebrate the completion of planting, occasions when he socialized freely with the black residents of Greenfield, who entertained themselves and their proprietor by singing and dancing (BL, 996–97, 1026). Blotner suggests explicitly that Faulkner created the stuff of his Lucas series out of his experience on the farm, and that he modeled Roth Edmonds's role upon his own (BL, 1036–37). In the completed novel, Roth is forty-three years old, Faulkner's age when he began his final revisions. Faulkner seems not to have been so legalistic in dealing with his tenants as Roth is with Lucas, but he certainly experienced something of Roth's exasperation with Negro guile. "A good servant is always a perfect tyrant," he would observe, and he seems to have had Ned mostly in mind. At the first Fourth of July barbecue, for example, Faulkner decided to slaughter Uncle Ned's favorite steer, "Black Bully," and ordered him to carry out the execution. Shortly after the picnic, however, he saw the very steer he had told Ned to slaughter, which he assumed the party had eaten, walking about alive and well. When he confronted Ned with the deception, the old man said, "Master, I calls them all Black Bully." Usually Faulkner humored such insubordination, allowing his servant insidiously to rule him (BL, 996–99).

Faulkner's attempt to revivify the plantation ideal was accompanied by an effort to discover its historical actuality. For example, in April 1940, he returned a book about antebellum plantations to a neighbor, from whom he had borrowed other books on the same subject (BL, 1042n). In a letter, he referred to them as "documentary-historical-personal records," and to the particular book he was returning as "THE PLANTATION OVER-SEER" (SL, 120). If Blotner is correct in identifying this as John Spencer Bassett's *The Southern Plantation Overseer, As Revealed in His Letters*, then Faulkner had exposed himself—at precisely the time he was writing the first "stories about Negroes"—to a sympathetic record of the trials and tribulations of those who must manage black people on farms. The book consists principally of the letters to James K. Polk from his overseers on a plantation in Yalobusha County, Mississippi, during the 1830s and 1840s. Because Polk remained an absentee landlord, he constructed no "great house" or planter's residence, and the men who functioned as masters were not "gentlemen" but uncultured semiliterates. [8] Blotner suggests that "Bassett's faithful reproduction of the letters' phonetic spelling may have been useful to [Faulkner] when he came to record the commissary ledger entries of Uncle Buck and Uncle Buddy in 'The Bear'" (BL, 1042n).

But the book may have affected *Go Down, Moses* even before the composition of "The Bear": "Almost" occurs both in a county and in a decade that adjoin the setting of Polk's correspondence, and the McCaslin twins resemble the overseers in their vernacular idiom and in the crudeness of their establishment. Furthermore, Faulkner would have noticed that, among the reports of acreage, yield, and price, and of illnesses and births in the Quarters, the abiding preoccupation of the overseers was the tendency of their slaves to run away. He would also have read there that "[i]t was a common rule that slaves should not marry slaves living off the plantation, since such marriages involved visiting and brought up the problem of discipling [sic] such visitors when on the plantation of the wife's master." Here perhaps lay the origin of Tomey's Turl's rebelliousness, reinforcing Faulkner's effort to revise the stereotype of the Negro as a passive though mischievous collaborator in his own subservience. The book may have contributed to a revision, in Faulkner's mind, of the general meaning of the plantation. In Bassett's words, the letters of the overseers reflect "a life that was not what the novelists have presented."[9]

Other experiences challenged his paternalistic attitude toward "his" blacks at about the same time. During mid-1939, he began a series of discussions with James McGlowan, a local black youth whose desire to attain an education and a profession he encouraged. Faulkner talked with McGlowan about teaching his childhood nurse, Mammy Caroline Barr, to read and write. Later, they discussed black and white relationships (BL, 1026). When Faulkner won the Nobel Prize in 1950, he would advance $3,000 to McGlowan to pay his tutition first at Hampton College and later at the University of Michigan (BL, 1371). In 1939, his contact with McGlowan must have caused him to question the limitations of black characterization.

An event the next year made Faulkner scrutinize his paternalism more closely than ever. In January 1940, Mammy Callie Barr died (BL, 1034–35). Faulkner eulogized her as "one of my earliest recollections, not only as a person, but as a fount of authority over my conduct . . . and of active and constant affection and love" (ESPL, 117). Her death followed the first Lucas Beauchamp story only by several months, and Faulkner wrote the other two within a fortnight afterward. In their portrait of Molly Beauchamp, they reflect a softening of the Negro burlesque he had purveyed in "A Point of Law." The relationship between Molly and Roth Edmonds corresponds closely to Faulkner's relationship with Callie, which may have helped to stimulate the complex inquiry into race that Go Down, Moses became. Faulkner's attitude toward Callie epitomized his ambivalence about black people. She was born in slavery and, in her dependency on him, provided a direct historical link with the antebellum plantation he was trying to reestablish. Still, Faulkner asserted in the sermon he delivered at her funeral that "the relationship between us never became that of master and servant" (ESPL, 117). She presented a human challenge to stereotype that he could not ignore. Ultimately, he dedicated Go Down, Moses to her; and he made it record the division within himself between the paternalistic formulae of the plantation tradition and the knowledge in his heart.

Faulkner and Plantation Literature

Faulkner's proprietorship of Rowan Oak and of Greenfield Farm and his composition of "stories about niggers" placed him in a tradition of literary pastoralism which affected his self-image more consequentially than his treatments of class and region. This tradition originated in the bucolic ideals of Theocritus, Virgil, Sannazzaro, and Pope; but it was diverted from its origins by the South's "peculiar institution."

Lewis P. Simpson has outlined a Southern tradition of pastoralism that differs fundamentally from the pastoral dream that has dominated New England intellectual history. The New England colonies were founded in accordance with the image of "a garden (or a vineyard) enclosed against a wilderness (or desert), which with some degree of poetic license we may call the garden of the covenant," where the gardener would be a man of God fulfilling the intellectual destiny of his community. In the South, however, the "vision of an errand into the wilderness" was quickly displaced by a vision of "commerce and reason"—by "an errand into an open, prelapsarian, self-yielding paradise," where man could "be made regenerate by entering into a redemptive relationship with a new and abounding earth." While the Puritans saw Massachusetts as a hostile wilderness, to be redeemed only by the efforts of men covenanted with God, the men who settled Virginia saw it as a paradise already accomplished— by Nature—in which they could achieve redemption by simple contact with the ground beneath them. [10]

Out of this Antaean configuration, according to Simpson, the Southern imagination molded the image of the plantation to symbolize the fruition of its "errand." He traces the development of this symbol through the writings of Robert Beverley, William Byrd II, Thomas Jefferson, John Taylor of Carolina, John Randolph of Roanoke, and John Pendleton Kennedy. Two contradictory elements affected that development. First, the "idea of the plantation as a homeland of the life of the mind" came to it from the classical tradition. Second, the rapid growth of chattel slavery forced the Southern intellectual to assimilate into classical pastoralism an institution that separated the gardener from his garden and the shepherd from his flock. For this assimilation led to the disturbing awareness that the slave more precisely fulfilled the "mission" than his white owner did, causing a "fear of slavery as being not simply a threat to the social order but of its being a subversion of the very source of order—that is, the mind and imagination." [11]

The effort to make the Southern plantation a pastoral environment of the mind failed because it was based upon the premise, later emphasized by proslavery apologists, that the mind could only function if it were *liberated* from direct contact with the soil by slave labor. Jefferson recognized the contradiction: though slavery did free him to think and to write, he favored a society of yeoman farmers rather than of idle slavemasters. In his *Notes on the State of Virginia*, he fully expressed an irony that later Southern intellectuals would struggle to overlook. While he suspected "that the blacks . . . are inferior to the whites in the endowments both of body and mind," he also believed—as a central tenet of his pastoral philosophy—that "[t]hose who labour in the earth are the chosen people of God, if ever he had a chosen people."[12] According to Simpson, Jefferson was temporarily able to acknowledge that "[s]lavery not only . . . severs the connection between the mind of the master class and the soil, but it defies the very scrutiny of mind. Slavery destroys the very capacity for rational criticism. It implies the drastic dispossession of the pastoral vision of the plantation as a dominion of mind." After writing the *Notes*, however, Jefferson never again voiced such doubts about the plantation ideal. When he retired from the Presidency, his letters depicted Monticello as a "patrician domain of the mind," where he spent his mornings "in my shops, my garden, or on horseback among my farms" and his evenings in his study reading and writing.[13]

Faulkner bought Rowan Oak and Greenfield Farm as a gesture toward securing the same conditions of "the independent mind."[14] (When he died in 1962, furthermore, he was negotiating the purchase of a 250-acre "estate-farm" in the horse country of Virginia [BL, 1831–32; BL1, 701].) Doubtless, he hoped to institute a routine like Jefferson's, whereby his supervision of the farming would both stimulate and subsidize his writing, for which it would leave him ample leisure—the condition Harry and Charlotte sacrificed everything to achieve in *The Wild Palms*. He bought his property to recapture the pastoral ideal of the Southern plantation as a refuge for the life of the mind, where he might be independent of the literary market to which he felt enslaved. *Go Down, Moses* records his appreciation of the inner contradictions in that ideal, as well as the fatigue induced in him by its failure. Consequently, it is a book in which, as much as in *The Wild Palms* or *The Hamlet*, one of his subjects is the fate of his vocation.

Simpson, preoccupied with the South as a "garden of the chattel," mostly disregards the firm presence of a white peasantry in the antebellum Southern imagination. The William Byrd whose observations on slavery he locates near the beginning of a self-contradictory tradition of race pastoralism also, according to Kenneth Lynn, inaugurated the Southern tradition of class pastoralism.[15] The continuity of Southern letters has relied largely upon the renewal in each generation of these two pastoral modes—both sometimes practiced separately, or indeed together, by the same author. *The Hamlet* belongs to the Southwestern-humor tradition, by reviving it; *Go Down, Moses* belongs to the tradition of plantation fiction, by rejecting it.

In Simpson's view, the plantation became the symbolic environment for the Southern perception of the Negro: "this garden of the mind had not only been made by slave labor, it had been made to function as the center of a large agricultural enterprise carried on by chattels and their overseers." As the contradiction inherent in this condition became more and more apparent in the early nineteenth century, the "mind of the South" had to defend it more and more irrationally, until it surrendered its own freedom of scrutiny in order to rationalize the institution it now argued was the guarantor of that freedom. It set about assimilating to its pastoral ideal a slave system that was inherently antipastoral, a system in which the life of the mind was preserved by its systematic separation from the earth and from labor. This endeavor was rehearsed in what Simpson calls the "novel of the literary plantation," for which John Pendleton Kennedy's *Swallow Barn* (1832) was the prototype.[16] This book offers meaningful comparisons with *Go Down, Moses*.

John Pendleton Kennedy

Kennedy (1795–1870) was a citizen of Baltimore who grew to manhood favoring the Southern heritage of his mother. A staunch Whig, like many of the Southwestern humorists, he championed the claims of the American ruling class against Jackson's disorderly commoners, and he strove to mollify Northern hostility toward the South by reconciling slavery with the South's pastoral vision of itself. His first novel purports to be an account by one Mark Littleton, a New Yorker, of his two-month visit to Swallow Barn, the plantation of his cousins the Meriwethers. Although Kennedy was actually writing about "Adam's Bower," the Shenandoah Valley home of the Pendleton family, which he had frequented in his boyhood, he set *Swallow Barn* on the southern shore of the James River below Richmond.[17] After describing his journey from the North and the estate at which he arrives, Littleton devotes a number of leisurely chapters to portraits of family members and miscellaneous plantation personnel. Throughout most of the remainder of what Kennedy himself called "a book of episodes, with an occasional digression into the plot," the chapters order themselves very loosely about two "suits"—one of law, one of love. Frank Meriwether, the master of Swallow Barn, is engaged in settling an ancient but friendly "boundary-line dispute" with Isaac Tracy, master of "The Brakes," the neighboring plantation four miles down the river. Frank's brother-in-law and heir, Ned Hazard, is engaged in weaving "a web of intricate love-plots"[18] to catch the heart and hand of Bel Tracy, Isaac's daughter. The litigation ultimately resolves itself in the marriage of Ned and Bel, but only after meandering through a variety of "scenes" that depict an assortment of Southern types engaged in legal deliberations and romantic intrigues.

Primarily, Littleton concentrates on the "amusements" by which the two families divert themselves, for the society of the plantation is founded on the arts of leisure. Behind these entertainments lies a pretension to "feudatory" culture that Kennedy presented as both endearing and faintly ridiculous. Inspired by Walter Scott, Bel Tracy has tricked out a pet hawk in leather bewets, silver varvels, and "I know not what other foppery." When she first tests the bird—which she has given a name, "Fairbourne," and a motto, "I live in my lady's grace"—it snaps its leash, "which she termed a creance," and flies away. In a gesture of "knight errantry," Ned and Mark succeed in recapturing Fairbourne the next day. For more than four hundred pages, *Swallow Barn* "exhibits a picture of country life in Virginia," as Kennedy described his purpose in his 1851 introduction to the second edition, without ever referring to the agricultural function of the plantation. The initial sketch of Swallow Barn includes "a succession of fields clothed with Indian corn, some small patches of cotton or tobacco plants, with the usual varieties of stubble and fallow grounds," but only as a picturesque background for the "aristocratical old edifice" which houses the family.[19] Likewise, these pages pay only passing attention to the slaves who work Swallow Barn.

Not until Littleton has exhausted the digressive potentialities of the two "suits" does he propose, in the forty-fourth of the novel's forty-nine chapters, to examine the economic foundations of the leisure he has enjoyed. Immediately, Negroes appear. What follows seems both to contain an afterthought and to set forth the true subject of Kennedy's book, from which he has tried to distract himself. Littleton accompanies Meriwether in an inspection of the Quarter, following visits to the "meadows," where pedigreed horses graze, and to the "farm-yard," where "a party of negroes were employed in treading out grain." At the former site the gentlemen are joined by Carey, Meriwether's "veteran groom," who governs by veto his master's decisions, just as Ned Barnett "tyrannized" Faulkner. "Rather than disturb the peace," Meriwether explains to Littleton, "I must submit to his authority." All the blacks enjoy a friendly though respectful familiarity with the white gentlemen. [20]

To reconcile slavery with the idea of the plantation as an "environment of the mind," Kennedy deliberately concealed its disagreeable features. In his final revision, for instance, he cancelled the last two sentences of a passage in which Littleton's granduncle, a quixotic old planter, reacts to a slave who has grinned "saucily and good-humoredly" at him: "[M]y . . . uncle looked up at the black with the most awful face he ever put on in his life. It was blood red with anger. But bethinking himself for a moment he remained silent, as if to subdue his temper. *He did not speak one word. If he had not constrained himself by this silence, he would probably have attacked his slave with his stick.*"[21] Kennedy struck out the reference to physical intimidation, for in the pastoral of race blacks and whites must not threaten each other. The only tyranny at Swallow Barn must be Carey's over Meriwether.

But Kennedy omitted much more than the slave-owner's disposition to beatings. The immediate historical context of *Swallow Barn* argues for its deceptiveness in a far more insistent way. According to a biographer, Kennedy began writing sketches of Virginia characters as early as 1825, which he developed into a continuous narrative during the next few years. He commenced the final draft in September 1830, added much "new matter" along the way, and completed the book on the last day of 1831.[22] During the fourth week of August 1831, while he was revising it, Nat Turner's rebellion occurred—an insurrection of slaves in Southampton County, Virginia, instigated by a thirty-year-old preacher who believed himself divinely chosen to lead his people out of bondage. In a day and a night, he and his followers butchered more than fifty whites; in the suppression that followed, a larger number of blacks were killed as well. This incident shocked the South. Almost every slaveholding state enacted new laws that greatly increased the severity of the slave codes, and the Abolition movement withered below the Potomac. "Perhaps the most important result of all," according to one historian, "was that never again was the slaveholding South free from the fear, lurking most of the time, of a wholesale and successful slave uprising."[23] Coincidentally, Kennedy shifted the scene of

Swallow Barn from the horse-breeding country of Jefferson County, where it belongs, to the tobacco land of the Tidewater, no more than fifty miles from the site of the insurrection, which he did not mention. His avoidance of that subject indicates his awareness of its incompatibility with the purpose of his book: to embody the Southern ideal of a pastoral "garden of the mind" in a form that included slavery.

But Kennedy did not avoid Nat Turner completely. In the chapter entitled "A Negro Mother," Meriwether's guided tour of the Quarter ends at the "cabin of old Lucy," the widow of Luke, whose services during the American Revolution had earned him the possession of "a few acres of grounds." When the gentlemen enter it, she greets them warmly, but her conversation quickly turns into an "exhibition of drivelling dotage" on the subject of her youngest son, Abraham, whose tragic loss she laments piteously. On their way home, Meriwether relates to Littleton the history of the case. Abe's brothers and sisters were selected for the prestigious employments of the plantation, as their family was "remarkable for its intelligence." Abe, however, was an exception. Although shrewd and energetic, he was corrupted by thieves with whom he molested the neighborhood, retreating to "fastnesses of the low-country swamps."[24] Abe's misdemeanors fell short of insurrection, but they might well have reminded Southern readers in 1832 of the atrocity in their recent memory. Nat Turner had planned to use the Great Dismal Swamp as his refuge and staging ground.

Abe did not suffer Nat Turner's fate, however. Unable to tolerate his transgressions any longer, his master was forced to remove him from the pastoral Eden he threatened. He bound him into the service of a Chesapeake Bay pilot, who could discipline him. The arrangement succeeded, and Abe developed into a capable seaman. Some years later, a great storm threatened the passengers and crew of a merchant brig that had run aground on a shoal. With a crew of black volunteers, Abe set out to rescue them, despite the fury of the storm. All were lost at sea.[25] Thus the renegade slave—a covert type of the black Moses, sent to deliver his people from bondage—was transformed into a black saint, who sacrificed himself attempting to save white lives; and Kennedy reasserted the ideal of interracial comity in the face of Nat Turner's bloody rebellion. Jean Fagan Yellin finds it "strange that in the first important book to celebrate the antebellum South, the closest approximation to a true hero is a rebellious slave."[26] But Abe earns his heroism in an act of total submission, not of rebellion: such a black hero was required by historical circumstance. Kennedy used him to preserve the fictional decorum of chattel slavery within the garden of Southern civilization, despite its actual disharmony; the plantation tradition was born in the impulse to repress facts. By counteracting that impulse, Faulkner moved to revise the tradition.

Faulkner's story "Go Down, Moses" offers some striking parallels with "Abe." In it, another black matriarch, Molly Beauchamp, grieves for another black manchild gone astray. Like Luke and Lucy, Lucas and Molly own their own homes, their white families having rewarded them with partial independence for years of devoted service. As Lucy had been "a nurse to the children at Swallow Barn,"[27] Molly was Roth Edmonds's black mammy, the only mother he ever knew. Thus, for both Frank Meriwether and Roth, the racial barrier against affection is broken by an almost filial obligation. Before breaking out of jail and disappearing from Yoknapatawpha County, Butch Beauchamp has put that obligation to as severe a test as Abe did.

But the cases of Abe and Butch are fundamentally different. Despite the similarity of their provocations, their white masters dispose of them in opposite ways. Frank Meriwether banishes Abe, but in such a way as to redeem his character; Roth Edmonds has already banished Butch, perfunctorily, after only one incident. "[I]t was Edmonds who had sent the boy into Jefferson; he had caught the boy breaking into his commissary store and had ordered him off the place and had forbidden him ever to return" (US, 259). Roth Edmonds has simply dismissed Butch, whose Chicago exile has resulted in more and increasingly serious misbehavior until he has become not the benefactor of whites but their murderer—a later, lesser Nat Turner.

As *Go Down, Moses* evolved, Faulkner shaped all of his black heroes into figures of rebellion against white hegemony—tentative types of a black Moses, to counter the stereotypes of "Abe" and "Uncle Tom." If he read John Spencer Bassett's book of "documentary-historical-personal records," he read that "there were always slaves who rebelled at the idea of bondage."[28] He set out to revise the plantation formulae in other ways as well.

"Almost," which became the first chapter in *Go Down, Moses*, presents the same antebellum way of life that Kennedy had idealized in the 1830s; but Faulkner treated it first as comic and finally as cruel. The McCaslin plantation and the Prim (later Beauchamp) plantation—like

"Swallow Barn" and "The Brakes"—are neighboring estates between which an amicable property dispute provides a reason for social visits. The tendency of Tomey's Turl to run away to the Prim/Beauchamp plantation constitutes a legal controversy between them; and Sophonsiba's pursuit of Uncle Buck corresponds to Ned Hazard's courtship of Bel Tracy. Whereas Bel's pretensions to chivalry were fetching though somewhat absurd, however, Sophonsiba's are only absurd. With her roan-tooth homeliness and her simpering manner, she is a parody of a Southern belle. She insists that her brother is the "true earl" of "Warwick" (GDM, 5), but this worthy is so irresolute that he has failed for years to replace a rotted floorboard in a main passageway of the mansion (GDM, 10). (Whether this portrait owes anything to the insolvent handyman-master of the grandly named "Rowan Oak" is a matter for conjecture.) At the gatepost of the estate, she stations a slave boy with a fox horn to announce the arrival of guests (GDM, 9), a gesture that would resemble such extravagancies of Bel Tracy as her attempt at falconry, except that it is even more incongruous in frontier Mississippi than in Tidewater Virginia. At "Warwick," even the gate upon whose post the slave boy sits has fallen away (GDM, 9). The master is a type of the irresponsible aesthete-planter whose genealogy W. R. Taylor traces back to John Randolph of Roanoke and Roderick Usher. [29] The "society"upon which Sophonsiba forces her delusions is not a company of clever young ladies and gentlemen as in Kennedy's Old Dominion, but a young boy and a rude complement of old men lacking any of the social graces. Her courtship of Buck McCaslin is a bizarre—and hilarious—imitation of romantic intrigue, in which their conversation seems a grotesque travesty of Bel Tracy's witty badinage with Ned Hazard. The bedroom scene and poker games that follow make a farce of the pleasant entertainment between households that animated most plantation fiction. Mark Littleton played cards with his Virginia gentlemen friends only to divert Ned from the momentarily unhappy course of his love. But at "Warwick," the game determines the possession of slaves. In other details as well, "Almost" seems to have been Faulkner's commentary on the iconography of the plantation genre it so comically imitates.

At the same time, however, Faulkner reproduced that iconography in his role as the master of Rowan Oak. He too created "entertainments" for his friends, including the "hunt breakfast" in 1938, at which he played the lord of the manor. The fox horn Miss Sophonsiba orderd her slave to blow upon the arrival of guests, Faulkner also blew. On one hand, he portrayed the social and intellectual life of the plantation as absurd. On the other, he relished even its absurdity. Both in his personal affairs and in the products of his imagination, he transmitted contradictory signals concerning his cultural situation. He resisted a stereotyped depiction of Negroes, yet he eagerly assumed a position that required him to patronize them. He criticized plantation life as it was supposed to have been lived, yet he risked his financial security and compromised his literary independence in attempting to replicate it. Even while he was writing *Go Down, Moses*, he dreamed, at least intermittently, the old dream of the plantation as a refuge for the mind. Consequently, his sense of his vocation necessarily came to reflect his shifting relationship with the black laborers in his pastoral garden.

Faulkner and the Liabilities of Black Characterization

By the time Faulkner wrote his first fiction, the imagery of the plantation tradition and the images of black people that derived from it had fossilized into a set pattern of conventions. The dominant image of the Negro was that of a carefree, illiterate, mischievous, and devoted servant. The primary texts of the tradition all "asserted the joy of negro existence." Above everything else, F. P. Gaines wrote in 1925 during Faulkner's late apprenticeship, "the popular conception thinks of race relations . . . as always happy." Out of this conception came the main types of black character, both on and off the plantation. The taxonomy of these types is familiar enough. Gaines divided them into the "uncle," the "mammy," and the clownish "Jim Crow." A book on the "history of blacks in American films" classifies them as *Toms, Coons, Mulattoes, Mammies, and Bucks*; a historian of "plantation life in the ante-bellum South" categorizes "the major slave characters" as "Sambo, Jack and Nat." In short, Negro character attracted stereotyping, and the types were immediately recognizable to the public. In Gaines's words, "If the popular conception is certain of one thing, that confidence is that 'it knows a nigger.'"[30]

During the 1920s, many white writers reacted against the old stereotypes of the Negro by inventing new ones. For young writers eager to rebel against Victorianism, the Negro became—in Robert Bone's words— "a symbol of that freedom from restraint for which the white intellectual longed so ardently." A "cult of the primitive" developed, to which Vachel Lindsay, Eugene O'Neill, Sherwood Anderson, Carl Van Vechten, Julia

Peterkin, DuBose Heyward, and Howard Odum made prominent contributions. But their idealization of unrepressed personalities, in effect, simply transformed the same old figure from an object of ridicule to an object of admiration. [31]

Faulkner's first novels manifested an unstable perception of black character that derived sometimes from the plantation stereotype and sometimes from its primitivist mirror image. [32] The ending of *Soldiers' Pay*, for example, reflects the primitivist ethic of Anderson's *Dark Laughter*. As Joe Gilligan and Rector Mahon walk into the countryside surrounding a small town in Georgia, they pass a Negro church that stands in contrast to the physical and spiritual anemia of white culture: "Within it was a soft glow of kerosene serving only to make the darkness and the heat thicker, making thicker the imminence of sex after harsh labor along the mooned land; and from it welled the crooning submerged passion of the dark race. It was nothing, it was everything; then it swelled to an ecstasy, taking the white man's words as readily as it took his remote God and made a personal Father of Him" (SP, 319). But only two years later, in *Sartoris*, Faulkner reverted to plantation types. Simon and Caspey Strother supply that novel with comic relief from the intensities of the self-destructive Sartorises by parodying their behavior. Simon, whom Faulkner based partly upon his "uncle" Ned Barnett (BL, 538), echoes the patrician views of his "master," the elder Bayard Sartoris, on the decline of antebellum life: " 'De ottomobile,' Simon philosophized, 'is all right fer pleasure en excitement, but fer de genu-wine gentlemun tone, dey ain't but one thing: dat's hosses' " (SAR, 231). He shares "his race's fine feeling for potential theatrics" (SAR, 3) and makes a ridiculously pompous figure. Caspey the gardener makes an even more ridiculous figure—a comic foil to young Bayard Sartoris and Horace Benbow, who, like him, have just returned from World War I: "Caspey returned to his native land a total loss, sociologically speaking, with a definite disinclination toward labor, honest or otherwise, and two honorable wounds incurred in a razor-hedged crap game." He spends his days loafing and fabricating war stories (SAR, 62).

When Faulkner let Caspey speak for three pages, the result constituted one of his few real indulgences throughout his career of the dialect fiction that formed the staple of the plantation genre after the Civil War. Faulkner often relinquished the narrator's platform to vernacular white voices, but he never told any stories completely in a black dialect. In "A Justice," for example, Quentin Compson recalls a story told by Sam Fathers, who is part Negro, and Blotner suggests that this narrative frame derived from the stories Faulkner had heard as a child from the Negro blacksmith on his grandfather's farm (BL, 566). But Sam's voice is controlled by his Indian, not his Negro, blood. He "talked like a nigger," Quentin says; "that is, he said his words like niggers do, but he didn't say the same words" (CS, 344). The words he does say are standardized in Faulkner's, or Quentin's, transcription of them.

Negro voices *speak* frequently enough in Faulkner, but they do not *narrate*. Caspey, perhaps, can help explain why. Sitting in the Sartoris kitchen on the morning after his return, he answers the questions of his father Simon, his sister Elnora, and his nephew Isom.

> "How many you kilt, Unc' Caspey?" Isom asked deferentially.
> "I ain't never bothered to count 'um up. Been times I kilt mo' in one mawnin' dan dey's folks on dis whole place. One time we wuz down in de cellar of a steamboat tied up to de bank, and one of dese submareems come up and stopped, and all de white officers run up on de bank and hid. Us boys downstairs didn't know dey wuz anything wrong 'twell folks started clambin' down de ladder. We never had no guns wid us at de time, so when we seed dem green legs comin' down de ladder, we crope up behin' 'um, and ez dey come down one of de boys would hit 'um over de haid wid a piece of scantlin' and another would drag 'um outen de way and cut dey th'oat wid a meat-plow. Dey wuz about thirty of 'um. . . . Elnora, is dey any mo' of dat coffee lef?" (SAR, 62–63)

Caspey's braggadocio is transparently a *routine*. The other exploits he alleges are equally ridiculous. His language, insofar as it reveals character, reveals ignorance, deceit, and uppitiness. Given the long tradition of dialect humor, it could have revealed little else. His performance derives fairly clearly from comic "darkies" in the fiction of Joel Chandler Harris, Thomas Nelson Page, Harry Stillwell Edwards, and other white Southerners.

In *The Sound and the Fury*, however, Faulkner began to display a conscious concern with the special difficulty of describing black characters accurately. In Part Two of that novel, for example, Quentin Compson experiences a moment of existential nausea when he notes the instability of his perception of black people. Deacon, a black man who makes a living by doing odd jobs for Southern students at Harvard, meets incoming trains wearing "a sort of Uncle Tom's cabin outfit, patches and all," and Quentin remembers that when Deacon first talked to him, he spoke in an obsequious parody of Southern Negro dialect: "Yes, suh. Right dis way, young marster, hyer we is. . . . jes give de old nigger yo room number, and hit'll be done got cold dar when you arrives" (SF, 120). Later, however, Deacon appears as a semi-respectable Bostonian in a Brooks Brothers suit, who marches in political parades and speaks standard English. When he momentarily reverts to his slavish demeanor, Quentin confuses him with Roskus, the Compson family's servant back in Mississippi:

> . . . suddenly I saw Roskus watching me from behind all his whitefolks' claptrap of uniforms and politics and Harvard manner, diffident, secret, inarticulate and sad. "You aint playing a joke on the old nigger, is you?"
> "You know I'm not. Did any Southerner ever play a joke on you?"
> "You're right. They're fine folks. But you cant live with them."
> "Did you ever try?" I said. But Roskus was gone. Once more he was that self he had long since taught himself to wear in the world's eye, pompous, spurious, not quite gross. (SF, 123)[33]

Elsewhere, Quentin reflects that "a nigger is not a person so much as a form of behaviour; a sort of obverse reflection of the white people he lives among" (SF, 106).[34] The ambiguity of Deacon's image casts into doubt all of the truisms about Negroes that Quentin has learned in the South. If Deacon's identity seems unclear, then what can Quentin say with certainty about Roskus, or Dilsey, or any of the other Negroes back home among whom he grew up? Do they really love to sing and dance? Do they really like to eat watermelon? Or does Roskus too have a Brooks Brothers suit hanging in *his* closet? What is the true life beneath their conditioned appearance?

Behind Quentin's nausea lurks Faulkner's suspicion about his own ability to see black people—to penetrate appearances—and then to describe the reality within. According to Blotner, "Even toward the end of his life, Faulkner would talk of the difficulty of understanding Negroes' thoughts and feelings. He seemed to feel that not only had they perforce developed a pattern of concealment from white people, but their modes of thought and feeling were often different and therefore difficult for a white person to understand" (BL, 1038–39).[35]

Faulkner never exactly defined the ways in which he felt that Negroes "differed" from Caucasians in their "modes of thought and feeling," though it was a question he posed all his life. But another perceptual shift in *The Sound and the Fury* provides an important clue to his attitude. In Part Four, when Dilsey takes her children to Easter services at her church, a guest minister has been invited from St. Louis to deliver the sermon. As the Reverend Shegog begins to speak, he sounds "like a white man"—"level and cold." But, as he warms to his message, "his intonation, his pronunciation became negroid"—"as different as day and dark from his former tone, with a sad, timbrous quality like an alto horn" (SF, 366–67).[36] As he moves from a white voice to a black one, something happens to his language that has special significance for any writer. It transcends itself: "He was like a worn small rock whelmed by the successive waves of his voice. With his body he seemed to feed the voice that, succubus like, had fleshed its teeth in him. And the congregation seemed to watch with its own eyes while the voice consumed him, until he was nothing and they were nothing and there was not even a voice but instead their hearts were speaking to one another in chanting measures beyond the need for words" (SF, 367–68).

A valuable analogy to Reverend Shegog's bilingualism appears in *Along This Way*, the autobiography of James Weldon Johnson. Johnson, with other black poets of the late nineteenth and early twentieth centuries, had been frustrated by a special literary predicament. To be published, they had had to adopt one of two equally dishonest voices: they could pass for white, writing in a colorless, genteel English, foreign to their own roots; or they could imitate the Negro dialects that had been invented by white authors. One of these voices rendered them invisible and unread; the other limited them to self-demeaning expressions of "quaint" humor and pathos. Johnson's friend Paul Lawrence Dunbar, throughout his brief career, practiced the art of impersonating his white readers' notion of how black people sounded. But Johnson, declaring that "Negro dialect is . . . not capable of giving expression to the varied conditions of Negro life in America," called for the discovery of "a form that will express the racial spirit by symbols from within rather than by symbols from without, such as the mere mutilation of English spelling and pronunciation."[37] In 1918, he located one such form when he heard a black evangelist deliver a sermon in Kansas City. At first, Johnson wrote, the preacher spoke from a formal text, apparently intimidated by Johnson's presence. When his audience responded apathetically, however, he suddenly shifted from standard English to the very different rhythms of "the rambling Negro sermon that begins with the creation of the world, touches various high spots in the trials and tribulations of the Hebrew children, and ends with the Judgment Day." In an instant, the congregation responded; and as the preacher "moaned," "pleaded," "blared," "crashed," and "thundered," it "reached a state of ecstasy." As Johnson sat listening, he found a piece of paper and began to write "The Creation," the first of seven verse sermons that comprise *God's Trombones* (1927), his most famous work.[38]

Although they could not have affected each other, Johnson's reminiscence and the scene in Faulkner's novel are remarkably similar. In each a black minister shifts from an explicitly white voice to an explicitly black one to stir a black audience. But they differ even more remarkably. For Johnson, the sermon provided an escape from the literary dispossession black writers had long suffered. It was a verbal resource, which directly stimulated him to write poetry. But for Faulkner the black sermon led toward silence. It intimated that black people have a nonliterary way of knowing and communicating—a way that goes "beyond words."[39] Faulkner's imagination of the difference between whites and blacks can most consistently be located in this nonverbal resource.

For the mature Faulkner, the most definitive characteristic of Negroes—certainly more definitive than any mere appearance or custom, and even more definitive than their capacity for "endurance"—was their alienation from literary formulations of experience. Writing about blacks presented Faulkner with a special case of pastoralism, of literature about nonliterate people. Except for Quentin Compson, Gavin Stevens, and a few others, his most powerful characters are people who either cannot or do not read. The pool of humanity from which he recruited his *dramatis personae* were people whom he could not readily conceptualize as an audience for his books about them—a situation that severely limited the degree to which he could experience his writing as a communicative act. The idiots, Benjy Compson and Ike Snopes, are the clearest examples of Faulkner's interest in articulating the experience of inarticulate people, but they are exceptional only in the totality of their illiteracy. Writing about poor whites involved a more limited communicative barrier. When he wrote *The Hamlet*, he probably did not anticipate that many of the people he regarded as Snopeses would ever read it; but such a possibility was sufficiently strong to affect the idiom in which that book speaks: through V. K. Ratliff's vernacular narrative voice, *The Hamlet* embodies a controlled conversation between Faulkner and the upwardly mobile rednecks he feared.[40]

But the possibility that the blacks he knew might read his books about them must have seemed as remote to him as that an idiot might read *The Sound and the Fury.* This is not to say that he believed blacks incapable of literacy. After all, he *had* discussed with James McGlowan the possibility of teaching Mammy Callie, the real-life model for Dilsey, how to read. But she never learned, and when he dedicated *Go Down, Moses* "To Mammy Caroline Barr," he did so in the knowledge that it could be a book "to" her in only the most abstract way. Nor did Faulkner's sense of Negro illiteracy prevent him from creating literate black characters in his fiction. Lucas Beauchamp can read and write, but he does so for only the most practical purposes. Charles Bon goes to a university, but his intellectual refinement is noteworthy because it departs monstrously from normality. And Reverend Shegog is clearly a literate man, but he transports his audience *away* from words, away from intellect.

What is crucial about Faulkner's perception of blacks is the discontinuity within it between their "modes of thought and feeling" and the resources of books. Whenever he wrote about them—as, to a lesser degree, when he wrote about poor whites—he inevitably felt the incongruity of his sophisticated, analytical intelligence brooding upon what he regarded as simple, customary spirits. No matter how sympathetic Faulkner was disposed to be toward his rustic characters, the constitutional incompatibility between their sensibility and his own inhibited his characterization of them. He was painfully aware of the inhospitality of the novel, as a form, to his subject matter. In the middle of his career, this awareness precipitated a crisis of confidence from which he never fully recovered.

John Faulkner

Even after *The Sound and the Fury,* Faulkner was capable of exploiting "darky" characters and comic black dialect. In his desperation for money, he was willing to try whatever formulae the magazines were buying. "Negro stories" sold briskly. Thus, in late 1933 he wrote "A Bear Hunt," in which V. K. Suratt (alias Ratliff) relates how Old Man Ash, the "Major's nigger," wreaks a grotesque vengeance upon Lucius Provine, a white man, for an old wrong (CS, 67). Twenty years before, Provine had burned Ad's celluloid collar as a practical joke. The last paragraph of the story, in which Ad lugubriously reveals his grievance, comes directly out of the plantation dialect tradition: "Hit wuz de collar. Back in dem days a top nigger hand made two dollars a week. I paid fo' bits fer dat collar. Hit wuz blue, wid a red picture of de race betwixt de Natchez en de Robert E. Lee running around hit. He burnt hit up. I makes ten dollars a week now. En I jest wish I knowed where I could buy another collar like dat un fer half of hit. I wish I did" (CS, 79).

If, in his desperation for money, Faulkner looked about for profitable story models in 1939, he could have found examples of successful plantation fiction in his own backyard. Among them were stories by Roark Bradford, his friend, and by John Faulkner, his brother, which were designed for *Collier's*, one of the highest paying magazines. Both these writers exploited precisely the Negro stereotypes Faulkner had upon occasion resisted, and his imitation of them would exact an ultimate reckoning.

According to John Faulkner's testimony, his brother William derived recognizable portions of the "nigger stories" at the core of *Go Down, Moses* from *his* fiction, which was unabashedly commercial and humorously racist. Miss Maud supported John's claim, much to William's consternation. Apparently, both "A Point of Law" and "Go Down, Moses" originated in stories that John showed William in manuscript.[41] We do not have the stories that William appropriated. But John did later place four other stories in *Collier's*, which probably resemble the earlier, lost ones in tone and method. These light diversions indicate that his outlook on the profession of letters was thoroughly mercantile. "Progress Report" (1941) humorously exposes a New Deal boondoggle: workers in a local WPA office satisfy a federal inspector by posting as their own progress charts the demonstration models that his office had sent them. "Good Neighbors" (1942) relates the failed attempt by some "prohibition agents" to apprehend two moonshiners, and the moonshiners' subsequent willing surrender to old Uncle Pete because he is a family friend whose good health means more to them than three or four years in prison. In "Treasure Trail" (1943), two Americans in Mexico win a treasure map in a poker game and lose it in an alcoholic interlude with "Siete Pistolas Pedro," a caricature of a bandito. Finally, "Lawd! Lawd!" (1942) presents what seems to be John Faulkner's amiable exposé of his own meager narrative powers. In it, a hack writer named Henry Moore, who resides on a farm in northern Mississippi, concludes a story that resists resolution by having previously unmentioned Japanese planes salvo his cast of characters during a bombing mission from Cuba to Memphis.[42]

John Faulkner devoted his belated literary apprenticeship to manufacturing gallimaufries of plot cliché and character type. He worked, furthermore, toward a purely economic goal: he told *Time* magazine in 1941 that "if he can make $150 a month writing (he is sure he can), he will never do any kind of work again in his life."[43] The stories that William read in manuscript belonged to a very early stage of this apprenticeship, and we can only assume that they resembled, even more than his published fiction, the potboiler by Henry Moore in "Lawd! Lawd!" When William acknowledged them as sources for "A Point of Law" and "Go Down, Moses," then, he was acknowledging the commercial and formulaic origins not only of these two stories but of Go Down, Moses itself, for which they were the genetic core.

We can also assume that John's plagiarized stories presented "nigger" types. A decade afterward, William's "moderate" stand in the civil rights controversy would divide the two brothers bitterly; but their views of the Negro had diverged well before the fifties, as Go Down, Moses itself testifies. John's fictional treatment of blacks in the late thirties probably did not differ greatly from his factual treatment of them in My Brother Bill, which he published in 1963. There, certain black people form an integral part, and usually an affectionate one, of his memory of his brother. His portrait of Mammy Callie Barr is especially appreciative, for she had nursed him too (MBB, 47–52). But John devotes his most characteristic description of Negroes to the tenants of Greenfield Farm, whom he associates with livestock: "We broke all our land with the tractor and only used Negroes and mules to cultivate the crops. That was light plowing and the exercise was good for the stock" (MBB, 178). At the Fourth of July barbecue, the Negro tenants appear as darky caricatures. When one of them plays "Jack o' Diamonds" on a mouth organ, for example, the others "all got stiller than before and one by one they began grinning and patting their feet." One of them hopped up and began dancing: "He'd snort and rear his head back just like a mule when you are trying to put the bridle on him" (MBB, 193–94). Undoubtedly, such scenes actually occurred; but John Faulkner selects them to represent completely the Negro presence in his brother's life. His stories about Negroes likely resulted from the same selection process, a process governed by the way in which white America in the thirties mostly perceived the Negro race.

Roark Bradford

Another writer whose stories about Negroes Faulkner may have imitated was Roark Bradford (1896–1943), a Tennesseean whom Faulkner had known in New Orleans during the twenties when both men belonged to the coterie associated with the *Double Dealer* and the *Times-Picayune* (BL, 394–95). In 1928, in *Ol' Man Adam and His Chillun*, he presented Negro-dialect versions of Old Testament stories. The success of these "Bible stories in blackface," which Marc Connelly adapted for the Broadway stage in *Green Pastures*, insured Bradford a wide audience for nearly a dozen more collections of Negro stories throughout the thirties. John Bradbury has explained why his fame did not outlive him: "Bradford's Negro preachers and folk heroes are essentially caricatures, and their stories a series of repetitious exaggerations calculated to please an undiscriminating public."[44]

To these stories, published mostly in *Collier's*, Faulkner's truncated Lucas Beauchamp series bears a resemblance. Bradford's stories treated two casts of characters: the black roustabouts of the riverboat *John D. Grace*, including Bugaboo and Iron Man; and, more extensively, the laborers on the Little Bee Bend Plantation near Shreveport, Louisiana— Giles Arnold, the plantation foreman who keeps his subordinates "in high gears"; the Widow Duck, senior usher of the "Ole Ship er Zion" Church; B'r Charlie, a "one-legged preacher-blacksmith" whose "backsliding" the Widow Duck must constantly correct; and Uncle Henry, the aged lot man who knows all about mules. The stories, most of which concern conflicts within this black community, contain some of the same plot elements that appear in the Lucas stories. Giles forever has to police his workers to keep them in their beds at night, so that they will apply themselves to the fields during the day. Otherwise they will be "wawkin' the bayou" with their neighbors' spouses, creating friction and reducing efficiency. Just so, Molly Beauchamp has to bring her husband under control after he has been "[w]awkin' de roads all night wid de ground cryin' to git planted" (US, 215). Contested weddings, like the one in "A Point of Law," and divorce proceedings, like those Molly initiates in "The Fire on the Hearth," proliferate at Little Bee Bend.

In their dealings with white people, Bradford's characters anticipate Lucas's manipulation of Roth Edmonds and the metal-detector salesman. In "The Cows in the Corn" (1938), for instance, Giles outmaneuvers the white "Bossman" and circumvents the rules of a federal "soil-rebuilding project" by ordering the field hands to drive the cattle into the corn at night and back out before dawn.[45] In "Manuscript Dice" (1940), the crew of the *John D. Grace* outwits Lucius Dolworthy, a professor of social sciences. To test his theory that "[t]he chance of an event happening is expressed by the fraction of which the numerator is the number of favorable ways and the denominator the whole number of ways," he engages them in a game of craps, of which the Negroes at first claim to be ignorant. After Iron Man substitutes his own dice for the professor's, he quickly wins more than forty dollars from him, much to the professor's astonishment.[46] The humor of the story depends upon the discrepancy between the Negroes' dialect and Dolworthy's "big words," and upon his innocence compared to their know-how. The natural shrewdness of the Negroes compensates them for their lack of book learning.

More than any particular plot device, however, Faulkner's "nigger stories" shared with Bradford's a quality of formulaic perception, which almost any excerpt from Bradford's stories will demonstrate. A controversy of the 1930s into which Bradford entered helps to define this quality. During that decade, sociologists and anthropologists promulgated a series of studies of the Negro that threatened to invalidate the plantation tradition as an accurate context for depicting blacks.[47] The most effective of these was probably John Dollard's *Caste and Class in a Southern Town* (1937), which recorded the research Dollard had conducted during the previous two years in Indianola, Mississippi, a county seat one hundred miles southwest of Faulkner's Oxford. His methodology "was the systematic gathering of life-history materials, especially from Negro people"; he argued that personality traits derive more directly from social position and acculturation than from racial heredity. According to Dollard, the Negro's so-called irresponsibility, for example, is less a reason *for* his subjugation than the result *of* it. His most damaging conclusion undermined the very foundation of "traditional" perception: "Since any new perception requires energy and courage, rare human qualities, [the] persistence of tradition probably is based on a fundamental human indolence and timorousness which prefer the historical routine of behavior to an active and independent perception of social fact. If inertia of habit and fixity of complex play a rôle on the pleasure side, social fear and wishes for security are equally important in stabilizing the ancestral routine. . . . This impotence in the grip of custom, always tangible in persons and personal relations, is the primary defense."[48]

Traditionalists naturally regarded the sociological model of Southern race relations as a threat. In a review of *Caste and Class*, the Agrarian Lyle Lanier refuted Dollard on professional grounds.[49] As an active practitioner of plantation fiction, Roark Bradford attacked Dollard in a less polemical way. He contrived "Lucius *Dol*worthy" as a caricature of him and tried to dramatize the faults in *his* perception. In "Manuscript Dice," this sociologist is "preparing a series of monographs on the social and psychological phases of existence among the lower income bracket groups." From the men of the *John D. Grace,* he solicits "life histories" of the kind Dollard had based his research on. But he is hopelessly unable to cope with his informants, who tell him only what they think he wants to hear.[50] In "Double-Yolk Hoodoo" (1942), Professor Dolworthy—now the "head of his university's department of Experimental Sociology"—comes to Little Bee Bend plantation to research the Cajun practice of "*vaudoo.*" He proves too naïve to discern that his "hoodoo lady" informant is really a fraud named Cissy Ringgold, who had "runned off wid a levee camp worker, fawty years ago, and . . . comed back home callin' herse'f Modom Aw-bear, and puttin' on juju Franch talk." Ultimately, she "hoodoos" him out of his shirt and pants and off the plantation, by which gesture Bradford indirectly ejected all scientists from the territory of the plantation myth.[51]

Faulkner would not have endorsed Dollard's "scientific" opinions, but neither was he satisfied with the "ancestral" perception of his brother and of Bradford. He rebelled against their inertia, attempting periodically and unsuccessfully to penetrate the inner lives of Negroes. When he tried to reverse his own formulaic portrayals of the Negro, his subject became, not the Negro, but what Thadious Davis calls "the Negro as an aesthetic problem."[52] He depicted the ordeal of depicting the Negro, the ordeal of trying to revitalize perception, the ordeal of writing itself.

"Delta Autumn": Paradigms of Depletion

During the summer and fall of 1940, Faulkner did not work on the "novella" that would complete what he then thought would be a short book but used his time instead to write stories he could sell in place of his property. Then, in November, he went hunting in the delta of the Big Sunflower River near Anguilla, Mississippi, more than one hundred miles southwest of the woods in Lafayette County where he had hunted as a boy.

One morning, after his normal time to rise, his companions found him still in bed, pale and stricken. At first, they thought he was sleeping off a hangover. But he did not look right even so, and one of them suggested that he might have suffered "a kidney seizure of some sort." By luck a motorboat happened to sputter past the riverside camp. They commandeered it to rush their unconscious friend the eight miles to a highway; then they drove him to a hospital in Oxford. A doctor there estimated that "a few hours more would have been too late": his new patient had been hemorrhaging, probably from a perforated ulcer (BL, 1063–64).

Faulkner's experiences at the camp affected Go Down, Moses definitively. In "Delta Autumn," the next story he wrote after his medical emergency, Faulkner appropriated the geography of the delta as a personal symbol for both his and the world's fatigue. Throughout the following decade and a half, he drew periodically upon the imagery of rivers, floods, and deltas to express gloom over his physical mortality, over the uncertain fate of his life's work, and over the violent course of human history. Near the outset of his career, in "The Leg," he had converted a flood (of sorts) into a symbol of the release from confinement that writing provided. He had revived the image of the flood in The Wild Palms. Now, in "Delta Autumn," a floodscape transformed the novel he was working on; and it announced his adoption of his vocation as one of his principal subjects. This story is a crucial document in his intermittent fictionalized autobiography: his premature portrait of the artist as an old man.

After Faulkner wrote "Delta Autumn," his plan for Go Down, Moses changed.[53] He continued to explore racial themes, but now he subsumed them within the more general subject of exhaustion, which his physical collapse had instigated. When he next addressed his editor on the subject, in May 1941, the projected book was much closer to its final shape than it had previously been. It no longer included the mystery "novella"; he had decided on its final title; and its contents would comprise "The Fire and the Hearth" (a combination of the three Lucas Beauchamp stories), "Pantaloon in Black," "The Old People" (appearing for the first time among his plans for the book), "Delta Autumn," and "Go Down, Moses" (SL, 139–40). In "The Old People," he had revived Sam Fathers, the multiracial narrator of "A Justice," to serve as the sponsor of a young boy's initiation into the mystery of hunting. After Sam ritualistically smears his face with the blood of his first kill, the boy is granted a vision of a magnificent phantom buck, symbolic of all the game that hunters slay. When he asks his father what it means, his father discloses that he had seen it too, when Sam taught him, and that it betokens the spiritual conservation of all natural creatures (US, 201–12).

He still anticipated a relatively painless unification of these stories. "I will rewrite them, to an extent," he informed Haas: "some additional material might invent itself in process. Book will be about the size and similar to THE UNVANQUISHED." Later the same month, he reported that he had added "Almost" to the list (SL, 140). With that, except for one major addition to come, he had determined the basic substance that after considerable revision became *Go Down, Moses*. Although he did not yet foresee it, "The Bear," rather than a mystery story about Lucas, would form the capstone that would unite the material he diversified by writing "Delta Autumn."

The story that effected this crystallization of Faulkner's plan concerns Uncle Ike McCaslin, a character who had appeared in previous fiction but never before as a protagonist. In "Delta Autumn," Faulkner transformed him from a random name—unless he chose him *because* his name was Isaac—into one of the focal characters of his *oeuvre*: his King Lear, his figure of wasted Age. The story takes place in 1940, the year Faulkner wrote it. Now the last surviving member of the original hunting party, Ike represents for his younger companions an obsolete ethic and a time that is outmoded, when the hunters rode to camp in wagons rather than automobiles, when the game was plentiful, when the code that Sam Fathers had taught in "The Old People" still prevailed (US, 267–68). Indeed, when Faulkner wrote "Delta Autumn," he had already decided to revise that other story by making Ike its main character too, and by having old Ike in "Delta Autumn" remember the scene in "The Old People" in which Sam Fathers coached him in his first kill and baptized him in the blood of the slain buck (US, 273–74). Thus, in "Delta Autumn," we see Ike both in his boyhood and in his old age. We see him receiving the wisdom of the past, the humility and pride of the true hunter; and we see the failure of his attempts to transmit the same ethic to the next generation.

Although childless himself, he stands in a paternal relation to the men with whom he rides: "two of the sons of his old companions, whom he had taught not only how to distinguish between the prints left by a buck and a doe but between the sound they made in moving" (US, 268). Will Legate has learned much. But Don Boyd demonstrates early that he has failed to master at least one of Ike's lessons, the futility of possessiveness. Ike knows that the wilderness "belonged to no man" (US, 275). But Boyd "owned . . . anything—animal, machine or human—which he happened to be using" (US, 268). Nor does Boyd reverence the life he takes. Ike had learned fifty years earlier from Sam Fathers to behave in a way that would not shame the blood he spilt. "I slew you," he had learned to address his prey; "my bearing must not shame your quitting life. My conduct forever onward must become your death" (US, 273–74). But Boyd behaves ignobly both in the woods and out. He carries a shotgun rather than a rifle, and he kills a doe although Ike had taught him enough woodcraft to know better. Shooting the doe corresponds to the central event of the story, Boyd's abandonment of the black mistress who has borne him a child—a correspondence the other hunters reinforce by making *double entendre* references to "coon-hunting" and two-legged does (US, 268). Like his rejection of his mistress and child, his violation of the hunting code epitomizes not only Ike's failure to transmit the old values but also the general absence of those values from twentieth-century civilization.

The day after Ike's party arrives in camp, the woman, a light-skinned Negro who has lived in the North, comes by motorboat to seek Boyd, but she finds only a bed-ridden Ike instead, with whom Boyd has left an envelope of money and a one-word message, "no." When Ike discerns that she is black, he reacts with shock and advises her to return North and marry a black man. "And then in a year's time," he tells her, "you will have forgotten all this; you will forget it even happened, that he ever existed." Her response defines Ike's failure: " 'Old man,' she said, 'have you lived so long that you have forgotten all you ever knew or felt or even heard about love?' " The remark evokes in him a sad reflection upon the Delta's history of natural destruction and social injustice (US, 276–80).

Faulkner wrote "Delta Autumn" at a time when he was especially worried about the nation and the world. He had watched the war in Europe with a growing apprehension that it would engulf him and all he was laboring to preserve. In May 1940, he had tried on his old British uniform (SL, 125). Soon afterward, he had mobilized in a minor way, serving as an advisor in the flight-instruction program at the University of Mississippi; and he had tried to gain a National Guard commission (SL, 136). One purpose for his retreat to the woods in November 1940 seems to have been to escape these uncharacteristically public worries. In a letter the next month, he described the deer country as a sanctuary from his anxieties: "One nice thing about the woods: off there hunting, I dont fret and stew so much about Europe. But I'm only 43, I'm afraid I'm going to the damn thing yet" (SL, 138).

If Faulkner escaped "fretting and stewing" about the European con-
flagration while hunting that November, Uncle Ike does not. On the drive
down to the camp, he and his companions discuss the current global
proliferation of dictatorships and wars. As they debate America's power to
resist tyranny, Faulkner arranges that they identify the hunting camp itself
with the nation's moral fortitude, and their banter about does assumes
geopolitical overtones. Their fear that civilization is going bankrupt
blends with their apprehension that the woods are vanishing. While Ike
and Legate argue that Americans will defend themselves against any dic-
tator, foreign or domestic, Boyd charges that America has already suc-
cumbed to injustice and chaos. "And *what have you got left?*" he asks,
"Half the people without jobs and half the factories closed by strikes. Too
much cotton and corn and hogs, and not enough for all the people to wear
and eat" (US, 269, my italics). What they have got left, Legate replies, is a
deer camp—and does.

When Ike recognizes, in the story's final sentence, that the deer Boyd
has shot "was a doe" (US, 280), he comprehends that his younger friend
will no longer defend the community's values, and he realizes that he has
failed to educate Boyd as Sam Fathers had educated *him*. By extension,
Faulkner implied—why else, in 1940, would he have inserted this political conversation?—that Boyd represents the national character more accurately than Ike does, or Sam Fathers, or the black woman. Further, the
camp and its setting come to stand for the diminishing fortitude not only
of the United States but of humanity.

Later in the narrative, Faulkner repeated the wording of Boyd's question
in order to emphasize Legate's answer: "*There was still some of it left*,
although now it was two hundred miles from Jefferson when once it had
been thirty" (US, 272, my italics). The antecedent of the pronoun "it"
here is both geographical and temporal: both an old time and a perennially new place—the wilderness, the Big Woods, hunting country. In the
paysage moralisé of "Delta Autumn," it becomes the final, contracting
sanctuary of the values Sam Fathers represented, which Ike can only imperfectly convey to the next generation because it is "dissolving" before his
eyes: "He had watched it . . . retreating southward through this shaped
section of earth between hills and river until *what was left of it* seemed
now to be gathered and for the time arrested in one tremendous density of
brooding and inscrutable impenetrability at the ultimate funnelling tip"
(US, 272, my italics).

The "shaped section" of earth is literally deltoid: on a map, the sector between the Sunflower, the Mississippi, and the northern hills is vaguely triangular. But the shape of the delta is less significant than its function as depository, as the terminus not only for the river but also for human history and for Ike McCaslin's single fate. Ike's life explicitly parallels the life of the wilderness, both of them "drawing yearly inward" (US, 267) toward extinction: "He seemed to see the two of them—himself and the wilderness—as coevals, . . . the two spans running out together, not into oblivion, nothingness, but into a scope free of both time and space where once more the untreed land warped and wrung to mathematical squares of rank cotton for the frantic old-world peoples to turn into shells to shoot at one another, would find ample room for both" (US, 275). In this allusion to cotton, Faulkner was referring again to the European war: during World War I the demand for cotton to use in making explosives had forced its price to records still unbroken in 1940. The consequent, temporary prosperity had resulted in a spurt of progress, including "the automobile invasion of the rural South," which further consumed the territory of the hunt.[54] The withdrawal of the wilderness, then, is a measure of "what people called progress" (US, 275), the epitome of which is warfare and the exhaustion of the very civilization—including literature—that progress ostensibly builds.

The war was not all that confronted Faulkner's jaundiced vision in the early 1940s. He had long viewed America as a threadbare raiment. In *The Hamlet*, he had recorded with a forced humor the depredations visited upon his region by the ludicrous but lethal forces of modernity. But Snopesism reigned throughout the land. For a minor example, when Franklin Roosevelt had moved the date of Thanksgiving forward a week in 1939 so that merchants could profit from an extra week of Christmas shopping, Faulkner "reacted vehemently against the changing of tradition for commercial purposes. . . . Later his wife would hear him say, 'I never did care much for Thanksgiving after Mr. Roosevelt got through messing around with it'" (BL, 1030–31). Roosevelt had messed with much more than Thanksgiving, and Faulkner disapproved of most of the New Deal measures. They especially rankled him when the Internal Revenue Service in 1940 billed him for $450 in back taxes (BL, 1042).

That these old provocations were on Faulkner's mind when he wrote "Delta Autumn" his next story confirms. In March 1941, he finished "The Tall Men" (BL, 1070), in which a Selective Service investigator from Jackson accompanies the Yoknapatawpha County marshal on a visit to the MacCallum family to arrest the twin sons of Buddy for draft evasion. In a plot that loosely resembles John Faulkner's "Good Neighbors," the marshal explains that the two boys would have enlisted unhesitatingly had war been declared but that otherwise they saw no need. He lectures the federal man on the pride of these independent hill people and on the apostasy of modern society. Significantly, he attributes America's moral decline to a failure of transmission: the values of life must be taught from generation to generation, as Buddy's Confederate father had taught them to him: "Life has done got cheap, and life ain't cheap. Life's a pretty durn valuable thing. I don't mean just getting along from one WPA relief check to the next one, but honor and pride and discipline that make a man worth preserving, make him of any value. That's what we got to learn again. Maybe it takes trouble, bad trouble, to teach it back to us; maybe it was the walking to Virginia because that's where his ma come from, and losing a war and then walking back, that taught it to old Anse. Anyway, he seems to learned it, and to learned it good enough to bequeath it to his boys" (CS, 60). The same belief in traditional values permeates "Delta Autumn," but there the transmission has been broken. The "honor and pride and discipline" that were "transmitted to" Ike he has been unable to inculcate in Don Boyd or even, completely, in Will Legate.

If "Delta Autumn" expresses Faulkner's despair over human history, it also captures a deep depression about his own fate that fused with his global concern. The parallel recession of Ike's life and of the wilderness is autobiographical: Faulkner too sensed the approaching terminus. He had only recently, and uncertainly, emerged from a crisis that almost forced him to change publishers. He was still chronically in debt and still holding off imminent dispossession from Rowan Oak and Greenfield Farm. His need for money still forced his talent into commercial detours about which he anguished, and he had never really exorcised his guilt over such prostitution.

In mid-1940, his insecurity about his vocation had assumed a new dimension. His complaint to Robert Haas in April that "maybe a man worrying about money cant write anything worth buying" (SL, 121) had been characteristic; but soon he was confessing that he found difficulty in writing anything at all. In a letter to Haas in late May or early June, Faulkner mentioned, for perhaps the first time, a problem that would beset him increasingly throughout the rest of his life. After surveying the lamentable state of the world, he wrote that "[m]aybe the watching of all this coming to a head for the last year is why I cant write, dont seem to want to write, that is" (SL, 125). Only two and a half years earlier, he had told a friend that it was easy: "You just keep the words coming. No trick to it at all if the writing is in yo'" (BL, 973). Now, in his fear of failure, he was placing his career in the context of world history and could not help doubting his own permanence. Faulkner's fiction began to exhibit an increasing concern with the fragility of his work and with its value as a testament worthy of protection from the vagaries of time. That concern is reflected in Uncle Ike's failure to secure *his* testament in the life of Don Boyd. Ike's greater success with Will Legate is signified by the latter's name, both halves of which denote bequeathal or legacy.[55]

Faulkner's self-doubt had intensified as autumn 1940 approached. When a visitor asked him in mid-July whether his writing had improved over the years, Faulkner smiled in response. "'Ten years ago I was much better,' he said. 'Used to take more chances. Maybe I'm tired'" (BL, 1053–54). Failure to take chances was the charge he would make against Hemingway six years later (BL, 1231–35). But even in 1940, his sense of his own decline had extended to other authors, and thus to literature generally. "What has happened to writing, anyway?" he asked in a letter to Bennett Cerf that same month. "[T]here are no young writers worth a damn that I know of" (SL, 134).

His sense of literary mortality must have been heightened by the intimation of physical mortality he received at the hunting camp that fall. The "autumn" in his title stands for *his* life as well as Uncle Ike's; and the solicitude Ike's friends exhibit for him—they let him "oversleep" the morning after the journey to camp—dimly reproduces the care Faulkner himself had required. Faulkner's concerns in "Delta Autumn" are the concerns of age. Though still forty-three years old, he was beginning to think like a man whose time was running out, whose cupboard of talent was bare.

The central subject of "Delta Autumn" is not race relations or the failure of love, or the wilderness, but the gradual depletion of energy from the earth, from history, from men's lives, from Faulkner's career. The two halves of the title refer to a single process. The river is an agent of entropy, a vital power seeking as its whole purpose the erosion of its sources. The delta is a zone of dissolution marking the river's leakage into the sea. The story opens with an entrance into that zone and with the "sensation" it arouses in Ike, upon whom weighs the principal exhaustion of the narrative.

In a long meditation on the history of the delta and its inhabitants, McCaslin focuses again on "what is left," the remnants of lost time and lost lives. After reciting the early record of settlement and cultivation, he notes that, despite its defeat of the wilderness, civilization has not replaced it with anything permanent. In the delta, as in the autumn of a declining talent, the very accumulation of the past works to defeat present creativity. Periodically constricted by the sediments that form the delta, the river overflows its banks and floods the flatland, depositing another layer of upstream dismantlement and preventing the erection of permanent structures downstream. In the resulting landscape, "there was no gradient anywhere and no elevation save those raised by forgotten aboriginal hands as refuges [sic] from the yearly water and used by their Indian successors to sepulchre their fathers' bones" (US, 271).

These "Indian mounds" help to explain how Faulkner began at this moment to feel a continuing identity between himself and the delta. For, despite their grossness, they are human artifacts that have endured as he hoped his books would do. At a time when he was trying desperately to create a comparable monument—his personal testament to future generations—Faulkner created in the river, the delta, and the mounds an allegory of his dilemma. He felt a slackening of his literary powers that resembled the deceleration of a stream meandering through its flood plain. His past masterpieces appeared as canyons and gorges cut in a highland youth, but they also acted as barriers to future creativity: what encore *can* one perform after having written *The Sound and the Fury* and *Absalom, Absalom!*? The future was clogged with sediments from the past—not only with unsurpassable accomplishments but also with uncompleted projects like the *Snopes* trilogy and the Lucas Beauchamp murder mystery, with uncollected stories that needed gathering, with the whole corpus of Yoknapatawpha fragments that had to be raised into a single coherent structure, and with unpaid debts and unrealized ambitions.

Like Isaac McCaslin brooding on his past and on the history of his "coeval" land, Faulkner even imitated the river's course. During the flood each year, he wrote in "Delta Autumn," the river "actually ceased to flow and then moved backward, spreading, drowning the rich land and then subsiding again, leaving it still richer" (US, 270). During Ike's geological reminiscence while traveling with Boyd and Legate, "it seemed to him that the retrograde of his recollection had gained an inverse velocity from their own slow progress and that the land had retreated . . . back toward what it had been when he first knew it" (US, 271). In the years to come, Faulkner also turned back increasingly upon his own career, to examine and straighten its course, to guide himself in its continuing flow, to inspect—and occasionally pilfer—the "mounds" he had erected for his self-preservation.

Faulkner probably knew of Indian mounds all his life. They pepper the map of Mississippi, including several in Lafayette County. [56] In 1933, he seemed to draw on his own memory in a story whose narrator recalls his childhood fascination with a "darkly enigmatic" local mound (CS, 65). [57] But if he saw mounds nowhere else, he saw them in books: in Lyle Saxon's *Father Mississippi*; and, more extensively, in another friend's book, Calvin S. Brown's *Archeology of Mississippi*, which came into his possession in 1938, in time to affect *The Wild Palms*. Writing "Old Man" that year, Faulkner beached his castaway hero and heroine on an Indian mound in the midst of the Great Flood of 1927. Thereafter, beginning with "Delta Autumn," he repeatedly created versions of the flooded-mound image as projections of a vocational self-image.

In the works Faulkner produced in the next decade and a half, flooding became a persistent figure for the passage of time, above which only the most enduring artifacts can persevere. In *Requiem for a Nun*, (1951) he traced the history of Mississippi from before the Ice Age and implicitly compared its principal feature, the river valley, with his writing. As the earth tilted on its axis eons ago, the sea receded southward, "baring to light and air the broad blank mid-continental page for the first scratch of orderly recording." Like Faulkner, the river functions as a record-keeper. The text it produces, its delta, is a "long signatureless chronicle" and "the land's slow alluvial chronicle" (REQ, 100–101).

In the final chapter of *Requiem*, however, he shifted from the constructive to the destructive aspects of the flood of history. There, the old Yoknapatawpha County jail stands, mound-like, as a survivor from the past. Like Isaac McCaslin in "Delta Autumn," it represents an "old time which had been exhausted, used up, to be no more and never return." A new age of progress and civilization has washed away the old in "one burst, one surge, one soundless roar filled with one word: town: city"; and that flood leaves the old jail "in the tideless backwater of an alley on a side-street . . . the mud-chinked log walls even carcerant of the flotsam of an older time"

(REQ, 222–23). Throughout the deluge of history, the jail endures as a record of the "unhurryable continuity against or across which the vain and glittering ephemerae of progress and alteration washed in substanceless repetitive evanescent scarless waves" (REQ, 250). Here is a figure of Faulkner's ambition as a writer: not only did he attempt to record the resistance of the old values to the flood of change; he wanted his own work to survive as the jail did. Floods and jails were natural companions in Faulkner's imagination: long before he dramatized the anal-urethral plea- sures of retention and release in *The Wild Palms*, *The Marble Faun* and "Carcassonne" had linked confinement and escape as opposite but simul- taneous components of his artistry.

In *A Fable* (1954) also, Faulkner consistently described public events in hydraulic terms. The opening scene of the book portrays crowds of French citizens circulating through the city of Chaulnesmont as if they were liq- uid: "hovel and tenement voiding into lane and alley and nameless *cul-de- sac*, and lane and alley and *cul-de-sac* compounding into streets as the trickles became streams and the streams became rivers, until the whole city seemed to be pouring down the broad boulevards converging like wheel spokes into the *Place de Ville*, filling the *Place* and then, pressed on by the weight of its own converging mass, flowing like an unrecoiling wave up to the blank gates of the *Hôtel*" (FAB, 4). The mob flings aside the cavalry sent to control it, "blotting the intersecting streets as it passed them as a river in flood blots up its tributary creeks, until at last that boulevard too was one dense seething voiceless lake" (FAB, 6). The pro- gress of the war is treated similarly: Faulkner rendered troop movements in the same language he had applied to the Great Flood in "Old Man." For example, one character realizes that the combat is in recess when he sees "the vast cumbrous machinery of war grinding to its clumsy halt in order to reverse itself to grind and rumble in a new direction—the proprietorless wave of victory exhausted by its own ebb and returned by its own con- comitant flux, spent not by its own faded momentum but as though *bogged down in the refuse of its own success*" (FAB, 71–72, my italics). Above these evanescent currents of history stand certain enduring monu- ments. Overlooking Chaulnesmont rises an ancient citadel that is "not Gothic but Roman: not soaring to the stars out of the aspiration of man's past but a gesture against them of his mortality like a clenched fist or a shield" (FAB, 343). At the end of the book, a Parisian crowd "flows" around the base of the Arc de Triomphe, which rises "toward the gray and grieving sky, invincible and impervious, to endure forever" (FAB, 434). Finally, in the section Faulkner published separately as *Notes on a Horse-thief*, two men steal a racehorse when the train they are riding north from New Orleans plunges through "a flood-weakened trestle" (FAB, 153). They save it from drowning and repair its broken hip on "a hummock, a small island in the swamp," that barely rises above the floodwaters (FAB, 154). The only literal flood in a book filled with figurative ones occurs not in Europe but in the same Cajun territory where "Old Man" is set.

At approximately the same time that Faulkner was adapting "Old Man" for television in 1953,[58] he wrote a travel piece about Mississippi for *Holiday* magazine, partially fulfilling a vague intention to write a book of memoirs. It remained the most direct effort he ever attempted at autobiography. Naturally enough, his urge to remember coincided with a fear of forgetting: he undertook to write the essay within a month after his attacks of "retrograde amnesia" propelled him into the psychiatric office of Dr. Wortis (BL, 1452–53). The Mississippi River, to which he primarily devoted the essay, thus came to signify an intensely personal experience of mortality and oblivion. As Mark Twain had done seventy-five years earlier in "Old Times on the Mississippi," Faulkner converted the river into a private symbol for his vocation. As Twain had learned his craft—narration as well as navigation—by "master[ing] the language of this water," so Faulkner would associate his career with the course of the "old man."[59]

Ostensibly about the whole state, "Mississippi" focuses on the Delta region and only reaches the remainder by following the tributaries of the "Big River" back up into the hills. Combining fiction with fact, it blends a history of the author's private world, including Compsons, McCaslins, Sartorises, and Snopeses, with a summary of Mississippi history borrowed chiefly from the W.P.A. State Guide by way of *Requiem for a Nun*.[60] At the same time, it juxtaposes that history with the life of a character named William, who experiences it first as "the boy," then as "the young man," and finally as "the middleaged." The essay thus presents Faulkner and the river valley as "coevals," like Isaac McCaslin and the Delta. These "two spans running out together" (US, 275) both begin in the Delta, where "some of the land was still virgin in the early nineteen hundreds when the boy himself began to hunt" and "where in the beginning the predecessors crept with their simple artifacts, and built the mounds and vanished." As Faulkner recapitulated centuries of history, he related them to the flow of the river. After the white men arrive, for example, the Indians watch an "ebb-flux-ebb-flux" of alien nationalities vying for possession (ESPL, 11–13). The Civil War is rendered in a scene drawn from the opening of *The Unvanquished*, except that it occurs fifty years later: "the boy" and his black playmate re-create the war in miniature "with empty spools and chips and sticks and a scraped trench filled with well-water for the River." The advent of cotton is described primarily in terms of its effect upon the "whole vast flat alluvial Delta-shaped sweep of land along the Big River" (ESPL, 17).

Faulkner's autobiographical history of his state climaxes in the Great Flood, which also marks his protagonist's passage from "young man" to "man." For five pages, the longest vignette in the piece, he described the rise of the river, the backward flow of its tributaries, the battle to save the "dykes" (ESPL, 24), their collapse, the subsequent rescue operations, and a gradual drying out. At the center of this sequence, he reverted to Saxon's *Father Mississippi*, describing in a purer form than in "Old Man" the two scenes he had conflated in 1938. Above the flood rose "the mounds of the predecessors on which, among a tangle of moccasins, bear and horses and deer and mules and wild turkeys and cows and domestic chickens waited patient in mutual armistice; and the levees themselves, where among a jumble of uxorious flotsam the young continued to be born and the old to die, not from exposure but from simple and normal time and decay, as if man and his destiny were in the end stronger even than the river which had dispossessed him, inviolable by and invincible to, alteration" (ESPL, 26). That Faulkner still returned to these scenes, sixteen years after he first appropriated them from Saxon, testifies to their grip on his imagination. The image of the flooded mound seems to reflect both the irresistible force of his own intermittent deluge of words and the enduring products shaped by that force, products he hoped would long outlive their execution.

If Faulkner's childhood corresponds to the virgin Delta, and if the noon of his vocation corresponds to the Great Flood, at the end of "Mississippi" another alluvial image embodies the last phase of his life. The taming of the river constitutes a loss for "William"—as it did for Twain. Where "Delta Autumn" postulates Ike's gradual dissolution along with that of the delta, "Mississippi" records the substitution of a new kind of delta for the old. The Tallahatchie River bottom where Faulkner and Ike both hunted as boys has been submerged beneath a "flood control project." What "the middle-aged" remembers as "dense river bottom jungle and rich farm land, is now an artificial lake twenty-five miles long." The force of the river, for both destruction and creativity, has been broken; and the flood, which once deposited a periodic layer of fertile soil, has been turned into a stagnant reservoir from which a much less attractive form of sedimentation precipitates. The site of the boyhood hunting camp is "now the bottom of a muddy lake being raised gradually and steadily every year by another layer of beer cans and bottle caps and lost bass plugs" (ESPL, 35–36).[61]

Here is the ultimate depletion: the delta has become a parody of a delta. By extension, in Faulkner's imagination, the writer whose life is "coeval" with the river has become a parody of a writer. If the sediment deposited by the floods corresponds in some way to the works periodically added by a writer to his *oeuvre*, these dregs suggest a talent no longer capable of settling an alluvium but only a debris, a talent for defecation rather than parturition. Beginning with *Go Down, Moses*, indeed, Faulkner composed most of his books not by building mounds upon which to withstand the fury of his own vision, but by combining or completing works he had already written, the flotsam of previous floods. From the time of his collapse in the hunting camp, Faulkner adapted the delta setting of his medical embarrassment to an ongoing commentary on his literary career. By the early fifties, his stagnation had become one of the few fresh subjects that propelled him forward. A self-consciousness of decline entered Faulkner's works with "Delta Autumn," and it transformed *Go Down, Moses*.

Revision

Before "Delta Autumn," Faulkner's main purpose as he constructed *Go Down, Moses* was to repudiate the Negro stereotypes he had exploited in his Lucas Beauchamp stories. After "Delta Autumn," he also needed to incorporate its theme of historical and personal decline into all of the stories. As he rewrote them between May and July 1941, his revisions fulfilled these two needs and one other: to unify them into a minimally coherent, loosely chronological narrative, he began to impose a number of repetitive patterns upon them.[62] Expecting to complete a final typescript of the book by August 1, he did not yet anticipate that his varied purposes would require reconciliation in a new story, or that that story would eventually comprise fully one-third of the book's final length. In the early summer, he attacked the accomplished stories in the order he had established in May: "Almost," "The Fire and the Hearth," "Pantaloon in Black," "The Old People," "Delta Autumn," and "Go Down, Moses" (BL, 1072–80).

"Almost" became "Was," a title that emphasized its initial position in the volume and fixed it in the long historical perspective Faulkner had built in "Delta Autumn." He detached it from the *Unvanquished* material by changing the boy narrator's name from Bayard Sartoris to McCaslin ("Cass") Edmonds and by shifting to the third person. The boy's new first name indicates that Faulkner had already decided he would be related to Uncle Ike, thus linking the story to "Delta Autumn." In an introductory segment, he identified him as Ike's elder cousin. The boy's new last name indicates that Cass was to be an ancestor of Roth Edmonds, whose family background Faulkner had not previously mentioned. By relating these two, Faulkner unified "Was" with the Lucas stories and, more important, conferred upon them a relationship of historical cause. He began to draw a line of genealogical transmission like the symbolic, broken one between Ike and Don Boyd, whom Faulkner may already have identified with Roth Edmonds. Also, by changing Jason and Sophonsiba Prim's name to Beauchamp, he signalled that he was drawing a parallel line from their slave Tennie, who thereby became Lucas Beauchamp's ancestress.

Thus, just as Ike McCaslin's memory had moved back through his past and through the "coeval" past of the Big Woods, Faulkner was moving backward through the genealogical sources of Roth and Lucas, the main characters in his "stories about niggers." Those stories were themselves partially revised by the revision of "Was." As the backward motion continued, the formulaic black stereotypes partially dissolved. As the revisions proceeded, Faulkner's elaboration of the genealogical patterns became his principal strategy for combining his racial theme with the theme of depletion from "Delta Autumn."

In June 1941, Faulkner finished revising "A Point of Law," which became Chapter One of "The Fire and the Hearth" (BL, 1076). It contained much new material which derived from the concerns of "Delta Autumn" and from Faulkner's need to revise Lucas's formulaic relationship with his proprietor. It placed that relationship in the context of a much fuller history than the simplistic stereotypes could survive. First, into a lengthy new opening for the story Faulkner introduced an Indian mound, the presence of which stimulated other additions. In the revision, Lucas conceals his still in a "secret place in the creek bottom" (US, 215), as he had done in the original, but now that secret place lies in the side of a "squat, flat-topped, almost symmetrical mound rising without reason from the floor-like flatness of the valley" (GDM, 37). As he digs beneath an overhang on the face of the mound, it collapses, covering his still and "hurling clods and dirt at him, striking him a final blow squarely in the face with some-thing larger than a clod." This final object, which delivers an "admonitory pat from the spirit of darkness and solitude, the old earth, perhaps the old ancestors themselves," turns out to be "a fragment of an earthenware ves-sel which, intact, must have been as big as a churn and which even as he lifted it crumbled again and deposited in his palm, as though it had been handed to him, a single coin" (GDM, 38). Afterward Lucas remembers that years earlier "a group of white men, including two women, most of them wearing spectacles" (GDM, 37), had spent a day digging about the hillock, which they called an Indian mound. He had watched them con-temptuously at the time, but now he assumes that they had been search-ing for the buried treasure of which he thinks he has found one part.

Faulkner never described the "single coin," except to say that Lucas knew from touch alone that it was gold. Then it disappears from *Go Down, Moses*. He did not support Lucas's theory that the coin was part of a cache Buck and Buddy had buried decades earlier. He implied instead that it is a more ancient "bequest," a legacy from "the old ancestors." If Calvin Brown's *Archeology of Mississippi* did attract Faulkner's attention when he received it in 1938, he would have read there about professional field trips like the one Lucas witnessed and about such acts of vandalism as the demolition, by "treasure hunters" in 1890, of a mound "in the Tal-lahatchie bottom." He would also have seen, among the illustrations of artifacts discovered throughout Mississippi, photographs of a silver "Jeffer-son medal" that came from an excavation near his birthplace, New Al-bany. The early federal government had distributed to the Southern Indi-ans Presidential medals bearing diplomatic slogans. The one in Brown's book portrays a profile bust of Thomas Jefferson on one side, and on the reverse the cuffed hand of a white man and the braceleted hand of an Indian clasping each other amid the legend "Peace and Friendship."[63] If Faulkner noticed the medal, the only artifact in the book that resembles a coin, he might have been intrigued that it came from his birthplace and that it depicted the man after whom he had named his fictional commu-nity. As the themes of *Go Down, Moses* developed, moreover, he might have recalled the friendship legend with particular irony: while the medal promises interracial harmony, Faulkner's revisions were leading him to recite a history of white betrayal. If that is the coin that strikes Lucas, the earth has good reason to throw it up, for it signifies the tradition of white deception that forms Lucas's actual inheritance from the McCaslins, and it foreshadows the truth about the past that Ike would later "dig up" in "The Bear."

The motif of the clasped hands pictured on the reverse side of Brown's coin prefigures a related motif that entered Faulkner's book soon after he described Lucas's discovery of the coin. As he revised, he punctuated the novel with images of hands grasping *wrists*. Bondage and escape had been central to Faulkner's imagination probably even before Miss Maud strapped him into her back brace; in *Go Down, Moses*, he allowed his private obsession to merge with the imagery of enslavement and liberation. Shortly following the scene at the mound, a long digression substantially alters the humorous characterization of Lucas in the *Collier's* version of the story. As Lucas walks toward the Edmonds house, he recalls the time of Roth's birth. Roth's mother had died in childbirth, and his father Zack had commandeered Molly to nurse Roth as well as her own son Henry. After six months, Lucas had successfully demanded Molly's return; but he still decided that his pride required bloodshed, and he entered the white man's house, intending to murder him with a razor. During a bedside struggle Lucas secured Zack's pistol and aimed it point-blank at him, but it misfired. Into these events, Faulkner twice introduced variations on the handclasp motif. When Lucas first found that Molly had returned, he also discovered that she brought Roth with her to nurse. As they confronted each other beside the bed where Roth lay, Lucas reached out toward the white infant and threatened it. Molly's hand suddenly caught Lucas by a wrist. They stood thus, "locked hand and wrist," until Lucas "broke his wrist free, flinging her hand and arm back" (GDM, 50). Later, when Lucas assaulted Zack, they agreed to settle their conflict by placing Zack's pistol on his bed, kneeling and clasping hands, and racing each other to the weapon. Lucas grabbed Edmonds's right wrist, and Edmonds tried to break free: "Even as he tried to snatch his hand free Lucas' hand closed on it. He darted his left hand toward the pistol but Lucas caught that wrist too" (GDM, 55). After Lucas secured the weapon, they leapt into an "embrace" over the center of the bed, where the pistol misfired as Lucas jammed it into Zack's side (GDM, 57).

In "Pantaloon in Black," for another example, Faulkner had already drawn vaguer, preliminary versions of the image of hands grasping arms which then break free. As Rider shovels dirt onto his wife's grave, one of his friends from the sawmill offers to finish the job for him, touching his arm as he does so. Rider's response echoes the revised "Point of Law": "He didn't even falter. He released one hand in midstroke and flung it backward, striking the other across the chest, jolting him back a step, and restored the hand to the moving shovel." As Rider walks away from the funeral, his aunt "grasped his forearm"; but he rejects her solicitude, "walking out from under her hand, his forearm like iron, as if the weight on it were no more than that of a fly" (GDM, 135–36). When he visits her the next day, she grasps his arm in the same way (GDM, 150). Still another gesture, later in the story, resembles Lucas's more closely. When Rider sees that the sawmill watchman is cheating at cards, he challenges him by seizing his arm— "his left hand grasping the white man's wrist . . . until the white man's hand sprang open and the second pair of dice clattered onto the floor beside the first two and the white man wrenched free" (GDM, 153).

Faulkner's repetitions of the clasped-hands image, here and in later revisions, appear much too contrived to have been either accidental or unconscious. Nor did he restrict his use of the image to racial situations. When he wrote "The Bear," for example, his account of Ike's relationship with his wife involved another hand-and-wrist passage. Attempting to extort from Ike a promise to retain his farm, his wife removes her clothing and beckons to him from their bed, "her hand moving as though with volition and vision of its own, catching his wrist at the exact moment when he paused beside the bed" (GDM, 313). Again, when Faulkner revised "Delta Autumn," he had Ike produce a weak imitation of his wife's gesture in "The Bear." In the original Ike demands that the Negro woman take Boyd's money, which she has tossed onto his bed. As she retrieves it in the new version, Faulkner added another passage of hand choreography. Ike reaches out to her hand: "He didn't grasp it, he merely touched it—the gnarled, bloodless, bone-light bone-dry old man's fingers touching for a second the smooth young flesh where the strong old blood ran after its long lost journey back to home" (GDM, 362).

The image of the handclasp is only one of many replicated elements in the book. Faulkner devoted a major part of the revision process to the proliferation of certain motifs. For another example, virtually every story in the book came to contain confrontations between two people beside a bed.

These include the struggle of Lucas and Zack in "The Fire and the Hearth," the encounters between Ike and his wife in "The Bear" and between Ike and Roth's mistress in "Delta Autumn," the entrapment of Buck McCaslin by Sophonsiba Beauchamp in "Was," and, marginally, the interview between Butch Beauchamp and a census taker at the beginning of "Go Down, Moses," throughout which Butch lies on a "steel cot" in his prison cell (GDM, 369). In the magazine version of "The Old People," the closing conversation between the boy and his father takes place in their surrey on the way home from the hunt; after Faulkner's revision, it occurs in the bed they share at Major de Spain's house.

"Pantaloon in Black" includes no confrontation beside a literal bed, but Rider's brief grapple with his friend happens beside a figurative one. The book came to reiterate that graveside encounter. In "The Bear," for example, two men "faced one another across" the grave of the dog, Lion. Lion's grave is a "low mound," suggesting the other mounds in the book, and it lies near the burial platform of Sam Fathers (GDM, 252–53). This juxtaposition, in turn, echoes backward through the book also, recalling other pairs of resting places. In the revised "Fire on the Hearth," for instance, Faulkner used "the bed and the pallet" of Roth Edmonds and his "black foster-brother," Henry Beauchamp, to represent the "old curse" of racial injustice (GDM, 110–11).

A motif of parallel motion also multiplied itself in the book, echoing Ike's "coeval" relationship with the delta and culminating in the plantation ledgers in "The Bear," where the record of supplies issued and the record of cotton gathered form "two threads frail as truth and impalpable as equators yet cable-strong to bind for life them who made the cotton to the land their sweat fell on" (GDM, 256). The cable image appears elsewhere too, as when Faulkner described the "arm and hand" of Ike's wife as a "piece of wire cable with one looped end" (GDM, 314) tightening around Ike's wrist.

As Faulkner revised, he turned *Go Down, Moses* into an echo chamber, where characters and events ricochet off each other and where motifs repeat themselves seemingly *ad infinitum*. The final redundancy of the book conveys a sense that historical differentiation is futile and novelty impossible, as if all human dramas have collapsed into one scene, as if every struggle will inevitably happen beside a bed or a grave, where hands will inevitably clutch wrists, which will then break free. Ultimately, Faulkner discovered that this redundancy was one of his major subjects. Although his repetition of images may have begun as a means of uniting the stories into a book, it soon became thematic in itself, coalescing with the theme of inertia from "Delta Autumn."

In their futile repetitiveness the various images follow a genealogical paradigm, which Faulkner began to construct while he revised "A Point of Law." He drafted a chart then, which indicated for the first time a blood relationship between the white Edmondses and McCaslins and the black Beauchamps. A patriarchal "McCaslin" appears at its head, from whose four children three lines of descent derive. Buddy remained a childless bachelor. Buck fathered Isaac. A daughter named Mary wedded an "Edmonds," whose son "Carothers" was the father of Zack and the grandfather of a second "Carothers," the aptly nicknamed Roth Edmonds of "The Fire and the Hearth." Finally, the progenitive "McCaslin" fathered one black child, "Tomey's Turl. N.," the father of Lucas (BL, 1077). This chart would change substantially—the first Carothers Edmonds would become "Cass" again, for example—but already it had established a permanent pattern in the book.

That pattern is one of betrayal. In each generation on the chart, Faulkner created black-white relationships in which a white man betrays his black companion, whether male or female. The original "McCaslin" committed the primordial act of treachery when he compelled a daughter to bed with him and refused to acknowledge their offspring. When his sons pursue their fugitive slave in "Was," we now learn, they are pursuing their own half-brother. Zack Edmonds shames Lucas by commandeering Molly and rejects his black cousin Henry. In "Go Down, Moses," Roth Edmonds has banished not just any defiant teenager but his kinsman. In "Delta Autumn" Roth recommits the sin of his great-grandfather by repudiating his black mistress, to whom he is also related, and their child. Only Ike attempts to end the repetition.

To turn the stories of *The Unvanquished* into a novel, Faulkner had reversed the pattern of the first six stories by writing "An Odor of Verbena," in which Bayard Sartoris repudiates the ethic of violence that controls the previous stories. In refusing to perpetuate the formulaic code of honor pressed upon him by his family, he alters the design of his past and makes a new future possible. Ike McCaslin pursues a similar goal in *Go Down, Moses*: to break the pattern of racial betrayal that has controlled his family's history. Faulkner began to define Ike's efforts immediately after he created the chart, suggesting that a futile, thwarted impulse to deviate and renovate was built into the genealogical pattern from its inception. In Chapter One of "The Fire and the Hearth," we learn that "old Isaac" has lost his "patrimony" to Edmondses. In Chapter Three, we begin to see that he gave it away. There Faulkner reverted to the McCaslin twins' "scheme for the manumission of their father's slaves," which he had described in *The Unvanquished*; and he revealed for the first time that their plan included "an especial provision . . . for their father's negro son." They left "a sum of money, with the accumulated interest," to Tomey's Turl, who declined it. Ike has relinquished his own inheritance from his father except for the "trusteeship" of his father's legacy to Turl, which he has administered to Turl's children, including Lucas (GDM, 105–6). He has attempted to amortize the sins of his ancestors and to remove himself from their self-perpetuating cycle of betrayal.

Unlike Bayard Sartoris, however, Ike cannot break the pattern that binds him. Faulkner had already illustrated its continuance in "Delta Autumn," where Ike recognizes that Roth's repudiation of his mistress and child has replicated the original sin of the founding "McCaslin." Thus his inability to transmit Sam Fathers's bequest is balanced there by his powerlessness to quash the legacy of shame from his grandfather. By repeating a faded version of the hands-and-wrists motif when he revised "Delta Autumn," Faulkner underscored Ike's weakness. When Ike reaches to touch the hand of Roth's mistress, he seems to enter the pattern of bondage he had rejected when he broke both his wife's grip on him and her resistance to his relinquishment. The redundancy of his gesture, coming as the final element in a series of similar images, emphasizes the futility of his previous efforts to interrupt the repetitive design. [64]

It also suggests that Faulkner was signalling his own failure. He could finally neither overcome the "inertia of habit"—Dollard's phrase—which bound the white perception of the Negro nor even alter his own formulae for scene and gesture. If Bayard Sartoris turned *The Unvanquished* into a coherent work by reversing the patterning of its first six stories, neither Ike McCaslin nor Faulkner himself could provide the same service for *Go Down, Moses*, which consequently follows the entropic pattern he first articulated in "Delta Autumn." As the starting point of Faulkner's revisions, that story governed the final shape of the book and provided it a model in the periodic floods it describes, which exhaust the lands they wash even in enriching them.

Faulkner's revisions imposed an order of graduated depletion upon the whole book. Through the recurrent motifs that he scattered through its pages, he created a feeling of repetition without effect. With each new occurrence of the same image or gesture, the preceding ones lose part of their vitality. When they become identifiable as motifs, they turn the experience of reading into an artificial act. The reader of this superficially chaotic book is threatened, at last, by the same monotonously inevitable patterning that governs its characters. The final story of Go Down, Moses accomplishes not a reversal or innovation, as "An Odor of Verbena" or "Knight's Gambit" does, but only the reenactment of a century-old drama, which Gavin Stevens cannot prevent any more effectively than Ike could.

The book's paradigm of depletion is the genealogical structure Faulkner worked into its fabric after composing "Delta Autumn." In his revision of "A Point of Law," for example, he began to imply, through Lucas, that the McCaslin-Edmonds line has diminished substantially with each passing generation. As Lucas approaches Roth Edmonds's home to incriminate George Wilkins, he notices "the gleam of electricity in the house where the better men than this one had been content with lamps and even candles." Modernization has inflicted a tractor and an automobile upon the farm also, which neither Cass nor Zack would have tolerated. "But they were the old days," Lucas reflects, "the old time, and better men than these" (GDM, 44). The original McCaslin, despite his rapacity, was the most vital of them all; and the links of his posterity incarnate a true descent. Within the compass of the book, the seminal vitality of the founder exhausts itself.

This record of decline is ultimately autobiographical. As he had done before, Faulkner was projecting his own family's diminution. In the aftermath of "Delta Autumn," he was also registering his experience of personal reduction. But the major failure Go Down, Moses so successfully embodies is his final inability to penetrate the Negro stereotypes he had set out at first to destroy. In the end he discovered that, although he could subvert the old formulae he had exploited, he could not erect a new image of the Negro in their place. In a variety of ways his revisions incorporated an effort, parallel with Ike's, to repudiate the plantation tradition out of which the stereotypes arose; before he completed them, he doubted the very possibility that the written word could accommodate the Negro.

When he revised "A Point of Law," Faulkner humanized his black characters. He standardized their English. Lucas's first words in the Collier's version were "Gwine down the road"; they became "Going down the road." Molly had responded, "Messin' around up yon in de bottom all last night; gittin' back just in time to hitch up and be in de field when de sun cotch you!" (US, 213). Now, she said, "Messing around up yonder in the bottom all last night! Getting back home just in time to hitch up and get to the field a good hour after sunup!" (GDM, 42). "Wawkin" became "walking"; "gonter" became "going to." Lucas even became capable of alluding loosely to *Macbeth*: "tomorrow and the one after that and the one after that as long as tomorrow" (GDM, 57).

Faulkner's invention of the struggle with Zack also humanized Lucas. Having attacked Edmonds, Lucas has become what John Pendleton Kennedy invented the plantation tradition to conceal—a renegade Negro. He has intentionally tempted "the rope, even the coal oil" (GDM, 58) to defend his honor. By turning Lucas into a former Nat Turner, Faulkner prepared us for the violence of "Pantaloon in Black," obscuring the fact that the original motive of that story was in reaction against the Lucas stories. He also rendered Turl's mild rebellion in "Was" more serious than it at first seems. The struggle with Zack also dignified Lucas's marriage to Molly. In the *Collier's* story, Molly is a comic shrew. When Lucas tells George Wilkins in the last sentence of the story that "I don't give no man advice about his wife" (US, 225), the line is intended to arouse laughter. When he delivers the same line in the revised version, it arouses pathos as well, for we have watched him attempt murder and risk lynching for Molly's sake. His forced separation from her for six months, moreover, renders more serious her threat to divorce him forty-three years later, and his extreme reaction intensifies the drama of that threat. Into "A Point of Law," also, Faulkner inserted references to the hearth that provides the central domestic symbol of the final narrative. During the six-month separation, for example, Lucas kept "alive on the hearth the fire he had lit there on their wedding day and which had burned ever since" (GDM, 46). Like the hands and beds, fires and hearths proliferated across the text of *Go Down, Moses*.

Until Faulkner wrote "The Bear," his revisions served the same needs that altered the two opening stories. He sufficiently reworked "Gold Is Not Always" and "The Fire on the Hearth" to insure their consistency with "A Point of Law." He continued to improve Lucas's language, and he inserted new material that reinforced the changes in the preceding story. Especially in Chapter Three of the new amalgam, Faulkner added information that neutralized the stereotype, including the revelation that Lucas is related to the Edmondses by blood. Because of the circumstances of Roth's birth, furthermore, Molly became not just another tenant but the landlord's "mammy," reflecting more explicitly Faulkner's own relationship with Caroline Barr.

When he finished complicating the relationship between the black and white families in the Lucas stories, Faulkner may have felt that his major business was behind him—his repudiation of the book's formulaic core. His treatment of "Pantaloon in Black" corroborates this supposition, for he made no substantial changes in it, reproducing it almost *verbatim* in his typescript of Go Down, Moses. Because this story had already embodied the repudiation that motivated him and because it anticipated the image patterns that ultimately pervaded the novel, he did not feel a need to change it, even though it remained unassimilated to the genealogy of the other stories.

The next story, "The Old People," required numerous changes, however, for when he annexed it to "Delta Autumn," its racial dimension remained unarticulated. He began by reassigning characteristics to Ike McCaslin and Cass Edmonds that had belonged, probably, to Quentin and Jason Compson, and by pushing back the time of the story several decades. He also inserted passages describing Ike's genealogy, thus integrating the story into its narrative environment. For example, he identified Cass as the "grandson of [Ike's] father's sister . . . more his brother than his cousin and more his father than either" (GDM, 164). At the same time, he added a passage strengthening Sam Fathers's figurative paternity of the boy. The hunt joined them forever, "so that the man would continue to live past the boy's seventy years and then eighty years, long after the man himself had entered the earth" (GDM, 165). He elaborated Sam's heritage as well, turning the hunting story into a story also about race. Thus, for example, the "slave woman who was to be Sam's mother" became not just Negro but a "quadroon" (GDM, 166), diluting Sam's Negro blood (so that the "only visible trace" [GDM, 167] of it lay in the color of his hair and fingernails and in the expression of his eyes) and intensifying the injustice of the society that renders him Negro nevertheless.

In other ways too, Faulkner bound "The Old People" more tightly to the stories about Negroes. For example, he changed the "farm" of the first narrator's family (US, 203) into a "plantation" (GDM, 168), thus projecting onto it, and onto the story, the connotations of the old Southern tradition to which he had contributed when he began the Lucas stories. He pursued those connotations to confound them, inserting an indirect Biblical commentary upon them that extended the Biblical allusions in the title story toward a general applicability to all the stories. In the early version of "The Old People," Sam Fathers asks the young narrator's father for permission to live permanently at the hunting camp by announcing, "I want to go. . . . I want to go to the big bottom to live" (US, 205). In the revision, he repeats the same words but adds, "I want to go. . . . Let me go" (GDM, 173), echoing Moses' demand (in Exodus and in the Negro spiritual from which Faulkner derived his novel's title) to "Let my people go." By adding this reference, Faulkner defined the rebellion against white dominance that each of the black characters came to undertake, to one degree or another, during the revision of *Go Down, Moses*. Faulkner had decided to create Negro types of Moses—Nat Turners rather than Christlike "suffering servants."

The pattern of black rebellion in the finished novel constitutes Faulkner's definitive revision of the plantation stereotype of racial harmony and black passivity epitomized by Abe's conversion in *Swallow Barn*. Nevertheless, the title story bespeaks a postponement of deliverance. Faulkner's decision, soon after writing "Delta Autumn," to place "Go Down, Moses" last in the book indicates that he intended none of his black equivalents of Moses to succeed. His choice for the title of the whole book suggests that the failure of an anticipated deliverance had gained a central thematic importance for him. The literal meaning of the title, moreover, amplifies the mood of decline that "Delta Autumn" introduced to the book, reinforcing Faulkner's expression of his own failure. Thus, indirectly, Faulkner himself was also the Moses of the title, who had hoped to liberate the Negro from literary bondage and whose mission, he knew, had failed.

As Faulkner proceeded to the revision of "Delta Autumn"—and of "Go Down, Moses," which he changed hardly at all—he could look back upon a manuscript in which the image of the Negro is inconsistent. In "Was," for example, Tomey's Turl is comic, but we later learn the tragic dimensions of his story. In "The Fire and the Hearth," Lucas has become a figure of dignity, but he has not shed all his comic, formulaic attributes. Reading *Go Down, Moses*, one's perception of the Negro comes to resemble Quentin's unfocused perception of Deacon in *The Sound and the Fury*. It shifts from perspective to perspective, sliding from caricature into something deeper and back out again. In "The Bear," Faulkner frankly confronted the fact that the subject of his book was not the Negro but the white man's failed experience of the Negro. Faulkner's suspicion that black lives are impenetrable to literary scrutiny grew into an anxiety about the writer's power to penetrate *anything*. This anxiety exploded in Part Four of "The Bear," a central preoccupation of which is . . . writing. That long, convoluted text contains a climax to Faulkner's crisis of vocation.

"The Bear"

After he finished reworking "The Old People," Faulkner turned to "Delta Autumn," the story that had determined the character of the whole revision process. Like "The Old People," it required many changes, beginning with Don Boyd's rechristening as Roth Edmonds. By the time he completed it nearly half a year later, he had introduced several other innovations— including especially the genealogical relationship of Roth's mistress to the McCaslins and Edmondses—which helped to tighten the story's linkage to the volume of which it was becoming a part. [65]

Midway through these alterations, however, in late June or early July 1941, Faulkner set "Delta Autumn" aside and took up an old story, "Lion," which, when first published in 1935, had been loosely connected to the material of "The Old People." Throughout the remainder of 1941, he modified it and expanded it until it became the longest and most meaningful chapter of *Go Down, Moses*, "The Bear." It not only provided the book with "new material for climactic effect," as Blotner suggests (BL, 885– 87, 1080–90); it also articulated the major tensions that control the whole work: between acceptance and repudiation of the plantation tradition, including its representation of the Negro; between Faulkner's faith in his literary talent and his acquiescence in its exhaustion; between an impulse to bequeath his substance through words and a virtual surrender to illiteracy.

When Faulkner began "The Bear," he was responding directly to the needs of "Delta Autumn." Its central interest is not race, but again exhaustion, waste, and failure. Only as the story developed did Faulkner connect these concerns to the question of race. "The Bear" grew out of the incongruity between "The Old People" and "Delta Autumn," stories that embody opposite reckonings of the bounty of nature and the renewability of history. "The Old People" asserts that the world's energies conserve themselves and postulates the spiritual immortality of wildlife, whereas "Delta Autumn" illustrates a principle of irreversible drainage. As Faulkner moved from revision of "The Old People" to revision of "Delta Autumn," their philosophical incompatibility triggered the transformation of "Lion," to which he returned because it mediated between the two contrary visions. It shares with "The Old People" its setting in the Big Woods in a time of plenitude, when "[t]here had been bear" (GDM, 335). But it also dramatizes the onset of a long slide toward the comparative scarcity in "Delta Autumn."

When Faulkner had written "Lion" in early 1935—partly to finance his interrupted work on *Absalom, Absalom!*, with which it shares its narrator, Quentin Compson—it reflected his personal involvement in an immediate ecological problem. Less than two months before he sent it to his New York agent, he and some friends had incorporated the "Okatoba Hunting and Fishing Club," to which "General" James Stone transferred the hunting and fishing rights on his property in the Tallahatchie River bottom. Much of this land, including the campsite where Faulkner had hunted as a boy, lay under the waters of Sardis Reservoir by the time he wrote about it in "The Bear"; but in 1935 he still hoped to preserve it from human depredation. Shortly before writing "Lion," he drafted a letter to the state game commissioner explaining the goals of the new hunting club: "It is our intention to protect the game which is fast being exterminated." The bylaws he drew up for the association included a provision that members might invite guests only with "due regard to the amount and condition of the game available" (BL, 879–85). When he wrote "Lion," he created in a character named Boon Hogganbeck an example of someone not to invite.

A forty-year-old, part-Indian ne'er-do-well with the intellect of a child, Boon provides a frame for the destructive action of "Lion." As the story opens, Major de Spain, who owns the camp, sends him with Quentin to Memphis to replenish the party's whiskey supply. On the train to and from the city, Boon boasts about the dog Lion, whom Quentin compares to the gods and heroes of primitive religions, and about Old Ben, the "head bear" of the Big Woods. On the following morning the two creatures keep an annual appointment, which the neighboring country has anticipated in the same way that "people talked about Sullivan and Kilrain or Dempsey and Tunney." Uncle Ike McCaslin, an old man and a minor character in "Lion" as he had been in "A Bear Hunt," puts Quentin on a stand "under a gum tree beside the bayou," where the boy reflects on the virgin luxuriance of the wilderness and fearfully anticipates the bear upon which he "had conferred supernatural powers." When he hears the dogs bay it, he returns with his father to the camp, where they spend the remainder of the day waiting for Boon and Lion to return from the chase. After dark, a bloodied and disheveled Boon enters the camp house carrying a fatally wounded Lion. Ad, the Negro cook, then describes "how Lion had bayed Old Ben against a down tree top . . . and how Old Ben caught Lion and had him on the ground, and Boon ran in with the hunting knife and jerked Lion back, but he would not stay out; and how this time Boon jumped straddle of Old Ben's back and got the knife into him . . . until he touched the life." Lion dies at the end of the next day, and the hunters then break camp. Sensing that the deaths of Lion and Old Ben have devitalized the Big Woods, Major de Spain never returns (US, 184–200).

Faulkner made clear in an epilogue that the story's primary subject is a Creation diminished by man's rapacity, more than it is Quentin's initiation into adulthood. There Boon, who in his love for Lion has proved an agent of destruction, provides a caricature of simple bloodlust. On a squirrel hunt during the summer after Old Ben's death, Quentin discovers Boon maniacally besieging a tree filled with squirrels, which he cannot kill because he has dismantled his gun in a rage of frustration and scattered its pieces about him on the ground. In a curiously masturbatory image, Quentin sees him "hunched over, hammering furiously at the part on his lap, his walnut face wild and urgent and streaming with sweat" (US, 200). The denizens of the Big Woods have been reduced from bears to squirrels, and Boon has changed the hunt from a ritual of pride and humility into a wasteful "expense of spirit."

When Faulkner converted "Lion" into "The Bear," the masturbatory connotations of Boon's destructiveness became self-referential, for he preceded the scene of the epilogue with the notorious fourth section of "The Bear," in which he made the decline of the wilderness emblematic of human history and of his own prospects as a writer. In the end the hunt came to serve as a remote metaphor for the act of writing, for pursuing through the perishable Big Woods of his depleted talent the spirit-buck of past achievement. The dead bear—Old *Has*-Been—stands as a loose equivalent to such unsurpassable trophies as *The Sound and the Fury* and *Absalom, Absalom!* Boon's scattered gun suggests the dismantling of Faulkner's creativity.

Except for Part Four, however, "The Bear" fleshes itself trimly upon the frame provided by "Lion." The major differences between the two stories are that Ike McCaslin has become sixty years younger and replaced "Quentin" as the central character, that a third-person narrative voice has replaced the first-person one, that Sam Fathers has entered the story in the preceptorial capacity he performed in "The Old People," and that Faulkner described in three new episodes the boy's previous experience of the mythic beast. The last change is the most important, for it establishes the bear as a permanently repetitive phenomenon whose demise depreciates Time itself.

Part One introduces Old Ben as an inheritance, a legacy "out of an old dead time," which "loomed and towered" in young Ike's dreams "before he even saw the unaxed woods" (GDM, 193). It presents the boy's first exposures to the bear: once, without seeing it, when the bear comes to look *him* over; then, in his eleventh year after he abandons his reliance on the "lifeless mechanicals" (US, 289)[66] of civilization, when the bear grants him a rendezvous on its own ground, on its own terms. In Part Two, a third level of exposure occurs when Ike pits his small "fice" against Old Ben but fails to take a clear shot at the bear. He throws down his rifle instead and runs in to remove the tiny dog from the bear's clutches. This incident prefaces the advent of Lion, whose capture and training occupy most of the second part. Part Three then recapitulates the basic text of "Lion," from the trip to Memphis through the death of the bear and the burial of Lion, elaborating it in places to meet the expanded requirements of the longer story. The boy not only hears about but witnesses directly the struggle between Old Ben, Lion, and Boon, in which "they almost resembled a piece of statuary" (GDM, 241). The deaths include not only Ben's and Lion's but Sam Fathers's too, whose passing reinforces the effect of closure and decline. Before his death, Sam echoes the Mosaic imperative he had uttered in "The Old People," insisting to Major de Spain that they "Let [him] go home" to his "dark little hut" to attend his own "[e]xhaustion" (GDM, 245–56). The section ends a few days later with an implication that Boon may have killed Sam, upon Sam's request.

Part Five of "The Bear" repeats and expands the epilogue to "Lion." As if consciously to accelerate the reduction of the Big Woods signalled by Old Ben's death, Major de Spain has "sold the timber-rights to a Memphis lumber company" (GDM, 316). Faulkner accentuated the loss by describing in detail Ike's return to the woods aboard the log train. As the little locomotive enters between the "twin walls of unaxed wilderness," it resembles "a small dingy harmless snake" (GDM, 318–19), which frightens a diminished wildlife, including a timorous, half-grown bear. When Ike returns to the grave-site of Old Ben and Lion, which has been washed by one of the many floods in *Go Down, Moses*, he encounters a real snake, "the old one, the ancient and accursed about the earth" (GDM, 329), whose fallen dominion the wilderness has become. That Boon's violent rapacity as a squirrel hunter was meant to indicate the same decline Faulkner made clear by producing a second figure of false prowess in Uncle Ad Bush. Ad's single venture into deer hunting had ended, the narrator here recounts, in the misfiring of three shells.

Faulkner's preoccupation with misfirings, which began at least as early as *Light in August* and which had surfaced recently in the revision of "The Fire and the Hearth," would culminate in *A Fable* with the blank ammunition that compels the young pilot Levine to commit suicide. In *Go Down, Moses*, as elsewhere, it serves as a correlative for impotency: in *A Fable*, for example, the removal of shrapnel from anti-aircraft shells is spoken of as "gelding" (FAB, 80). In the metaphor of the hunt as writing, that impotency is not so much physical as vocational. The fruitless spendings of Ad and Boon provide an immediate introduction to another false hunter, Roth Edmonds in "Delta Autumn," but they also echo Part Four, in which Faulkner directly voiced his otherwise sublimated anxieties.

While the beginning and ending of "The Bear" straightforwardly expand "Lion" to resolve the inconsistency between "The Old People" and "Delta Autumn," the middle departs drastically from "Lion" in order to adapt it to the full novelistic context. Part Four of "The Bear" was the final piece of new writing that entered *Go Down, Moses*. In it Faulkner attempted not only to assimilate one narrative entity into a larger one but also to make sense of the total construction, to analyze the very forces that had produced the book he was writing.

First, it captures Faulkner's ambivalence about the plantation tradition, which had provided the original impetus for the first stories and for the idea of collecting them. Part Four consists primarily of an argument between Ike and his cousin Cass Edmonds over the morality of owning land worked by Negroes. When he is twenty-one years old, Ike repudiates his inheritance of the McCaslin plantation, because he has discovered in its commissary ledgers the legacy of betrayal which that inheritance includes. There, his Uncle Buck and Uncle Buddy have recorded their father's acts of miscegenation and incest, along with their efforts to redeem his transgressions. Having learned at age sixteen of this skeleton in the family closet, Ike abjures the entire edifice upon attaining his majority, refusing even to acknowledge that he has a claim to relinquish. "I cant repudiate it. It was never mine to repudiate," he tells Cass, denying the very principle of possession (GDM, 256–57). Against Ike's idealism, Cass maintains a pragmatic conservatism, arguing for preservation of the status quo despite its tainted origins and for the orderly transmission of property and values from generation to generation. He defends the legitimacy of Ike's legacy, praising the strength of Carothers McCaslin, "who saw the opportunity and took it, bought the land, took the land, got the land no matter how, held it to bequeath, no matter how" (GDM, 256).

The two cousins also dispute their responsibilities to "their" Negroes. Ike hopes that his repudiation will help "to set at least some of His lowly people free" (GDM, 259). Cass stands as defender of "that whole edifice intricate and complex and founded upon injustice and erected by ruthless rapacity" (GDM, 298). Ike professes to admire the Negroes as a race, finding them "better than we are. Stronger than we are" (GDM, 294). Cass takes the stereotypic view of blacks as lazy and untrustworthy, rebutting Ike's defense of them point by point.

The question of who wins the debate in Part Four is controversial. Some readers assume that Faulkner cannot have agreed with the Cass Edmonds whose derogation of the "wilderness of wild beasts and wilder men" so sharply contradicts the nostalgia for the wilderness elsewhere in "The Bear." They also note that Cass's rather casual acceptance of racial injustice is inconsistent with the evident sympathy Faulkner displayed toward the blacks in the other stories in the volume. But other readers call attention to the inadequacy of Ike's idealism, suggesting that his effort to break the patterns of betrayal and rapacity fails because it is negative. They point to his final recognition in "Delta Autumn" that Roth Edmonds's treatment of his mistress continues the old pattern despite his abdication—or indeed *because* he has abdicated—and to his realization that the legacy from Sam Fathers, which he has tried to perpetuate, will die with him, while the legacy of betrayal, which he hoped to cancel, will survive.

The truth is probably that neither view prevails. The center of *Go Down, Moses* is a dialogue because the experiences it distills were contradictory and because Faulkner sympathized with both sides of the argument. On one hand, he had first conceived of the book as a repudiation of plantation preconceptions and black stereotypes, which he himself had exploited. Just as the only McCaslin legacy Ike accepts is the execution of his grandfather's bequest to his black heirs, so Faulkner's dedication of *Go Down, Moses* "To Mammy Caroline Barr" resembles a bequest also. The book is one payment of his hereditary debt to the Negro race. On the other hand, Faulkner portrayed Ike's repudiation and self-dispossession just at a time when he was fighting desperately to retain his own ersatz plantation. He wrote the very stories that undermine the plantation stereotype in order to earn enough money to retain his paternal relationship to the blacks at Greenfield Farm.

The opposition between Ike and Cass expresses other divisions within Faulkner as well. Besides the author's ambivalence about his attempt to reconstruct a plantation heritage, their dialogue captures a powerful longing within him to escape from all domestic duties, whether they followed antebellum precedents or not. He derived great pride from having reversed the depletion of his family's fame and fortune over several preceding generations. When he spoke of his accomplishments, he could sound both bitter about his forced independence and boastful about having replenished the Falkner legacy. Thus, in May 1940, shortly after *Go Down, Moses* was first conceived, he complained to Robert Haas that "I inherited my father's debts and his dependents, white and black without inheriting yet from anyone one inch of land or one stick of furniture or one cent of money. . . . I bought without help from anyone the house I live in and all the furniture; I bought my farm the same way" (SL, 122–23). Nevertheless, while his pride in his property explains the tenacity with which he held on to it, that property was also a prison. The household it sheltered became a setting from which Faulkner yearned to escape. In June 1942, he described his mood to Harold Ober as claustrophobic: "I have been trying for about ten years to carry a load that no artist has any business attempting: oldest son to widowed mothers and inept brothers and nephews and wives and other female connections and their children, most of whom I dont like and with none of whom I have anything in common, even to make conversation about." He regretted that he was "either not brave enough or not scoundrel enough to take my hat and walk out" (SL, 153). In Part Four of "The Bear," Ike McCaslin not only relinquishes his property; he also rejects his wife's control and renounces paternity, thus denying the most literal form of bequeathal. Faulkner undoubtedly considered Ike's renunciation to be irresponsible, but it was an irresponsibility with which he deeply sympathized. His letters disclose simultaneously an intense possessiveness and a yearning to dispossess himself.[67]

Cass accuses Ike of wanting to escape not merely from domestic encumbrances but from the whole weight of human history. Whereas Cass stands for the uninterrupted transmission of the social order, even if that order bears flaws, Ike views history as a process of decay that requires periodic regeneration. While Cass concedes that "the old world" "col-lapsed" after Rome fell and that "men fought over the fragments of that collapse" for a thousand years, Ike holds that God then revealed America as a "new world" where mankind could redeem itself (GDM, 257–58). In a lengthy rehearsal of Southern history, Ike argues for a similar interpreta-tion of the Civil War as a divinely sanctioned interruption of the evil pattern that had corrupted the new world in its turn; he hopes to correct the evil that the war failed to repair, by breaking the pattern that remains. Throughout their debate, both men refer to history as a process of inheri-tance, a succession of transmissions from generation to generation. Ike is said to have "inherited" the Civil War, although it preceded his birth, just "as Noah's grandchildren had inherited the Flood although they had not been there to see the deluge" (GDM, 289). Thus the idea of bequeathal comes to stand for the very principle of history, which Cass upholds de-spite its confusion and which Ike would negate because of its injustice.

Presumably, Ike's disaffection from history results in part from his nega-tive experience of inheritances of all sorts. To emphasize the connection Faulkner strewed Part Four of "The Bear" with depleted legacies, includ-ing especially the "silver cup filled with gold pieces" which his Uncle Hubert Beauchamp kept for Ike at "Warwick" until he should turn twenty-one (GDM, 301). On Ike's visit to Warwick with his mother, they see that Uncle Hubert has taken Negro mistresses to his bed, a discovery that strengthens Ike's rejection of the McCaslin legacy when he learns from the commissary ledgers about his grandfather's miscegenation. They also see successive stages in the dismantlement of Warwick's grandeur: piece by piece, Uncle Hubert sells off the crumbling mansion to which Ike is the sole heir, until finally it burns to the ground. When Ike reaches his major-ity, he finds that his other "Legacy" has dwindled also. The "silver cup" has become a tin coffee-pot, and the "gold pieces" have become copper coins, muffled by "a collection of minutely-folded scraps of paper suffi-cient almost for a rat's nest, of good linen bond, of the crude ruled paper such as negroes use, of raggedly-torn ledger-pages and the margins of newspapers and once the paper label from a new pair of overalls" (GDM, 306). Upon these, Hubert Beauchamp has signed IOU notes to Ike for the previous contents of the cup, which he intermittently removed during the ten years he lived after Ike's birth. They constitute a fragmented record of graduated depletion that matches the depletion on the other side of Ike's genealogy, recorded in the similarly intermittent ledger entries.

That both legacies come to Ike on "scraps of paper" is significant, for throughout Part Four of "The Bear" Faulkner referred indirectly to various acts of writing and reading, suggesting that the subject of literary communication was one which the task of resolving *Go Down, Moses* required him to address.[68] The association of the written "Legacy" with the diminished "silver cup" confirms this suggestion, for Faulkner had often used a similar image to denote his artistic ideal. One version of it appeared as early as *Sartoris*, in which Horace Benbow produces with the glass-blowing equipment he brings with him from Europe "one almost perfect vase of clear amber," which he called by his sister's name and addressed as "Thou still unravished bride of quietness" (SAR, 182). In an early draft of his long-unpublished "Introduction" to *The Sound and the Fury*, Faulkner applied the Keatsian imagery more closely to his own work, comparing what was to remain his favorite novel to a similarly feminine vessel:

> There is a story somewhere about an old Roman who kept at his bedside a Tyrrhenian vase which he loved and the rim of which he wore slowly away with kissing it. I had made myself a vase, but I suppose I knew all the time that I could not live forever inside of it, that perhaps to have it so that I too could lie in bed and look at it would be better; surely so when that day should come when not only the ecstasy of writing would be gone, but the unreluctance and the something worth saying too. It's fine to think that you will leave something behind you when you die, but it's better to have made something you can die with.[69]

Already in 1933, Faulkner could sound elegiac about himself. In the final draft of the "Introduction," he even described the series of novels that followed *The Sound and the Fury* as a sequence of increasing failure, recalling that in *Sanctuary, As I Lay Dying,* and *Light in August* he had tried to recapture a "quality which The Sound and the Fury had given me" but that, with growing distance, "[i]t did not return."[70] Even then, he characterized his career as a graduated decline.

It is fitting that Faulkner associated the vase metaphor with the idea of legacy.[71] Writing was always for him something he could "leave behind" when he died, the "decipherable scar" he would scratch on "the face of the supreme Obliteration." But an opposite impulse toward anonymity contributed to the same result. While he frequently expressed a wish to deface history with his unique "Kilroy was here" (LG, 253), he also frequently voiced a hope that the books he wrote would be sufficient for him to "*die* with," that they would enable him to *escape* history, as Ike attempted to do. Thus, in 1949 he wrote to a journalist who had solicited personal information that "[i]t is my ambition to be, as a private individual, abolished and voided from history, leaving it markless, no refuse save the printed books. . . . It is my aim, and every effort bent, that the sum and history of my life, which in the same sentence is my obit and epitaph too, shall be them both: He made the books and he died" (BL, 1276; SL, 125, 285).

The Tyrrhenian vase embodies the fulfillment of both these contrary motives, but it also signifies failure. It represents the solid accomplishment that, even in 1933, he knew would outlive him; but he claimed then that he had created *The Sound and the Fury* without an audience in mind, and he knew that the essential experience it imperfectly expressed would indeed die with him. In later years, he consistently referred to *The Sound and the Fury* as a failure, the "best failure" (FU, 61) among his books but representative of them in its failure nonetheless. The vision it contains was too private. He felt that it had not adequately transmitted the meaning he had hoped to convey. Like all books, it was a legacy from author to reader, which depletes itself in every imperfect act of reading. The vase image attracted Faulkner precisely because it defies the erosion to which he increasingly felt his work was susceptible. Like a dam or levee, the vase *contains* whatever it holds.

Faulkner's purest use of the vase image occurs in Part Four of "The Bear," a few pages before the appearance of Hubert Beauchamp's silver cup, through a direct allusion to the "Ode on a Grecian Urn" itself.[72] In the scene that provides the dénouement for the *Saturday Evening Post* condensation of "The Bear," a younger Cass tries to explain to a younger Ike why the latter has failed to fire at Old Ben when he had the clear shot described in Part Two. From a bookcase in the plantation library, Cass removes a volume and reads the poem aloud, evoking the eternal criteria of "[c]ourage and honor and pride, and pity and love of justice and of liberty" (GDM, 297) that Ike has recognized in Old Ben. In his embodiment of Keats's urn, Ben corresponds to Ike's depleted "Legacy," another well-wrought vessel. Both derive ultimately from Faulkner's visualization of his own fate.

That Part Four of "The Bear" is about writing Faulkner confirmed by filling it with books. Indeed, it is as replete with manuscripts and published texts as the rest of *Go Down, Moses* is empty of them; and the contrast implies a discontinuity between literary and nonliterary experience. With one important exception in the title story, the only books in *Go Down, Moses* outside of "The Bear" are Roth Edmonds's commissary ledger and the bank "pass book" in which Lucas records the deposit of his McCaslin legacy when Ike gives it to him in "The Fire and the Hearth." Even in "The Bear," except in Part Four, the references to books that do appear simply introduce Faulkner's qualms about books. After the death of Old Ben, for example, young Ike asks for permission to stay at the camp so that he may tend Sam Fathers. Cass, ever an advocate of book learning and other "legacies" from the past, refuses on the ground that Ike should return to school; and Boon, practically illiterate himself, supports Cass. But General Compson intervenes on Ike's behalf, arguing successfully that the understanding Ike has gained from the Big Woods surpasses what schools can offer. "If missing an extra week of school is going to throw you so far behind you'll have to sweat to find out what some hired pedagogue put between the covers of a book, you better quit altogether," he tells Ike (GDM, 250).[73] The opposition between books and life also appears at the very beginning of "The Bear," where Faulkner described the wilderness as "bigger and older than any recorded document" (GDM, 191). Again, in Part Two, Faulkner described the woods as an alternative (and superior) form of school: "If Sam Fathers had been [Ike's] mentor and the backyard rabbits and squirrels his kindergarten, then the wilderness the old bear ran was his college and the old male bear itself, so long unwifed and childless as to have become its own ungendered progenitor, was his alma mater" (GDM, 210).

But only in Part Four do bibliographical images begin to accumulate, turning it into a microcosm of the book into which it entered—a text filled with texts that must be integrated, just as *Go Down, Moses* consists of story fragments that readers must manipulate into a narrative whole.[74] Simultaneously, Faulkner cranked up his Truebloodian language machine. The plantation ledgers obviously occupy the center of Part Four, but a host of other manuscripts and published texts crowd its perimeter. The first slave mentioned in the Compson archives, for example, is Percival Brownlee, whom Buck and Buddy bought as a "bookkeeper" (GDM, 264) to handle the plantation accounts. Ironically, he turns out to be illiterate; and the irony is significant, for the Negro race proves to be the main repository of the knowledge that competes with books. The Negro's foreignness to books is emphasized in a later scene in Part Four, when Ike discovers the husband of his black cousin Fonsiba reading a book through "gold-framed spectacles" that "did not even contain lenses" (GDM, 278). Reading is a technique to which blacks are clearly unhabituated, in Faulkner's imagination, and Ike registers an appropriate perception of incongruity.

Other texts abound within Part Four. When Cass reads Keats's "Ode," for example, Faulkner again casts doubt upon the validity of book experience. Ike tests the poem against his memory of the hunt and concludes that "[s]omehow it had seemed simpler than that, simpler than somebody talking in a book about a young man and a girl he would never need to grieve over because he could never approach any nearer and would never have to get any further away" (GDM, 297). Here, and in a spate of other references to "books," "chronicles," "scraps of paper," and other written records, Faulkner substantiates Gail Hightower's discovery in *Light in August* of "how false the most profound book turns out to be when applied to life" (LA, 455).[75]

To fulfill Hightower's recognition as precisely as possible, the debate between Ike and Cass even includes an extended discussion of the most profound of all Western books, the Bible. Ike's argument dominates. Although he accepts the Bible's authority and quotes it to support his interpretation of history, he refuses to read it literally as Cass would have him do. Instead, he presents it as a model of the ideal relationship between an author and his readers, which transcends mere literacy and overcomes all the normal barriers to communication. Proceeding from the pen of a writer as uncompromising with readers as Faulkner had always been, Ike's explanation of how the Bible transcends its message is elaborately paradoxical: "He [God] didn't have His Book written to be read by what must elect and choose, but by the heart, not by the wise of the earth because maybe they dont need it or maybe the wise no longer have any heart, but by the doomed and lowly of the earth who have nothing else to read with but the heart. Because the men who wrote his [sic] Book for Him were writing about truth and there is only one truth and it covers all things that touch the heart" (GDM, 260). The authors of the Bible, Ike says, wrote not only with a sense of responsibility to the meaning they conveyed but also with an awareness of the limitations of their audience:

> They were trying to write down the heart's truth out of the heart's driving complexity, for all the complex and troubled hearts which would beat after

them. What they were trying to tell, what He wanted said, was too simple. Those for whom they transcribed His words could not have believed them. It had to be expounded in the everyday terms which they were familiar with and could comprehend, not only those who listened but those who told it too, because if they who were that near to Him as to have been elected from among all who breathed and spoke language to transcribe and relay His words, could comprehend truth only through the complexity of passion and lust and hate and fear which drives the heart, what distance back to truth must they traverse whom truth could only reach by word-of-mouth? (GDM, 260–61)

Thus, pastoralism fulfills its natural inclination to self-parody. The writer writing about illiterates naturally discovers that his real subject, all along, has been not their illiteracy but his doubts about his own eloquence. The Moses of the book's title appears here in his role as author of Scripture as well as in his role as liberator, and in both roles he "goes down" to defeat. Having rejected the popular formulae of such writers as Bradford, Faulkner concluded his novel about black people by offering a testimonial to accommodating one's readers—ironically, in the midst of his most notoriously baroque prose. Insofar as he agreed with Ike, then, he was repudiating his own practice as a writer.76 If David Minter correctly identifies the "paradigm" of Go Down, Moses as "that of reader and text,"77 it is a paradigm that constantly risks self-destruction.

Just how thoroughly Faulkner was questioning his own vocation, an intriguingly self-allusive passage later in Part Four of "The Bear" makes clear. Ike tries to convince Cass that the War Between the States was God's revenge upon Americans for their failure to renew human history after He had given them a new world in which to do so.78 Faulkner inserts the titles of his own novels into this treatise on exhaustion:

. . . He [God] could have *repudiated* them [the American people] since they were *his creation* now and forever more throughout all their generations until not only that old world from which He had rescued them but this new one too which He had revealed and led them to as a *sanctuary* and refuge were become the same worthless tideless rock cooling in the last crimson evening except that out of all that *empty sound and bootless fury* one *silence*, among that loud and moiling all of them just one simple enough to believe that horror and outrage were first and last simply horror and outrage and was crude enough to act upon that, *illiterate and had no words* for talking or perhaps was just busy and had no time to. (GDM, 284, my italics)

Man's "sanctuary" here proves illusory, as it had in the novel of the same title. "The sound and the fury" are "empty" and "bootless," and followed ominously by "silence." Moreover, Faulkner's references to his own works occur in the same sentence with a creator considering the repudiation of his creation, and they immediately precede Ike's prophecy that history will be redeemed by an illiterate person with "no words."

Of course, Cass Edmonds argues against Ike's negative view of literacy, but their debate is never resolved in Go Down, Moses. At the end of the novel, Gavin Stevens is returning to his desk to resume his translation of the Old Testament "back" into classic Greek—the same "vocation" (GDM, 371) he would pursue in "Knight's Gambit," which Faulkner first drafted immediately after concluding the manuscript of Go Down, Moses (BL, 1093–97). On a symbolic level, Stevens's translation suggests the purity of Faulkner's intentions as a writer: to recapture the lost Word of some divine truth. But in reality, Stevens's task (like Faulkner's?) is quixotic and doomed to failure: even were he to succeed in resurrecting the dead words of Scripture, fewer people would be able to read them properly in classic Greek than have actually been able to read Faulkner's own, American Greek. Stevens may return to *his* desk, but his resumption of his writing preceded the longest silence in *Faulkner's* career.[79]

Faulkner further undercut Stevens as an affirmative representative of the literary vocation by juxtaposing him with an illiterate old black woman, Molly Beauchamp. Although Molly cannot read, she insists that her nephew's death be reported in the local newspaper. She does not care to know the literal facts in the case, which are sordid; but she does know, "with the heart," that she must fulfill the obligations of human kinship. Although her knowledge of Scripture is imprecise, she quotes its spirit accurately; and it is from her illogical utterances, not from Gavin Stevens's book-learning, that the whole novel derives its title. In the end, Faulkner's attribution of illiteracy to blacks subverted his own literacy. The successive waves of Shegog's voice ultimately overwhelmed Faulkner too.

The division within Faulkner between Cass's bookishness and Ike's anti-literalism derived from the contradictions in the Southern intellectual heritage that Lewis Simpson describes in *The Dispossessed Garden*. In the beginning of the plantation myth, the library was the main facility for which men undertook the "errand into paradise." It stood as the *raison d'être* of Byrd's Westover and Jefferson's Monticello. During the nineteenth century, however, the plantation justified itself less and less as a "homeland of the mind." When plantation writers shifted their attention from the Big House to the Quarter after the Civil War, they largely forsook the idea of the plantation as an environment of thought. Instead, their writing enunciated a positively anti-intellectual reaction against the original vision of the plantation. One of the chief assets of the dialect genre became the opportunity it afforded its authors to express covertly their disenchantment with the value of writing. Joel Chandler Harris, for example, put into the mouth of Uncle Remus a typical dialect-fiction statement of the evils of erudition: "W'at a nigger gwineter l'arn outen books? I kin take a bar'l stave an' fling mo' sense inter a nigger in one minnit dan all de school-houses betwixt dis en de State er Midgigin. . . . Hit's de ruination er dis country. . . . Put a spellin'-book in a nigger's han's, en right den en dar' you loozes a plow-hand."[80] In the popular "Christmas-Night in the Quarters," Irwin Russell extended the case against books to both races, and he based upon it an invidious comparison that favors the Negro:

In this our age of printer's ink
'Tis books that show us how to think—
The rule reversed, and set at naught,
That held that books were born of thought.
We form our minds by pedants' rules,
And all we know is from the schools;
And when we work, or when we play,
We do it in an ordered way—
And nature's self pronounce a ban on,
Whene'er she dares transgress a canon.
Untrammeled thus the simple race is
That "wuks the craps" on cotton places.
Original in act and thought,
Because unlearned and untaught.[81]

In *Scarlet Sister Mary* (1928), Julia Peterkin provided a twentieth-century, "primitivist" example of the same theme. The black heroine of that novel discourages her son from going to school, because she distrusts the white perception of the world: "Instead of reading all the time out of books and papers covered with printed words, he would do better to learn how to read other things: sunrises, moons, sunsets, clouds and stars, faces and eyes. . . . Book-learning takes people's minds off more important things."[82]

Had any of these writers listened to themselves as they wrote, we would not have the books in which they said what they did. A pastoralist who really believed in pastoralism would quit writing books and take up farming or sheepherding. Only rarely did a Southern dialect writer before the mid-twentieth century seem to face the consequences of his blackface pretensions. Irwin Russell, for one unusual example, did write a poem about a professor who invents a machine, the "polyphone," that will translate speech from one language into another. He contructs two of the instruments, places one upstairs "upon the study table" and the other "downstairs in the stable," hires a boy to speak English into the stable "phone," and expects to hear German upstairs. But the boy

> Was not in a regenerate state:
> His language did not smack of schools,
> Or go by proper laws and rules.

He speaks only slang, which, "having no equivalent / In German," clogs the apparatus.

> And shattered were the polyphones,
> And eke the intellect of Jones![83]

In short, translation from one "high" language to another is difficult but safe, while translation between "high" and "low" forms of language—Russell's stock in trade—is not only impossible but *intellectually* disastrous.

Like Russell, Harris, and Peterkin, Faulkner was led by his material to anti-intellectual postures. But, much more than they, he listened to what he found himself saying. Or, rather, he could hear something he had not even yet begun to say, which was so implicit in his subject that it required utterance. When he came to write *Go Down, Moses* in the early forties, Faulkner was ready to question the contradictory logic of pastoralism—of writing books about people whom one praises for their superiority to, or immunity from, books. It represents a climactic moment in his career, when his attitude toward his rustic characters backfired, undercutting significantly his very will to write about them. *Go Down, Moses* began as a book about Negroes, but it ended as a book partly about the inadequacy of books. It remains, nevertheless, a very bookish book: encountering inarticulate people, Faulkner reacted in "The Bear" by executing portentous gestures of articulateness.

Ike's attitude toward the Bible seems to derive from the dialect tradition also. His assertion that the Bible was meant to be read with the heart rather than the mind, by the "lowly of the earth" rather than the wise, conforms to the frequent suggestion in dialect writing that some Negroes, despite their ignorance, understand the Scripture more fully than most whites. For a prominent nineteenth-century example, Mark Twain demonstrated humorously that Huckleberry Finn, as a momentary champion of book knowledge, understands the story of King Solomon's wisdom less well than Nigger Jim does. Although Jim misconstrues the text, he sees the true meaning: "En mine you, de *real* pint is down furder—it's down deeper. It lays in de way Sollermun was raised. You take a man dat's got on'y one er two chillen; is dat man gwyne to be waseful o' chillen? No, he ain't; he can't 'ford it. *He* know how to value 'em."[84] Jim may sound mercenary, but he really *does* know how to value children.

Similarly, the dialect sermon, a conventional subgenre which Johnson's "Creation" and Faulkner's Shegog transcend, has typically presented darky misconstructions of Biblical texts. While the facts may be confused, the spirit of the Bible is accurately rendered. John Charles McNeill, a popular white dialect poet in North Carolina at the turn of the century, has his black preacher transform Nicodemus into "Nigger Demus" and John the Baptist into a Baptist minister. But the same preacher introduces his sermon with advice that should disconcert any writer:

> Dis is anudder Sunday when I done fugit my specks.
> I'll hatter 'pen', my bruddern, 'pon de 'memb'ance er de tex'.
> 'N' if you-all wants a snow-white tent up hyander in de skies
> You better keep de Scripters in yo' head, en not yo' eyes.[85]

Too much reliance on the printed word can endanger one's very soul.

Bruce Rosenberg, a student of the American folk sermon, verifies the content of McNeill's poem, if not its doggerel expression: the "spiritual preacher," according to folk tradition, "need not be learned, in fact should not be educated, except in the ways of the Bible," and the Bible itself authorizes departures not only from textual accuracy but even from intelligibility. Glossolalia, based on Acts 2:2–4, is one model of the preacher's vocation. The sermon may begin with a passage from Scripture, but then it should lead away from the rationality of books toward pure emotion: "The entire sermon is divinely inspired and everything in it is an expression of God's will; the preacher simply lends his voice to God at those moments so that He may express Himself." To communicate the Word of God, the preacher must "translate" the prose on the Biblical page into terms that a congregation can understand, since "he has to speak the language of his flock." Even language is not fully necessary, however, as one of Rosenberg's preachers—the Rev. D. J. McDowell, speaking in 1967—makes plain:

> Jesus of Nazareth, the son of Joseph; the Christ of the Bible cannot be described in words
> Language loses its signifisence [sic], tryin' to pay proper homage to the Christ of the Bible . . .
> You see words, are only symbols of an artist, that are used in creating images in the human mind
> But mere words fall short—Amen—and become insufficient and images dissolve and vanish because the Christ of the Bible is not an aggregation of words but the perfect embodyment [sic] of the living God Himself—Isaiah chapter six verse three, Colossians, chapter two and verse nine.[86]

Insofar as black Christianity provides a model for Southern authorship, the writer's goal is a Word-made-flesh rather than a typographical text.

Traces of this model appear, often with ironic effect, in many texts by white Southerners. In the 1920s and 1930s, for example, Faulkner's friend Roark Bradford made his reputation writing "Bible stories in blackface"; his tales of the Little Bee Bend Plantation also include many Biblical "allusions." "The Bible Boys' Cotton" (1940), for example, centers on a struggle between the Widow Duck's faith in Scripture and the foreman Giles's skepticism. The Scripture in which Duck believes, however, is her own version of the Bible, and her "text" is contested by the literal-minded B'r Charlie. When she avers that "De Book say . . . 'twile ye tharfo' in de field for ninety days and shall unto you be given a crop er cotton next fall,'" Charlie challenges the accuracy of her quotation. "De Bible," he tells her, "don't speak nothing' 'bout cotton, on account er hit wa'n't no cotton in de Bible." But the Widow Duck's version is validated when the Bossman's son, Mr. Junior, informs her that Egyptian cotton had been grown since "[l]ong before the Bible times."[87] Although her translation is technically inaccurate, Bradford would have us sentimentally see, her good faith enables her to approach what Faulkner would call the "lost Hebrew infancy" of the Bible's meaning (KG, 207). Some of his Negro characters are fools, but as a race they are wiser than white people not only in the ways of the world but in the ways of the Lord as well. What they lack in book learning, they make up for in Book "learning."

If Faulkner read this story when *Collier's* printed it in November 1940, he likely noticed some resemblances between it and "Gold Is Not Always," which appeared in the *Atlantic Monthly* during the same month. The climax of "The Bible Boys' Cotton" occurs when Widow Duck goes to the plantation store, where she discovers the Bossman's son "working on the commissary books."[88] "Gold Is Not Always" begins as Lucas enters Roth Edmonds's commissary and discovers his landlord "writing in a ledger" (US, 226), much "as one of Faulkner's own tenants might have found him at Greenfield Farm" (BL, 1036). When Molly enters the same commissary at the beginning of "The Fire on the Hearth," she too finds Roth at work on his accounts. *Her* "quotation" from the Bible provides a tacit criticism of the white man's book, in which mere transactions of property are recorded: "God say, 'What's rendered to My earth, it belong to Me unto I resurrect it. And let him or her touch it, and beware'" (GDM, 102).

This scene is instructive, for in the original Lucas Beauchamp stories Roth Edmonds served as Faulkner's surrogate. When Faulkner began to write a book about black people, his own relationship to them manifested itself in the image of a white man writing in a book the "accounts" of his Negro tenants, which mostly they cannot read. The futility of his words is emphasized by their irrelevance in the face of the Negro's fidelity to a higher Word, which his do not touch. Ike's comments on the Bible in the final writing for the book thus had their origin in its earliest germ.

"Go Down, Moses" offers the same lesson in its juxtaposition of Molly with Gavin Stevens. Referring to the same "Bible Boys" who exercised Widow Duck, Molly gives the whole volume its title in her ranting indictment of hard-hearted Roth for expelling her grandson Butch from the plantation: "Roth Edmonds sold my Benjamin. Sold him in Egypt. Pharaoh got him—" (GDM, 371). Though she fumbles the letter of the Word, she perceives its spirit accurately enough. Though illiterate, she values literacy for better reasons than Stevens's. Just as illiterate Dilsey has faith that her name will "be in the Book . . . Writ out" (SF, 71), Molly insists that Butch's name be recorded in the local newspaper, though she cannot read it there. The *idea* of writing is more important than the fact. Molly's understanding of the Book contrasts eloquently with the book-learning of Stevens, whose "twenty-two-year-old unfinished translation of the Old Testament back into classic Greek" (GDM, 371) signifies his ensnarement in its letter.

In this contrast, brought to dialectical intensity in Part Four, Faulkner clearly demonstrated the intellectual incapacitation of his depleted Southern heritage. In Stevens's "Translation," a more "serious vocation" (GDM, 371) than the law, Faulkner imaged forth his own calling, and he embodied the mission the plantation had first been meant to support. In 1940, when he wrote "Go Down, Moses," he himself had been a professional writer for about twenty-two years, having first achieved publication in 1919 with his *translation* of Mallarmé's "L'Après-Midi d'un Faune." In Stevens's "rendering" of the Bible back into "the classic Greek into which it had been translated from its lost Hebrew infancy" (KG, 207), Faulkner expressed his nostalgia for the half-consumed sources of his own creativity, his need to transform the boiling "coffee-pot" of commerce back into the "silver cup" of art, and his desire to overcome the natural erosion that diminishes all texts, all signals, all legacies. But in Molly's lament, he voiced a suspicion that those for whom learning comes by "word-of-mouth" were better able to "traverse" the "distance back to truth" (GDM, 260–61) than scholars and thinkers, whose "old books" are "fixed immutably, finished, unalterable, harmless" (GDM, 268). He expressed a suspicion that all writing petrifies, formulates, and distorts life. Throughout the next decade, Faulkner repeatedly reverted to this conflict between the letter and the spirit, between exhaustion and replenishment, between parodying and celebrating his life's work.

HEART IN CONFLICT

There is a ridge; you drive on beyond Seminary Hill and in time you come upon it: a mild unhurried farm road presently mounting to cross the ridge and on to join the main highway leading from Jefferson to the world. And now, looking back and down, you see all Yoknapatawpha in the dying last of day beneath you. . . .

. . . And you stand suzerain and solitary above the whole sum of your life beneath that incessant ephemeral spangling. . . .

. . . .

And you, the old man, standing there while there rises to you, about you, suffocating you, the spring dark peopled and myriad. . . . the cup, the bowl proffered once to the lips in youth and then no more; proffered to quench or sip or drain that lone one time and even that sometimes premature, too soon. Because the tragedy of life is, it must be premature, inconclusive and inconcludable, in order to be life; it must be before itself, in advance of itself, to have been at all.

Faulkner, The Town

William Faulkner's "Address upon Receiving the Nobel Prize for Literature" is a classic statement of humanist affirmation. Newspaper editorialists and commencement speakers quote it when they want to simulate inspiration, and it appears in countless college-English anthologies. It is more widely known than anything else Faulkner wrote. It enables instructors of his other works to demonstrate to their skeptical students that the horror stories they think they are reading are actually testaments of faith in man's heroic potentiality. Even those readers who reject such *ex post facto* pacifications of *The Sound and the Fury* or *Absalom, Absalom!* usually assume that Faulkner's view of the world had "mellowed" by 1950.

I decline to accept the Nobel Speech as evidence of "mellowing." As an abstract pronouncement, the Stockholm Address deserves the scriptural status it has achieved. But as a particular utterance by William Faulkner in 1950, it is an entirely different phenomenon. The text that appears in college anthologies is a noble statement, a model of rhetoric transcending platitude. But the text that Faulkner delivered to the Swedish Academy—albeit an identical one—is not completely sincere. Faulkner did not fully believe what he was saying.

The first half—yes. He did believe what he said about other writers: that they had "forgotten the problems of the human heart in conflict with itself which alone can make good writing," and that those who fail to confront the "old verities and truths of the heart" doom themselves to write "not of the heart but of the glands." These sentiments he had long felt. But the final, longest paragraph of the Speech presents a teleological defense of his foregoing remarks which contradicts not only the pessimism implicit in his early works but attitudes he was expressing in current books as well. That paragraph is familiar to most students of modern literature:

> Until [the writer] relearns [the old universal truths], he will write as though he stood among and watched the end of man. I decline to accept the end of man. It is easy enough to say that man is immortal simply because he will endure: that when the last ding-dong of doom has clanged and faded from the last worthless rock hanging tideless in the last red and dying evening, that even then there will still be one more sound: that of his puny inexhaustible voice, still talking. I refuse to accept this. I believe that man will not merely endure: he will prevail. He is immortal, not because he alone among creatures has an inexhaustible voice, but because he has a soul, a spirit capable of compassion and sacrifice and endurance. The poet's, the writer's, duty is to write about these things. It is his privilege to help man endure by lifting his heart, by reminding him of the courage and honor and hope and pride and compassion and pity and sacrifice which have been the glory of his past. The poet's voice need not merely be the record of man, it can be one of the props, the pillars to help him endure and prevail. (ESPL, 120)

This stirring assertion of immortality for the human spirit, and of the writer's contribution to that immortality, presents only one side of the internal debate that preoccupied Faulkner from the late thirties into the fifties. It therefore provides a false resolution to a question Faulkner was still struggling to answer, a question that touched him personally in a way the Speech conceals: not only "Will mankind prevail?" (that is, does human history have meaning?) but also "Is it meaningful for me, William Faulkner, to write?" (is *my* voice "inexhaustible"?).

This context of internal debate is evident throughout the history of the central image in the last paragraph of the Speech—that of the lone man standing upon the last rocky island in an apocalyptic seascape. From early in his career, Faulkner used variants of this image to report on his literary situation: floods, mound-like refuges from floods, and urns (inverted mounds, which *contain* floods rather than merely rising above them) had marked important shifts in his attitude toward his vocation. In "The Leg," the opening of a river lock had embodied the cathartic gratifications Faulkner sought by becoming a writer. In *The Sound and the Fury*, Reverend Shegog had resembled "a worn small rock whelmed by the successive waves of his voice." Faulkner's "Introduction to *The Sound and the Fury*" had proposed a vase as an image of literary immortality. "Old Man" had turned a flood into an objective correlative for the vocational self-doubt Faulkner suffered in the late thirties. In "Delta Autumn," he had consolidated the flood-and-mound imagery into a sustained and almost explicit metaphor for his stalled career. (In "Mississippi," the metaphor would be explicit.)

Throughout this evolution of the Nobel Prize imagery, it had remained distinctly ambivalent. The flood could be enriching, or it could be destructive. Sometimes the river was a beneficial source of fertility and eloquence. At other times it was an instrument of oblivion, embodying all of Faulkner's fears for himself and the world; and the mounds were necessary for survival. In 1929, Faulkner could seem to envy Reverend Shegog's ability to communicate with his congregation "in chanting measures beyond the need for words" (SF, 367); he could feel the imperative voice within himself too strongly to resist a desire to move beyond it. In 1950, however, he was too fearful of his own exhaustion, and too disillusioned with the idea that language can transcend itself, to speak favorably of an eloquent silence. Whereas Reverend Shegog uttered his words only to release the flood of passion that impelled him to speak them, Faulkner the Nobel laureate hoped to build a memorial mound of words that would insure the immortality of himself and his kind.

A significant change did occur between 1928 and 1950, but it pertained less to Faulkner's supposed conversion from nihilism to affirmation than to the advent of serious doubts about the efficacy of his vocation—doubts he had to appease in order to continue writing. In the teens and twenties, Faulkner had forged his artistic identity out of internal division. In the late thirties, under the onslaught of middle age, commercial failure, critical obscurity, marital discord, amatory disappointment, and international up-heaval, he reactivated the debate that had remained relatively dormant within him throughout the years of his masterpieces. The Nobel Address expressed only the hopeful half of that debate. While advising his listeners to write about "the human heart in conflict with itself," Faulkner wish-fully ignored the conflict within himself, which his books continued to reveal whether he wished them to or not.

Faulkner wrote a first draft of the Speech's last paragraph ten years be-fore he delivered it in Stockholm. In "Delta Autumn," the river is an instrument of oblivion, embodying all of Faulkner's fears for his own ca-reer and for human history. *Go Down, Moses* also contains a hopeful vision, however, and Faulkner first rehearsed the Nobel language within the confrontation between his faith in the durability of writing and his assumption of its futility. Ike McCaslin, disillusioned by his social heri-tage, chooses to reject the past, to erase his historical memory, and to dispense with written records. An exponent of the flood of oblivion, the younger Ike articulates Faulkner's own deep suspicion of the inertia and ineffectuality of words. Against this position stands Ike's cousin Cass Ed-monds, who defends inherited evils and cultivates book-knowledge—con-sulting Keats's poetry, for example, to explain an experience Ike would rather leave to instinct. Thus, Faulkner entrusted his optimism about the human race to a man who belittles the value of writing and his defense of literacy to a man who accepts a bleak vision of history—a confusion he only artificially disentangled in the Nobel Speech. The debate in Part Four of "The Bear" culminates in the same passage in which Ike imagines a God repudiating His creation and in which Faulkner virtually repudiates his own titles against the backdrop of a "worthless tideless rock cooling in the last crimson evening" (GDM, 284). Here, the Nobel imagery was associated long before the Speech itself with Faulkner's crisis of confi-dence. Throughout the 1940s and into the 1950s, both before and after the Speech, Faulkner's books displayed the same contradictions about lit-erature, about history, and about his career that defined Part Four of "The Bear."

We have already seen that, after the skepticism expressed in *Go Down, Moses*, Faulkner temporarily reasserted the value of books in his revision of "Knight's Gambit" in 1949. Among the many "translations" that occur in that story is Chick Mallison's reading of the *Cid* in Spanish. But Chick is ready to abandon the passivity of mere book knowledge: in his eagerness for direct action, he resembles the young Ike McCaslin. His longing to go to the war in Europe reiterates the tension between literary and nonliterary experience that informs "The Bear." To the heroism accomplished in the *Cid*, he prefers another kind of "writing": "he couldn't have explained, to anyone, least of all a man fifty years old, even his uncle, how to assuage the heart's thirst with the dusty chronicle of the past when not fifteen hundred miles away in England men not much older than he was were daily writing with their lives his own time's deathless footnote" (KG, 213).

Gavin Stevens resolves this tension in such a way that books prevail. When he is trying to make Chick understand what happened between himself and Melisandre Backus Harriss, he recommends that Chick visit a street in Paris where, he implies, he and she had met in the twenties. His advice changes, though, when he recalls that the street "doesn't exist any more now"; and when Chick proposes to "look at where it used to be," Stevens replies that "[y]ou can do that here. . . . In the library." He then quotes a descriptive passage from "the right page in Conrad" (KG, 244), which preserves the setting of his meeting more effectively than it has been preserved in reality. The Conrad passage thus comes closer to being "deathless" than any merely historical experience.

Conversely, *Requiem for a Nun* (1951) reasserts the suspicion of letters that characterizes Faulkner's fiction about Negroes. From its first page, which lists the records that impelled the founders of Jefferson to construct a courthouse, it represents white civilization as an edifice of paper, founded largely upon injustice: "even the simple dispossession of Indians begot in time a minuscule of archive, let alone the normal litter of man's ramshackle confederation against environment" (REQ, 3). A conflict between written records and unspoken deeds pervades *Requiem*, materializing most clearly in the very structure of the book, which alternates between segments of narrative prose and segments of dramatic action. The prose segments are almost as replete with books, records, and papers as Part Four of "The Bear." In "The Courthouse," for example, the founders of Jefferson solve their first civic controversy—over the administration of a federal debt—by agreeing to "[p]ut it on the Book," a decision "which not only solved the problem but abolished it; and not just that one, but all problems, from now on into perpetuity" (REQ, 20). The subtitle of "The

Golden Dome" asserts that in the "Beginning Was the Word" (REQ, 99); this chapter presents the history of Mississippi as a geological palimpsest, and it incorporates literal as well as figurative "chronicles" by including long passages borrowed from the Mississippi State Guide.[1] The final prose segment, in turn, presents the town jail as a repository of overlapping chronicles, including the signature the jailor's daughter scratched in a window in 1861 which is "apparently no more durable than the thin dried slime left by the passage of a snail, yet which has endured a hundred years" (REQ, 253). Against these assertions of the word, Nancy Mannigoe, the black murderess, offers a brief but sufficient refutation in her closing exchange with Temple Drake:

> TEMPLE: . . . At least, dont blaspheme. But who am I to challenge the language you talk about Him in, when He Himself certainly cant challenge it, since that's the only language He arranged for you to learn?
> NANCY: What's wrong with what I said? Jesus is a man too. He's got to be. Menfolks listens to somebody because of what he says. Women dont. They dont care what he said. They listens because of what he is. (REQ, 273–74)

Such an understanding signifies a major dilemma for anyone, like Faulkner, whose identity derived almost wholly from "what he said." The dilemma appears again in A *Fable* (1954)—Faulkner's strenuous attempt to "traverse" "the distance back" to the truth of the Word (GDM, 260–61)—in which the French Army corporal who corresponds allegorically to Christ is an illiterate (FAB, 366). A *Fable* contains a lengthy paraphrase of the Nobel Speech, amounting almost to an act of self-quotation or -parody, in a context that belies its affirmativeness. The climax of this novel is a dialogue, similar to the one between Ike and Cass in "The Bear," in which the supreme commander of the allied forces in World War I tries to persuade the corporal, who has led a mutiny in the French army, to save himself and give up his idealistic dream of justice. One of the general's ploys is to argue that mankind is durable enough without the corporal's sacrifice. Man, he says, will survive even an atomic holocaust: "Oh yes, he will survive it because he has that in him which will endure even beyond the ultimate worthless tideless rock freezing slowly in the last red and heartless sunset, because already the next star in the blue immensity of space will be already clamorous with the uproar of his debarkation, his puny and inexhaustible voice still talking, still planning; and there too after the last ding dong of doom has rung and died there will still be one sound more: his voice, planning still to build something higher and faster and louder" (FAB, 354). He goes on to declare, cynically rather than optimistically, that man will not merely endure but prevail.

By placing these words in the mouth of a character who utters them in the quite literal role of devil's advocate, perhaps Faulkner was revealing his suspicion of their inauthenticity in his own mouth. The final reckoning of man's fate and of the value of writing, in A *Fable*, is problematic. Ostensibly, this novel is a retelling of the Christian Passion, a "Translation"—to use Gavin Stevens's word—of the Scripture into modern terms. But Faulkner's allegorical correspondences break down. The illiterate modern Christ is not resurrected, except ironically. He becomes the Unknown Soldier instead, a monument to the war he had tried to end; and his voice, for all the good it does, has been extinguished.

The immortality of mankind and, implicitly, the future of Faulkner's artistic legacy remain doubtful in A *Fable*. The debate between the general and the corporal, which is no more resolved than Ike's and Cass's in Go *Down, Moses*, articulates the division between faith and despair that afflicted Faulkner throughout the forties and into the fifties. At about the time he began complaining of his inability to write and denigrating the works he managed to produce anyway, he also began busily to promote his own reputation and to revise the shape of his career so as to enhance its durability. Like Ike McCaslin recollecting his youth "in retrograde," he returned repetitively to his literary *corpus*, borrowing from it and making adjustments in it. In its clearest form, this retrospective attitude resulted in conventional anthologies: the *Portable Faulkner* (1946), the *Collected Stories* (1950), the *Faulkner Reader* (1954), *Big Woods* (1955). But his "original" writing also reverted to the past. Every book he published after Go *Down, Moses* he had conceived before 1943. Though the immediate source of A *Fable* was Humphrey Cobb's *Paths of Glory*, its true germ may lie in the speculations about the Bible in Part Four of "The Bear." Faulkner had included the plot idea for *Intruder in the Dust* among his early plans for Go *Down, Moses*. *Knight's Gambit* was a specialized by-product of the editing of the *Collected Stories;* most of its stories had been published a full decade before it appeared. *Requiem for a Nun* was a sequel to, and redemption of, *Sanctuary*, which he had contemplated since the early thirties. In *The Town* and *The Mansion*, he concluded the Snopes trilogy he had long delayed. The idea for *The Reivers* had first occurred to him in 1940 (BL, 1044). By the fifties, Faulkner's principal subject had become the viability of his own career.

His awareness of the self-contradictions inherent in his vocation had first beset him during the period when he wrote his "anthology novels." More than any other grouping of his books, these derived their meaning and their form from Faulkner's need to bridge the gaps between literary and vernacular experience, between social mobility and the status quo, between acceptance and repudiation of his cultural heritage, between speech and silence, between immortality and oblivion. That he was conscious of his inner divisions is suggested by a portrayal of the act of writing which he conceived for Hollywood.

In June 1944 he drafted a treatment for Warner Brothers of a movie called *Fog over London*, the "remake" of a profitable film of the thirties, *The Amazing Dr. Clitterhouse.* The original story concerns a medical doctor who conducts a valuable scientific investigation into criminal behavior by entering the underworld and participating in robberies so that he can observe the culprits he has joined. Faulkner's version, which the studio did not use, renders Clitterhouse schizophrenic: he seems at home both in the lofty world of experimental science and in the vulgar society of thieves and murderers. As a scientist, he writes his notes and speculations with his right hand; as a criminal, he writes jeering letters in an underworld argot to the ruthless prosecutor whose methods he hopes to expose, and he disguises these letters by writing them with his left hand. In a crucial scene, after he has achieved his main purpose, he writes a letter to the prosecutor with his right hand and in genteel language, promising that the series of robberies he has perpetrated will cease. As he signs his name, the scene cuts to blackness, which

> then DISSOLVES to: Clitterhouse at the desk as before. A new sheet of paper lies before him. He is writing with his *left* hand. In an ashtray before him a final wisp of smoke is rising from the charred carbon of the first letter. Clitterhouse seems to wake, jerks himself up, seems dazed, recovers, looks down, moves his *right* hand as if to write again, then sees with horror that his LEFT hand holds the pen. He looks down with slow horror at the letter.
> INSERT: LETTER IN DISGUISED HAND addressed to the [prosecutor]. It is another jeering, taunting letter, warning the [prosecutor] of the next robbery.[2]

Faulkner's own division was never psychotic, but some internal competition—between hands, voices, visions, identities—controlled most of his writing during the late thirties and throughout the forties. In working itself out, it determined the climax of his career.

NOTES

Chapter One
"William Faulkner" and "Ernest V. Trueblood"

1. *Furioso* 2 (Summer 1947): 5–17, with "Notes on Mr. Faulkner" by Reed Whittemore, 18–25.
2. BL, 902–68; ALG, 15–195; CNC, 129–58; BLRO, 100.
3. My translation from Coindreau's "Note" to "L'Après-Midi d'une Vache, par Ernest V. Trueblood," 66. ("Le texte était de ceux qui nécessitent un effort soutenu; les périodes enchevêtrées, coupées d'incidentes et de parenthèses, enveloppaient la pensée d'arabesques perfides.") See also SL, 99–100.
4. Coindreau, "Note" to "L'Après-Midi d'une Vache," 66. ("Nous étions tous trop attentifs pour pouvoir même songer à rire.")
5. Compare Maury Bascomb's letter to his nephew in *The Sound and the Fury*: "For naturally I shall employ this sum as though it were my own and so permit your Mother to avail herself of this opportunity which my exhaustive investigation has shown to be a bonanza—if you will permit the vulgarism— of the first water and purest ray serene" (SF, 278–79).
6. See also Coindreau, "Note" to "L'Après-Midi d'une Vache," 66–67.
7. Maurice Edgar Coindreau, "The Faulkner I Knew," in *The Time of William Faulkner: A French View of Modern American Fiction*, 96. See also BL, 963. Coindreau and Blotner disagree on some details of fact, but their accounts are identical in substance.
8. Reed Whittemore, "Notes on Mr. Faulkner," 18.
9. Its place in a lifelong association among anality, accidents, and suffocating maternal females will bear further attention in Chapter Two.
10. Whittemore, "Notes on Mr. Faulkner," 18.
11. Coindreau, "The Faulkner I Knew," in *The Time of William Faulkner*, 95.
12. See his "Introduction for *The Sound and the Fury*" of 1933, in which he states that he wrote that novel after having "shut a door between me and all publishers' addresses and book lists" (*Southern Review* [Autumn 1972]: 710). For a variant of the same statement, see "An Introduction to *The Sound and the Fury*," in *A Faulkner Miscellany*, 158.

13. According to Meta Carpenter Wilde, Faulkner was still telling the tale about cow-patty baseball in 1937, but she remembers the sliding runner's name as Buck Smeegers rather than Ernest Trueblood (ALG, 226).

14. Blotner attributes the transcript to 1946, when Faulkner was in Hollywood working for Warner Brothers (BL, 1207n). As Faulkner was embroiled with that studio in an effort to break his contract, he may have written this piece simply to vent the frustration he suffered from writing for Hollywood—if not to prove to the studio that he was not worth retaining. However, "One Way to Catch a Horse" includes one event that suggests an earlier composition. Ernest Trueblood flies home from Moscow in a Russian plane making a good-will flight across the North Pole. The first such transpolar flight occurred in June 1937, making headlines in the *Los Angeles Times* during the very week of Coindreau's visit.

    The conclusive dating of "One Way to Catch a Horse" awaits an explanation of the address Faulkner wrote on the first page of the typescript: 1410 No. Berendo. See Bruce F. Kawin, *Faulkner and Film*, 178; George F. Hayhoe, "Faulkner in Hollywood: A Checklist of His Film Scripts at the University of Virginia," 416. For Faulkner's designation of Frank Norfleet's memoir *Norfleet* as the source of "One Way to Catch a Horse," see George F. Hayhoe, "Faulkner in Hollywood: A Checklist of his Filmscripts at the University of Virginia: A Correction and Additions," 471–72.

15. William Faulkner, "One Way to Catch a Horse," 36-page typescript.

16. For example, Meta Carpenter Wilde records the disappointment she felt when she learned, after Faulkner's death, that he had lied to her about having a silver plate in his skull (ALG, 46–47; see also Panthea Reid Broughton, "An Interview with Meta Carpenter Wilde," 780). In 1942, Phil Stone still believed that Faulkner had hurt "his head and foot a little in a plane accident" (Louis Daniel Brodsky and Robert W. Hamblin, eds., *Faulkner: A Comprehensive Guide to the Brodsky Collection, Volume II: The Letters*, 21–24). Faulkner's stepson, Malcolm Franklin, writes as if still unaware, in 1977, that Faulkner, with whom no one else had "spent more man-hours," had not flown Sopwith Camels in France (BLRO, "Preface" and 102). Faulkner even lied about his flying experience to the man who finally taught him how to fly in 1933 (BL, 795, 797), though he had confessed his secret to a pilot from whom he took a few clandestine lessons in 1920 (BL1, 79–80).

17. For the best discussion of the relationship of Faulkner's vocation to his impostures, see Judith L. Sensibar, *The Origins of Faulkner's Art*. Sensibar reduces all of Faulkner's impersonations to what she calls *pierrotisme* and thereby associates them with the Symbolist ethos in which he steeped himself in his youth. She then argues that, when Faulkner rejected Symbolist narcissism as a vocational model, he "chose not to become an impostor" (p. 43).

She attributes this decision to the year 1921, when he completed *Vision in Spring*. I believe that Faulkner's fraudulence was far more generalized and far more persistent.

18. According to Malcolm Franklin, Faulkner wore his R.A.F. uniform every Armistice Day and every Bastille Day well into the 1930s (BLRO, 46, 85).

19. H. Edward Richardson, *William Faulkner: The Journey to Self-Discovery*, 79.

20. According to one hypothesis, Faulkner began to adopt his bohemian slovenliness in 1918: "After he lost Estelle Oldham" to another man, "he quit caring how he dressed" (Carvel Collins, "Biographical Background for Faulkner's *Helen*," in HEL, 24).

21. For example, "David" is the name Faulkner attributes to the protagonist of "Out of Nazareth," published in April 1925. The narrator of this sketch introduces a grammatically imperfect text by a young vagabond, who serves as a figure of the kind of artist Faulkner may have hoped to incarnate during his imminent walking tour of Europe (NOS, 46–54). Donald Mahon, the wounded hero of *Soldiers' Pay*, was called "David" in that book's earliest draft, which Sherwood Anderson read in manuscript in early 1925 (Margaret J. Yonce, "The Composition of *Soldiers' Pay*," 295). Faulkner gave the same name to the protagonists of "Carcassonne," in that story's manuscript, and of "The Leg," both of which he probably wrote in the years immediately following his first European trip (BL, 478–79, 502). David West's infatuation with Patricia Robyn, in *Mosquitoes*, may reflect Faulkner's unrequited affection for Helen Baird or Estelle Oldham (BL1, 185). Max Putzel reveals that the manuscript of *The Sound and the Fury* contains a slip of the pen that rendered Benjy Compson's name as "Davy" (*Genius of Place: William Faulkner's Triumphant Beginnings*, 153). Perhaps Faulkner identified with the Biblical David, a diminutive giant-killer who became both an artist and a warrior (and the father of Absalom).

22. Sherwood Anderson, "A Meeting South," 269–79. Ben Wasson reports that Faulkner, like "David," attributed his drinking to pain from his "leg injury" (CNC, 49).

23. BL, 101; Jack Ewing, "Collector Finds Consolation Stone," 2; *St. Nicholas: An Illustrated Magazine for Young Folks* 38 (November 1910, January 1911): 23–28, 213–18; *Youth's Companion* 85, nos. 1 (January 5, 1911), 2 (January 12, 1911), 3 (January 19, 1911); George Lawrence Parker, "The Body Guard," 640–41; M. A. DeWolfe Howe, "The Humorist's Honor," 5.

24. Theodore Peterson, *Magazines in the Twentieth Century*, 171.

25. Martin Kreiswirth, "Faulkner as Translator: His Versions of Verlaine," 430–31.

26. *St. Nicholas* 47 (February 1920): 359.

27. To Faulkner's correct spelling of Verlaine's title, "Fantoches," the *Mississippian's* typesetter added a *u* to make "Fantouches"—perhaps as a comment on Faulkner's addition of the *u* to his own name (BL1, 80).
28. "Faulkner's 'Ode to the Louver,'" 333–35.
29. "Faulkner's 'Ode to the Louver,'" 333–35.
30. BL, 534–36; William Faulkner, "Foreword" to *Sherwood Anderson & Other Famous Creoles: A Gallery of Contemporary New Orleans.*
31. When Faulkner accepted membership in the Legion of Honor in October 1951, he called France "la mere universelle des artists" [sic] (BL, 1403). According to his stepson, Malcolm Franklin, Faulkner celebrated Bastille Day annually, well into his middle years: "In the late afternoon, champagne would be served on the east verandah [of Rowan Oak], followed by appropriate toasts to France" (BLRO, 85).
32. For evidence of Faulkner's similarly positive attitude toward the peasantry of Mississippi during his early twenties, see CNC, 47–48.
33. See Judith Bryant Wittenberg, *Faulkner: The Transfiguration of Biography,* 56.

Chapter Two
The Psychopathology of Vocation

1. Jay Martin, "'The Whole Burden of Man's History of His Impossible Heart's Desire': The Early Life of William Faulkner," 611–14.
2. Martin, "'The Whole Burden,'" 619–22.
3. Martin, "'The Whole Burden,'" 620.
4. A. I. Bezzerides would remember that "he had a way of leaning backward when he walked" (Louis Daniel Brodsky, "Reflections on William Faulkner: An Interview with Albert I. Bezzerides," 377). See also MBB, 81–82.
5. Martin, "'The Whole Burden,'" 622–24.
6. Louis D. Brodsky and Robert W. Hamblin, eds., *Faulkner: A Comprehensive Guide to the Brodsky Collection, Volume II: The Letters,* xviii, 82, 89, 96. On the relationship between Maud's corset and William's accident-proneness, see Judith L. Sensibar, *The Origins of Faulkner's Art:* "Looked at together, these disparate details spanning Faulkner's lifetime describe a pattern of identity conflict. Relief was ultimately sought by returning to the physical site where conflict was first experienced, i.e., in Faulkner's back. For it was in his back that he first felt the pain and punishment for not measuring up to one of his ideals, the stiff-backed Civil War hero with military bearing, Colonel William Clark Falkner" (p. 236).

7. H. Edward Richardson, *William Faulkner: The Journey to Self-Discovery*, 19–20.
8. Robert Waelder, *Basic Theory of Psychoanalysis*, 178. Two months before he died in 1962, when he was asked about Hemingway's death the previous year, Faulkner said "that Hemingway was too good a man to be the victim of accidents; only the weak are victims of accidents unless a house falls on them" (FWP, 49). Or a horse?
9. Panthea Reid Broughton, "An Interview with Meta Carpenter Wilde," 780.
10. Faulkner exhibited an interest in knees throughout his post-war poetry. In "L'Après-Midi d'un Faune," for example, the immobilized faun longs to pursue a nymph who has "lascivious dreaming knees." This phrase attracted particular scorn during Faulkner's Pastoral War (EPP, 39; BL, 268). For a discussion of the imagery of dance and paralysis in *Vision in Spring* (1921), see Sensibar, *The Origins of Faulkner's Art*, 138–49.
11. Compare Judith L. Sensibar's introduction to *Vision in Spring*: "Faulkner represents [his mother] in his poetry as the Marble Faun's and Pierrot's 'moon mother.' She always 'snares' her young victim, making him impotent, even as he is simultaneously obsessed with and repelled by a desire to experience an adult love relationship" (VS, xxviii). Compare also the roughly contemporaneous "After Fifty Years," in which a young man is "bound" by a woman whose "heart is old": "he feels her presence like shed scent, / Holding him body and life within its snare" (EPP, 53).
12. Sensibar attributes the faun's paralysis and silence to Faulkner's inability to overcome the powerful literary influences of the past. The marble form of the statue represents "achieved artistic creation," while the mute faun's inner voice represents "artistic creation striving for expression" (*The Origins of Faulkner's Art*, 12).
13. Compare the first line of *Vision in Spring*: "And at last, having followed a voice that cried within him . . ." (VS, 1).
14. Patricia Merivale, *Pan the Goat-God: His Myth in Modern Times*, 1–16, 111–22.
15. For a treatment of the anti-Christian Pan in Faulkner, see Lewis P. Simpson, "Faulkner and the Legend of the Artist"; and Simpson, "Sex & History: Origins of Faulkner's Apocrypha."
16. Ovid, *The Metamorphoses*, trans. Horace Gregory, 51.
17. For similar appearances of the upward-raised palms, see VS, 59, 67, 80.
18. See Karl F. Zender, "Faulkner and the Power of Sound." Although Zender characterizes Pan's call in *The Marble Faun* as revivifying and joyous (p. 92), he asserts that Faulkner, in the last half of his career, "created a kind of boundary art, making speech out of his desire to be free of speech" (p. 101). In the prison scenes of *Requiem for a Nun* and *A Fable*, according to Zender,

Faulkner "depict[ed] meaning as somehow entrapped or imprisoned" (p. 103).

19. The paradox of a self-defeating call to poetry is already present in Mallarmé's original poem. See Steven F. Walker, "Mallarmé's Symbolist Eclogue: The 'Faune' as Pastoral." Walker's analysis confirms the self-parodic tendency of the whole pastoral tradition. See also Renato Poggioli, " 'L'Heure du Berger': Mallarmé's Grand Eclogue," in *The Oaten Flute: Essays on Pastoral Poetry and the Pastoral Ideal,* 283–311.

20. In 1974, Blotner attributed the two stories ("Black Music" and "Carcassonne") to early 1926 (BL, 501–2). In 1984, he placed them in his chapter on 1929–1930, while acknowledging that "Black Music" resembled stories Faulkner wrote in 1925 (BL1, 253–54). Max Putzel speculates that one of two surviving typescripts of "Carcassonne" may have been written in 1926 and that the other, "typed on the same rarely used bond paper" that Faulkner employed for seven sheets of the *Sound and the Fury* manuscript, may belong to 1928 (*Genius of Place: William Faulkner's Triumphant Beginnings,* 152). Martin Kreiswirth asserts that "[t]he quality of writing in 'Carcassonne' . . . definitely suggests Faulkner's more mature style" (*William Faulkner: The Making of a Novelist,* 80).

21. For a discussion of the sinister matron as a recurrent character in Faulkner's fiction in the late twenties, see Noel Polk, " 'The Dungeon Was Mother Herself': William Faulkner: 1927–1931."

22. In 1957, he called "Carcassonne" "a piece that I've always liked" (FU, 22). He also liked "Black Music" well enough to try publishing it in 1933 even though he knew he could not *sell* it (SL, 75–76). For explications of "Carcassonne," see Richard A. Milum, "Faulkner's 'Carcassonne': The Dream and the Reality"; Robert W. Hamblin, " 'Carcassonne': Faulkner's Allegory of Art and the Artist"; and Noel Polk, "William Faulkner's 'Carcassonne.' "

23. Putzel notes that, in *Sartoris,* Aunt Jenny Du Pre "wears her pince nez in a 'small gold case pinned to her bosom' " (*Genius of Place,* 109).

24. In 1958, he admitted to a self-destructive element in his horsemanship: "I'm scared to death of horses," he told someone, "that's why I can't leave them alone." A fall from a horse in June 1962 was an indirect cause of his death the next month (BL, 1709, 1828). See also "Race at Morning" (1954), in which an old man named *Ernest* rides his horse under a vine which hooks under the saddle horn, pulling the saddle girth tighter and tighter until it breaks, spilling Ernest and his passenger onto the ground (BW, 184). For discussions of the significance of horses throughout Faulkner's fiction, see Mary Jane Dickerson, "Faulkner's Golden Steed"; Richard A. Milum, "Continuity and Change: The Horse, the Automobile, and the Airplane in Faulkner's Fiction"; John M. Howell, "Faulkner, Prufrock, and Agamemnon: Horses, Hell,

and High Water." See also Faulkner's description of the statue of Man o' War—"the golden effigy of the golden horse"—in his account of the 1955 Kentucky Derby (ESPL, 56).

25. BL, 138–39, 1702; A. I. Bezzerides, *William Faulkner: A Life on Paper*, 70–71.

26. See also Hamblin, "'Carcassonne': Faulkner's Allegory of Art and the Artist," 356–57. Hamblin quotes a statement Faulkner made to Jean Stein late in his life: "I prefer silence to sound, and the image produced by words occurs in silence. That is, the thunder and the music of the prose take place in silence."

27. For a review of attitudes toward language and silence in Faulkner—and in Faulkner criticism—see John T. Matthews, *The Play of Faulkner's Language*, 36–45.

28. William Faulkner, "An Introduction to *The Sound and the Fury*," in *A Faulkner Miscellany*, 158, 160.

29. See Matthews, *The Play of Faulkner's Language*, 72–73: "Benjy's inescapable muteness confers a kind of tranquillity and order that a novelist might dream about and then forswear in order to write" (p. 72). See also François L. Pitavy, "Idiocy and Idealism: A Reflection on the Faulknerian Idiot," 97–104.

30. Walter Slatoff recognized long ago "the deep-seated tendency in Faulkner to view and interpret experience in extreme terms and to see life as composed essentially of pairs of warring entities." His pairs included "Motion and Immobility," "Sound and Silence," and "Quiescence and Turbulence" (*Quest for Failure: A Study of William Faulkner*, 79). See also Gail L. Mortimer, *Faulkner's Rhetoric of Loss: A Study in Perception and Meaning*. Mortimer's Faulkner is a creature—and creator—of dualities and polarities including, for example, the "rhythm" that "oscillates" between narrative "control" and relaxed "flowing" (p. 28).

31. John T. Irwin, *Doubling and Incest/Repetition and Revenge: A Speculative Reading of Faulkner*, 30, 31, 158. See also David Wyatt, *Prodigal Sons: A Study in Authorship and Authority*, 72–100; Claire Rosenfield, "The Shadow Within: The Conscious and Unconscious Use of the Double," 327–29; and Lee Jenkins, *Faulkner and Black-White Relations: A Psychoanalytic Approach*, 1–60.

32. Irwin, *Doubling*, 43. See also Putzel, *Genius of Place*, 33–35, 106–7, for an application of Rank's *The Double* to Faulkner's *Soldiers' Pay*.

33. According to Joel Kovel, psychologists who have studied white racism agree that it derives in part from the projection of incestuous guilt onto blacks (*White Racism: A Psychohistory*, 71–75). On the inverse relationship between incest and miscegenation, see also Eric J. Sundquist, *Faulkner: The House Divided*, 19–25.

34. Irwin, *Doubling*, 42.
35. Irwin, *Doubling*, 114, 120. See also Sundquist, *Faulkner: The House Divided*, 17–19, 117–23.
36. Irwin, *Doubling*, 158–59.
37. Irwin, *Doubling*, 160, 164–65.
38. In *The Reivers*, a character named Everbe Corinthia is a prostitute.
39. "In dreams as in mythology, the delivery of the child *from* the uterine waters is commonly presented by distortion as the entry of the child *into* water" (Sigmund Freud, *The Interpretation of Dreams*, 437).
40. Compare a much later story, "The Tall Men" (1941), in which a Mississippi farmer named Buddy McCallum proves his superior manhood by waiving anesthesia during the amputation of his leg. A U.S. Marshal at the scene contrasts McCallum's behavior with that of most Americans, who, he says, have "slipped" their spines: "we have about decided a man don't need a backbone any more; to have one is old-fashioned" (CS, 59). The association of spinal fortitude with an enabling dismemberment fits a minor Faulknerian pattern. The five-foot-five author of "The Tall Men" must have found consolation in an amputation that heightens stature and enhances virility.
41. Faulkner, "An Introduction to *The Sound and the Fury*," in *A Faulkner Miscellany*, 159.
42. Erik H. Erikson, *Identity: Youth and Crisis*, 91–141.
43. Erikson, *Identity*, 26, 27, 29, 67, 73, 87, 133–34.
44. Erikson, *Identity*, 129, 132, 143.
45. Erik H. Erikson, *Young Man Luther: A Study in Psychoanalysis and History*, 49–67; *Gandhi's Truth: On the Origins of Militant Nonviolence*, 79, 132; Robert Coles, *Erik H. Erikson: The Growth of His Work*, 12–31.
46. James Hurt, "All the Living and the Dead: Lincoln's Imagery," 353, 357, 360, 364–80; Maynard Solomon, *Beethoven*, 10–24, 29, 40.
47. Richard Lebeaux, *Young Man Thoreau*, 25, 29–38, 41–43, 47, 55.
48. Lebeaux, *Young Man Thoreau*, 64, 68, 71, 73.
49. Lebeaux, *Young Man Thoreau*, 33, 59, 79–85, 215.
50. For an Eriksonian biography of Faulkner, see Judith Bryant Wittenberg, *Faulkner: The Transfiguration of Biography*.
51. Lebeaux, *Young Man Thoreau*, 47.
52. For a brief Eriksonian analysis of Murry's relationship to his father, see Sensibar, *The Origins of Faulkner's Art*, 49.
53. Lebeaux, *Young Man Thoreau*, 32.
54. Murry C. Falkner, *The Falkners of Mississippi: A Memoir*, 11–12.
55. Sensibar, *The Origins of Faulkner's Art*, 3.
56. He told his own "son," Malcolm Franklin, that "Mr. Murry was a kind and

gentle man, who always made sure that I had two feet under the table"
(*BLRO*, 97).

57. Brodsky and Hamblin, eds., *Faulkner: A Comprehensive Guide to the
Brodsky Collection, Volume II: The Letters*, 135. For her part, Jill revealed
the strain of being Faulkner's child when she chose as her husband a man
who had never heard of him (BL, 1491). Later, she could say frankly, "I think
he cared about me. But, I also think I could have gotten in his way and he
would have walked on me" (Bezzerides, *William Faulkner*, 67).

58. But Faulkner's brother John remembers his father encouraging William to
believe that he would be able to read after his first day of school and then
teasing him when he could not read the funny papers (MBB, 35).

59. Bezzerides, *William Faulkner*, 38.

60. Lebeaux, *Young Man Thoreau*, 36.

61. Lebeaux, *Young Man Thoreau*, 41, 43.

62. But Murry did keep a "kind of journal," in which he recorded random
pieties, notations of family travel, and—once—an idea for "a novel with a
very melodramatic story line" (BL1, 69, 132, 207, 276).

63. Sensibar, *The Origins of Faulkner's Art*, 7.

64. For an instructive contrast, consider Quentin Compson, who corresponds
only with his father and who laments his lack of a mother: "*if I'd just had a
mother so I could say Mother Mother*" (SF, 213). Gary Harrington points out
the similarity of Harry Wilbourne's magazine story in *The Wild Palms:* "If I
had only had a mother's love to guard me on that fatal day" ("Distant Mirrors:
The Intertextual Relationship of Quentin Compson and Harry Wilbourne,"
43).

65. Coles, *Erik H. Erikson*, 214.

66. Lewis P. Simpson, *The Man of Letters in New England and the South:
Essays on the History of the Literary Vocation in America*, 233, 235.

67. Walter Slatoff, though he was not concerned with Faulkner's biography, defined Faulkner's temperament concisely in the title of his book, *Quest for
Failure*. See Michael Millgate's modification of Slatoff's thesis in "William
Faulkner: The Two Voices," 73–74. See Leon S. Roudiez's elevation of it
into Marxist dialectic in "*Absalom, Absalom!* The Significance of Contradictions," 62–63.

68. For similar formulations of the same notion, see LG, 119, 217, 238; FU, 4,
22, 145, 207; FWP, 48, 78, 118.

69. For Faulkner's original formulation of this opinion, see LG, 58. For Hemingway's reaction, see BL, 1231–35. For Faulkner's later efforts to clarify his
statement, see BL, 1266, 1334, 1428–29, 1526; LG, 81, 88–89, 90–91,
107, 137–38, 179–80, 225; FU, 15, 143–44, 206; FWP, 78.

70. Erikson, *Young Man Luther*, 83.
71. I suppose a Freudian would attribute Faulkner's doctrine of endurance to his anality. In the classic scheme, a child's experience of "holding" his urine and of "waiting" to move his bowels determines his attitude toward time. When *delay* results in parental reward, in physical pleasure, and in narcissistic self-esteem, it can encourage a temperamental commitment to (anxious) *patience*. By extension, a prose style that persistently defers syntactical closure, as Faulkner's Truebloodian style notoriously does, gratifies the same pleasure in delay. See Norman N. Holland, *The Dynamics of Literary Response*, 39–41. Because language acquisition normally begins during the "anal period," and because the child's earliest experience of words occurs most forcefully in connection with toilet training, "it is . . . as much in this anal stage as in the oral that attitudes toward language are formed" (Holland, 39).
72. Erikson, *Identity*, 67, 133.
73. Bertram Wyatt-Brown, *Southern Honor: Ethics and Behavior in the Old South*, vii, xi, xvii, 20–22.
74. Wyatt-Brown, *Southern Honor*, xv, 4, 14, 74.
75. Wyatt-Brown, *Southern Honor*, 22.
76. Bezzerides, *William Faulkner*, 48.
77. Wyatt-Brown, *Southern Honor*, 46–47.
78. Thomas Nelson Page, *The Old South: Essays Social and Political*, 70–71.
79. Willard Thorp, "The Writer as Pariah in the Old South," 4, 7, 12. See also Elmo Howell, "Southern Fiction and the Pattern of Failure: The Example of Faulkner."
80. Page, *The Old South*, 72.
81. Manly Wade Wellman, "Introduction" to *Adventures of Captain Simon Suggs, Late of the Tallapoosa Volunteers*, by Johnson Jones Hooper, xxi.
82. Drew Gilpin Faust, *A Sacred Circle: The Dilemma of the Intellectual in the Old South, 1840–1860*, x–xi, 9–10, 59, 112.
83. Thomas W. Cutrer, ed., "Conference on Literature and Reading in the South and Southwest, 1935," 267, 269.
84. Faulkner, "An Introduction to *The Sound and the Fury*," in *A Faulkner Miscellany*, 156–57.
85. Faulkner, "An Introduction to *The Sound and the Fury*," in *A Faulkner Miscellany*, 157–58.
86. Louis D. Rubin, Jr., "The Dixie Special: William Faulkner and the Southern Literary Renascence," 72.
87. Rubin, "The Dixie Special," 73–75. For an elaboration of this dichotomy, and for a substantiation of Faulkner's fears for the masculinity of his vocation, see also Rubin, "William Faulkner: The Discovery of a Man's Vocation."

88. On the tension between Faulkner's insistence on the sanctity of his personal privacy and his efforts in later life to create a public role for himself, see Lewis P. Simpson, "The Loneliness of William Faulkner."

Chapter Three
The Wild Palms

1. Meta Carpenter Wilde asserts that Faulkner had begun writing *The Wild Palms* before she broke off their affair in late 1936 (ALG, 140; Panthea Reid Broughton, "An Interview with Meta Carpenter Wilde," 787). But Faulkner mentioned it as a "novel in my bean" in a letter he wrote on December 28, 1936, soon *after* her engagement to Wolfgang Rebner, and it does not seem to have started coming *out* of his "bean" until almost a year later (SL, 97, 99, 102; BL, 950, 953). See also Carvel Collins, "Biographical Background for Faulkner's *Helen*," in HEL, 87–89.

2. In *A Loving Gentleman*, Wilde remembers having been in New York for several weeks before Faulkner's visit (218–21). In her interview with Panthea Reid Broughton, she seems to acknowledge that Faulkner actually met her and her husband at the dock upon their return from Germany ("Interview," 794), as Carvel Collins asserts (HEL, 89).

3. ALG, 221–30; Broughton, "Interview," 795; BL, 974–76; WP, 324.

4. See Thomas L. McHaney, *William Faulkner's "The Wild Palms": A Study*, 21–24, 45; Cleanth Brooks, *William Faulkner: Toward Yoknapatawpha and Beyond*, 210–11, 406; Collins, "Biographical Background for Faulkner's *Helen*," in HEL, 9–98.

5. See Pamela Rhodes and Richard Godden, "*The Wild Palms*: Degraded Culture, Devalued Texts," 98–99, for a brief suggestion that "the 'strange land' might well be Hollywood," within a Marxist interpretation of the abandoned title: "If so, the singer in Babylon must learn the language of commodity, and be prepared to cut out his tongue by ravaging his own earliest and most 'precious' art work." See also the treatments of this psalm by McHaney in *William Faulkner's "The Wild Palms*," xiii–xiv, and by François L. Pitavy in "Forgetting Jerusalem: An Ironical Chart for *The Wild Palms*."

6. Faulkner, "Introduction to *The Sound and the Fury*," in *A Faulkner Miscellany*, 158.

7. On Faulkner's debt to Conrad Aiken for the musical metaphor here, see Judith L. Sensibar, *The Origins of Faulkner's Art*, 124–25, 255.

8. Ben Ray Redman, "Faulkner's Double Novel," 5.

9. Alfred Kazin, "A Study in Conscience," 2; Wallace Stegner, "Conductivity in Fiction," 446.

10. Edwin Berry Burgum, "Faulkner's New Novel," 23.

11. Hyatt H. Waggoner, *William Faulkner: From Jefferson to the World*, 141.

12. Carolyn Reeves, "*The Wild Palms*: Faulkner's Chaotic Cosmos," 148–57. On Helen Baird's "yellow" eyes, see Collins, "Biographical Background for Faulkner's *Helen*," in HEL, 93.

13. W. T. Jewkes, "Counterpoint in Faulkner's *The Wild Palms*," 39–41 (his italics).

14. Joseph J. Moldenhauer, "Unity of Theme and Structure in *The Wild Palms*," 313, 321.

15. Malcolm Cowley, "Sanctuary," 349. See also Marion W. Cumpiano, "The Motif of Return: Currents and Counter Currents in 'Old Man' by William Faulkner."

16. Jewkes, "Counterpoint," 52.

17. For a recent example of the latter judgment, see Doreen A. Fowler, "Measuring Faulkner's Tall Convict."

18. Burgum, "Faulkner's New Novel," 23.

19. But compare his response in 1953 to the prospect of publishing "Wild Palms" and "Old Man" in consecutive order rather than in alternation: "Dismembering THE WILD PALMS will in my opinion destroy the over-all impact which I intended" (BL, 1462). See also Gary Harrington, "Distant Mirrors: The Intertextual Relationship of Quentin Compson and Harry Wilbourne."

20. BL, 1456; William Faulkner, "Old Man," 22-page typescript. This is the television treatment, not the original story. For a description of the scenario that was actually dramatized on *Playhouse 90* in 1958 (Louis Daniel Brodsky and Robert W. Hamblin, eds., *Faulkner: A Comprehensive Guide to the Brodsky Collection, Volume II: The Letters*, 118), see Horton Foote, "On First Dramatizing Faulkner."

21. Faulkner frequently wished aloud that his works might have been published anonymously, because "[t]he artist is of no importance. Only what he creates is important." Just as frequently, however, he said that writing was his way of "scribbling 'Kilroy was here' on the wall of the final and irrevocable oblivion" (LG, 238, 253). He often quoted the lines in Gray's "Elegy" about unrealized genius ("Full many a gem of purest ray serene . . . Some mute inglorious Milton here may rest"), suggesting a complex connection in his mind between his own genius and the anonymous country people he had written about to gain *his* immortality.

22. William Empson, *Some Versions of Pastoral*, 25, 28–29, 32.

23. Empson, *Some Versions*, 41, 46–47.

24. Thomas L. McHaney, "Anderson, Hemingway, and Faulkner's *The Wild Palms*," 472, 474; McHaney, *William Faulkner's "The Wild Palms*," 38.

25. Léon Moussinac, *Sergei Eisenstein: An Investigation into His Films and Philosophy*, 208. See also George Sidney, "Faulkner in Hollywood: A Study of His Career as a Scenarist," 48: "According to the Twentieth Century-Fox research files, Faulkner worked for . . . Universal, where he did a treatment of *Sutter's Gold.* . . . If Faulkner did actually work on *Sutter's Gold*, he would have been in a position to have met Sergei Eisenstein, the great Russian director who came to Hollywood in 1930 and wrote, among other things, a screenplay of *Sutter's Gold.*" According to Bruce Kawin, "it seems evident . . . that Faulkner worked from Eisenstein's 1930 treatment" of *Sutter's Gold* ("Faulkner's Film Career: The Years with Hawks," 175). Eisenstein does not mention Faulkner in his *Immoral Memories: An Autobiography.*

26. McHaney, *William Faulkner's "The Wild Palms*," 127–28n.

27. See Bruce Kawin's discussion of Faulkner and Eisenstein in "The Montage Element in Faulkner's Fiction," 107–19.

28. Sergei Eisenstein, "Dickens, Griffith, and the Film Today," in *Film Form: Essays in Film Theory*, 204–5, 217, 223, 234–35, 239 (his italics).

29. Eisenstein, "Dickens, Griffith," in *Film Form*, 235–36, 238, 240 (his italics).

30. Sergei Eisenstein, "Through Theater to Cinema," in *Film Form*, 4. For a Marxist reading of *Absalom, Absalom!* as "two separate narratives" (Sutpen's and Quentin's), out of which "a third one materializes" through "a dialectic process," see Leon S. Roudiez, "*Absalom, Absalom!* The Significance of Contradictions," 58–62.

31. For a contrary view of the political implications of *The Wild Palms*, see Rhodes and Godden, "*The Wild Palms*," 92–110. These authors turn Faulkner into a proto-Marxist with a "radical perspective," and they argue that *The Wild Palms* illustrates the evils of "commodity fetishism" and "reified consciousness." For them, E. B. Burgum correctly identified the convict as a "representative of the proletariat" rather than as a "pastoral" character: "The Tall Convict is hardly an Arcadian shepherd, and he is certainly no primitive. Unlike the Noble Savage, the convict is carried towards class consciousness" (p. 102).

32. Louis D. Rubin, Jr., *The Writer in the South: Studies in a Literary Community*, 84–85.

33. John Donald Wade, "Southern Humor," 616–28.

34. James M. Cox, "The South Once More," 169.

35. John Fox, Jr., *"Hell fer Sartain" and Other Stories*, 3, 11.

36. Rubin, *The Writer in the South*, 84.

37. See Rhodes and Godden, *"The Wild Palms,"* 95: "The more the artificial longings expand their own artificiality through deepening layers of parody, the more an excess of artifice comes to signify only its own falsity, leaving the novel in danger of collapsing upon itself, as fabricated as the fabric it sought to comprehend."

38. See Rhodes and Godden, *"The Wild Palms,"* 98: "Certainly, the various elements of self-parody and the literary cross-referencing within 'Wild Palms' serve not only to present the afflictions of the characters, but set on display Faulkner's own moral problems as a producer for the market, as he seems ingeniously to introduce himself into the narrative."

39. Note Margaret Powers's similar language in *Soldiers' Pay*: "Am I cold by nature, or have I spent all my emotional coppers, that I don't seem to feel things like others?" (SP, 39).

40. See David Minter, *William Faulkner: His Life and Work*, 175.

41. For a treatment of *The Wild Palms* in the context of Hollywood novels, especially Horace McCoy's *They Shoot Horses, Don't They?* and James M. Cain's *The Postman Always Rings Twice*, see Rhodes and Godden, *"The Wild Palms,"* 87–92.

42. BL, 981–82; McHaney, *William Faulkner's "The Wild Palms,"* 21–24; Brooks, *William Faulkner: Toward Yoknapatawpha and Beyond*, 210–11; Collins, "Biographical Background for Faulkner's *Helen*," in HEL, 86–87.

43. Maxwell Geismar, "A Cycle of Fiction," 1309, 1312, William Phillips, "What Happened in the 30's," 211, 212, Granville Hicks, "Writers in the Thirties," 99.

44. See Richard Pearce, " 'Pylon,' 'Awake and Sing!' and the Apocalyptic Imagination of the 30's." For a Marxist estimation of the "political mood of *Absalom, Absalom!*" within a treatment of this novel as a Depression document, see Roudiez, *"Absalom, Absalom!,"* 72–76. For a general treatment of Southern writing during the Depression, see Louis D. Rubin, Jr., "Trouble on the Land: Southern Literature and the Great Depression," in A *Gallery of Southerners*, 152–73.

45. Robert L. Snyder, *Pare Lorentz and the Documentary Film*, 56–65; Frank S. Nugent, "The Screen: Samuel Goldwyn Turns Nordhoff-Hall 'Hurricane' Loose Across the Screen of the Astor," 31.

46. W. L. White, "Pare Lorentz"; C. M. Black, "He Serves Up America"; Andrew Bergman, *We're in the Money: Depression America and Its Films*, 165–66; Snyder, *Pare Lorentz and the Documentary Film*, 56–65; Pare Lorentz, dir., *The River*. For a transcript of the movie and still photographs from it, see Pare Lorentz, *The River* (Stackpole Sons).

47. See Nugent, "The Screen," 31; "The New Pictures: *Hurricane*," 41–42.

48. Charles Nordhoff and James Norman Hall, *The Hurricane*, 22.

49. He also would have seen, during the climactic storm, a church in which most of the islanders seek refuge; and he would have heard, throughout the hurricane scene, the church's bell tolling in the wind. If Faulkner did indeed see *The Hurricane*, it may have provided one source for the final image in the Nobel Prize Speech: the "last ding-dong of doom," the destruction of which will be survived by some "puny inexhaustible voice" on "the last worthless rock hanging tideless in the last red and dying evening" (ESPL, 120). The bell is destroyed when the church collapses; the church's ruin is all that remains on a mound of coral fragments after the hurricane.

50. Peter Drucker's metaphor typifies Depression memoirs: "The American response to the Depression was the response to a natural disaster. As after an earthquake, a flood, a hurricane, the community closed ranks and came to each other's rescue" (*Adventures of a Bystander*, 299–300).

51. See also CNC, 81–82; McHaney, *William Faulkner's "The Wild Palms,"* 45.

52. BL, 952–53; Broughton, "An Interview with Meta Carpenter Wilde," 777.

53. Joseph Blotner, comp., *William Faulkner's Library: A Catalogue*, p. 51.

54. Lyle Saxon, *Father Mississippi*, vi, 65–67, 279–306, 309–11, 314–40. For a more extended treatment of Faulkner's debt to Saxon, see my "Lyle Saxon's *Father Mississippi* as a Source for Faulkner's 'Old Man' and 'Mississippi.'"

    A more remote influence may be Twain's *Life on the Mississippi*, which includes in an appendix an account of the great flood of 1882 as it was reported in the New Orleans *Times-Democrat*. Twain toured the Mississippi River in April 1882, one month after the flood. The appendix includes several elements that reappear both in *Father Mississippi* and in "Old Man." It includes newspaper headlines. The Atchafalaya appears, prominently. Relief boats ply swollen waters, rescuing victims "out of trees and off of cabin roofs." Indian mounds are described: "These elevations, built by the aborigines hundreds of years ago, are the only points of refuge for miles. When we arrived we found them crowded with stock, all of which was thin and hardly able to stand up. They were mixed together, sheep, hogs, horses, mules, and cattle" (Mark Twain, *Life on the Mississippi*, in *Mississippi Writings*, 586–96). Faulkner possessed a copy of the first edition of *Life on the Mississippi*, which had belonged to his grandfather (Blotner, comp., *William Faulkner's Library*, 23).

55. William Stott, *Documentary Expression and Thirties America*, 33–35, 41–45.

56. Bergman, *We're in the Money*, 96. Compare Tom Joad's description of prison life in John Steinbeck's *The Grapes of Wrath*, 35–36: "'You eat regular, an' get clean clothes, and there's places to take a bath. It's pretty nice some ways. . . .' Suddenly he laughed. 'They was a guy paroled,' he said. ''Bout a month he's back for breakin' parole. A guy ast him why he bust his parole.

"Well, hell," he says. "They got no conveniences at my old man's place. Got no 'lectric lights, got no shower baths. There ain't no books, an' the food's lousy." Says he come back where they got a few conveniences an' he eats regular. He says it makes him feel lonesome out there in the open havin' to think what to do next. So he stole a car an' come back. . . . The guy's right, too,' he said. 'Las' night, thinkin' where I'm gonna sleep, I got scared.'" For a nonliterary analogue, consider Charlie Chaplin's resistance to his release from prison in *Modern Times* (1936): "Can't I stay a little longer? I'm so happy here."

57. Burgum, "Faulkner's New Novel," 23.

58. George B. Tindall, *The Emergence of the New South: 1913–1945*, 415.

59. James Agee and Walker Evans, *Let Us Now Praise Famous Men: Three Tenant Families*, 103.

60. For a further updating, note the concentration of prison scenes in Faulkner's novels of the late 1940s and early 1950s: *Intruder in the Dust* (1948), *Requiem for a Nun* (1951), *A Fable* (1954).

61. Stott, *Documentary Expression*, 251–52.

62. Quoted in Stott, *Documentary Expression*, 37–39.

63. Nathan Asch, *The Road: In Search of America*, 23.

64. The relationship of *The Wild Palms* to "screwball comedy," perhaps the most successful film genre of the late 1930s both artistically and commercially, deserves attention. Stanley Cavell, in *Pursuits of Happiness: The Hollywood Comedy of Remarriage*, discusses a "screwball" subgenre which he calls "the comedy of remarriage." In each of the films he examines, a man and a woman—the latter an autonomous "new" woman—are thrust into a romantic "green world" (p. 49), where they have the leisure to be together, to "waste time together" (p. 88). No children exist to divert them from a search for their own childhood within marriage. Beginning in divorce, they reconstitute the institution of marriage as a framework for "festival" (p. 239). In their "pursuits of happiness," they must create a private erotic bastion against the pressures of civilization (pp. 64–65). Faulkner, imprisoned in his less-than-festive marriage, must have dreamed of escaping with "the right sort of a girl" to "an island in the Pacific" (p. 97), just as Peter Warne (Clark Gable) does in *It Happened One Night*. "Wild Palms" amounts to a *tragedy* of remarriage, roughly contemporary with Cavell's films, which also include *The Awful Truth* (1937), *Bringing Up Baby* (1938), *The Philadelphia Story* (1940), *His Girl Friday* (1940), and *The Lady Eve* (1941).

65. See also Erskine Caldwell's parody of on-the-road books, in his and Margaret Bourke-White's *Say, Is This the U.S.A.?*, 10–12.

66. Stott, *Documentary Expression*, 37; Clara Weatherwax, *Marching! Marching!*, 6.

67. Stott, *Documentary Expression*, 38.

68. Fay M. Blake, *The Strike in the American Novel*.

69. Ernest Hemingway, *To Have and Have Not*, 176.

70. Carlos Baker, *Hemingway: The Writer as Artist*, 216.

71. For a discussion of Richard Wright's more conventionally "proletarian" treat-
ment of the Great Flood of 1927 and of sharecropping in "The Man Who
Saw the Flood" (1937) and "Down by the Riverside" (1938), see William
Howard, "Richard Wright's Flood Stories and the Great Mississippi River
Flood of 1927: Social and Historical Backgrounds."

72. For an essential differentiation between these two terms, see Empson, *Some
Versions*, 3–23.

Chapter Four
The Hamlet

1. BL, 995–1001; Panthea Reid Broughton, "An Interview with Meta Carpenter
Wilde," 777.

2. Michael Millgate, *The Achievement of William Faulkner*, 185.

3. Cleanth Brooks, *William Faulkner: The Yoknapatawpha Country*, 174.

4. Wallace Stegner, "The New Novels," 464; Helen White and Redding Sugg,
Jr., comps., *From the Mountain: Selections from "Pseudopodia" (1936), "The
North Georgia Review" (1937–1941), and "South Today" (1942–1945)*, 209;
Robert Littell, "Outstanding Novels," x.

5. Robert Penn Warren, "The Snopes World," 257; Robert Penn Warren, "Cowley's Faulkner," 236.

6. Warren, "The Snopes World," 256; Warren Beck, *Man in Motion: Faulkner's
Trilogy*; James Gray Watson, *The Snopes Dilemma: Faulkner's Trilogy*; Flor-
ence Leaver, "The Structure of *The Hamlet*"; Peter Lisca, "The Hamlet:
Genesis and Revisions"; Viola Hopkins, "William Faulkner's *The Hamlet*: A
Study in Meaning and Form"; T. Y. Greet, "The Theme and Structure of
Faulkner's *The Hamlet*"; Olga W. Vickery, *The Novels of William Faulkner:
A Critical Interpretation*, 167.

7. Arthur F. Kinney, *Faulkner's Narrative Poetics: Style as Vision*, 254; Joseph
W. Reed, Jr., *Faulkner's Narrative*, 240; John T. Matthews, *The Play of
Faulkner's Language*, 165; Donald M. Kartiganer, *The Fragile Thread: The
Meaning of Form in Faulkner's Novels*, 114.

8. Kartiganer, *The Fragile Thread*, xiii, 109.

9. Brooks. *William Faulkner: The Yoknapatawpha Country*, 179.

10. Irving Howe, *William Faulkner: A Critical Study*, 244, 246.

11. Carey Wall, "Drama and Technique in Faulkner's *The Hamlet*," 17.

12. Kartiganer, *The Fragile Thread*, 118.

13. John M. Bradbury, *Renaissance in the South: A Critical History of the Literature, 1920–1960*, 5.

14. R. W. B. Lewis, *The American Adam: Innocence, Tragedy, and Tradition in the Nineteenth Century*, 1–2.

15. Only in the past decade have scholars begun paying real attention to twentieth-century Southern intellectual history. See Michael O'Brien, *The Idea of the American South, 1920–1941*; Richard H. King, *A Southern Renaissance: The Cultural Awakening of the American South, 1930–1955*; Daniel Joseph Singal, *The War Within: From Victorian to Modernist Thought in the South, 1919–1945*. For "dialectical" models of Southern intellectual history, see Fred Hobson, *Tell About the South: The Southern Rage to Explain*; and Singal, *The War Within*. Hobson identifies a "school of remembrance" and a "school of shame and guilt" who, respectively, defended and criticized Southern society between the 1850s and the 1960s. Singal describes a generational dialogue between early twentieth-century "Victorians" and mid-twentieth-century "Modernists."

16. Lewis, *The American Adam*, 2.

17. For an attempt to locate the dialogue's origins in the mid-nineteenth century, see Hobson, *Tell About the South*.

18. See Marion D. Irish, "Proposed Roads to the New South, 1941: Chapel Hill Planners vs. Nashville Agrarians"; Bradbury, *Renaissance in the South*, 140; King, *A Southern Renaissance*, 39–76.

19. George B. Tindall, *The Emergence of the New South, 1913–1945*, 576–88; George B. Tindall, "The Significance of Howard W. Odum to Southern History: A Preliminary Estimate." For Gunnar Myrdal's estimation of the political impact of Southern liberalism, see *An American Dilemma: The Negro Problem and Modern Democracy*, 466–67.

20. Tindall, *The Emergence of the New South*, 583–88; Alexander Karanikas, *Tillers of a Myth: Southern Agrarians as Social and Literary Critics*, 100–22; Singal, *The War Within*, 147–52.

21. John Dollard, *Caste and Class in a Southern Town*; Hortense Powdermaker, *After Freedom: A Cultural Study in the Deep South*; Allison Davis, Burleigh B. Gardner, and Mary R. Gardner, *Deep South: A Social Anthropological Study of Caste and Class*; Arthur F. Raper, *Preface to Peasantry: A Tale of Two Black Belt Counties*; Arthur F. Raper, *Tenants of the Almighty*; Gunnar Myrdal, *An American Dilemma*; Clarence E. Cason, *90° in the Shade*; Jonathan Daniels, *A Southerner Discovers the South*; Virginius Dabney, *Below the Potomac: A Book About the New South*; James Agee and Walker

Evans, *Let Us Now Praise Famous Men: Three Tenant Families*; W. J. Cash, *The Mind of the South.*

22. Tindall, *The Emergence of the New South*, 576–82.

23. See, for example, John Crowe Ransom, "Poetry: A Note in Ontology"; and Robert Penn Warren, "Knowledge and the Image of Man."

24. Wallace W. Douglas, "Deliberate Exiles: The Social Sources of Agrarian Poetics," 286; King, *A Southern Renaissance*, 67; John Crowe Ransom, "Poetry: A Note in Ontology," 176 (my italics); Warren, "Knowledge and the Image of Man," 191 (Warren's italics).

25. John Crowe Ransom, "Modern with the Southern Accent," 192, 193–94, 198 (my italics). For a similar bisection of Southern writing into two camps, the worthy "traditionists" and the unworthy "provincials," see Allen Tate, "The New Provincialism," in *Essays of Four Decades*, 543–45.

26. Stanley J. Kunitz and Howard Haycraft, eds., *Twentieth Century Authors: A Biographical Dictionary of Modern Literature* (1942), 1359; Donald Davidson, "The Trend of Literature: A Partisan View," 190; Bradbury, *Renaissance in the South*, 82, 86, 102–3.

27. Donald Davidson, "Critic's Almanac," *Nashville Tennesseean*, 18 April 1926, rpt. in *The Spyglass: Views and Reviews, 1924–1930*, 11–16; Robert Penn Warren, "T. S. Stribling: A Paragraph in the History of Critical Realism"; Allen Tate, "T. S. Stribling"; John Donald Wade, "Two Souths." But see also the generous revaluation in *American Literature: The Makers and the Making*, ed. Cleanth Brooks, R. W. B. Lewis, and Robert Penn Warren, 2560–61.

28. Warren, "T. S. Stribling," 463–64, 477, 481–83, 485.

29. Byrom Dickens, "T. S. Stribling and the South," 341, 345, 349.

30. Howard W. Odum, *Southern Regions of the United States*, 529–31; W. J. Cash, *The Mind of the South*, 380; Joseph L. Morrison, *W. J. Cash, Southern Prophet: A Biography and Reader*, 238–41; Thomas Wolfe, *The Web and the Rock*, 242–43.

31. Tindall, "The Significance of Howard W. Odum," 286; Morrison, *W. J. Cash*, 6–12; Kunitz and Haycraft, eds., *Twentieth Century Authors* (1942), 237–38.

32. Louise Cowan, *The Fugitive Group: A Literary History*, 3–22.

33. O'Brien, *The Idea of the American South*, 128.

34. For discussions of the ideological biases of Faulkner criticism, see Myra Jehlen, *Class and Character in Faulkner's South*, 14–17; Susan Willis, "Aesthetics of the Rural Slum: Contradictions and Dependency in 'The Bear,'" 82–86. For placements of Faulkner within the literary politics of the Southern Renaissance, see Richard H. King, "Framework of a Renaissance";

Cleanth Brooks, "Faulkner and the Fugitive Agrarians"; Floyd C. Watkins, "What Stand Did Faulkner Take?"; Watkins, "The Hound Under the Wagon: Faulkner and the Southern Literati."

35. Morrison, W. J. Cash, 156–59.
36. White and Sugg, comps., From the Mountain, 153, 208–10.
37. Tindall, The Emergence of the New South, 667–69; John Crowe Ransom, The New Criticism, xi–xii; Hyatt H. Waggoner, "The Current Revolt Against the New Criticism," 211–25; Douglas, "Deliberate Exiles."
38. Tindall, The Emergence of the New South, 669; Ransom, "Modern with the Southern Accent," 197.
39. O'Donnell's essays on tenant farming include "Looking Down the Cotton Row" and, with Richmond Croom Beatty, "The Tenant Farmer in the South."
40. George Marion O'Donnell, "Faulkner's Mythology," 285, 286. See also Tindall, The Emergence of the New South, 669–70.
41. Warren, "Cowley's Faulkner," 177. See Lewis P. Simpson, "O'Donnell's Wall," in The Man of Letters in New England and the South: Essays on the History of the Literary Vocation in America, 192–200.
42. Robert Penn Warren, "Faulkner: Past and Present," 17. For an elaboration of Warren's judgment, see Richard H. King, "A Fable: Faulkner's Political Novel?"
43. King, A Southern Renaissance, 64.
44. Grace Lumpkin, To Make My Bread; Erskine Caldwell, God's Little Acre, 213–21; Caroline Gordon, The Garden of Adonis, 7, 48–49: George Sessions Perry, Hold Autumn in Your Hand; BL, 1184; Agee and Evans, Let Us Now Praise, 92–95, 120–21.
45. Tindall, The Emergence of the New South, 580. Faulkner may have been exposed to the public discourse when he attended the Southern Writers Conference in Charlottesville in 1931, where Donald Davidson and Paul Green debated "whether the creative mind could function in a machine age" (Hobson, Tell About the South, 219).
46. For an example of liberal proposals, see W. T. Couch, "An Agrarian Programme for the South," American Review 3 (Summer 1934): 313–26; for an example of conservative proposals, see Troy J. Cauley, Agrarianism: A Program for Farmers, especially the last chapter, "Toward the Restoration of Agrarianism," 187–211.
47. Herman Clarence Nixon, Forty Acres and Steel Mules, especially 83–86.
48. King, A Southern Renaissance, 47.
49. John Crowe Ransom, "Reconstructed but Unregenerate," in I'll Take My Stand: The South and the Agrarian Tradition, by "Twelve Southerners," 14.

50. Edd Winfield Parks, *Segments of Southern Thought*, 31.
51. John Donald Wade, "Southern Humor," 620–21.
52. For example, see Allison Davis's definition of six "subclasses" in addition to three "main class divisions"—each "characterized by its particular behavior pattern and by a distinctive ideology" (Davis, Gardner, and Gardner, *Deep South*, 63).
53. Lyle H. Lanier, "Mr. Dollard and Scientific Method."
54. Donald Davidson, "The Class Approach to Southern Problems," 262, 268–70. On Nixon's *Forty Acres*, see King, *A Southern Renaissance*, 50.
55. Davidson, "The Class Approach," 272.
56. Cash, *The Mind of the South*, 34, 351.
57. The subsistence farmers Ransom described in "The Aesthetic of Regionalism" were New Mexican Indians rather than white sharecroppers; but the ideological results of the contact were the same, and the comparison was implicit.
58. O'Donnell and Beatty, "The Tenant Farmer in the South," 80–81.
59. Faulkner repeated the image in all his books of the late thirties and the forties. In "An Odor of Verbena," Colonel Sartoris sent money to the hill woman whose husband he had slain. She "walked into the house two days later while we were sitting at the dinner table and flung the money at Father's face" (UNV, 255). For similar rejections of money in *The Wild Palms*, see Chapter 3. For the two scenes in "The Long Summer," see HAM, 176–78, 240. Roth Edmonds's mistress rejects his money in "Delta Autumn" (GDM, 358–61). Lucas Beauchamp "spurns" Chick Mallison's money in *Intruder in the Dust*, 15–16. In "Tomorrow," Jackson Fentry tosses the money purse the Thorpes try to give him "over behind the chopping block" (KG, 102–3).
60. For examples of the opposed viewpoints, see Cauley, *Agrarianism*, 187 ("If the farmer cannot make a great deal of money, relief is obviously to be found in reducing the amount of money which the farmer needs"), and Nixon, *Forty Acres*, 95 ("[I]t behooves the South and Southerners to be concerned with an immediate improvement of the region's low production and income status. It is pertinent to note that the ills of the South are the ills of class more than of region or section").
61. John Arthos, "Ritual and Humor in the Writing of William Faulkner"; Carvel Collins, "Faulkner and Certain Earlier Southern Fiction"; Frank M. Hoadley, "Folk Humor in the Novels of William Faulkner"; Cecil D. Eby, "Faulkner and the Southwestern Humorists"; M. Thomas Inge, "William Faulkner and George Washington Harris: In the Tradition of Southwestern Humor"; Otis B. Wheeler, "Some Uses of Folk Humor by Faulkner"; Richard K. Cross, "The Humor of *The Hamlet*"; John T. Flanagan, "Folklore in

Faulkner's Fiction"; Thomas W. Cooley, Jr., "Faulkner Draws the Long Bow"; Helen Swink, "William Faulkner: The Novelist as Oral Narrator"; Myra Jehlen, *Class and Character in Faulkner's South*, 133–51.

62. Kenneth S. Lynn, *Mark Twain and Southwestern Humor*, 3–22, 52, 58, 61, 64, 145. See also Louis D. Rubin, Jr., "The Great American Joke," 87–94.

63. Augustus Baldwin Longstreet, *Georgia Scenes: Characters, Incidents, Etc., in the First Half Century of the Republic*, 52.

64. See John Q. Anderson, "Scholarship in Southwestern Humor–Past and Present." Anderson couches his objections to Lynn's "socio-political explanation of Southwestern humor" (p. 78) in arguments derived from Agrarianism. He rejects the application of Marxist economic interpretations to antebellum literature as anachronistic: "Assumptions that Southwestern humor had the ulterior motive of keeping the lower class in its place and of discriminating against it is a kind of twentieth century thinking that did not exist in the nineteenth century" (p. 81). Anderson argues further that "the assumption that Southwestern humor favored only the upper class is not borne out in the sketches themselves" (pp. 80–81). He shows that the genre encompassed more political variety than Lynn seems prepared to admit. However, as part of his evidence, he cites John Donald Wade's biography of Longstreet, which "shows that eight of the eighteen stories in *Georgia Scenes* deal 'with what anybody would have called the upper element of Georgia society'" (p. 81). Anderson would have done well to notice that the upper-class sketches *alternate* with the vernacular sketches. *Georgia Scenes* is another double text, like John Fox, Jr.'s *"Hell fer Sartain" and Other Stories* or Faulkner's *The Wild Palms*. If Longstreet or his editors were unconscious of class differentiation, one might ask, how did they happen to gather his sketches into such a "socio-politically" symmetrical order? One might also suggest that the Whiggish pretense of "homogeneity" is well served by such intermingling and, further, that the satire directed against the "upper element" is different from the satire directed at vulgar ruffians. "[W]hen Longstreet satirized the elite he showed himself lounging within the select circle," as Louis J. Budd has written, but he "was careful to dissociate himself from illiterate crackers" ("Gentlemanly Humorists of the Old South," 233, 234). See James B. Meriwether's redefinition of Longstreet as a "pioneer of literary realism" rather than merely a Southwestern humorist, in "Augustus Baldwin Longstreet: Realist and Artist."

65. Longstreet, *Georgia Scenes*, 1, 2.

66. Lynn, *Mark Twain and Southwestern Humor*, 68–69.

67. Longstreet, *Georgia Scenes*, 55.

68. Charlotte Renner, "Talking and Writing in Faulkner's Snopes Trilogy," 66. Renner's argument that the Snopes trilogy achieves a "synthesis of spoken and

written narration" (p. 69) is more convincing for *The Town* and *The Mansion* than for *The Hamlet*.

69. Lynn, *Mark Twain and Southwestern Humor*, 146.

70. My search for a more satisfactory term has yielded only *diglossia*, which the linguist Charles Ferguson coined to describe "speech communities" in which "two . . . varieties of the same language are used by some speakers under different conditions." His examples of "diglossic" communities include Egypt, where modern Egyptian and classical Arabic are used for separate purposes, German Switzerland (Swiss German and standard German), Haiti (Haitian Creole and French), and Greece (*katharévusa*, the prestige language, and *dhimotikí*, the demotic language). Southern literary texts are not quite diglossic, however, because no one in a diglossic community regularly uses the "higher" speech pattern as "a medium of ordinary conversation," whereas the nonvernacular characters in Southern fiction are identifiable with the social class of their authors precisely because they speak "standard English" rather than the dialect of lower-class characters (Charles A. Ferguson, "Diglossia," in *Language Structure and Language Use: Essays by Charles A. Ferguson*, 1, 3, 16–17).

71. Raymond Williams, *The Country and the City*, 169.

72. Richard Poirier, *The Performing Self: Compositions and Decompositions in the Languages of Contemporary Life*, 4, 5.

73. Compare Beck, *Man in Motion*, 119: "Frequently the dialogues between Ratliff and Gavin Stevens, especially in *The Town*, suggest Faulkner's self-examination, in an attempt to be accountable to his deepest insights and most comprehensive judgments."

74. See Floyd C. Watkins and Thomas Daniel Young, "Revisions of Style in Faulkner's 'The Hamlet,'" 327–36; Joanne V. Creighton, *William Faulkner's Craft of Revision: The Snopes Trilogy, "The Unvanquished," and "Go Down, Moses,"* 21–48.

75. Cecil D. Eby, "Ichabod Crane in Yoknapatawpha"; Edward Stone, "William Faulkner."

76. John Crowe Ransom, *Grace After Meat*, 15.

77. Williams, *The Country and the City*, 171.

78. T. Harry Williams, *Huey Long*, 70. For a similar assessment of the bilingualism of Mississippi's Governor Theodore Bilbo, see Calvin S. Brown, "Faulkner's Localism," 19.

79. Poirier, *The Performing Self*, 4.

80. Williams, *The Country and the City*, 168.

81. For a contrary view, see David Minter, *William Faulkner: His Life and Work*, 182: "[*The Hamlet*] does not dramatize minds and voices engaged in the

crucial acts of knowing and articulating, and so does not overtly play with its own fictive status."

82. Empson, *Some Versions*, 23. See also François L. Pitavy, "Idiocy and Idealism: A Reflection on the Faulknerian Idiot," 103–7.
83. Empson, *Some Versions*, 11.
84. William Stott, *Documentary Expression and Thirties America*, 216, 261, 262–64. See also Laurence Bergreen, *James Agee: A Life*, 158–82.
85. Agee and Evans, *Let Us Now Praise*, 12–13.
86. Agee and Evans, *Let Us Now Praise*, 134.
87. Stott, *Documentary Expression*, 291.
88. Agee and Evans, *Let Us Now Praise*, 64, 197.
89. Agee and Evans, *Let Us Now Praise*, 328, 340.
90. Agee and Evans, *Let Us Now Praise*, 97–111.

Chapter Five
Knight's Gambit

1. On Faulkner's stories set in Memphis, see Max Putzel, *Genius of Place: William Faulkner's Triumphant Beginnings*, 242–53.
2. Frank Luther Mott, *A History of American Magazines*, vol. 4, 1885–1905, 701, 702.
3. Hans H. Skei, *William Faulkner: The Short Story Career: An Outline of Faulkner's Short Story Writing from 1919 to 1962*, 31.
4. *Sanctuary, Intruder in the Dust*, and *Knight's Gambit* are not Faulkner's only books into which the conventions of detective fiction entered. For discussions of the detective elements in Faulkner's fiction generally, see George R. Stewart and Joseph M. Backus, "'Each in Its Ordered Place': Structure and Narrative in 'Benjy's Section' of *The Sound and the Fury*," 455; Warren French, "William Faulkner and the Art of the Detective Story"; C. Hugh Holman, "*Absalom, Absalom!*: The Historian as Detective"; Julian Symons, *Mortal Consequences: A History—From the Detective Story to the Crime Novel*, 140–41; Mick Gidley, "Elements of the Detective Story in William Faulkner's Fiction"; Peter J. Rabinowitz, "The Click of the Spring: The Detective Story as Parallel Structure in Dostoyevsky and Faulkner"; Edmond L. Volpe, "Faulkner's 'Monk': The Detective Story and the Mystery of the Human Heart"; Hans H. Skei, "Faulkner's *Knight's Gambit*: Detection and Ingenuity."
5. Louis Daniel Brodsky, "Reflections on William Faulkner: An Interview with A. I. Bezzerides," 387.

6. Joseph Blotner, comp., *William Faulkner's Library: A Catalogue*, 9.
7. Resemblances between *Knight's Gambit* and Post's *Uncle Abner* have been noticed by some historians of the detective story. When "An Error in Chemistry" appeared in *Ellery Queen's Mystery Magazine*, the editors (in a headnote) remarked the "richness of kinship" between Faulkner's story and Post's series. After conceding that Faulkner may have "never read an Uncle Abner story in all his life," they enumerated the similarities between "the characters, the backgrounds, and the moods of the storytelling" of the two authors. Then they exclaimed, "Who would have dreamed that William Faulkner of all the writers in America would, by accident or design, carry on the legend of Uncle Abner, create a modern Uncle Gavin in the great tradition?" (*Ellery Queen's Mystery Magazine*, June 1946, 5). Julian Symons more soberly observes that Gavin Stevens is "rather like Uncle Abner" (*Mortal Consequences*, 176).

   For a similar analogue to *Knight's Gambit*, see Cleanth Brooks's discussion of "The Influence on Faulkner of Irvin S. Cobb," in *William Faulkner: Toward Yoknapatawpha and Beyond*, 375–76.
8. Stanley J. Kunitz and Howard Haycraft, eds., *Twentieth Century Authors: A Biographical Dictionary of Modern Literature* (1942), 1120. See also Charles A. Norton, *Melville Davisson Post: Man of Many Mysteries*.
9. For Abner's secret romance, see Melville Davisson Post, "The Broken Stirrup-Leather," 12.
10. Melville Davisson Post, *Uncle Abner: Master of Mysteries*, 41–81, 303–22.
11. Post, *Uncle Abner*, 30.
12. Post, *Uncle Abner*, 1, 43.
13. Post, *Uncle Abner*, 8.
14. For an elaboration of this conundrum, see W. E. Schlepper, "Truth and Justice in *Knight's Gambit*."
15. Post, *Uncle Abner*, 3.
16. Renato Poggioli, "Naboth's Vineyard, or the Pastoral View of the Social Order," in *The Oaten Flute: Essays on Pastoral Poetry and the Pastoral Ideal*, 194–95, 199, 216.
17. For discussions of the relationship of "outlanders" to the community as a unifying factor for *Knight's Gambit*, see Jerome F. Klinkowitz, "The Thematic Unity of *Knight's Gambit*"; and Skei, "Faulkner's *Knight's Gambit*."
18. For a treatment of "Monk" as a story about Chick's "interpretive act," in which "the art of detection, the art of narration, and the art of reading" are equated, see David Minter, *William Faulkner: His Life and Work*, 214–15. See also Volpe, "Faulkner's 'Monk.'"
19. On Faulkner's ambivalence toward the peasant class, in "Monk," see Myra Jehlen, *Class and Character in Faulkner's South*, 165–68.

20. George B. Tindall, *The Emergence of the New South: 1913–1945*, 254–58.
21. Tindall, *The Emergence of the New South*, 257.
22. William Faulkner, "Knight's Gambit," 23-page typescript.
23. Tindall, *The Emergence of the New South*, 492.
24. David Wyatt, *Prodigal Sons: A Study in Authorship and Authority*, 72–100.
25. Faulkner, "Knight's Gambit," 23-page typescript.
26. Faulkner, "Knight's Gambit," 23-page typescript.
27. Symons, *Mortal Consequences*, 176.
28. For a discussion of "Knight's Gambit" as a story *about* sentimentality, see Edmond L. Volpe, "Faulkner's 'Knight's Gambit': Sentimentality and the Creative Imagination."
29. For evidence that Faulkner may have based Stevens's romantic past upon Phil Stone's unsuccessful courtship of Katrina Carter, see Susan Snell, "William Faulkner, Phil Stone, and Katrina Carter: A Biographical Footnote to the Summer of 1914," 85–86.

Chapter Six
Go Down, Moses

1. For a similar "p'int of law" in a dialect poem, see Irwin Russell, "The Mississippi Witness," in *Poems*, 36.
2. Compare "Sunset," one of the sketches Faulkner wrote in New Orleans in 1925, in which the events leading to another lynching are told from two points of view: an "objective" account and a racist newspaper report (NOS, 76–85). See Walter Taylor, *Faulkner's Search for a South*, 15–17.
3. James Early, *The Making of "Go Down, Moses,"* 15.
4. Both in the magazine version of "Go Down, Moses" and in the version that appears as the final chapter of the novel, this character's name is spelled "Mollie." I have regularized the spelling to "Molly," in conformity with Faulkner's practice elsewhere in *Go Down, Moses*.
5. Michael Millgate, *The Achievement of William Faulkner*, 39.
6. "The WP&A," *Time*, 11 August 1941, 71.
7. A. I. Bezzerides, *William Faulkner: A Life on Paper*, 71.
8. John Spencer Bassett, *The Southern Plantation Overseer, As Revealed in His Letters*, 35, 49, 261.
9. Bassett, *The Southern Plantation Overseer*, 10, 17.
10. Lewis P. Simpson, *The Dispossessed Garden: Pastoral and History in Southern Literature*, 3, 12, 13, 15. See also Simpson, "The Southern Literary Vocation." For a placement of *Go Down, Moses* within a definition of South-

ern pastoral as a nostalgic dream of an idealized golden age, see Lucinda Hardwick MacKethan, *The Dream of Arcady: Place and Time in Southern Literature*, 153–80.

11. Simpson, *The Dispossessed Garden*, 22–24.
12. Thomas Jefferson, *Notes on the State of Virginia*, 143, 164–65.
13. Simpson, *The Dispossessed Garden*, 30, 32.
14. But see Lewis P. Simpson's argument, in "Faulkner and the Southern Symbolism of Pastoral," that "Faulkner rejected the pastoral mode" (p. 403) of the literary vocation, adopting instead an urban ideal of the writer's life, grounded in history.
15. Kenneth S. Lynn, *Mark Twain and Southwestern Humor*, 6–20.
16. Simpson, *The Dispossessed Garden*, 25–26, 43.
17. William R. Taylor, *Cavalier and Yankee: The Old South and American National Character*, 167–72; Charles H. Bohner, *John Pendleton Kennedy: Gentleman from Baltimore*, 8, 79.
18. John Pendleton Kennedy. *Swallow Barn, or a Sojourn in the Old Dominion*, vii, 91, 436.
19. Kennedy, *Swallow Barn*, 8, 27, 29, 229, 232–34, 356–57.
20. Kennedy, *Swallow Barn*, 75, 442, 446, 448.
21. Bohner, *John Pendleton Kennedy*, 86 (Bohner's italics).
22. Bohner, *John Pendleton Kennedy*, 79; J. V. Ridgely, *John Pendleton Kennedy*, 37–38.
23. [J. G. deR. Hamilton], "Turner, Nat," *Dictionary of American Biography*, 19:69–70.
24. Kennedy, *Swallow Barn*, 460, 463, 465, 466, 467–68.
25. Kennedy, *Swallow Barn*, 468–84.
26. Jean Fagan Yellin, *The Intricate Knot: Black Figures in American Literature, 1776–1863*, 59.
27. Kennedy, *Swallow Barn*, 465.
28. Bassett, *The Southern Plantation Overseer*, 263.
29. Taylor, *Cavalier and Yankee*, 137–40.
30. Francis Pendleton Gaines, *The Southern Plantation: A Study in the Development and the Accuracy of a Tradition*, 17, 219; Donald Bogle, *Toms, Coons, Mulattoes, Mammies, and Bucks: An Interpretive History of Blacks in American Films*; John W. Blassingame, *The Slave Community: Plantation Life in the Antebellum South*, 133.
31. Robert Bone, *The Negro Novel in America*, 59–60.
32. See Thadious Davis, *Faulkner's "Negro": Art and the Southern Context*, 32–64 passim; Taylor, *Faulkner's Search for a South*, 31–35, 42–51.
33. For a possible real-life source of Deacon's Uncle-Tom theatrics, see Ben Wasson's description of Faulkner's reaction to "Blind Jim" (CNC, 43–44).

34. For a discussion of Deacon as "Quentin's double," see Thadious Davis, *Faulkner's "Negro,"* 94–95. For a discussion of race as a repressed subject in *The Sound and the Fury*, see Eric J. Sundquist, *Faulkner: The House Divided*, 26–27.

35. Compare Faulkner's remarks to an audience in Virginia in 1958: "[T]he white man can never really know the Negro, because the white man has forced the Negro to be always a Negro rather than another human being in their dealings, and therefore the Negro cannot afford, does not dare, to be open with the white man and let the white man know what he, the Negro, thinks" (ESPL, 157). For a discussion of the contradictions among Faulkner's statements about blacks, see Donald A. Petesch, "Faulkner on Negroes: The Conflict Between the Public Man and the Private Art."

36. For a confirmation of the authenticity of Shegog's sermon, including his shift from one voice to another, see Bruce Rosenberg, *The Art of the American Folk Preacher*, 117, 258. For a judgment of Shegog's sermon as a "not completely successful" but "admirable attempt," see Thadious Davis, *Faulkner's "Negro,"* 122n. See Davis, 111–23, on the relationship between "linguistic transformations" and black characterization. See also Stephen M. Ross, "Rev. Shegog's Powerful Voice."

37. James Weldon Johnson, "Preface," in *The Book of American Negro Poetry*, 41–42.

38. James Weldon Johnson, *Along This Way: The Autobiography of James Weldon Johnson*, 335–36. See Louis D. Rubin's treatment of this episode in "The Search for a Language, 1746–1923," 19–26.

39. On Shegog as a "double of the novelist," who "signals the writer's willing renunciation of his authorial pride and of his prerogatives as a fiction-maker," see André Bleikasten, *The Most Splendid Failure: Faulkner's "The Sound and the Fury,"* 200–201. But see also John T. Matthews's contrary view, in *The Play of Faulkner's Language*, 42–43.

40. In 1924, Faulkner actually presented a copy of *The Marble Faun* to Joe Parks, a probable model for Flem Snopes (Louis Daniel Brodsky and Thomas Verich, *William Faulkner's Gifts of Friendship: Presentation and Inscribed Copies from the Faulkner Collection of Louis D. Brodsky*, item 4.

41. BL, 1057, 1069; MBB, 207–9. For William's firm denial of having read John's *novels*, see BLRO, 99.

42. John Faulkner, "Lawd! Lawd!" 62.

43. "The WP&A," *Time*, 71.

44. John Bradbury, *Renaissance in the South: A Critical History of the Literature, 1920–1960*, 82–83; Lewis P. Simpson, "Roark Whitney Wickliffe Bradford," in *Southern Writers: A Biographical Dictionary*, ed. Robert Bain, Joseph M. Flora, and Louis D. Rubin, Jr., 44–45. Faulkner renewed their acquain-

tance in 1934, when he went to New Orleans to observe an air show. He stayed with the Bradfords while he was there, and he took home with him one of Bradford's books, *Let the Band Play Dixie and Other Stories*, as a memento. In *Pylon*, written later in the year, the character Hagood seems to have been based on Bradford (BL, 835–36, 870; Joseph Blotner, comp., *William Faulkner's Library: A Catalogue*, 19).

45. Roark Bradford, "The Cows in the Corn," 28.
46. Roark Bradford, "Manuscript Dice," 20, 70, 72–73.
47. They include Hortense Powdermaker, *After Freedom: A Cultural Study in the Deep South*; Allison Davis, Burleigh B. Gardner, and Mary R. Gardner, *Deep South: A Social Anthropological Study of Caste and Class*; Arthur Raper, *Preface to Peasantry: A Tale of Two Black Belt Counties*; Gunnar Myrdal, *An American Dilemma: The Negro Problem and Modern Democracy.*
48. John Dollard, *Caste and Class in a Southern Town*, 21, 368.
49. Lyle H. Lanier, "Mr. Dollard and Scientific Method," 657–72.
50. Bradford, "Manuscript Dice," 70.
51. Roark Bradford, "Double-Yolk Hoodoo," 15, 34, 37.
52. Thadious Davis, *Faulkner's "Negro,"* 214.
53. Before Blotner's biography, the best account of the novel's composition history was James Early's *The Making of "Go Down, Moses."* Early's work is flawed, however, by his assumption that "The Bear" rather than "Delta Autumn" constituted the turning point in its composition. He attributed the revisions in the previously published stories of the volume to the necessity of adapting them to "the genealogical plan and the powerful themes of 'The Bear'" (p. 71). But Blotner revealed that Faulkner began the revision process soon after composing "Delta Autumn," and that he did not start writing "The Bear" until that process was nearly complete (BL, 1064–80).
54. George B. Tindall, *The Emergence of the New South, 1913–1945*, 60–61.
55. See Peter L. Hays, "Significant Names in 'Delta Autumn.'"
56. Federal Writers' Project of the Works Progress Administration, *Mississippi: A Guide to the Magnolia State*, 48; Calvin S. Brown, *Archeology of Mississippi*, 4–9; Blotner, comp., *William Faulkner's Library*, 113. Brown's book describes many mounds in great detail. According to Faulkner's stepson Malcolm Franklin, Faulkner "knew" and "liked" the book (BLRO, 16).
57. See also Horace Benbow's yearning for a refuge from his sterile marriage: "I thought that maybe I would be all right if I just had a hill to lie on for a while— It was that country. . . . That Delta. Five thousand square miles, without any hill save the bumps of dirt the Indians made to stand on when the River overflowed" (SY, 16).
58. Faulkner typed the television version of "Old Man" onto the verso pages of an early draft of "Mississippi" ("Old Man," 22-page typescript).

59. Mark Twain, "Old Times on the Mississippi," in *Great Short Works of Mark Twain*, 27.
60. Thomas L. McHaney, "Faulkner Borrows from the Mississippi Guide," 116–20.
61. Faulkner was describing Sardis Reservoir, a TVA dam which the government completed in 1937 to *prevent* floods on the Tallahatchie, Sunflower, and Yazoo rivers. According to Elizabeth Kerr, "the Indian Mound referred to in 'A Bear Hunt,'" which lay "[f]ive miles down the river from the camp," became "almost an island, as no doubt it was during floods in ancient days." Perhaps this phenomenon, occurring at about the time he wrote "Old Man," affected his symbolic use of Indian mounds (Elizabeth M. Kerr, *Yoknapatawpha: Faulkner's "Little Postage Stamp of Native Soil"*, 56–57). For Faulkner's irate response to the damming of a favorite fishing stream in the late forties, see Louis Daniel Brodsky, "Reflections on William Faulkner: An Interview with A. I. Bezzerides," 388.
62. For one explication of the "patterns of action" and the "patterns of meaning" that unify the stories of *Go Down, Moses* into a novel, see Dirk Kuyk, Jr., *Threads Cable-strong: William Faulkner's "Go Down, Moses."*
63. Brown, *Archeology of Mississippi*, 7, 349–53; Jack D. L. Holmes, "Spanish Policy toward the Southern Indians in the 1790s," 71–72.
64. But see Walter Taylor's hopeful estimation of the woman's future, to which Ike is blind, in *Faulkner's Search for a South*, 133–35.
65. On the revision of "Delta Autumn," see Carol C. Harter, "The Winter of Isaac McCaslin: Revisions and Irony in Faulkner's 'Delta Autumn.'"
66. This phrase appears only in the *Saturday Evening Post* version of "The Bear," which Faulkner "carefully tailored" to "a mass audience," according to Blotner (BL, 1085–86).
67. Karl Zender, in "Faulkner at Forty: The Artist at Home," explores the autobiographical origins of both the dialogue between Ike and Cass and the struggle between Lucas and Roth. Cass and Roth are figures of social responsibility; Ike and Lucas are figures of artistic freedom. In both pairings, "Faulkner opposed himself to himself" (p. 299). See also Margaret M. Dunn, "The Illusion of Freedom in *The Hamlet* and *Go Down, Moses*."
68. On the relationship of inheritance to textuality in *Go Down, Moses*, see David Minter, *William Faulkner: His Life and Work*, 187; Matthews, *The Play of Faulkner's Language*, 248–49.
69. Faulkner, "An Introduction to *The Sound and the Fury*," in *A Faulkner Miscellany*, 161.
70. Faulkner, "An Introduction for *The Sound and the Fury*," *Southern Review*, 709.

71. See J. Douglas Canfield, "Faulkner's Grecian Urn and Ike McCaslin's Empty Legacies."

72. For a survey of the ambivalent echoes of this poem throughout Faulkner's writing, see Joan S. Korenman, "Faulkner's Grecian Urn."

73. Contrast the end of "Race at Morning," written in 1954, where Mister Ernest sends the illiterate young narrator to school because "just to belong to the farming business and the hunting business ain't enough. You got to belong to the business of mankind" (BW, 175, 196).

74. See Minter, *William Faulkner: His Life and Work*, 189: *Go Down, Moses* "defines every text as an ur-text and pre-text, and then requires us to begin making connections and patterns that we must then revise or even repudiate."

75. See Karl Zender, "Reading in 'The Bear,'" for an examination of "The Bear's" "intimations of Faulkner's loss of faith in the power of reading to reveal the world" (p. 96). See also Patrick McGee, "Gender and Generation in Faulkner's 'The Bear.'" McGee characterizes Ike's response to the "Ode" as mistaken and Cass's as "shrewd" (p. 51), suggesting that Faulkner was actually *confirming* the power of reading.

76. But see Matthews, *The Play of Faulkner's Language*, 259–60. Matthews substitutes for the "substantially naïve model of language" that "one might infer" from Ike's words a "more problematic analysis," according to which the truth is equivalent to "the play of complexities in a text."

77. Minter, *William Faulkner: His Life and Work*, 188.

78. For a discussion of late-nineteenth-century interpretations of Southern history as Providential, see Fred Hobson, *Tell About the South: The Southern Rage to Explain*, 85–87. For Robert Lewis Dabney and other apologists for the Confederacy, Hobson writes, "the defeat came to be seen as *felix culpa*: the South had fallen *because* it was God's Chosen. It needed to be taught to fail and to suffer, and it would profit from the lesson in the end" (p. 86). For a mid-twentieth-century assertion of God's role in Southern history, see Hobson's discussion of James McBride Dabbs, 335–48.

79. For a contrary view of Stevens's *"poésie pure,"* as evidence that Stevens is "a type of the literary creator," see Patrick Samway, S.J., "Gavin Stevens as Uncle-Creator in *Knight's Gambit*," 150–51, 162.

80. Joel Chandler Harris, "As to Education," in *Uncle Remus: His Songs and His Sayings*, 216.

81. Russell, *Poems*, 4. A radio station in Charlottesville, Virginia, recorded Faulkner reading this poem in December 1961 (BL, 1806).

82. Julia Peterkin, *Scarlet Sister Mary*, 196–97.

83. Russell, "The Polyphone," *Poems*, 79–81.

84. Mark Twain, *Adventures of Huckleberry Finn*, in *Mississippi Writings*, 701.

85. John Charles McNeill, *Lyrics from Cotton Land*, 15.
86. Rosenberg, *The Art of the American Folk Preacher*, 23, 44–45, 97, 102, 111, 188, 255.
87. Roark Bradford, "The Bible Boys' Cotton," 11, 40–43.
88. Bradford, "Bible Boys' Cotton," 42.

Epilogue

1. Thomas L. McHaney, "Faulkner Borrows from the Mississippi Guide," 116–20.
2. George R. Sidney, "Faulkner in Hollywood: A Study of His Career as a Scenarist," 100–104.

WORKS CITED

Works by Faulkner

"Afternoon of a Cow." Under the pseudonym Ernest V. Trueblood. *Furioso* 2 (Summer 1947): 5–17.

"L'Après-Midi d'une Vache, par Ernest V. Trueblood." *Fontaine* 27–28 (June–July 1943): 66–81.

As I Lay Dying. New York: Vintage, 1964.

Big Woods. New York: Random House, 1955.

Collected Stories of William Faulkner. New York: Random House, 1950.

Elmer. Edited by Dianne L. Cox. Foreword by James B. Meriwether. *Mississippi Quarterly* 36 (Summer 1983): 337–460.

"An Error in Chemistry." *Ellery Queen's Mystery Magazine* 7 (June 1946): 4–19.

Essays, Speeches and Public Letters. Edited by James B. Meriwether. New York: Random House, 1966.

A Fable. New York: Random House, 1954.

Father Abraham. Edited by James B. Meriwether. New York: Random House, 1983.

Faulkner at West Point. Edited by Joseph L. Fant and Robert Ashley. New York: Vintage, 1969.

Faulkner in the University: Class Conferences at the University of Virginia, 1957–1958. Edited by Frederick L. Gwynn and Joseph L. Blotner. New York: Vintage, 1965.

"Faulkner's 'Ode to the Louver.'" Edited by J[ames] B. M[eriwether]. *Mississippi Quarterly* 27 (Summer 1974): 333–35.

Go Down, Moses. Modern Library issue. New York: Random House, 1955.

A Green Bough. 1933. Reprint with *The Marble Faun*. New York: Random House, 1965.

The Hamlet. 3rd ed. New York: Random House, 1964.

Helen: A Courtship. With *Mississippi Poems*. Introduction by Carvel Collins. New Orleans and Oxford, Miss.: Tulane University and Yoknapatawpha Press, 1981.

"An Introduction for *The Sound and the Fury.*" Edited by James B. Meriwether. *Southern Review* 8 (Autumn 1972): 705–10.

"An Introduction to *The Sound and the Fury.*" In *A Faulkner Miscellany,* edited by James B. Meriwether, 156–61. Jackson: University Press of Mississippi, 1974.

Intruder in the Dust. New York: Random House, 1948.

"Knight's Gambit," 23-page typescript. Series IA, Box 12, Item 15fl. William Faulkner Collections, Alderman Library, University of Virginia.

Knight's Gambit. New York: Random House, 1949.

Light in August. New York: Harrison Smith & Robert Haas, 1932.

Lion in the Garden: Interviews with William Faulkner: 1926–1962. Edited by James B. Meriwether and Michael Millgate. New York: Random House, 1968.

The Marble Faun. 1924. Reprint with *A Green Bough.* New York: Random House, 1965.

Mississippi Poems. With *Helen: A Courtship.* Introduction by Joseph Blotner. New Orleans and Oxford, Miss.: Tulane University and Yoknapatawpha Press, 1981.

Mosquitoes. New York: Boni & Liveright, 1927.

New Orleans Sketches. Edited by Carvel Collins. New York: Random House, 1968.

"Old Man," 22-page typescript. Series IV, Box 10, Item 3a. William Faulkner Collections, Alderman Library, University of Virginia.

"One Way to Catch a Horse," 36-page typescript. Series IV, Box 10, Item 4. William Faulkner Collections, Alderman Library, University of Virginia.

Pylon. New York: Harrison Smith & Robert Haas, 1935.

The Reivers. New York: Random House, 1962.

Requiem for a Nun. New York: Random House, 1951.

Sanctuary. Introduction by the author. Modern Library issue. New York: Random House, 1932.

Sartoris. New York: Harcourt, Brace, 1929.

Selected Letters of William Faulkner. Edited by Joseph Blotner. New York: Random House, 1977.

Sherwood Anderson & Other Famous Creoles: A Gallery of Contemporary New Orleans. By William Faulkner and William Spratling. New Orleans: Pelican, 1926.

Soldiers' Pay. New York: Liveright, 1970.

The Sound and the Fury. New York: Vintage, 1963.

The Town. New York: Random House, 1957.

Uncollected Stories of William Faulkner. Edited by Joseph Blotner. New York: Random House, 1979.

The Unvanquished. New York: Random House, 1938.

Vision in Spring. Introduction by Judith L. Sensibar. Austin: University of Texas Press, 1984.

The Wild Palms. New York: Random House, 1939.

William Faulkner: Early Prose and Poetry. Compiled and with an introduction by Carvel Collins. Boston: Atlantic-Little, Brown, 1962.

Secondary Works

Agee, James, and Walker Evans. *Let Us Now Praise Famous Men: Three Tenant Families.* 1941. Reprint. Boston: Houghton Mifflin, 1960.

Allen, James Lane. *A Kentucky Cardinal: A Story.* 1895. Reprint. Ridgewood, N.J.: Gregg, 1968.

Anderson, John Q. "Scholarship in Southwestern Humor—Past and Present." *Mississippi Quarterly* 17 (Spring 1964): 67–86.

Anderson, Sherwood. "A Meeting South." *Dial* 78 (April 1925): 269–79.

Arthos, John. "Ritual and Humor in the Writing of William Faulkner." *Accent* 9 (Autumn 1948): 17–30.

Asch, Nathan. *The Road: In Search of America.* New York: Norton, 1937.

Bain, Robert, Joseph M. Flora, and Louis D. Rubin, Jr., eds. *Southern Writers: A Biographical Dictionary.* Baton Rouge: Louisiana State University Press, 1979.

Baker, Carlos. *Hemingway: The Writer as Artist.* 4th ed. Princeton: Princeton University Press, 1972.

Bassett, John Spencer. *The Southern Plantation Overseer, As Revealed in His Letters.* Northampton, Mass.: Smith College, 1925.

Basso, Hamilton. *Courthouse Square.* New York: Scribner's, 1936.

Beck, Warren. *Man in Motion: Faulkner's Trilogy.* Madison: University of Wisconsin Press, 1961.

Bergman, Andrew. *We're in the Money: Depression America and Its Films.* New York: Harper & Row, 1972.

Bergreen, Laurence. *James Agee: A Life.* New York: Dutton, 1984.

Bezzerides, A. I. *William Faulkner: A Life on Paper.* Edited by Ann Abadie. Introduction by Carvel Collins. Jackson: University Press of Mississippi, 1980.

Black, C. M. "He Serves Up America." *Collier's* (3 August 1940): 22, 38.

Blake, Fay M. *The Strike in the American Novel.* Metuchen, N.J.: Scarecrow, 1972.

Blassingame, John W. *The Slave Community: Plantation Life in the Antebellum South.* New York: Oxford University Press, 1972.

Bleikasten, André. *The Most Splendid Failure: Faulkner's "The Sound and the Fury."* Bloomington: Indiana University Press, 1976.

Blotner, Joseph. *Faulkner: A Biography.* 2 vols. New York: Random House, 1974.

————. *Faulkner: A Biography.* One-volume edition. New York: Random House, 1984.

————, ed. *Selected Letters of William Faulkner.* New York: Random House, 1977.

————, comp. *William Faulkner's Library: A Catalogue.* Charlottesville: University Press of Virginia, 1964.

Bogle, Donald. *Toms, Coons, Mulattoes, Mammies, and Bucks: An Interpretive History of Blacks in American Films.* New York: Viking, 1973.

Bohner, Charles H. *John Pendleton Kennedy: Gentleman from Baltimore.* Baltimore: Johns Hopkins Press, 1961.

Bone, Robert. *The Negro Novel in America.* 2nd ed., rev. New Haven: Yale University Press, 1965.

Bradbury, John M. *Renaissance in the South: A Critical History of the Literature, 1920–1960.* Chapel Hill: University of North Carolina Press, 1963.

Bradford, Roark. "The Bible Boys' Cotton." *Collier's* (2 November 1940): 11, 40–43.

————. "The Cows in the Corn." *Collier's* (15 October 1938): 14–15, 27–28.

————. "Double-Yolk Hoodoo." *Collier's* (12 September 1942): 15, 34, 36–37.

————. "The Manner of Heaven." *Collier's* (20 January 1940): 21, 37–38.

————. "Manuscript Dice." *Collier's* (9 November 1940): 20, 70, 72–73.

Brodsky, Louis Daniel. "Reflections on William Faulkner: An Interview with Albert I. Bezzerides." *Southern Review* 21 (Spring 1985): 376–403.

————, and Robert W. Hamblin, eds. *Faulkner: A Comprehensive Guide to the Brodsky Collection, Volume I: The Biobibliography.* Jackson: University Press of Mississippi, 1982.

————, and Robert W. Hamblin, eds. *Faulkner: A Comprehensive Guide to the Brodsky Collection, Volume II: The Letters.* Jackson: University Press of Mississippi, 1984.

————, and Thomas Verich, eds. *William Faulkner's Gifts of Friendship: Presentation and Inscribed Copies from the Faulkner Collection of Louis D. Brodsky.* Oxford: University of Mississippi, 1980.

Brooks, Cleanth. "Faulkner and the Fugitive-Agrarians." In *Faulkner and the Southern Renaissance: Faulkner and Yoknapatawpha, 1981,* edited by Doreen Fowler and Ann J. Abadie, 22–39. Jackson: University Press of Mississippi, 1982.

————. *William Faulkner: Toward Yoknapatawpha and Beyond.* New Haven: Yale University Press, 1978.

————. *William Faulkner: The Yoknapatawpha Country.* New Haven: Yale University Press, 1963.

————, R. W. B. Lewis, and Robert Penn Warren, eds. *American Literature: The Makers and the Making*. 2 vols. New York: St. Martin's, 1973.

Broughton, Panthea Reid. "An Interview with Meta Carpenter Wilde." *Southern Review* 18 (October 1982): 776–801.

Brown, Calvin S. *Archeology of Mississippi*. 1926. Reprint with introduction by Philip Phillips. New York: AMS, 1973.

Brown, Calvin S.[, Jr.]. "Faulkner's Localism." In *The Maker and the Myth: Faulkner and Yoknapatawpha*, 1977, edited by Evans Harrington and Ann J. Abadie, 3–24. Jackson: University Press of Mississippi, 1978.

Budd, Louis J. "Gentlemanly Humorists of the Old South." *Southern Folklore Quarterly* 17 (December 1953): 232–40.

Burgum, Edwin Berry. "Faulkner's New Novel." *New Masses* (7 February 1939): 23–24.

Caldwell, Erskine. *God's Little Acre*. New York: Duell, Sloan and Pearce, 1949.

————, and Margaret Bourke-White. *Say, Is This the U.S.A.?* New York: Duell, Sloan and Pearce, 1941.

Canfield, J. Douglas. "Faulkner's Grecian Urn and Ike McCaslin's Empty Legacies." *Arizona Quarterly* 36 (Winter 1980): 359–84.

Cash, W[ilbur] J[oseph]. *The Mind of the South*. New York: Knopf, 1941.

Cason, Clarence E. *90° in the Shade*. Chapel Hill: University of North Carolina Press, 1935.

Cauley, Troy J. *Agrarianism: A Program for Farmers*. Chapel Hill: University of North Carolina Press, 1935.

Cavell, Stanley. *Pursuits of Happiness: The Hollywood Comedy of Remarriage*. Cambridge: Harvard University Press, 1981.

Chaplin, Charles, dir. *Modern Times*. With Chaplin, Paulette Goddard, Chester Conklin. United Artists, 1936.

Coindreau, Maurice Edgar. "On Translating Faulkner." *Princeton University Library Chronicle* 18 (Spring 1957): 108–13.

————. *The Time of William Faulkner: A French View of Modern American Fiction*. Edited and translated by George McMillan Reeves. Columbia: University of South Carolina Press, 1971.

Coles, Robert. *Erik H. Erikson: The Growth of His Work*. Boston: Little, Brown, 1970.

Collins, Carvel. "Biographical Background for Faulkner's *Helen*." In *Helen: A Courtship and Mississippi Poems*, by William Faulkner, 9–110. New Orleans and Oxford, Miss.: Tulane University and Yoknapatawpha Press, 1981.

————. "Faulkner and Certain Earlier Southern Fiction." *College English* 16 (November 1954): 92–97.

Cooley, Thomas W., Jr. "Faulkner Draws the Long Bow." *Twentieth Century Literature* 16 (October 1970): 268–77.

Couch, W. T. "An Agrarian Programme for the South." *American Review* 3 (Summer 1934): 313–26.

———, ed. *Culture in the South.* Chapel Hill: University of North Carolina Press, 1934.

Cowan, Louise. *The Fugitive Group: A Literary History.* Baton Rouge: Louisiana State University Press, 1959.

Cowley, Malcolm. *The Faulkner-Cowley File: Letters and Memories, 1944–1962.* New York: Viking, 1966.

———. "Sanctuary." *New Republic* (25 January 1939): 349.

Cox, James M. "The South Once More." *Sewanee Review* 82 (Winter 1974): 163–78.

Creighton, Joanne Vanish. *William Faulkner's Craft of Revision: The Snopes Trilogy, "The Unvanquished," and "Go down, Moses."* Detroit: Wayne State University Press, 1977.

Cross, Richard K. "The Humor of *The Hamlet.*" *Twentieth Century Literature* 12 (January 1967): 203–15.

Cullen, John B., and Floyd C. Watkins. *Old Times in the Faulkner Country.* Chapel Hill: University of North Carolina Press, 1961.

Cumpiano, Marion W. "The Motif of Return: Currents and Counter Currents in 'Old Man' by William Faulkner." *Southern Humanities Review* 13 (Summer 1978): 185–93.

Cutrer, Thomas W., ed. "Conference on Literature and Reading in the South and Southwest, 1935." *Southern Review* 21 (Spring 1985): 260–300.

Dabney, Virginius. *Below the Potomac: A Book About the New South.* New York: Appleton-Century, 1942.

———. *Liberalism in the South.* Chapel Hill: University of North Carolina Press, 1932.

Daniels, Jonathan. *A Southerner Discovers the South.* New York: Macmillan, 1938.

Davidson, Donald. "The Class Approach to Southern Problems." *Southern Review* 5 (Autumn 1939): 261–72.

———. *The Spyglass: Views and Reviews, 1924–1930.* Selected and edited by John T. Fain. Nashville: Vanderbilt University Press, 1963.

———. "The Trend of Literature: A Partisan View." In *Culture in the South,* edited by W. T. Couch, 183–210. Chapel Hill: University of North Carolina Press, 1934.

Davis, Allison, Burleigh B. Gardner, and Mary R. Gardner. *Deep South: A Social Anthropological Study of Caste and Class.* Chicago: University of Chicago Press, 1941.

Davis, Thadious M. *Faulkner's "Negro": Art and the Southern Context.* Baton Rouge: Louisiana State University Press, 1983.

Dickens, Byrom. "T. S. Stribling and the South." *Sewanee Review* 42 (July–September 1934): 341–49.

Dickens, Charles. *Oliver Twist.* New York: Dodd, Mead, 1949.

Dickerson, Mary Jane. "Faulkner's Golden Steed." *Mississippi Quarterly* 31 (Summer 1978): 369–80.

Dictionary of American Biography. Edited by Allen Johnson and Dumas Malone. 20 vols. New York: Scribner's, 1928–37.

Dollard, John. *Caste and Class in a Southern Town.* 3rd ed. Garden City, N. Y.: Doubleday, [1957].

Douglas, W. W. "Deliberate Exiles: The Social Sources of Agrarian Poetics." In *Aspects of American Poetry: Essays Presented to Howard Mumford Jones,* edited by Richard M. Ludwig, 273–300. Columbus: Ohio State University Press, 1962.

Drucker, Peter F. *Adventures of a Bystander.* New York: Harper & Row, 1978.

Dunn, Margaret M. "The Illusion of Freedom in *The Hamlet* and *Go Down, Moses.*" *American Literature* 57 (October 1985): 407–23.

Early, James. *The Making of "Go Down, Moses."* Dallas: Southern Methodist University Press, 1972.

Eby, Cecil D. "Faulkner and the Southwestern Humorists." *Shenandoah* 11 (Autumn 1959): 13–21.

———. "Ichabod Crane in Yoknapatawpha." *Georgia Review* 16 (Winter 1962): 465–69.

Eisenstein, Sergei. *Film Form: Essays in Film Theory.* Edited and translated by Jay Leyda. New York: Harcourt, Brace & World, 1949.

———. *Immoral Memories: An Autobiography.* Boston: Houghton Mifflin, 1983.

Ellison, Ralph. *Shadow and Act.* New York: Random House, 1964.

Empson, William. *Some Versions of Pastoral.* 1935. Reprint. Norfolk, Conn.: New Directions, 1960.

Erikson, Erik H. *Gandhi's Truth: On the Origins of Militant Nonviolence.* New York: Norton, 1969.

———. *Identity: Youth and Crisis.* New York: Norton, 1968.

———. *Young Man Luther: A Study in Psychoanalysis and History.* New York: Norton, 1958.

Ewing, Jack. "Collector Finds Consolation Stone." *Faulkner Newsletter & Yoknapatawpha Review* 1, no. 3 (July–September 1981): 2.

Falkner, Murry C. *The Falkners of Mississippi: A Memoir.* Baton Rouge: Louisiana State University Press, 1967.

Faulkner, John. "Good Neighbors." *Collier's* (7 November 1942): 17, 60, 62–66.

———. "Lawd! Lawd!" *Collier's* (10 October 1942): 62–65.

———. *My Brother Bill: An Affectionate Reminiscence.* New York: Trident, 1963.

―――. "Progress Report." *Collier's* (14 June 1941): 18, 25–27, 30.

―――. "Treasure Trail." *Collier's* (6 March 1943): 60, 65–68.

Faust, Drew Gilpin. *A Sacred Circle: The Dilemma of the Intellectual in the Old South, 1840–1860.* Baltimore: Johns Hopkins University Press, 1977.

Federal Writers' Project of the Works Progress Administration. *Mississippi: A Guide to the Magnolia State.* New York: Viking, 1938.

Ferguson, Charles A. *Language Structure and Language Use: Essays by Charles A. Ferguson.* Selected and introduced by Anwar S. Dil. Stanford, Calif.: Stanford University Press, 1971.

Flanagan, John T. "Folklore in Faulkner's Fiction." *Papers on Language and Literature* 5 (Summer supplement 1969): 119–44.

Foote, Horton. "On First Dramatizing Faulkner." In *Faulkner, Modernism, and Film: Faulkner and Yoknapatawpha, 1978,* edited by Evans Harrington and Ann J. Abadie, 49–65. Jackson: University Press of Mississippi, 1979.

Ford, John, dir. *The Hurricane.* With Jon Hall, Dorothy Lamour, Thomas Mitchell, Raymond Massey. Produced by Samuel Goldwyn, 1937.

Fowler, Doreen A. "Measuring Faulkner's Tall Convict." *Studies in the Novel* 14 (Fall 1982): 280–84.

Fox, John, Jr. *"Hell fer Sartain" and Other Stories.* New York: Harper & Brothers, 1897.

Franklin, Malcolm. *Bitterweeds: Life with William Faulkner at Rowan Oak.* Irving, Tex.: Society For The Study Of Traditional Culture, 1977.

French, Warren. "William Faulkner and the Art of the Detective Story." In *The Thirties: Fiction, Poetry, Drama,* edited by Warren French, 55–62. Deland, Fla.: Everett Edwards, 1967.

Freud, Sigmund. *The Interpretation of Dreams.* Translated by James Strachey. New York: Avon, 1965.

Gaines, Francis Pendleton. *The Southern Plantation: A Study in the Development and the Accuracy of a Tradition.* New York: Columbia University Press, 1925.

Geismar, Maxwell. "A Cycle of Fiction." In *Literary History of the United States,* edited by Robert E. Spiller, Willard Thorp, Thomas H. Johnson, and Henry Seidel Canby, rev. ed., 1296–1316. New York: Macmillan, 1953.

Gidley, Mick. "Elements of the Detective Story in William Faulkner's Fiction." *Journal of Popular Culture* 7 (Summer 1973): 97–123.

Gordon, Caroline. *The Garden of Adonis.* New York: Scribner's, 1937.

Greet, T. Y. "The Theme and Structure of Faulkner's *The Hamlet.*" PMLA 72 (September 1957): 775–90.

Grimwood, Michael. "Lyle Saxon's *Father Mississippi* as a Source for Faulkner's 'Old Man' and 'Mississippi.'" *Notes on Mississippi Writers* 17 (1985): 55–62.

Hamblin, Robert W. "'Carcassonne': Faulkner's Allegory of Art and the Artist." *Southern Review* 15 (Spring 1979): 355–65.

[Hamilton, J. G. deR.] "Turner, Nat." *Dictionary of American Biography.* Vol. 19: 69–70. New York: Scribner's, 1936.

Harrington, Gary. "Distant Mirrors: The Intertextual Relationship of Quentin Compson and Harry Wilbourne." *Faulkner Journal* 1 (Fall 1985): 41–45.

Harris, Joel Chandler. *Uncle Remus: His Songs and His Sayings.* Edited by Robert Hemenway. Harmondsworth, England: Penguin, 1982.

Harris, Julia Collier. *The Life and Letters of Joel Chandler Harris.* Boston: Houghton Mifflin, 1918.

Harter, Carol Clancey. "The Winter of Isaac McCaslin: Revisions and Irony in Faulkner's 'Delta Autumn.'" *Journal of Modern Literature* 1 (1970–71): 209–25.

Hayhoe, George F. "Faulkner in Hollywood: A Checklist of His Film Scripts at the University of Virginia." *Mississippi Quarterly* 31 (Summer 1978): 407–19.

———. "Faulkner in Hollywood: A Checklist of his Filmscripts at the University of Virginia: A Correction and Additions." *Mississippi Quarterly* 32 (Summer 1979): 467–72.

Hays, Peter L. "Significant Names in 'Delta Autumn.'" *Notes on Modern American Literature* 6 (Winter 1982): item 19.

Hemingway, Ernest. *To Have and Have Not.* New York: Scribner's, 1937.

Hicks, Granville. "Writers in the Thirties." In *As We Saw the Thirties: Essays on Social and Political Movements of a Decade,* edited by Rita James Simon, 76–101. Urbana: University of Illinois Press, 1967.

Hoadley, Frank M. "Folk Humor in the Novels of William Faulkner." *Tennessee Folklore Society Bulletin* 23 (September 1957): 75–82.

Hobson, Fred. *Tell About the South: The Southern Rage to Explain.* Baton Rouge: Louisiana State University Press, 1983.

Holland, Norman N. *The Dynamics of Literary Response.* New York: Oxford University Press, 1968.

Holman, C. Hugh. "*Absalom, Absalom!*: The Historian as Detective." *Sewanee Review* 79 (Autumn 1971): 542–53.

Holmes, Jack D. L. "Spanish Policy toward the Southern Indians in the 1790s." In *Four Centuries of Southern Indians,* edited by Charles M. Hudson, 65–82. Athens: University of Georgia Press, 1975.

Hooper, Johnson Jones. *Adventures of Captain Simon Suggs, Late of the Tallapoosa Volunteers.* Introduction by Manly Wade Wellman. Southern Literary Classics Series. Chapel Hill: University of North Carolina Press, 1969.

Hopkins, Viola. "William Faulkner's *The Hamlet*: A Study in Meaning and Form." *Accent* 15 (Spring 1955): 125–44.

Howard, William. "Richard Wright's Flood Stories and the Great Mississippi River Flood of 1927: Social and Historical Backgrounds." *Southern Literary Journal* 16 (Spring 1984): 44–62.

Howe, Irving. *William Faulkner: A Critical Study*. 2nd ed. New York: Random House, 1962.

Howe, M. A. DeWolfe. "The Humorist's Honor." *Youth's Companion* 85, no. 1 (5 January 1911): 5.

Howell, Elmo. "Southern Fiction and the Pattern of Failure: The Example of Faulkner." *Georgia Review* 36 (Winter 1982): 755–70.

Howell, John M. "Faulkner, Prufrock, and Agamemnon: Horses, Hell, and High Water." In *Faulkner: the Unappeased Imagination: A Collection of Critical Essays*, edited by Glenn O. Carey, 213–29. Troy, N.Y.: Whitston, 1980.

Hurt, James. "All the Living and the Dead: Lincoln's Imagery." *American Literature* 52 (November 1980): 351–80.

Inge, M. Thomas. "William Faulkner and George Washington Harris: In the Tradition of Southwestern Humor." *Tennessee Studies in Literature* 7 (1962): 47–59.

Irish, Marion D. "Proposed Roads to the New South, 1941: Chapel Hill Planners vs. Nashville Agrarians." *Sewanee Review* 49 (January–March 1941): 1–27.

Irwin, John T. *Doubling and Incest/Repetition and Revenge: A Speculative Reading of Faulkner*. Baltimore: Johns Hopkins University Press, 1975.

Jackson, Blyden, and Louis D. Rubin, Jr. *Black Poetry in America: Two Essays in Historical Interpretation*. Baton Rouge: Louisiana State University Press, 1974.

Jefferson, Thomas. *Notes on the State of Virginia*. Edited by William Peden. New York: Norton, 1972.

Jehlen, Myra. *Class and Character in Faulkner's South*. New York: Columbia University Press, 1976.

Jenkins, Lee. *Faulkner and Black-White Relations: A Psychoanalytic Approach*. New York: Columbia University Press, 1981.

Jewkes, W. T. "Counterpoint in Faulkner's *The Wild Palms*." *Wisconsin Studies in Contemporary Literature* 2 (Winter 1961): 39–53.

Johnson, James Weldon. *Along This Way: The Autobiography of James Weldon Johnson*. New York: Viking, 1933.

————, ed. *The Book of American Negro Poetry*. Rev. ed. 1931. Reprint. New York: Harcourt, Brace & World, 1959.

Johnston, Richard Malcolm. *Dukesborough Tales: The Chronicles of Mr. Bill Williams*. 1871. Reprint. Ridgewood, N. J.: Gregg, 1968.

Karanikas, Alexander. *Tillers of a Myth: Southern Agrarians as Social and Literary Critics*. Madison: University of Wisconsin Press, 1966.

Kartiganer, Donald M. *The Fragile Thread: The Meaning of Form in Faulkner's Novels*. Amherst: University of Massachusetts Press, 1979.

Kawin, Bruce F. *Faulkner and Film.* New York: Frederick Ungar, 1977.

——. "Faulkner's Film Career: The Years with Hawks." In *Faulkner, Modernism, and Film: Faulkner and Yoknapatawpha, 1978,* edited by Evans Harrington and Ann J. Abadie, 163–81. Jackson: University Press of Mississippi, 1979.

——. "The Montage Element in Faulkner's Fiction." In *Faulkner, Modernism, and Film: Faulkner and Yoknapatawpha, 1978,* edited by Evans Harrington and Ann J. Abadie, 103–26. Jackson: University Press of Mississippi, 1979.

Kazin, Alfred. "A Study in Conscience." *New York Herald Tribune Books* (22 January 1939): 2.

Kennedy, John Pendleton. *Swallow Barn, or A Sojourn in the Old Dominion.* 2nd ed. 1853. Reprint. New York: Hafner, 1962.

Kerr, Elizabeth M. *Yoknapatawpha: Faulkner's "Little Postage Stamp of Native Soil."* New York: Fordham University Press, 1969.

King, Richard H. "*A Fable:* Faulkner's Political Novel?" *Southern Literary Journal* 17 (Spring 1985): 3–17.

——. "Framework of a Renaissance." In *Faulkner and the Southern Renaissance: Faulkner and Yoknapatawpha, 1981,* edited by Doreen Fowler and Ann J. Abadie, 3–21. Jackson: University Press of Mississippi, 1982.

——. *A Southern Renaissance: The Cultural Awakening of the American South, 1930–1955.* Oxford: Oxford University Press, 1980.

Kinney, Arthur F. *Faulkner's Narrative Poetics: Style as Vision.* Amherst: University of Massachusetts Press, 1978.

Klinkowitz, Jerome F. "The Thematic Unity of *Knight's Gambit.*" *Critique* 11 (1969): 81–100.

Korenman, Joan S. "Faulkner's Grecian Urn." *Southern Literary Journal* 7 (Fall 1974): 3–23.

Kovel, Joel. *White Racism: A Psychohistory.* New York: Pantheon, 1970.

Kreiswirth, Martin. "Faulkner as Translator: His Versions of Verlaine." *Mississippi Quarterly* 30 (Summer 1977): 429–32.

——. *William Faulkner: The Making of a Novelist.* Athens: University of Georgia Press, 1983.

Kunitz, Stanley J., and Howard Haycraft, eds. *Twentieth Century Authors: A Biographical Dictionary of Modern Literature.* New York: H. W. Wilson, 1942.

Kunitz, Stanley J., ed. *Twentieth Century Authors: A Biographical Dictionary of Modern Literature, First Supplement.* New York: H. W. Wilson, 1955.

Kuyk, Dirk, Jr. *Threads Cable-strong: William Faulkner's "Go Down, Moses."* Lewisburg, Penn.: Bucknell University Press, 1983.

Lanier, Lyle H. "Mr. Dollard and Scientific Method." *Southern Review* 3 (Spring 1938): 657–72.

Leaver, Florence. "The Structure of *The Hamlet.*" *Twentieth Century Literature* 1 (July 1955): 77–84.

Lebeaux, Richard. *Young Man Thoreau.* Amherst: University of Massachusetts Press, 1977.

Leonardo da Vinci. *The Notebooks of Leonardo da Vinci.* Compiled from the original manuscripts by Jean Paul Richter. 2 vols. New York: Dover, 1970.

LeRoy, Mervyn, dir. *I Am a Fugitive from a Chain Gang.* With Paul Muni. Warner Brothers, 1932.

Lewis, R. W. B. *The American Adam: Innocence, Tragedy, and Tradition in the Nineteenth Century.* Chicago: University of Chicago Press, 1955.

Lisca, Peter. "The Hamlet: Genesis and Revisions." *Faulkner Studies* 3 (Spring 1954): 5–13.

Littell, Robert. "Outstanding Novels." *Yale Review* 29 (Summer 1940): viii, x.

Longstreet, Augustus Baldwin. *Georgia Scenes: Characters, Incidents, Etc., in the First Half Century of the Republic.* Introduction by B. R. McElderry, Jr. American Century Series. New York: Sagamore, 1957.

Lorentz, Pare, dir. *The River.* With score by Virgil Thompson. Farm Security Administration, 1937.

———. *The River.* New York: Stackpole, 1938.

Lumpkin, Grace. *To Make My Bread.* New York: Macaulay, 1932.

Lynn, Kenneth S. *Mark Twain and Southwestern Humor.* Boston: Atlantic-Little, Brown, 1959.

McGee, Patrick. "Gender and Generation in Faulkner's 'The Bear.'" *Faulkner Journal* 1 (Fall 1985): 46–54.

McHaney, Thomas L. "Anderson, Hemingway, and Faulkner's *The Wild Palms.*" *PMLA* 87 (May 1972): 465–74.

———. "Faulkner Borrows from the Mississippi Guide." *Mississippi Quarterly* 19 (Summer 1966): 116–20.

———. *William Faulkner's "The Wild Palms": A Study.* Jackson: University Press of Mississippi, 1975.

MacKethan, Lucinda Hardwick. *The Dream of Arcady: Place and Time in Southern Literature.* Baton Rouge: Louisiana State University Press, 1980.

McNeill, John Charles. *Lyrics from Cotton Land.* Charlotte, N. C.: Stone, 1907.

Martin, Jay. "'The Whole Burden of Man's History of His Impossible Heart's Desire': The Early Life of William Faulkner." *American Literature* 53 (January 1982): 607–29.

Matthews, John T. *The Play of Faulkner's Language.* Ithaca, N.Y.: Cornell University Press, 1982.

Maxwell, Allen. "The Wild Palms." *Southwest Review* 24 (April 1939): 357–60.

Merivale, Patricia. *Pan the Goat-God: His Myth in Modern Times.* Cambridge: Harvard University Press, 1969.

Meriwether, James B. "Augustus Baldwin Longstreet: Realist and Artist." *Mississippi Quarterly* 35 (Fall 1982): 351–64.

———. "Early Notices of Faulkner by Phil Stone and Louis Cochran." *Mississippi Quarterly* 17 (Summer 1964): 136–64.

Millgate, Michael. *The Achievement of William Faulkner.* New York: Random House, 1966.

———. "William Faulkner: The Two Voices." In *Southern Literature in Transition: Heritage and Promise,* edited by Philip Castille and William Osborne, 73–85. Memphis: Memphis State University Press, 1983.

Milum, Richard A. "Continuity and Change: The Horse, the Automobile, and the Airplane in Faulkner's Fiction." In *Faulkner: the Unappeased Imagination: A Collection of Critical Essays,* edited by Glenn O. Carey, 157–74. Troy, N.Y.: Whitston, 1980.

———. "Faulkner's 'Carcassonne': The Dream and the Reality." *Studies in Short Fiction* 15 (Spring 1978): 133–38.

Minter, David. *William Faulkner: His Life and Work.* Baltimore: Johns Hopkins University Press, 1980.

Moldenhauer, Joseph J. "Unity of Theme and Structure in *The Wild Palms.*" In *William Faulkner: Three Decades of Criticism,* edited by Frederick J. Hoffman and Olga W. Vickery, 305–22. East Lansing: Michigan State University Press, 1960.

Morrison, Joseph L. *W. J. Cash, Southern Prophet: A Biography and Reader.* New York: Knopf, 1967.

Mortimer, Gail L. *Faulkner's Rhetoric of Loss: A Study in Perception and Meaning.* Austin: University of Texas Press, 1983.

Mott, Frank Luther. *A History of American Magazines.* 5 vols. Cambridge: Harvard University Press, 1930–1968.

Moussinac, Léon. *Sergei Eisenstein: An Investigation into His Films and Philosophy.* Translated by D. Sandy Petrey. New York: Crown, 1970.

Myrdal, Gunnar. *An American Dilemma: The Negro Problem and Modern Democracy.* New York: Harper & Brothers, 1944.

"The New Pictures: *Hurricane.*" *Time* (15 November 1937): 41–42.

Nixon, Herman Clarence. *Forty Acres and Steel Mules.* Chapel Hill: University of North Carolina Press, 1938.

Nordhoff, Charles, and James Norman Hall. *The Hurricane.* Boston: Little, Brown, 1935.

Norton, Charles A. *Melville Davisson Post: Man of Many Mysteries.* Bowling Green, Ohio: Bowling Green University Popular Press, 1973.

Nugent, Frank S. "The Screen: Samuel Goldwyn Turns Nordhoff-Hall 'Hurricane' Loose Across the Screen of the Astor." *New York Times* (10 November 1937): 31.

O'Brien, Michael. *The Idea of the American South, 1920–1941*. Baltimore: Johns Hopkins University Press, 1979.

O'Donnell, E. P. *Green Margins*. Boston: Houghton Mifflin, 1936.

O'Donnell, George Marion. "Faulkner's Mythology." *Kenyon Review* 1 (Summer 1939): 285–99.

———. "Looking Down the Cotton Row." In *Who Owns America? A New Declaration of Independence*, edited by Herbert Agar and Allen Tate, 161–77. Boston: Houghton Mifflin, 1936.

———, and Richmond Croom Beatty. "The Tenant Farmer in the South." *American Review* 5 (April 1935): 75–96.

Odum, Howard W. *Southern Regions of the United States*. Chapel Hill: University of North Carolina Press, 1936.

Ovid. *The Metamorphoses*. Translated by Horace Gregory. New York: New American Library, 1958.

Page, Thomas Nelson. *The Old South: Essays Social and Political*. New York: Scribner's, 1894.

Parker, George Lawrence. "The Body Guard." *St. Nicholas* 39 (May 1912): 640–41.

Parks, Edd Winfield. *Segments of Southern Thought*. Athens: University of Georgia Press, 1938.

Pearce, Richard. "'Pylon,' 'Awake and Sing!' and the Apocalyptic Imagination of the 30's." *Criticism* 13 (Spring 1971): 131–41.

Perry, George Sessions. *Hold Autumn in Your Hand*. New York: Viking, 1941.

Peterkin, Julia. *Scarlet Sister Mary*. Indianapolis: Bobbs-Merrill, 1928.

Peterson, Theodore. *Magazines in the Twentieth Century*. Urbana: University of Illinois Press, 1964.

Petesch, Donald A. "Faulkner on Negroes: The Conflict Between the Public Man and the Private Art." *Southern Humanities Review* 10 (Winter 1976): 55–64.

Phillips, William. "What Happened in the 30's." *Commentary* 34 (September 1962): 204–12.

Pitavy, François L. "Forgetting Jerusalem: An Ironical Chart for *The Wild Palms*." In *Intertextuality in Faulkner*, edited by Michel Gresset and Noel Polk, 114–27. Jackson: University Press of Mississippi, 1985.

———. "Idiocy and Idealism: A Reflection on the Faulknerian Idiot." In *Faulkner and Idealism: Perspectives from Paris*, edited by Michel Gresset and Patrick Samway, S.J., 97–111. Jackson: University Press of Mississippi, 1983.

Poggioli, Renato. *The Oaten Flute: Essays on Pastoral Poetry and the Pastoral Ideal*. Cambridge: Harvard University Press, 1975.

Poirier, Richard. *The Performing Self: Compositions and Decompositions in the Languages of Contemporary Life*. New York: Oxford University Press, 1971.

Polk, Noel. "'The Dungeon Was Mother Herself': William Faulkner: 1927–1931." In *New Directions in Faulkner Studies: Faulkner and Yoknapatawpha, 1983*, edited by Doreen Fowler and Ann J. Abadie, 61–93. Jackson: University Press of Mississippi, 1984.

———. "William Faulkner's 'Carcassonne.'" *Studies in American Fiction* 12 (Spring 1984): 29–43.

Post, Melville Davisson. "The Broken Stirrup-Leather." *Saturday Evening Post* (3 June 1911): 12–13, 65–66.

———. *Uncle Abner: Master of Mysteries*. New York: Appleton-Century, 1937.

Powdermaker, Hortense. *After Freedom: A Cultural Study in the Deep South*. New York: Viking, 1939.

Pruvot, Monique. "Faulkner and the Voices of Orphism." In *Faulkner and Idealism: Perspectives from Paris*, edited by Michel Gresset and Patrick Samway, S.J., 127–43. Jackson: University Press of Mississippi, 1983.

Putzel, Max. *Genius of Place: William Faulkner's Triumphant Beginnings*. Southern Literary Series. Baton Rouge: Louisiana State University Press, 1985.

Rabinowitz, Peter J. "The Click of the Spring: The Detective Story as Parallel Structure in Dostoyevsky and Faulkner." *Modern Philology* 76 (May 1979): 355–69.

Rank, Otto. *The Double: A Psychoanalytic Study*. Translated and edited by Harry Tucker, Jr. Chapel Hill: University of North Carolina Press, 1971.

Ransom, John Crowe. "The Aesthetic of Regionalism." *American Review* 2 (January 1934): 290–310.

———. *Grace After Meat*. Introduction by Robert Graves. London: Leonard & Virginia Woolf, 1924.

———. "Modern with the Southern Accent." *Virginia Quarterly Review* 11 (April 1935): 184–200.

———. *The New Criticism*. Norfolk, Conn.: New Directions, 1941.

———. "Poetry: A Note in Ontology." *American Review* 3 (May 1934): 172–200.

Raper, Arthur F. *Preface to Peasantry: A Tale of Two Black Belt Counties*. Chapel Hill: University of North Carolina Press, 1936.

———. *Tenants of the Almighty*. With FSA photographs by Jack Delano. New York: Macmillan, 1943.

Redman, Ben Ray. "Faulkner's Double Novel." *Saturday Review of Literature* (21 January 1939): 5.

Reed, Joseph W., Jr. *Faulkner's Narrative*. New Haven: Yale University Press, 1973.

Reeves, Carolyn. "*The Wild Palms*: Faulkner's Chaotic Cosmos." *Mississippi Quarterly* 20 (Summer 1967): 148–57.

Renner, Charlotte. "Talking and Writing in Faulkner's Snopes Trilogy." *Southern Literary Journal* 15 (Fall 1982): 61–73.

Rhodes, Pamela, and Richard Godden. "*The Wild Palms:* Degraded Culture, Devalued Texts." In *Intertextuality in Faulkner,* edited by Michel Gresset and Noel Polk, 87–113. Jackson: University Press of Mississippi, 1985.

Richardson, H. Edward. *William Faulkner: The Journey to Self-Discovery.* Columbia: University of Missouri Press, 1969.

Ridgely, J. V. *John Pendleton Kennedy.* New York: Twayne, 1966.

Rosenberg, Bruce A. *The Art of the American Folk Preacher.* New York: Oxford University Press, 1970.

Rosenfield, Claire. "The Shadow Within: The Conscious and Unconscious Use of the Double." In *Stories of the Double,* edited by Albert J. Guerard, 311–31. Philadelphia: Lippincott, 1967.

Ross, Stephen M. "Rev. Shegog's Powerful Voice." *Faulkner Journal* 1 (Fall 1985): 8–16.

Roudiez, Leon S. "*Absalom, Absalom!* The Significance of Contradictions." *Minnesota Review* 17 (Fall 1981): 58–78.

Rovere, Richard H. "New Books: Faulkner, Mrs. Roosevelt, and Social History." *Harper's* (December 1949): 106, 110.

Rubin, Louis D., Jr. "The Dixie Special: William Faulkner and the Southern Literary Renascence." In *Faulkner and the Southern Renaissance: Faulkner and Yoknapatawpha, 1981,* edited by Doreen Fowler and Ann J. Abadie, 63–92. Jackson: University Press of Mississippi, 1982.

———. *A Gallery of Southerners.* Baton Rouge: Louisiana State University Press, 1982.

———. "The Great American Joke." *South Atlantic Quarterly* 72 (1973): 82–94.

———. "The Search for a Language, 1746–1923." In *Black Poetry in America: Two Essays in Historical Interpretation,* by Blyden Jackson and Rubin, 1–35. Baton Rouge: Louisiana State University Press, 1974.

———. "William Faulkner: The Discovery of a Man's Vocation." In *Faulkner: Fifty Years After "The Marble Faun,"* edited by George H. Wolfe, 43–68. Univeristy: University of Alabama Press, 1976.

———. *The Writer in the South: Studies in a Literary Community.* Mercer University Lamar Memorial Lectures, No. 15. Athens: University of Georgia Press, 1972.

Russell, Irwin. *Poems.* Introduction by Joel Chandler Harris. New York: Century, 1888.

St. Nicholas: An Illustrated Magazine for Young Folks 38 (November 1910, January 1911).

Samway, Patrick, S.J. "Gavin Stevens as Uncle-Creator in *Knight's Gambit.*" In

Faulkner and Idealism: Perspectives from Paris, edited by Michel Gresset and Patrick Samway, S.J., 144–63. Jackson: University Press of Mississippi, 1983.

Saxon, Lyle. *Father Mississippi.* New York: Century, 1927.

Schlepper, W. E. "Truth and Justice in *Knight's Gambit.*" *Mississippi Quarterly* 37 (Summer 1984): 365–75.

Sensibar, Judith L. *The Origins of Faulkner's Art.* Austin: University of Texas Press, 1984.

Sidney, George R. "Faulkner in Hollywood: A Study of His Career as a Scenarist." Ph.D. diss., University of New Mexico, 1959.

Simpson, Lewis P. *The Dispossessed Garden: Pastoral and History in Southern Literature.* Mercer University Lamar Memorial Lectures, No. 16. Athens: University of Georgia Press, 1975.

———. "Faulkner and the Legend of the Artist." In *Faulkner: Fifty Years After "The Marble Faun,"* edited by George H. Wolfe, 69–100. University: University of Alabama Press, 1976.

———. "Faulkner and the Southern Symbolism of Pastoral." *Mississippi Quarterly* 28 (Fall 1975): 401–15.

———. "The Loneliness of William Faulkner." *Southern Literary Journal* 8 (Fall 1975): 126–43.

———. *The Man of Letters in New England and the South: Essays on the History of the Literary Vocation in America.* Baton Rouge: Louisiana State University Press, 1973.

———. "Sex & History: Origins of Faulkner's Apocrypha." In *The Maker and the Myth: Faulkner and Yoknapatawpha, 1977,* edited by Evans Harrington and Ann J. Abadie, 43–70. Jackson: University Press of Mississippi, 1978.

———. "The Southern Literary Vocation." In *Toward a New American Literary History: Essays in Honor of Arlin Turner,* edited by Louis J. Budd, Edwin H. Cady, and Carl L. Anderson, 19–35. Durham, N.C.: Duke University Press, 1980.

Singal, Daniel Joseph. *The War Within: From Victorian to Modernist Thought in the South, 1919–1945.* Chapel Hill: University of North Carolina Press, 1982.

Skei, Hans H. "Faulkner's *Knight's Gambit:* Detection and Ingenuity." *Notes on Mississippi Writers* 13 (1981): 79–93.

———. *William Faulkner: The Short Story Career: An Outline of Faulkner's Short Story Writing from 1919 to 1962.* Oslo: Universitetsforlaget, 1981.

Slatoff, Walter J. *Quest for Failure: A Study of William Faulkner.* Ithaca, N.Y.: Cornell University Press, 1960.

Snell, Susan. "William Faulkner, Phil Stone, and Katrina Carter: A Biographical Footnote to the Summer of 1914." *Southern Literary Journal* 15 (Spring 1983): 76–86.

Snyder, Robert L. *Pare Lorentz and the Documentary Film*. Norman: University of Oklahoma Press, 1968.

Solomon, Maynard. *Beethoven*. New York: Schirmer, 1977.

Spofford, Harriet Prescott. "Billy's Way." *St. Nicholas* 47 (February 1920): 359.

Stegner, Wallace. "Conductivity in Fiction." *Virginia Quarterly Review* 15 (September 1939): 443–47.

———. "The New Novels." *Virginia Quarterly Review* 16 (Summer 1940): 459–65.

Steinbeck, John. *The Grapes of Wrath*. New York: Viking, 1939.

Stewart, George R., and Joseph M. Backus. " 'Each in Its Ordered Place': Structure and Narrative in 'Benjy's Section' of *The Sound and the Fury*." *American Literature* 29 (January 1958): 440–56.

Stone, Edward. "William Faulkner." In *A Certain Morbidness: A View of American Literature*, 85–120. Carbondale: Southern Illinois University Press, 1969.

Stonum, Gary Lee. *Faulkner's Career: An Internal Literary History*. Ithaca, N.Y.: Cornell University Press, 1979.

Stott, William. *Documentary Expression and Thirties America*. New York: Oxford University Press, 1973.

Stuart, Jesse. *The Thread That Runs So True*. New York: Scribner's, 1951.

Sturges, Preston, dir. *Sullivan's Travels*. With Joel McCrea and Veronica Lake. Paramount, 1941.

Sundquist, Eric J. *Faulkner: The House Divided*. Baltimore: Johns Hopkins University Press, 1983.

Swink, Helen. "William Faulkner: The Novelist as Oral Narrator." *Georgia Review* 26 (Summer 1972): 183–209.

Symons, Julian. *Mortal Consequences: A History—From the Detective Story to the Crime Novel*. New York: Harper & Row, 1972.

Tate, Allen. *Essays of Four Decades*. Chicago: Swallow, 1968.

———. "T. S. Stribling." *Nation* 138 (20 June 1934): 709–10.

Taylor, Walter. *Faulkner's Search for a South*. Urbana: University of Illinois Press, 1983.

Taylor, William R. *Cavalier and Yankee: The Old South and American National Character*. Garden City, N.Y.: Doubleday, 1963.

Thorp, Willard. "The Writer as Pariah in The Old South." In *Southern Writers: Appraisals in Our Time*, edited by R. C. Simonini, Jr., 3–18. Charlottesville: University Press of Virginia, 1964.

Tindall, George B. *The Emergence of the New South: 1913–1945*. Vol. 10, A *History of the South*. Baton Rouge: Louisiana State University Press, 1967.

———. "The Significance of Howard W. Odum to Southern History: A Preliminary Estimate." *Journal of Southern History* 24 (August 1958): 285–307.

Trueblood, Ernest V. [William Faulkner.] "Afternoon of a Cow." *Furioso* 2 (Summer 1947): 5–17.

Twain, Mark [Samuel Clemens]. *Mississippi Writings: The Adventures of Tom Sawyer; Life on the Mississippi; Adventures of Huckleberry Finn; Pudd'nhead Wilson.* New York: Library of America, 1982.

———. "Old Times on the Mississippi." In *Great Short Works of Mark Twain,* edited by Justin Kaplan, 1–78. New York: Harper & Row, 1967.

———. *Pudd'nhead Wilson and Those Extraordinary Twins.* Edited by Sidney E. Berger. Norton Critical Edition. New York: Norton, 1980.

"Twelve Southerners." *I'll Take My Stand: The South and the Agrarian Tradition.* Introduction by Louis D. Rubin, Jr. 1930. Reprint. New York: Harper & Row, 1962.

Vickery, Olga W. *The Novels of William Faulkner: A Critical Interpretation.* Baton Rouge: Louisiana State University Press, 1959.

Volpe, Edmond L. "Faulkner's 'Knight's Gambit': Sentimentality and the Creative Imagination." *Modern Fiction Studies* 24 (Summer 1978): 232–39.

———. "Faulkner's 'Monk': The Detective Story and the Mystery of the Human Heart." *Faulkner Studies* 1 (1980): 86–90.

Wade, John Donald. "Southern Humor." In *Culture in the South,* edited by W. T. Couch, 616–28. Chapel Hill: University of North Carolina Press, 1934.

———. "Two Souths." *Virginia Quarterly Review* 10 (October 1934): 616–19.

Waelder, Robert. *Basic Theory of Psychoanalysis.* New York: International Universities Press, 1960.

Waggoner, Hyatt H. "The Current Revolt Against the New Criticism." *Criticism* 1 (Summer 1959): 211–25.

———. *William Faulkner: From Jefferson to the World.* Lexington: University of Kentucky Press, 1959.

Walker, Steven F. "Mallarmé's Symbolist Eclogue: The 'Faune' as Pastoral." *PMLA* 93 (January 1978): 106–17.

Wall, Carey. "Drama and Technique in Faulkner's *The Hamlet.*" *Twentieth Century Literature* 14 (April 1968): 17–23.

Warren, Robert Penn. *At Heaven's Gate.* New York: Random House, 1943.

———. "Cowley's Faulkner." *New Republic* 115 (12 and 26 August 1946): 176–80, 234–37.

———. "Faulkner: Past and Present." In *Faulkner: A Collection of Critical Essays,* edited by Robert Penn Warren, 1–22. Englewood Cliffs, N.J.: Prentice-Hall, 1966.

———. "Knowledge and the Image of Man." *Sewanee Review* 63 (Spring 1955): 182–92.

———. "The Snopes World." *Kenyon Review* 3 (Spring 1941): 253–57.

———. "T. S. Stribling: A Paragraph in the History of Critical Realism." *American Review* 2 (February 1934): 463–86.

Wasson, Ben. *Count No 'Count: Flashbacks to Faulkner.* Jackson: University Press of Mississippi, 1983.

Watkins, Floyd C. "What Stand Did Faulkner Take?" In *Faulkner and the Southern Renaissance: Faulkner and Yoknapatawpha, 1981,* edited by Doreen Fowler and Ann J. Abadie, 40–62. Jackson: University Press of Mississippi, 1982.

———. "The Hound Under the Wagon: Faulkner and the Southern Literati." In *Faulkner and the Southern Renaissance: Faulkner and Yoknapatawpha, 1981,* edited by Doreen Fowler and Ann J. Abadie, 93–119. Jackson: University Press of Mississippi, 1982.

———, and Thomas Daniel Young. "Revisions of Style in Faulkner's 'The Hamlet.'" *Modern Fiction Studies* 5 (Winter 1959–60): 327–36.

Watson, James G. "Literary Self-Criticism: Faulkner in Fiction on Fiction." *Southern Quarterly* 20 (Fall 1981): 46–63.

———. *The Snopes Dilemma: Faulkner's Trilogy.* Coral Gables, Fla.: University of Miami Press, 1968.

Weatherwax, Clara. *Marching! Marching!* New York: John Day, 1935.

Webb, James W., and A. Wigfall Green, eds. *William Faulkner of Oxford.* Baton Rouge: Louisiana State University Press, 1965.

Wheeler, Otis B. "Some Uses of Folk Humor by Faulkner." *Mississippi Quarterly* 17 (Spring 1964): 107–22.

White, Helen, and Redding Sugg, Jr., comps. *From the Mountain: Selections from Pseudopodia (1936), The North Georgia Review (1937–1941), and South Today (1942–1945).* Memphis: Memphis State University Press, 1972.

White, W. L. "Pare Lorentz." *Scribner's* (January 1939): 7–11, 42.

Whittemore, Reed. "Notes on Mr. Faulkner." *Furioso* 2 (Summer 1947): 18–25.

Wilde, Meta Carpenter, and Orin Borsten. *A Loving Gentleman: The Love Story of William Faulkner and Meta Carpenter.* New York: Simon & Schuster, 1976.

Williams, Raymond. *The Country and the City.* New York: Oxford University Press, 1973.

Williams, T. Harry. *Huey Long.* New York: Knopf, 1969.

Willis, Susan. "Aesthetics of the Rural Slum: Contradictions and Dependency in 'The Bear.'" *Social Text* 2 (Summer 1979): 82–103.

Wilson, Edmund. *The American Jitters: A Year of the Slump.* New York: Scribner's, 1932.

Wittenberg, Judith Bryant. *Faulkner: The Transfiguration of Biography.* Lincoln: University of Nebraska Press, 1979.

Wolfe, Thomas. *The Web and the Rock.* New York: Harper & Brothers, 1939.

"The WP&A." *Time* (11 August 1941): 68–71.

Wyatt, David. *Prodigal Sons: A Study in Authorship and Authority.* Baltimore: Johns Hopkins University Press, 1980.

Wyatt-Brown, Bertram. *Southern Honor: Ethics and Behavior in the Old South.* New York: Oxford University Press, 1982.

Yellin, Jean Fagan. *The Intricate Knot: Black Figures in American Literature, 1776–1863.* New York: New York University Press, 1972.

Yonce, Margaret J. "The Composition of *Soldiers' Pay.*" *Mississippi Quarterly* 33 (Summer 1980): 291–326.

The Youth's Companion 85, Nos. 1 (5 January 1911), 2 (12 January 1911), 3 (19 January 1911).

Zender, Karl F. "Faulkner and the Power of Sound." *PMLA* 99 (January 1984): 89–108.

―――. "Faulkner at Forty: The Artist at Home." *Southern Review* 17 (Spring 1981): 288–302.

―――. "Reading in 'The Bear.'" *Faulkner Studies* 1 (1980): 91–99.

INDEX